EDUCATING FOR BUSINESS, PUBLIC SERVICE AND THE SOCIAL SCIENCES

A HISTORY OF THE FACULTY OF ECONOMICS AT THE UNIVERSITY OF SYDNEY 1920–1999

Peter Groenewegen
Professor Emeritus (Economics), University of Sydney

SYDNEY UNIVERSITY PRESS

Published 2009 by Sydney University Press
SYDNEY UNIVERSITY PRESS
University of Sydney Library
www.sup.usyd.edu.au

© Peter Groenewegen 2009
© Sydney University Press 2009

Reproduction and Communication for other purposes

Except as permitted under the Act, no part of this edition may be reproduced, stored in a retrieval system, or communicated in any form or by any means without prior written permission. All requests for reproduction or communication should be made to Sydney University Press at the address below:

Sydney University Press
Fisher Library F03
University of Sydney NSW 2006 AUSTRALIA
Email: info@sup.usyd.edu.au

National Library of Australia Cataloguing-in-Publication entry

Author: Groenewegen, P. D. (Peter Diderik)

Title: Educating for business, public service and the social sciences : a history of the Faculty of Economics at the University of Sydney 1920-1999 / Peter Groenewegen.

ISBN: 9781920899219

Notes: Includes index.
Bibliography.

Subjects: University of Sydney. Faculty of Economics--History
Economics--Study and teaching (Higher)--New South Wales--Sydney--History.

Dewey Number:
330.07119441

Cover image reproduced with permission of Stacy Atkins
Cover design by Court Williams, the University Publishing Service

CONTENTS

List of illustrations iv

List of abbreviations v

Dean's preface vii

Author's preface and acknowledgements ix

Prelude. Pragmatism versus principle: bringing commercial
and economics education to the University of Sydney xiii

1. Two professors, many part-time teachers, brilliant graduates
   and fine social occasions: beginnings of the new, professional,
   Faculty of Economics (1920–28) 1

2. The faculty in Depression and war, 1929–45 27

3. Post-war reconstruction and shortening the BEc degree
   (1945–62) 57

4. The Merewether Building (1965) and a Golden Jubilee (1970):
   the faculty (1963–72) 91

5. Turmoil in the cloisters: University governance, student
   participation, and the Political Economy dispute, 1973–1984 131

6. Towards a Faculty of Economics and Business: new degrees
   and increased opportunities for specialisation, 1985–99 175

Epilogue. The Faculty of Economics and Business in its first decade 221

Bibliography 227

Index 231

LIST OF ILLUSTRATIONS

1. The author as graduate (BEc 1961) and professor. Reproduced with permission of the Author x
2. Economics and Commerce III: 1909. Reproduced with permission of University Archives xvi
3. Eight Deans (and one acting Dean): 1920–99. Reproduced with permission of Faculty of Economics Handbooks.. xxiv
4. Nine eminent faculty members: 1920–99. Reproduced with permission of University Archives 26
5. Final year Economics students in 1930 in the Great Hall. Reproduced with permission of University Archives 53
6. Staff and final-year students in the final decade of the 'old' by-laws: the classes of 1950 on the steps of the R.C. Mills Building. Reproduced with permission of University Archives 53
7. Staff and final-year students in the final decade of the 'old' by-laws: the classes of 1951 and 1953 on the steps of the R.C. Mills Building. Reproduced with permission of University Archives and John Pullen........... 54
8. Staff and final-year students in the final decade of the 'old' by-laws: the classes of 1954 and 1955 on the steps of the R.C. Mills Building. Reproduced with permission of University Archives and Economics Review..................... 55
9. R.C. Mills Building Floor Plan 1953. Reproduced with permission of Faculty of Economics Handbooks... 73
10. Merewether Building Floor Plan 1992. Reproduced with permission of Faculty of Economics Handbooks... 104
11. Merewether under construction. Reproduced with permission of Judy Butlin... 106
12. The official opening of Merewether (14 June 1966). Reproduced with permission of Judy Butlin... 107
13. Economic Society Office bearers (1966–67). Reproduced with permission of the Economics Review 122
14. Changing covers for the *Economics Review* (1955–75). Reproduced with permission of the Economics Review... 123

15. Administering the faculty as graduate assistant to the Dean: Joyce Fisher. Reproduced with permission of Mrs M. L. Ashby 150

16. Turmoil in the cloisters: advancing the cause of 'Political Economy' in the University. Reproduced with permission of University Archives 159

17. Demonstration in the Quadrangle in the 1980s. Reproduced with permission of University Archives 160

18. Economic Statistics staff and Honours graduates (1973). Reproduced with permission of University Archives 169

19. The faculty enters the computer age: a computing room in Merewether. Reproduced with permission of University Archives 176

LIST OF ABBREVIATIONS

ANZAAS: Australian and New Zealand Association for the Advancement of Science

FH: Faculty Handbook

FM: Faculty Minutes

SUES: Sydney University Economics Society

SM: Senate Minutes

UC: University Calendar

UCS: 1965 University Calendar Supplement

DEAN'S PREFACE

I am delighted to write a brief preface to this history of the Faculty of Economics in the University of Sydney over 80 years—from its inception in 1920 until 1999, when it was renamed the Faculty of Economics and Business. It could have no finer author than one of our distinguished graduates and professors, Professor Emeritus Peter Diderik Groenewegen FASSA. Having a continuous association with this faculty since 1957 when he first entered its halls as an undergraduate student, Professor Groenewegen earned the degrees of BEc and MEc at Sydney before leaving for the London School of Economics to complete his PhD. He returned as a Lecturer in Economics in 1965, was appointed to a Chair of Economics in 1980 and, as Professor Emeritus since 2002, remains actively engaged in the scholarly and intellectual life of the faculty.

This history is a labour of love—and the product of skilful and meticulous inquiry. With scholarly care, Peter Groenewegen presents a broad overview of the staff, students and academic programs of the Faculty of Economics from the beginnings of commerce teaching at The University of Sydney, and concludes with an Epilogue covering the first decade of the Faculty of Economics and Business. The account has been composed on the basis of archival research and correspondence with graduates. It contains several illustrations and individual reminiscences. It is a tribute to the contributions of the dedicated staff and graduates of the faculty to commercial, intellectual and public life.

This is a faculty with a rich and influential history. Several of its graduates are persons of significant achievement who, over the years, have been found in the highest public offices, at the head of Australia's principal economic regulatory institutions, in the most distinguished and influential board rooms and executives suites, and in faculty positions in the world's finest universities. Many have not only distinguished themselves in professional life, but have rendered extraordinary service to a wide array of community, cultural, humanitarian and sporting organisations.

Reading this history, we can all be grateful for, and proud of, the many benefits provided by this faculty over the 80 years chronicled within its pages. We can do this even more, in the knowledge that these and further benefits will continue to flow over the years to come to all who participate in what is now the Faculty of Economics and Business. In recent years, the faculty has earned the accreditations of the world's leading accrediting bodies for business schools—the US-based AACSB International and European-based EQUIS—and was selected as the Australian member school of the prestigious European-based global Community of European Management Schools and International Companies (CEMS). More importantly, the faculty continues to attract and retain high quality staff and students from all around the world.

Apart from its substantial value as an historical record, I trust that this history will evoke fond memories and inspire pride and engagement within the community of Economics and Business at the University of Sydney.

Peter W. Wolnizer
Dean of the Faculty of Economics and Business
The University of Sydney

AUTHOR'S PREFACE AND ACKNOWLEDGEMENTS

When at the start of the new millennium in 2000, the Faculty of Economics changed its name to Faculty of Economics and Business, it seemed a good opportunity to review the experience of the now defunct Faculty of Economics over the eight decades of its existence (1920–99). In what follows, this history is broken up into six chapters, together with a prelude indicating what was happening in economics and commercial education at the University of Sydney before the formation of the faculty. A short epilogue looks briefly at major events in the experience of the new Faculty of Economics and Business within the first decade of its existence; that is, until 2009, with its two Schools of Business and of Economics and Political Science, each situated in its own building.

I began my association with the Faculty of Economics just over 50 years ago when I started as a first-year student for its BEc degree in 1957. My experience as a student, both graduate and undergraduate, and as a staff member (teaching fellow 1962–63, lecturer 1965–67, senior lecturer, 1968–72, associate professor, 1973–80, professor 1980–2002 and emeritus professor from 2003) provides good qualifications to become also its first historian. Whether this assumption is correct is best left to the judgement of my readers. They will have shared my experience in the faculty for at least some of these years.

In writing this history, I have concentrated on the people who made up the faculty as its teaching and other staff, its students and its graduates. I have also outlined the formal teaching structures the faculty prescribed over the years, and the manner in which they were put together. Although departments of study, by the end of the 1960s evolved into Economics, Government and Public Administration, Accounting, Economic Statistics, Economic History, and Industrial Relations, feature as important parts of the faculty, their activities are not the major focus of attention. Their intersection at faculty level is what counts, through the participation therein of academic and other staff, their teaching and research.

Each chapter includes material on students and graduates for the period it covers. Those graduates, whose prominence in their fields is signalled by their inclusion in *Who's Who in Australia*, are invariably mentioned. Recollecting their names is to acknowledge that over the decades, the Faculty of Economics has produced many such graduates. They include one Australian prime minister, several state premiers, a substantial number of members of parliament, as well as many leaders in business, commerce, financial institutions, the public service, the media, and academic life. Academics associated with the faculty have been elected to academies such as the Australian Academy of the Social Sciences from its very beginning, and so far include one winner of the Nobel Prize for Economics.

In preparing this history, help was received from many people. First of all, I wish to thank those former graduates who responded to my invitation in the *University [alumni] Gazette* to send me reminiscences of their years in the faculty. I have used these shamelessly in

The author as graduate (BEc 1961) and professor.

what follows, since they add substantially to the human flavour of this faculty history. In addition, some former members of staff (Jules Ginswick, Ken Buckley and Neil Conn) allowed me to interview them about their individual faculty experience and reminiscences. They also gave me access to documents relevant to the faculty's story. Other people assisted with photographs. I am very grateful to Judith Butlin, Michael Hogan and John Pullen for helping out in this way. Many colleagues provided information on specific matters. Michael Jackson lent me material on the governance debates in the Government Department during the 1970s; Bob Brown donated his extensive collection of lecture notes and course outlines for the 1970s when he took his degree; Frank Stilwell made available his copy of the final issue of the *Economic Review*; David Hensher gave me his copies of faculty papers for the 1990s, the official copies of which, as signed by the then dean, had gone missing.

Official University publications provided much information for writing this history. The *University Calendar* was particularly valuable for the early decades of this story, as were issues of the *Faculty Handbook* which started in the 1950s. I also drew heavily on Senate Minutes when able to do so, on Faculty Minutes, on Professorial Board Minutes and on those of its successor, the Academic Board.

Special thanks are due the following. The Dean, Peter Wolnizer, and his staff, gave tangible support by providing occasional research assistance and retrieving faculty documents relevant to this story. Carl Harrison-Ford copy-edited the initial draft giving useful criticisms on various matters of style and content. Thanks also go to the staff of the Fisher Library, in particular the University Archivist and his invariably helpful assistants, as well as the staff of its Rare Book Library. Louis Haddad and Tony Aspromourgos read all chapters in draft, thereby saving me from a variety of errors. The second draft was carefully scrutinised by Frank Clarke, Graeme Dean, Russell Lansbury and Greg Patmore, for whose suggestions and comments I am very grateful. Some persons commented on drafts of individual chapters, or assisted in other ways. Merrill Bouckly from the University's Research Office retrieved Faculty Research Reports for 1994 to 1999, not published for those years by the University. Finally, special thanks go to Kathryn Borkovic, part-time research assistant for 2004–05, who diligently read files of relevant University periodicals (the *University News*, *Honi Soit* and the *Union Recorder*) to abstract information pertinent to this history. Her work greatly enhances the comprehensiveness of this book. Needless to say, errors of omission and commission are my responsibility.

Writing this history of the Faculty of Economics was a very enjoyable experience. Undertaking this task has allowed me to place on the record an account of an educational institution which, generally speaking, well served its students, its staff and society at large by providing a useful starting point for an education in Economics, Commerce, Business and the Social Sciences. I hope that the faculty's students, members of its staff, and other interested parties to its development will get as much enjoyment from reading this book, as I had in its writing.

Peter Groenewegen, February 2009

PRELUDE

Pragmatism versus principle: bringing commercial and economics education to the University of Sydney

The Faculty of Economics established by the University of Sydney in 1920 formalised the availability of Economics and associated subjects in the education it provided. However, this subject had been of concern to the University and its teaching staff from its very inception 70 years earlier. On the eve of enacting the University, the government committee investigating Sydney's need for its own university recognised that although the University started with the then traditional studies of Classics, Mathematics and the Natural Sciences, new fields of study, including history and political economy 'will soon be found indispensable' (cited in Goodwin, 1966, p. 546). The University's foundation Professor of Classics, John Woolley, offered optional lectures in political economy, two of which were published in the 1855 *Sydney University Magazine*. These did not set out its principles but stressed the usefulness of its 'laws' for promoting social harmony and preserving freedom and individual liberty. Woolley invited a Prize Essay on 'The Influence of Political Economy on the Course of History' and asked his Logic students in an examination paper to evaluate critically the proposition that 'Political Economy is the science of social well-being' (Goodwin 1966, p. 547; Groenewegen and McFarlane 1990, pp. 47–49; and Groenewegen 1990, pp. 21–23). His colleague, Morris Birkbeck Pell, a Cambridge senior wrangler and foundation Professor of Mathematics, in 1856 read a paper to the Sydney Philosophical Society on the principles of political economy as applied to railways, a topic he also addressed in the first issue of the *Sydney University Magazine*. Pell in addition did actuarial work and constructed mortality tables in his capacity as a consultant for the colony's life insurance offices (see Goodwin 1966, pp. 286–89, 438–40; Groenewegen and McFarlane 1990, pp. 49–50). Lack of formal recognition of political economy in the new University's syllabus of studies in the 1850s went together with recognition of the subject's importance by the actions of two of its three foundation professors, making its future introduction very likely.

Early formal lectures in Economics and Political Science

Both before and after the establishment of the University of Sydney, Sir Henry Parkes' newspaper the *Empire* lamented the omission of social science teaching from its proposed educational program. An editorial (January 1854) deplored the absence of political science and political economy from the University syllabus, all the more regrettable given the introduction of responsible government in New South Wales, which generated a real need for citizens versed in the art of government. Its success likewise depended on opportunities for being adequately informed on developments in these political subjects. Parkes' pleas fell on deaf ears. The new University did not offer political economy classes as part of its degree courses until 1866–67, and then for only two years. Lectures were then given by James Paterson, a Sydney LLD who had been appointed 'Reader' (that is, part-time lecturer) in Political Economy by the University in 1866 (SM: 6 March 1866). The 1866 *University Calendar* (p. vii) gave some details of this course. It was given during Michaelmas term, one lecture per week on Wednesdays at 8 pm. Paterson, the appointed teacher for the course (SM: 6 March 1866), held four degrees from the University of Sydney: BA in 1857, MA in 1859, LLB in 1864 and LLD in 1866. His interest in economics may therefore have come from attending John Woolley's lectures.

Why the course was so short lived is not known. Low enrolments are a possible explanation. Paterson's poor teaching ability is another. A year later, Senate Minutes (6 March 1867) record receipt of an application from Dr Aldcorn for the position of lecturer in Political Economy (La Nauze 1949, p. 18 and n. 13). The *University Calendar* (1866, p. v) mentioned a political economy segment in the courses on logic. Hence duplication with existing courses may also explain the rapid demise of Paterson's political economy course.

During the 1880s and 1890s, political economy appeared in the University syllabus in two distinct ways. One was the practice of including some political economy in Logic classes, subsequently (1888–89) followed in political philosophy courses. Earlier (in 1886) A.C. Wyllie had offered a course to MA students combining political philosophy with political economy. Texts recommended were Smith's *Wealth of Nations,* Mill's *Principles of Political Economy* and Bastiat's *Economic Harmonies* and *Economic Sophisms* (1887 UC: pp. 269–70). During the 1890s, the School of Logic continued to offer courses in political economy for the MA, now largely based on the political economy of John Stuart Mill (for example, 1890 UC: pp. cxvii–cl). Under Professor Arnold Wood, these courses also became acceptable for history students (see Crawford, 1975 chapter 7, esp. pp. 129, 140–41).

Extension Board teaching enacted in 1884 provided a second route for taking political economy courses at the University of Sydney. A.C. Wyllie offered a one-term course in it in 1886. This course was expanded in 1887 into weekly lectures on production, distribution and practical applications over three terms (1887 UC: p. 284). Butlin (1970, p. 8) mentioned that the Professor of Classics, Walter Scott, also lectured on political economy for the Extension Board, as did his successor, Professor Thomas Butler. Scott had in fact been a major force in establishing Extension Board teaching by the University. He was also active in first establishing and then running the Australian Economic Association, writing for its journal, the *Australian Economist* (Groenewegen and McFarlane 1990, pp. 86–87).

Extension Board courses continued during the early decades of the twentieth century (and after), attracting lecturers from within the University and from outside specialists. Among the latter was H.S. Jevons, son of W.S. Jevons, the famous economist and social philosopher. When in Sydney in the 1850s, W.S. Jevons himself had befriended two of the foundation professors of its University, and was acquainted with some of their economic views. H.S. Jevons lectured on political economy in 1904, as part of an attempt to test the water for successful teaching of commercial and economics topics to downtown business people in this way. His lectures were published by Angus and Robertson, publishers to the University (Jevons 1905).

Political economy, even more than political philosophy, had therefore a mixed reception at the University. Additional to its two-year existence as a separate subject for the BA, political economy was taught as part of the philosophy offerings in the School of Logic, either in Logic or Political Science courses. Moreover, political economy found a home as an Extension Board course taught from 1886. Pressure to provide opportunities for sound commercial training at the University came to a head during the first decade of the twentieth century.

An aborted proposal for a Faculty of Commerce (1903) and further initiatives in commercial education

Moves to have commercial subjects taught at the University in the first instance came from the Sydney Chamber of Commerce. Both its vice-president (George Littlejohn) and its secretary (Henry Braddon) actively supported these moves, best implemented in their opinion by establishing a faculty of commerce at the University. The chamber made its first formal request for this introduction in 1903. Given the University's initial strong opposition, the request was repeated the following year.

The Extension Board also showed an interest in supplying commercial education to the city. Its report submitted to the University's Senate recommended an increased membership to facilitate a new lecture course on commercial subjects 'for the benefit of clerks' (SM: 2 March 1903). Five subjects were suggested: business practice, commercial law, banking and exchange, economic and commercial history, and commercial geography and technology. Both the University Senate and Professorial Board remained cautious about closer University involvement in commercial education. Several of its leading members, including the then chancellor, Sir Normand MacLaurin, described opposition to these moves as 'scotching the snake'.

The press now came to assist the 'city men' from the Chamber of Commerce and other proponents of university commerce teaching. Articles and letters in the *Daily Telegraph* (18 and 19 August 1904) and in the *Sydney Morning Herald* (22 August 1904) drew attention to relevant overseas experience at the universities of London, Birmingham and Manchester. These had all introduced commerce courses and degrees. In addition, articles commented on the need for advanced commercial training in Australia to strengthen protection of Australian business and industry against foreign competition, and thereby to lead them more effectively to victory in imminent trade wars with Germany, the United States and Japan. Cost of the proposal was estimated by an anonymous member of the University Senate as ranging from £2000 to £3000, with a minimum enrolment of 84 students to make such courses viable.

The University responded quickly. A Senate committee, appointed in September 1904, reported in December (SM: 5 December 1904). It proposed a junior commercial

Economics and Commerce III: 1909.

examination and the award of a university commercial certificate, acceptable to both Senate and Chamber of Commerce. Senior and junior commercial examinations were to be introduced in 1905 with an evening course of 30 lectures on economics, accounting, business methods and techniques, to be followed in 1906 with a further evening course of 30 lectures on commercial law, commercial history and geography, and banking and finance. More delays and committees were generated by the New South Wales Teachers Association and resolved over three days in May 1906. As a result, a professorship in economics was to be quickly established for funding by the New South Wales Treasury; a new scheme of commercial education and examination was to be prepared; and business interests in the city were urged to accept both the new commercial education scheme and that its successful students be suitably certified.

In November 1906, a Senate committee unanimously approved implementation of this scheme. Commerce and Economics would become a subject of instruction for the BA. Commerce courses were to be given over three years and were to be open to non-matriculated students as well as to ordinary degree students. Non-matriculated students who had completed the three courses satisfactorily were to be awarded a Diploma of Commerce. The proposed first-year course, Commerce I, was to start in 1907. It was to include lectures on the principles of economics, accountancy, business methods and technology, commercial geography and the economic position of Australia. Four teachers in the new course were to be appointed (Report of the Senate, 1906, p. 311). Butlin (1970, p. 8) concisely outlined the next phase in the story:

> Working out of details passed to the Faculty of Arts which gave the scheme a rough passage. MacCallum (Professor of English and later Sir Mungo), having lost a motion to approve courses in Economics only, succeeded with one approving three years in 'Economics and Commerce' from which 'the more technical and professional branches of economic study' should be excluded. An amendment to reject the entire proposal was defeated only on the Dean's casting vote. What finally emerged was a programme for a three-year, part-time, Diploma of Economics and Commerce, and a Department of the same name, within the Faculty of Arts. In adopting this in November 1907 the Senate appointed six part-time staff, headed by Irvine … Arts was still unhappy and having failed in its demand for a full-time professor or lecturer in Economics urged transfer of the unclean thing to Law.

Despite fears expressed by the newspapers about a possible lack of students, the diploma was a success. It attracted 84 students for its first year of operations in 1907. By 1913, enrolments had more than doubled to 174, and reached their peak in the immediate post-war years of 1919 and 1920 with 298 and 296 students.

Opposition from the Arts Faculty meant that the Department of Economics and Commerce was initially housed in the Law Faculty. During 1912, it shifted to the Faculty of Arts, as originally intended. This remained the case until 1920, when commerce teaching found a permanent home in the then newly created Faculty of Economics. A BEc degree course came into effect in 1913. Only matriculated students were eligible for this degree, which mainly drew on courses offered by the Department of Economics and Commerce.

Two original appointees for teaching the Diploma of Commerce courses participated in the teaching of the Faculty of Economics on its establishment in 1920. The first was Henry Braddon, who for some years taught the Business Principles segment of the BEc degree; the second was Robert Irvine, the first dean and professor in the new faculty. They had been staunch allies in the downtown fight for the introduction of commercial teaching at the University. Braddon had done so in his capacity as secretary to the Chamber of Commerce, and Irvine did so from his involvement in the education and training of public servants for the New South Wales Public Service Board (*Union Recorder*, 10 July 1941, p. 21). Some background on these founders is interesting, starting with Braddon.

Henry Braddon (1863–1955) was born in India, and educated in Germany (Dusseldorf) and Dulwich College (London) with a year in Caen (Normandy) in between. In 1878, he joined his father in Tasmania, worked briefly there in one of its banks, then worked for a bank in New Zealand before returning to Sydney in 1884 as a member of the New Zealand rugby union team. There he stayed, making a career with Dalgety's, marrying, and being actively engaged in the Sydney Chamber of Commerce. This brought him into the fight to introduce commerce teaching at the University of Sydney (McCredie 1979, pp. 380–81). From its commencement he taught Business Principles and Practice for the Diploma of Commerce and later for the BEc degree as well (1907–23). He published a text on the subject (Braddon 1909), which stayed in print until the 1930s. In addition, he wrote on money, credit and banking, delivered two Joseph Fisher lectures on commerce

(Braddon 1912 and 1925), and published a volume of essays and addresses (Braddon 1930) which included an interesting study of the French assignats (the paper money issued by the French republic during the years following the French Revolution of 1789). Braddon was knighted (KBE) in 1920, he was a member of the University's Senate during the 1920s, served as a member of the Legislative Council from 1917 to 1938, and on his retirement from Dalgety's in 1928 he held a number of directorships in financial enterprises, giving freely of his time to many charities. His political and economic views tended to be on the conservative side and it is interesting to speculate how he got on with Irvine, his comrade in arms in the struggle for commerce education at the University, after the publication of Irvine's rather heretical views on monetary subjects (Irvine 1916, 1933). An account of Irvine's career is given below.

From Department of Economics and Commerce to Faculty of Economics

When in 1911 the Diploma of Economics and Commerce courses had been running for four years with enrolments just under the 100 mark (McLeod 1955, p. 41), Irvine, the sole teacher of its substantial economic content, was appointed to the Public Service Board. He had been associated with its work before taking up a lectureship in economics and Commerce in 1906, and intended to resign his university teaching position in order to accept the new appointment. Irvine was persuaded to stay on as lecturer with the prospect that a chair in Economics and Commerce would be created in the not too distant future. At the start of 1912, the state government provided the additional £3000 needed to establish the chair to which Irvine was appointed on the motion of the vice-chancellor (SM: 4 March, 1 April 1912). Irvine accepted the new position that same month and commenced professorial duties at the start of Lent term 1913. He spent the second half of 1912 in visiting major schools of economics in North America, Great Britain and Europe, to inform himself on developments in economics and commerce teaching in other parts of the world.

The Diploma of Commerce at this stage required unmatriculated students to take Economics and Commerce I, II and III as compulsory courses (1910 UC: p. 145). Until 1912, lectures were given in the evening at the Law School. Economics and Commerce I involved one lecture a week in Introductory Economics and in Accountancy for the whole year, for two terms in Business Principles and Practice and in first term in Economic Geography. Economics and Commerce II required one lecture a week in Economics II (dealing with finance, trade, business cycles and associated issues); one lecture per week for two terms in Accountancy II, and in Commercial Law I and History of Elementary Technology and Commercial Products for one term. For Economics and Commerce III, students took one lecture per week in Economics III on the theory of distribution, the labour movement, combinations and monopolies, public finance and commercial and industrial history; one lecture per week for two terms in Accountancy III, and one lecture per week for one term in Commercial Law II and the choice of either statistical methods, insurance, banking practice and accounts, and local government. Teaching staff had grown to eight, all part-time with the exception of Irvine (1910 UC: pp. 145–47). This course structure, less of a hotchpotch` than that improvised at the start of the Diploma of Commerce, contained the seeds for the course mix later offered by the Faculty of Economics for its degree.

Not long after his appointment as professor, Irvine drafted new by-laws for a revised curriculum in the Department of Economics and Commerce. These were gazetted on 21 January 1913 as Chapter XVIB of the University by-laws. They provided for a degree of Bachelor of Economics, open to all students who had passed the matriculation examination for university entry. Two of its subjects had to be completed at a 'higher standard', of which one had to be either French or German. Students had to complete ten courses to graduate: Economics I, II and III, three Arts courses, of which one had to be either French or German, and two courses combining the two half courses Commercial and Industrial Law and Economic Geography, and those in Accountancy I and Business Principles and Practice. The remaining two courses were either another Arts course not previously attempted, or combining two commercial half courses; or by combining four commercial half courses from the following: Commercial and Industrial Law [II], Accountancy [II and III], Technology and Commercial Products, Principles and Practice of Banking, Methods and Application of Statistics, Public Administration (including Local Government), Business Technique and Organisation of the Principal Australian Industries, Principles of Company and Industrial Organisation and Management (1913 UC: pp. 54–55). Students intending to take Actuarial Studies were advised to take Insurance Mathematics. No more than four qualifying courses for the degree could be taken per annum, making three years the minimum time for completing.

The new by-laws also enabled conversion of the Diploma of Commerce into a new BEc degree, by exempting holders of the diploma from taking commercial courses already completed for the diploma, including Economics I–III. They were, however, required to attend lectures on public finance, economic history and the history of economic thought not included in Economics I–III as taught previously for the diploma (1913 UC: pp. 55–57). BEc and diploma courses were now given as evening lectures within the Faculty of Arts, but only the three economics courses as revised were acceptable for BA students. By then, the Department of Economics and Commerce was housed 'in a cramped corner of the old Geology Building' (bordering Parramatta Road) where some of its classes were also held (Butlin 1970, p. 9).

Details of the revised Economics I–III courses were provided (1913 UC: pp. 180–82). Economics I now dealt with the Theory of Production, Consumption and Exchange (Part I), and with the Evolution of the Industrial System (Part II). Economics II covered Value and Price, Money, Exchange, Crises and Business Fluctuations, Speculation, and Australian Foreign Trade (Part I) and Economic History (Part II). Economics III added Public Finance and History of Economic Thought to its previous treatment of labour, socialism and other forms of the social organisation of industry. Segments of Economics III made Irvine unpopular with more conservative University elements and in downtown business and financial circles.

Irvine, who had been born in Scotland in 1861, was educated in New Zealand (BA in 1883, MA in 1888) and had subsequently worked there as journalist and in temporary academic posts at Canterbury University College. He migrated to Australia in 1891 and initially worked as a teacher before joining the New South Wales Public Service in 1897 as secretary to the Board of Examiners for the Public Service Board. He had actively cooperated with the Chamber of Commerce and others in promoting university-provided commercial education, and became a University Extension Board lecturer in History and Economics. When appointed to the chair, Irvine's few publications included an 1899 article on Impressionism in art; a joint 1902 book (with O.T.J. Alpers) on progress in New Zealand in the nineteenth century, and a 1913 report for the New South Wales government on the housing of workers in Europe and America. From 1914 to 1921 he published two or three items a year: on town planning, the importance of social science teaching at a university, war finance and public finance, money, contemporary labour issues and newspaper articles for the *Sunday Times* (McFarlane 1966, pp. 48–49 gives a detailed bibliography). Irvine saw his teaching role as important, both within the University and in the wider community. He later described his students as 'youthful comrades ... cheerful, sociable, keen and open-minded ... [who endured] ... our texts and far too many tedious lectures on top of them ... [so that class discussion was frequently substituted] for some of the lectures' (Irvine 1933, pp. 2–3). His ideas differed greatly from those of the 'conventional' economists and his teaching became more and more heretical in content (Groenewegen and McFarlane 1990, pp. 57–60).

Few BEc degrees were awarded by the University during the seven years following their establishment. The first was conferred as early as 1914, surprisingly, given the type of subjects offered by the Economics and Commerce Department, to a woman student, Edith Swain. Eight BEc degrees were conferred in 1916, in 1917 only three; and so on. Twenty-five BEc degrees were conferred prior to the formal establishment of the Faculty of Economics in 1920, a small fraction (15 per cent) of the Diplomas of Economics and Commerce awarded over these years. In all, 170 diplomas were awarded during the decade of its existence, with the maximum annual award of 24 achieved in its first year, 1910, and again in 1919 (UCS). Seven women (4 per cent of the total) received a diploma as did a future faculty teacher of Business Principles, W.J. Cleary. Little else can be said about these diploma and early degree students. Were they 'the clerks' mentioned by the Senate in its discussion of Extension Board endeavours to expand into commercial education or, more likely, middle-grade employees from banks, other financial institutions and segments of the world of business, or from the public service? Such details cannot be gleaned from the names recorded in the student records.

Staff for the Economics and Commerce courses continued to grow. Apart from Irvine as professor, Atkins was added as lecturer in Economic History, H. Dunstan Vane and Braddon continued to teach Accountancy and Business Principles, F.A.Russell taught Commercial and Industrial Law, F.B.Guthrie Technology and Commercial Products, E.M. Moors (a former—1887–1908—assistant lecturer in Mathematics) Actuarial Mathematics and Statistics, and G.M.Allard taught Banking Practice. In 1914, J.D.Fitzgerald lectured on

Local Government (Law and Administration); and G.S. Beeby in 1915 lectured on public administration (a course then added to the list of half courses for the BEc and the diploma). From 1917, public administration was taught by P.R.Watts and F.A.Bland (1915 UC: pp. 47, 450; 1916 UC: pp. 346–47).

To encourage their students, some lecturers offered prizes. The first such prize (introduced in 1910) was one of two guineas for Business Methods donated by Braddon; Russell in 1914 donated a one guinea prize to the student most proficient in Commercial and Industrial Law, while Irvine donated several prizes (all initially worth a guinea) for the best students in Economics I, II and III and for the diploma course as a whole (1916 UC: pp. 346–47).

The list of half courses on offer continued to expand. New half courses for 1918 were Business Techniques, Organisation of the Principal Australian Industries, Sociology (for the University teaching of which Irvine [1914] had made a cogent plea), Political Science and Constitutional History. The last was described as of special significance for Commerce and Economics students, given the growing importance of sections of the Constitution for trade, industry and commerce (1917 UC: p. 147).

A new degree was added by the Department of Economics and Commerce with the introduction in 1916 of the MEc as a postgraduate degree. No MEc degrees were conferred prior to the establishment of the Faculty of Economics, with the first masters awarded to Bradney William Goodwin in 1925 (1965 UCS: p. 312).

Further changes to the Bachelor of Economics degree were gazetted in 1918 as part preparation for transforming the Department of Economics and Commerce into a faculty. Moves for professional faculties had begun in 1918 with a proposal from the Professor of Engineering Science, Samuel Barraclough (later Sir Samuel), for the creation of a separate Faculty of Engineering. Eventually six additional faculties joined Arts, Law, Medicine and Science in 1920 (Butlin 1970, p. 9): Economics, Engineering, Dentistry, Veterinary Science, Agriculture and Architecture.

The new BEc degree requirements were succinctly stated in Chapter XVIB of the by-laws. First of all, they increased the minimum period for completing the degree to four years. First-year students had to complete Economics I, one Group A subject (that is, Mathematics I, French I, German I or a Science), and one Group B course (English I or II, Modern History I, Philosophy I or II or a Group A course not already selected). Mathematics I was compulsory for those intending to take a full course of Insurance Mathematics. Second-year students took three of the following four course combinations: (1) Economics II; (2) the two half courses Business Principles and Practice and Economic Geography; (3) a half course in Statistics and one, or two, half courses in Accountancy I, the students taking the second Accountancy course being exempt from taking History of Economic Thought in the final year; (4) Insurance Mathematics I. Third-year students completed (1) Economics III or Insurance Mathematics II; (2) Economic History; and (3) Commercial and Industrial Law. Finally, fourth-year students completed (1) either Public Administration or two from the half courses Principles and Practice of Banking, Technology and Commercial Products, Economics of Transport, Elements of Political Science, Municipal Administration,

Philosophy II (Sociology) if not already taken or Philosophy I (Psychology) if not already taken; (2) a subject not already taken from Group A or Group B or Accountancy II (including Auditing); and (3) the History of Economic Thought (unless exempted by having taken the additional Accountancy I course during second year). In addition, the fourth-year examinations would test student proficiency in translating either French or German if they had not completed French I or German I.

Compared to later regulations and by-laws of the Faculty of Economics, this degree structure had some remarkable features. Three years of compulsory Economics studies were not required for those taking Insurance Mathematics I and II. Those intending to become professional accountants were only advised to take Accountancy II and Auditing, but not the two Accountancy I courses offered in second year and the Commercial and Industrial Law course. Thirdly, Political Science and Public Administration were courses available to BEc students but not from a single department within the faculty. Two social sciences (Sociology, Psychology) were also included for the BEc degree. The course structure for students taking the Diploma of Commerce and Economics was also revised, but its status as a course which could be completed in three years continued.

Chapter XVIB of the by-laws was amended in 1917 to provide for a Board of Studies in Economics and Commerce. The chair of the new Economics Board was the Professor of Economics, 'but in his absence, the members then present shall elect a chairman from among themselves'. Its membership comprised 'all lecturers in the subjects primarily prescribed for degrees in Economics'. The chancellor, vice-chancellor and the University warden and registrar were ex officio members (1918 UC: p. 51). Similar boards had been created for the other five 'professional' departments which were given faculty status in 1920. This new organisational structure was therefore little more than a halfway house to full faculty status.

From the preserved record it appears that the Board of Studies in Economics and Commerce met only once (15 November 1917) at the University Chambers in Phillip Street. This was the same place where Faculty of Economics meetings were held for several years from 1920. Five members of the board attended: Irvine, who took the chair, together with F.A.Bland, G.W.Cotton, F.B.Guthrie and P.R. Watts. The meeting discussed the changes in the by-laws outlined previously and the mechanics by which students enrolled in first year in 1917 could transfer to the new structure in 1918. In addition, and probably suggested by Bland, it decided to add Municipal Administration to degree and diploma syllabus.

A consequence of the general improvements in university commercial and economic education was the expansion of the array of university clubs by a new society. The 1912 UC (pp. 560–61) recorded that an Economics and Commerce Association of New South Wales had been registered under the Companies Act in March 1911

> to stimulate interest and research in the Economics of Industry and Commerce by granting fellowships, prizes and scholarships and by the holding of lectures … It would also collect and diffuse information on all such subjects [including the printing, publishing and circulation of papers], establish a library and a reading

room, provide rooms and other facilities for holding of meetings … [and] prolong and sustain the interest of students in Economics after the completion of the University course.

The new association provided four categories of membership. Honorary members included every professor at the University and any other persons whom the council of the association chose to admit to this status. Fellows included the teaching staff in Economics and Commerce and any diploma holders who had contributed by research 'to the general stock of economic knowledge'. Associate members included all those who had successfully completed courses in Economics and Commerce either for degrees or diplomas subject to approval by the chief lecturer in the department or any other persons deemed fit by the council to be an associate member. Finally, there were student members subject to approval by the council. Ironically, given his attitude to university commercial education, Sir Normand MacLaurin (the chancellor) was listed as patron of the association; its president was Professor Irvine, there were four vice-presidents (of whom two were teachers), two honorary secretaries, an honorary treasurer and seven councillors. This very ambitious university club seems not to have lasted long, if it in fact ever started. No records of any of its meetings appear to be extant. Subsequent *University Calendars* do not mention its activities, and from 1918 dropped all references to its existence. It seems to have gone the way of many such organisations, started with the best of intentions but with far too ambitious a program and set of objectives to be ever effectively realisable.

Concluding remarks

Systematic economics and commerce teaching at the University of Sydney was a product of the twentieth century. Despite the interest in economics of two of its foundation professors, university economics teaching when tried in the nineteenth century was either a short-lived failure, or occasionally included as part of the Logic and Political Philosophy syllabus or, more frequently, in tutorial classes and similar courses offered to the outside public by the University's Extension Board. Demands for university teaching of commerce, economics and related subjects had been made by business and political leaders even before the establishment of the University in 1852. Nothing came of this until strong pressure from the Sydney Chamber of Commerce, those involved in public service education and especially the press, produced action from the University. This was done initially by establishing a Department of Economics and Commerce for organising such teaching, despite opposition from University leaders, including the chancellor and a majority of Faculty of Arts members.

Early teaching of economics and commerce was therefore conducted under the auspices of the Faculty of Law. Only after a Professor of Economics and Commerce was appointed did this teaching move to the Faculty of Arts. The range of Commerce courses introduced from 1907 could initially only be taken by Diploma of Commerce students. From 1913, they could also count towards a BEc for matriculated students. Hence a specialised economics degree preceded the start of a faculty of economics by seven years. A masters degree, MEc,

Eight deans (and one acting dean): 1920–1999.

was introduced in 1916. Their naming as economics degrees is explained by the fact that calling them commerce degrees (as in Melbourne) would not have differentiated them sufficiently from the diplomas also offered by the department. As acceptance of university-provided teaching for professional qualifications grew, the push for professional faculties additional to Medicine and Law grew with it. Engineering launched the first plea to turn its department into a faculty, and the departments of Dental Science, Agriculture, Veterinary Science, Architecture and Economics and Commerce soon followed. After serving brief apprenticeships for their imminent faculty status by way of boards of studies, these six areas of professional education became fully-fledged faculties in 1920. The teaching of economics and associated commerce, business and public administration subjects was by then firmly entrenched at the University of Sydney. Its teachers and syllabus were preserved in the new faculty structure to a significant extent. 'Scotching' the commercial snake proved not to be a long-term option for university traditionalists.

CHAPTER 1

Two professors, many part-time teachers, brilliant graduates and fine social occasions: beginnings of the new, professional, Faculty of Economics (1920–28)

The preface of the 1920 *University Calendar* (p. viii) announced that the University now consisted of ten faculties instead of four, and that the Faculty of Economics was one of the six 'professional' newcomers. More precisely, the faculty was the ninth faculty (1920 UC: p. 38). Its 'new' by-laws and the preface to the *Calendar* indicated its major functions as the provision of teaching for two degrees and one diploma. Little therefore changed in 1920, except for the new name for an existing organisational structure, signifying a change in status and heralding a promise for the future.

Butlin (1970, p. 9) concisely stated that:

> initially for the Faculty of Economics, the change was largely formal. It [the same full-time staff of the new faculty] continued to be housed in a cramped corner of the old Geology Building, its curriculum was unchanged. But it did double its full-time staff by the appointment in 1921 of R.C. Mills as lecturer. The following year Irvine resigned and Mills succeeded to the chair.

The 1920s was therefore the decade when the Faculty of Economics at the University of Sydney took a more definite shape by building up its teaching resources and its course structure, and attracting students eager to master its various offerings in economics, commerce and public administration.

The formal establishment of the new faculty

When can it be said that a new faculty is actually established? Is it when the University's highest governing body, the Senate, favourably reports on the establishment of the new faculty, indicating in its report the date by which implementation of its resolution was to be achieved? Or is it when the new faculty opens its doors to its first students, as the Faculty of Economics did at the start of Lent term 1920? If, however, faculty is simply seen as an organisation of members of the University overseeing the teaching of a specific array of subject recognised for the degrees and diplomas for which it examines, then its establishment is perhaps best dated by the first faculty meeting, which for the new faculty took place in July 1920.

The by-laws for the new faculty differed only nominally from those approved in 1918 for the Board of Studies in Economics and Commerce as Chapter XVIB. Chapter XVIII (note the alteration in numbering) of the new by-laws approved in 1920 altered the first section of the 1918 Economics and Commerce by-laws to read as follows: 'The Chancellor, the Vice-Chancellor, the Warden [and registrar], the Professors of Economics, Law and History, and the lecturers in the subjects primarily prescribed for degrees in Economics shall constitute the Faculty of Economics' (1920 UC: p. 84). Faculty Minutes, however, first recorded attendance by the professors of Law and History in March 1923 and September 1929.

Further sections of the by-laws then indicated the two degrees offered by the faculty—that is, the BEc and MEc—and the course requirements for the first of these degrees. These replicated the wording of the 1918 by-laws, as did the sections on the requirements, brief though they were, for the MEc. In addition to these degrees, the new faculty continued to provide for a Diploma of Commerce. However, the final sections of the 1920 by-laws were also altered, to make them conform to the usual provisions of faculties for its degree students. Section 18 indicated that students who failed to attend or to pass the annual examination had to re-attend the lectures for these courses before they could be eligible to sit these examinations again, unless specifically exempted by faculty. Judging from the minutes of subsequent faculty meetings, this requirement generated a great deal of work for its members in considering requests for exemptions from lectures by failed students. Section 19 prescribed the rules for progression from year to year, and for sequential courses of study. Permission from the faculty had to be obtained before a student was able to carry a failed subject among the courses of the following year, unless there were exceptional circumstances. In addition, students had to pass Economics I before they could attempt Economics II or Economics III. This final requirement implicitly acknowledged the shortage of teaching staff in Economics, which only permitted the presentation of lectures for Economics II and Economics III in alternate years.

The new faculty held its first meeting on 15 July 1920. As in the case of the Board of Studies meeting for which minutes remain, the venue was the University Chambers in Phillip street. The occasion attracted a large attendance: no less than nine part-time teaching members together with Professor Irvine, the faculty's one full time member of staff. It was to be one of the largest faculty meetings for the whole of the decade, exceeded only by the September 1923 meeting which attracted eleven. Average attendance at faculty meetings for the 1920s was 6.1, with three the lowest recorded attendance, and it may be observed here that it was not until 1930 that Senate set the quorum for a faculty meeting at three (SM: 1 December 1930).

The first action taken at the inaugural faculty meeting was to elect Irvine unanimously to the position of dean. It then moved into what rapidly became its routine business of dealing with individual student cases for exemptions of subjects or examinations and other types of special consideration. In addition, it formed a special committee (the first of many in its history) for the purpose of preparing and publishing a pamphlet to explain the services the new faculty intended to provide to its prospective clients. A special faculty meeting was called within a few weeks to seek leave from Senate for the speedy appointment of a full-time lecturer in economics to assist the professor (and newly elected dean).

Staff, enrolments and timetable

How little in fact changed in 1920 in the new faculty is indicated by the staff. The 1920 *Calendar* (pp. 526–27) assigned the following teachers to the Faculty of Economics, together with the subjects for the teaching of which they were responsible. Irvine was responsible for Economics, Carter for Accountancy, Moors for Actuarial Mathematics and Statistics, Allard for Banking Practice, Braddon for Business Principles and Practice, Cotton for Commercial Geography, Russell for Commercial and Industrial Law, Portus for Economic History, Hodgson and Jefferson for Economics of Transport, Watts for Political Institutions, Guthrie for Technology and Commercial Products and Bland for Municipal Administration and Public Administration. Of these thirteen faculty teachers, only Carter, Hodgson and Jefferson were appointed in 1920 and all, with the exception of Irvine, were part-time, temporary lecturers whose contracts had to be continually renewed. Portus and Bland were also teaching for the University in Adult Education.

Portus and Bland, who subsequently had distinguished academic careers, require more detailed introduction. Garnet Vere (Jerry) Portus (1883–1954) gained degrees from the University of Sydney and as a Rhodes Scholar (he was a distinguished football player), he studied at Oxford as well. He taught Economic History in the Faculty of Economics, as well as Adult Education classes until 1934. He then became Professor of History and Political Science at the University of Adelaide, until his retirement in 1950. Francis Armand Bland (1882–1967) was educated in arts, law and economics at the University of Sydney, and assisted Irvine on the New South Wales Public Service Board early in his career. This made him interested in teaching Public Administration part time in the faculty, while in addition he taught adult education classes with Portus. In 1937, he became the foundation Professor of Public Administration until his retirement in 1947. As a respected teacher in the faculty, he will be encountered later in this, and in the next two chapters.

As indicated previously, the full-time staff of the faculty was doubled in 1921 with the appointment to a lectureship in economics of R.C. Mills, a Melbourne graduate with a doctorate from the London of School of Economics. This followed the request from a special faculty meeting, on which the Senate had quickly acted (FM: 17 July 1920; 1921 UC: p. 550). Mills declined the offer of a chair at Otago to take up the Sydney lectureship (Irvine's proposal of appointment, 22 November 1920, Mills' appointment file, University Archives).

Preliminary enrolment figures augured well for the new faculty and indicate why the doubling of its full-time teaching staff was so quickly agreed to by the Senate. Four hundred and thirty-four students enrolled in the new faculty in 1920, nearly all of them evening students. Two hundred and ninety-seven were enrolled for the Diploma of Commerce courses, the other 137 for the BEc degree. In terms of student numbers, this made the new faculty the third largest in the University, behind Medicine and Arts. The 1920 enrolments were five times the number who had entered Economics and Commerce studies in its foundation year of 1907, and more than three times the numbers of students enrolled in 1912, the year preceding introduction of the BEc. Enrolments subsequently declined.

In 1922 they totalled 120 (93 men and 27 women), and the faculty slipped into fourth position in terms of student numbers behind Arts, Medicine and Engineering. In 1923, they declined to 113 (87 men and 26 women); in 1924, 112 (78 men, 34 women) of whom 88 students enrolled for the Commerce Diploma and 10 were special students. Only 107 enrolled in 1925 (78 men and 29 women) of whom 80 were Diploma students; so that the initial enthusiasm for the offerings of the new faculty was not sustained. By 1927 enrolments recovered to 125 (95 men and 30 women) for the degree, and an additional 60 for the Diploma, with 22 students attending faculty courses without being degree or diploma students (SM: 4 September 1922, 17 September 1923, 10 October 1924, 10 August 1925, 11 June 1928).

The lecture timetable reflected the substantial evening student component of the new faculty, an enrolment pattern which continued for its first two decades. Lectures for all courses offered specifically for the faculty only took place in the evening, as did those for the Arts subjects required for the BEc degree, other than Economics I.

A student such as Stacy Atkin, whose extant lecture notes for the first three years of his studies are discussed later in this chapter, had the following timetable over the four years he took to complete his degree. For first year (1923), his lectures for Economics I were either at 2 pm on Mondays and 11 am on Tuesdays and Fridays, or at 6 pm on Mondays and Fridays and 5 pm on Wednesdays; his lectures in English I at 8 pm on Wednesdays and Thursdays and those for Psychology I and Logic at 7 pm on Tuesdays and Thursdays, and 5 pm on Wednesdays. For second year (1924), his lectures for Economics II were at 7 pm on Mondays, Wednesdays and Fridays, for Statistics from 6.30 to 8 pm on Thursday nights; for Business Principles and Practice at 8 pm on Mondays and Wednesdays; for Accountancy IA and B, at 7 and 8 pm on Tuesdays (a double lecture) and 8 on Thursdays, and Economic Geography at 6 pm on Tuesdays and 5 pm on Fridays. In his third year (1925), Economics III lectures were given at 7 pm on Mondays, Wednesdays and Fridays; Economic History lectures were at 6 pm on Mondays, Tuesdays and Wednesdays and those for Industrial and Commercial Law at 8 pm on Mondays and 6 and 8 pm on Fridays. For his final, fourth year (1926), Atkin attended Economics IV (History of Economic Thought) at 7 pm on Mondays and Tuesdays; Public Administration at 6 pm on Mondays, Wednesdays and Fridays; and Accountancy II at 6 and 7 pm on Thursdays (another double lecture). In third year, his timetable implied three hours of lectures in a row on Mondays. It was therefore no wonder that the evening students who recorded their reminiscences at this time invariably mentioned their high potential for dozing off during lectures, if not actually falling asleep. Full-time students had a similar regime, except that Economics I was given during the day from 1921 (when Mills was available to help Irvine), and many of the arts subjects available for economics degree students were given at day times as well. In 1927, day classes in Economics II and III were introduced, but these had to be abandoned a few years later for lack of staff (Mills 1940, p. 15).

Sir Hermann Black, as chancellor of the University, recalled his experience of these evening classes as follows:

> We dined before the lectures in the Union … dined is the operative word … because the tables were resplendent in white cloth, serviettes were de rigeur, waitresses, neat and courteous stood to bring the young lords their cottage pie and pallid coffee, and those who, like Madgwick and myself, were day students, were thus brought into continuous contact with the genre 'Evening Student', a rare and splendid bird, with some choicer feathers among them. Look where those sons of evening toil lifted themselves today. (Black 1970, p. 14)

Requirements for the degree did not greatly vary from those approved for the four-year BEc degree in 1918. Revisions to that structure were not considered by faculty until 1923, for approval by Senate in 1924. The need to review the whole curriculum, and in particular that for the fourth year, had been explicitly acknowledged at the 28 March 1922 faculty meeting, which set up a committee of Irvine, Mills and Portus to look into the matter. However, Irvine's forced resignation within six months of that meeting induced the effective postponement of this review by a good twelve months.

The Faculty of Economics did make several significant changes to its by-laws and regulations during its first two years. The publicity pamphlet for the new faculty, finalised during 1920, became the effective forerunner of the *Faculty Handbook* introduced in 1926. At the July 1921 meeting, Portus raised the need for standardising faculty practice in the award of honours. He pointed out that Arts and Engineering awarded honours on the basis of special examinations taken in March, while Science and Medicine recorded honours results for meritorious performance in the ordinary December pass examinations, with high distinctions, distinctions and credit results yielding first-, second- and third-class honours in these subjects. The Economics Faculty used both methods: Economics and Economic History followed the special examinations practice of the Faculty of Arts; the other degree subjects followed the practice of Science and Medicine. The method of awarding honours raised a further ambiguity in Portus' view, peculiar to the Faculty of Economics. This arose from its use of the term 'economics', a word simultaneously referring to the whole array of courses taught within the faculty and to the specific subject taught by Irvine and Mills. Portus claimed this ambiguity was easily removed by placing the adjective 'pure' before 'economics' when conceived as an individual sequence of subjects. The suggested remedy raised ambiguities of its own from the various nuances associated with the phrase, 'pure economics'. It was not pursued, unlike the need to standardise faculty practice in the award of honours.

In October 1921, faculty resolved that it would provide for special distinction examination papers in March, as well as the usual pass papers in December. A total of four distinctions, of which at least two had to come from either Economics I, II or III, would be sufficient to secure an honours result for students on completion of their degree. Revised honours proposals were approved during 1922. In May 1923, five BEc students graduated with honours; eighteen received an ordinary pass degree.

It was subsequently decided (FM: 22 June 1923) that only successful honours graduates would be eligible for award of the University medal or, more specifically, that the medal would be awarded to 'the most distinguished honours graduate throughout the whole degree, provided he [*sic!*] is of sufficient merit'. Not long thereafter in 1927, the first University medals in the faculty were awarded jointly to Hermann Black and Robert Madgwick, who both graduated BEc with first-class honours in Economics, equal first. This probably explains why this pair, who subsequently became lecturers in the faculty, were collectively described by their fellow students as 'Black Magic'. In 1929, faculty agreed that a first-class honours result was a prerequisite for taking the masters degree by thesis only, that is, without having to sit the preliminary examinations provided for in the by-laws.

The early faculty meetings also raised the issue of providing the faculty with a suitable secretariat, something which did not come into effect for some time. Although Irvine unofficially had a personal assistant from at least mid-1916, such assistance was not generally provided for deans at this time, except for the work carried out traditionally by the registrar's staff. The 17 September 1925 faculty meeting (and many subsequent ones) record the presence of a faculty secretary, Brigadier General Iven G. Mackay, but he was in fact a University appointment covering all faculties, while he also had duties as student adviser (SM: 10 August 1925).

Professor Irvine's forced resignation, 1922

On 6 September 1922, Robert Irvine informed the registrar by letter of his intention to resign as Professor of Economics and Dean of the Faculty of Economics from the beginning of that month. The reasons he gave for his resignation were ill health from January 1922 and a severe breakdown due to lack of leave from his arduous University duties. A desire to devote more time to writing was a further reason Irvine gave for seeking early retirement. By today's standards, Irvine at 63 would not be considered too young to retire, but in the 1920s professors were expected to continue teaching until the retirement age of 65. On 12 September 1922, H.E. Barff as registrar informed Irvine that his resignation had been accepted by the Senate and that the sum of £275 would be paid to him on retirement in lieu of leave entitlements. Subsequently, the University made a payment of £2000 by way of Irvine's 'superannuation', a sum based on the aggregate premiums paid for the customary insurance policy by which the University at that stage provided for this contingency.

The minutes of the Senate meeting which had accepted Irvine's resignation at a special meeting on 11 September 1922 dealt with these financial matters. They also clearly imply that this was not the full story, and that Irvine's resignation had been forced on him because of circumstances other than ill health. In its minutes Senate recorded 'that the resignation of Professor Irvine as Professor of Economics is accepted by the Senate not on the grounds advanced in Professor Irvine's letter of the 6th instant but by reason of other matters that he has disclosed to the University Solicitor and which have been brought to the notice of the Senate'. In June 1921, Senate Minutes recorded that Irvine's leave had been postponed because of pressures of his teaching, but at its meeting of 14 August the chancellor had referred to an unspecified 'confidential matter' which he had asked the University solicitor to investigate. As a result of this investigation, he reported at the special meeting of 11 September that 'the University Solicitor had informed him that Professor Irvine had asked to be permitted to retire voluntarily from the Chair of Economics as from the 1st of September' (SM: 11 September 1922). Debate in June 1925 at a special meeting of Senate called to consider the resignation of Associate Professor Christopher Brennan on grounds of adultery and divorce explains the likely subject of this investigation. It produced the remark that the circumstances surrounding the demands for Brennan's dismissal were exactly the same as in the Irvine case and that 'Senate would be inconsistent if it had asked for Irvine's resignation [on such grounds] but not for Brennan's'. In the end, Senate voted sixteen to four that Brennan would be asked to resign (SM: 15 June 1922).

Irvine's entry in the *Australian Dictionary of Biography* (McFarlane 1983, p. 438) therefore correctly records that 'Irvine was forced to resign in 1922 when his adultery was brought to the attention of the University authorities'. Further documented quarrels (in 1928) about the share of Irvine's superannuation money to go to his wife and the reprimand Irvine had received from Barff in 1916 support the view that matrimonial misdemeanours forced Irvine's resignation by the Senate. Barff's reprimand had come in the context of an item in the *Daily Telegraph* (7 July 1916) on Miss Elsie Simpson, an American lady, who was claimed to have been assisting Professor Irvine at the University of Sydney. Vastly changed attitudes to divorce and adultery make Irvine's forced resignation difficult to understand today. However, it is instructive to recall in this context that during the 1950s the Australian academic world was set ablaze by extensive debate over the Orr case, in which the University of Tasmania obtained the dismissal of its Professor of Philosophy on somewhat similar grounds (Eddy 1961).

The public explanation of reasons for Irvine's departure was therefore of a face-saving nature for all parties concerned. *Hermes*, the University magazine (November 1922, pp. 183–40) reported that the news of Irvine's resignation 'on the grounds of ill health was received by his students with dismay'. This article, written by Irvine's faculty colleague, F.A. Bland, added that 'however vividly his lecture discussions may be recollected, they will not oust the affectionate memory of the less formal help he managed to give his students outside the lecture room'. *Hermes* also recognised that Irvine's 'influence extended far beyond the University sphere', that it covered economics, art, literature and history, and that 'he [had] developed a school of economics which stands unrivalled in the Empire outside the United Kingdom'. In the same issue (p. 184), the secretary of the Sydney University Economics Society indicated 'a sad gloom hangs over the Society … Professor Irvine … has resigned'. The following issue described Irvine as 'the father of Political Economy' and as 'a big hearted, fearless and cultured gentleman' (*Hermes*, June 1923, p. 40). Much later, Sir Leslie Melville, who had attended some of Irvine's lectures in the early 1920s, recalled in an interview:

> Irvine was an interesting teacher, though I wouldn't say he was a very good economist. He was unorthodox in his teaching on money and banking, emphasising the idea of money as a veil. He was influenced by the ideas of Hobson … At this time there was a great amount of discussion about Douglas social credit. We spent quite some time arguing about money and credit. That debate certainly impressed … He certainly was not a Marxist. He had I think Labor leanings. Maybe Fabian socialism … But he was certainly a supporter of Hobson's views on a lot of things. (Cornish 1993, p. 438)

The faculty (FM: 19 October 1922) passed the following resolution for transmission to Irvine: 'that the Faculty receives with regret the tidings of Professor Irvine's resignation. It wishes to place on record its appreciation of the great service he has rendered to the teaching of Economics both at the University and in the State'.

McFarlane (1983, p. 438) also reports that Irvine was unpopular in some University circles because of his radical political views, increasingly evident from the unorthodox opinions he presented in his lectures and published articles (cf. McFarlane 1966, esp. pp. 15–18). Buckley and Wheelwright (1998, p. 95) more strongly assert that 'Irvine antagonised powerful conservative forces within the University and outside, and in 1922, when he was accused of adultery, he was forced to resign from his University Chair'. Although the matter of Irvine's unorthodox economic views seems never to have been brought explicitly to the Senate's notice, the matter was informally raised by a Senator and former colleague of Irvine, Sir Henry Braddon. On 24 February 1921, Barff wrote to the vice-chancellor that Sir Henry Braddon wished to see both him and the chancellor about Irvine's articles in the *Sunday Times* (a paper run by Labor leader and one-time premier, William Holman) which were appearing on a weekly basis from early January 1921. These addressed matters of finance, credit, debt, tax incidence and the need for radical social change. This included the most recent manifestation of such change in the 1917 Bolshevik revolution, Major Douglas' heretical ideas on social credit and the inherent deficiency of purchasing power in capitalist society, as well as syndicalist ideas on social organisation and reform.

Braddon himself had received letters critical of Sydney University Economics and its professor from members of the public on that day. A letter from Arthur Eedy, general secretary of the MLC insurance company, reported that recent Diplomas of Commerce and Economics from the University of Sydney constituted a 'disqualification [in] seeking employment with this Company ... because the effects of the training in the School of Economics are in my opinion not good, and I attribute the unsettling of some members of our staff to it'. A letter from a Mr R.D. Miller to Braddon on Irvine's thirteen articles described them as an 'extraordinary mass of false economics', as an 'attack on the gold standard' and as 'ignorant rubbish on the subject of credit', views all the more disgraceful because they came from a man who was entrusted to teach the subject 'at our University'. Miller's letter concluded, '[t]ruly Professor Irvine is a very dangerous man to have as Professor of Economics at the University. Brainy young men will be disgusted with his teaching, while those of poor mentality will be encouraged to indulge in foolish if not dangerous ideas' (Sydney University Archives, File 11055). This same file contains Irvine's 1912 professorial contract with the stipulation that 'the tenure of office [as professor] is during good behaviour and that the Senate shall have power to remove the Professor from his office for misconduct'. There is no doubt that ten years later the Senate exercised that power over Irvine. Whether the misconduct was confined to Irvine's adultery or also included his increasingly unorthodox views and lectures is not easily deduced. The adverse views on Irvine's teaching from members of the public, of which the chancellor and vice-chancellor were well aware, undoubtedly made members of the University Senate eager to demand Irvine's resignation for moral misconduct, because it conveniently bypassed the thorny issue of academic freedom raised by dismissal for the contents of his teaching.

The elevation of R.C. Mills to dean and professor

At its meeting of 9 October 1922, Senate decided to offer R.C. Mills the now vacant chair of economics. Mills had been appointed immediately as acting professor at the Senate meeting which discussed Irvine's resignation and which had also appointed the selection committee for the vacant chair (SM: 11 September 1922). That committee never met, being bypassed by the decision of the Senate's October meeting.

At its meeting of 19 October 1922, the first after Irvine's resignation, the faculty asked Mills to take the chair on the motion of Sir Henry Braddon, elected him unanimously to dean (on the motion of Braddon and Portus) and (on the motion of Russell and Braddon) congratulated him on his newly acquired professorship. Mills thereafter was repeatedly re-elected until his resignation in 1945 as Professor of Economics and Dean of the Faculty of Economics on entering the Commonwealth Public Service as full-time chairman of the Universities Commission.

Richard Charles Mills was born in Mooloopna, Victoria, in 1886, and had studied law, history and political economy at the University of Melbourne as part of his law studies, graduating LLB (1909) and LLM (1910). He lectured on law, especially constitutional history, at the University of Melbourne in 1911. In 1912–15 Mills studied at the London School of Economics under Graham Wallas, winning the Hutchinson Medal and graduating DSc in Economics. His thesis, published as *The Colonisation of Australia, 1829–42* (Mills 1915) became an authoritative work on colonial history, and heralded further publications by Mills on Australian economic history and the history of economic thought. After distinguished service in World War I, Mills returned to Melbourne in 1919 to lecture on history and to serve on a Victorian Royal Commission on prices, the first of many official appointments he obtained. As already indicated, he was appointed lecturer in economics at Sydney University in late 1920 and rapidly rose to professor and dean after Irvine's resignation (Butlin 1953, pp. 177–80; Groenewegen 1986).

During the 1920s, Mills was active in promoting the value of economic and business studies both at the University and in the wider community. He strongly supported establishment of the Economic Society of Australia and New Zealand in 1924, including its New South Wales Branch, and served as adviser to the editor of its journal, the *Economic Record*, from 1925 to 1945. With his 1920s Sydney colleague, Fred Benham (see below), he published a text on the *Principles of Money, Banking, and Foreign Exchange and their Application to Australia* (Mills and Benham 1925) and many articles in the *Economic Record* (five during the 1920s). *Hermes* (November 1922, pp. 182–83) greeted the new professor as a student of Cannan and Hobson (wrongly, as Mills, who had declined the offer of a chair at Otago to come to Sydney, was never Hobson's student and his real mentors at the London School of Economics besides Cannan were Lillian Knowles and Graham Wallas). It also mentioned Mills, as someone well versed in the French language, in law and constitutional history, to which the author of the article (F.A. Bland, signing himself JFB) could personally attest.

Further changes to academic staff, 1922–28

As lecturer in economics, Mills was replaced in 1923 by F.C. Benham, like Mills a graduate of the London School of Economics and an admirer of Cannan. Benham left Sydney on a Rockefeller Fellowship in 1928 and resigned his Sydney lectureship not long thereafter to take up a lectureship at London. During his six years at Sydney, Benham published four articles in the *Economic Record*, wrote a text with Mills on *Money, Banking and Foreign Exchange* and in 1928 published an important and original work, *The Prosperity of Australia* (Benham 1928). Butlin described the Benham of those days as

> a self-confident, brash young man ... He usually lectured in a room with a very long dais, walking to and fro on its very edge, without notes, and his eyes either straight ahead or roving over the class whose pleasurable anticipation that he must some day walk over the edge was never realised. But his students enjoyed his lectures for their clarity and logical development, and they liked the man who joined freely and enthusiastically in the less academic activity of the University Economics Society. (1962, pp. 386–87)

A sample of Benham's lecture content in economics has been preserved in the notes taken by Stacy Atkin (discussed below), and his influence on economics teaching at the University lasted until the late 1950s because his text, *Economics*, was until then regarded as quite satisfactory for Economics I students as one of a number of recommended textbooks.

The vacancy created by Benham's resignation was filled by Ronald Walker, a graduate of the faculty who had earlier (7 February 1927) been appointed to the three-year 'Albert lectureship' in economics, so called because it had been financed by Frank Albert, a generous friend of the Faculty of Economics in many ways. On taking up the lectureship left vacant by Benham, Walker was in turn replaced for the remaining duration of the temporary Albert lectureship by Robert Madgwick, who later replaced Portus as lecturer in Economic History.

Most of the temporary lecturing staff in the non-economics subjects offered by the faculty were regularly reappointed. The Senate Minutes for the 1920s records the reappointment of Bland to teach Municipal and Public Administration courses, of Hodgson to teach the Economics of Railway Transport, of Cleary to teach Business Principles and Practice, of P.R. Watts to teach Political Institutions, of Portus to teach Economic History and of D.T. Sawkins to teach Elementary Statistics. In 1925, Wolfenden was appointed to teach the two accountancy courses, to be replaced on his resignation in 1927 by Ivo Kerr, a faculty graduate. Cleary as teacher of Business Principles was replaced for a year (1928) because of ill health, and in February 1930 resigned his long-held Business Principles teaching post because its duties were incompatible with his appointment as New South Wales Chief Commissioner for Railways. Cleary had been the first BEc on the faculty's teaching staff, and made the generous gesture of donating the whole of his salary as part-time lecturer to a University appeal fund which had been launched in 1928.

Butlin (1970, p. 9) singled out Sawkins as the most notable of these teachers. He gave the half course in Elementary Statistics, which was then, Butlin added, 'the only such course in the University', hence obviating the adjective 'economic'. This only became necessary, as Butlin put it, when 'the scientists discovered statistics'. That Sawkins was a genuine character was also illustrated by Butlin:

> Sawkins was too good a mathematician to be a first-rate teacher of elementary statistics and mediocre students were reduced to confusion by his minor eccentricities, such as his parlour tricks with arithmetic, and his attaché case, opened on a high lectern, behind whose lid his head disappeared at intervals—for a quick nip, it was gleefully alleged. Sawkins was well aware of the effect he created, and enjoyed playing the part. Few students had reason to complain of the justice of his examination results, though they were the despair of his colleagues and of the Examinations Department. Sawkins awarded numerical marks according to the arithmetical accuracy of answers to a long series of questions, far too long for anyone to complete but of which students were told to do as many as they could. But he awarded gradings in complete disregard of the marks according to his judgement of the student's understanding of the problems set. Fortunately, these curious procedures were unknown to students, to whom it would have been difficult to explain that the final results were really proper, and showed good correspondence with students' other results.

The faculty's growing number of full-time staff and students, together with the completion of the University quadrangle in 1924, meant that the faculty was given better accommodation. The Senate's Building and Grounds Committee recommended that Economics be given two lecture theatres and three staff rooms on the dormer floor, in the corner of the quadrangle near the vice-chancellor's office. From their scattered locations of the previous years, which at one stage included staff accommodation in the stone cottage adjoining the Union Building, the small faculty teaching staff could now be housed together (SM: 10 October 1924; Butlin 1970, p. 10). This spot was to be the faculty's home until it moved in 1951 to what is now called the R.C. Mills Building (and which then, equally appropriately, was simply called the Economics Building).

Change in by-laws governing the degree curriculum, 1924

During 1923 and 1924 the Faculty of Economics contemplated new by-laws for its degree curriculum, for implementation in 1925. At the same time, changes were made to the Diploma of Economics and Commerce. Its name was shortened to Diploma of Commerce (FM: 17 October 1923; SM: 2 June 1924) and its subjects were simply prescribed as follows. In first year, Diploma students attempted Accountancy I (A and B), Business Principles and Practice, and a special course in English; in second year, they took Accountancy II, Modern Political Institutions and Part I of Commercial and Industrial Law; in third year, they took Economics I, Economic Geography and Part II of Commercial and Industrial Law (SM: 2 June 1924). The altered syllabus for the diploma fully justified the removal of 'Economics' from its name. The Diploma of Commerce survived in this way until its effective abolition during the final years of World War II.

Changes in the structure of the BEc included in the by-laws from 1925 were far more significant. They made four successive years of economics studies the core of the degree, and included training in the subject areas which formed the *raison d'être* of the first four departments other than Economics created in the faculty from the late 1930s. These were Government and Public Administration, Accounting (including Commercial and Industrial Law), Economic History and Economic Statistics. Moreover, the 1925 by-laws made the first two years of studies for the BEc common to all students (even if they permitted limited choice in some subjects); the third and fourth years were subdivided into two streams (known as Groups A and B) of which Group B was designed to enable specialisation in Accounting.

In the common first year, students were now required to take Economics I, Philosophy I (Logic and Psychology) which was largely devoted to scientific method, and the two half courses Business Principles and Practice (a general introduction to commercial activity) and Economic Geography (a course whose subject matter covered material similar to the later faculty course, Descriptive Economics, subsequently called The Australian Economy). Compared to the 1918 by-laws, this significantly reduced choice for first-year students by removing it from a wide range of Arts subjects for two of the first-year subject slots.

For second year, students had to take Economics II, the two half courses Modern Political Institutions and Part I of Commercial and Industrial Law, and as third subject a Faculty of Arts course from the list in Chapter X section 4 of the by-laws (that is, either Greek, Latin, English, French, German, Japanese, History, Philosophy, Psychology, Roman Law, Constitutional Law, Jurisprudence or Public Interest Law), or from various Science subjects if not previously taken.

For third year, students had to take Economics III in both Groups A and B, the half course Statistics together with Accountancy IA (Group A) or Part II of Commercial and Industrial Law (Group B), and as third subject, Public Administration (Group A) and Accountancy IA and B (Group B). Again, this differed significantly from the 1918 by-laws for the degree in which Economics III was not compulsory (students who had completed Insurance Mathematics I could continue with Insurance Mathematics II instead), while Economic History and Industrial and Commercial Law (that is, its Parts I and II) constituted the two additionally required courses.

Fourth year required Economics IV and Economic History for all students and, in addition for Group A students, a full course from the list of Arts subjects specified for second year, if not already taken, and Accountancy II for Group B students. Compared to the 1918 by-laws, Public Administration was removed from fourth year, as well as the choice of any combination of two from a long list of available half courses or taking the specified Arts courses Philosophy I (Psychology) or Philosophy II (sociology), or Accountancy II, while History of Economic Thought was no longer the compulsory third subject in fourth year. However, compulsory history of economic thought studies remained in the degree, since the new (compulsory) Economics IV syllabus was essentially a seminar course, given by Mills (cf. Black 1970, pp. 14–15) on the development of modern economic doctrines, in which the textbooks were all histories of economic thought, that is, those by Cannan, Gide and Rist, Haney and Ingram (1925 UC: p. 226).

There were only minor alterations to the new BEc curriculum in the second half of the decade. These arose from changes in the Philosophy I (Psychology) syllabus, making revision of the specification of subjects for first year desirable. More generally, these revisions to the by-laws heralded the structure of what in the 1950s became known as the 'old' by-laws, which more readily embodied the developing departmental structures. The new 1925 structure, to reiterate, incorporated two of the principles on which faculty undergraduate teaching was to be based over the next quarter century: compulsory Economics I, II, III and IV as the core of the degree and a large measure of compulsion over the remaining courses, designed to encourage specialisation. In the opinion of its teachers, this new curriculum went further to meet the requirements of what the BEc was intended to achieve in educating people either for business or for the public service.

Some prominent graduates from the first decade

As compared with later decades, the enrolment data provided earlier indicate that BEc student numbers included a significant number of women. For the 1920s, about a quarter of the students enrolled in the Faculty of Economics were women, the peak occurring in 1922 when this proportion reached 30 per cent. This compared with an average of 22.3 for the University as a whole and to 46.4 per cent for the Faculty of Arts (Turner, Bygott and Chippendale 1991, Appendix 4; SM). Teaching was a major motivation for women taking the degree, future commercial employment may have been another, though the ratio of women enrolled for the Diploma of Economics was much lower than that for the BEc degree. The men, largely evening students, tended to come from financial institutions (especially banking and insurance) and were either eager to improve their qualifications or aimed at better careers in general commercial activity, the public service or education.

An indication of the later activities of prominent faculty graduates adds to the information about their employment as graduates. Some of them were previously mentioned in other contexts: W.J. Cleary, a 1918 graduate, was part-time teacher in business principles for most of the 1920s before his appointment as chief commissioner in the New South Wales Railways; Ivo Kerr, the Accountancy lecturer appointed in 1927, was a 1917 graduate; Hermann Black and Robert Madgwick also became university teachers, while Black subsequently became Chancellor of the University of Sydney and Madgwick Vice-Chancellor of the University of New England. Other economics students were arts students. They included Ronald Walker and George Duncan who both completed MAs and were later employed as university teachers and, in the case of Walker, in the diplomatic service.

More than 40 years later, Black recalled the type of student of his undergraduate days in the following manner:

> We were all secretly proud to be members of the University of Sydney. There is an occasional current fashion which asserts that in some ways we were "privileged". But the numbers of those who struggled at expense to themselves belied this. One

> was lucky to have an Exhibition ... a mere two hundred for the whole State; or a Bursary ... a mere thirty for N.S.W.; or a Teacher's College Scholarship to admit one to a degree course. Even the latter facility had its conditions ... one had, in "my day", to secure a credit in at least one subject to be permitted to continue, or at least give a good account of oneself in the Examinations. Sprinkled among us were returned soldiers, come back after the bloodiest of wars, to complete their degrees; and what was outstanding among them was not a compulsive desire to talk about the trenches of France or the wide spaces of Mesopotamia, or the rocky crags of Gallipoli, but a remarkable gaiety, a sort of gusty joie de vivre. (1970, p. 14)

Other names of faculty students are easily recalled because of fame gained in their subsequent careers. They include Leslie Melville (later Sir Leslie, and BEc with first-class honours in 1925) who had a distinguished career in university teaching (the youngest economics professor at Adelaide), banking and the public service; Clarey Martin (MEc with honours in 1932), who started his career in teaching tutorial classes at Newcastle before moving into politics, becoming Attorney-General in New South Wales in 1941; William Ian (later Sir Ian) Potter who graduated in 1928 with a distinguished academic record to become a well known stockbroker and later chairman of the Stock Exchange; Eric Scott became a noted educationist, working at the Teachers' College for many years and supervising the Economics syllabus for the Leaving Certificate; and finally, A.F. Albert, a graduate in 1930, the son of Frank Albert the music publisher who generously financed a temporary lectureship in economics and funded many academic prizes for students of the faculty. The last included the Frank Albert Prizes for proficiency in each year of the bachelor degree course, which entitled the winners not only to the usual cash prize but to a sumptuous lunch with the donor. (I qualified for this honour in 1960 as one of the last Frank Albert Prize winners in the faculty and recall with pleasure the splendid three-course lunch, with wines to match, in the Union Withdrawing Room.)

Faculty first-year enrolments in 1928 introduced quite a few students with distinguished subsequent careers. In alphabetical order, they included S.J. Butlin, who in 1946 succeeded Mills as dean and as Professor of Economics, and therefore features strongly in subsequent chapters; John Crawford (later Sir John), BEc in 1932 and MEc in 1940, a hard-working evening student who after a career as an agricultural economist and banker was co-author with Colin Clark of a book on national income statistics (Clark and Crawford 1938), headed the Department of Trade in Canberra, was director of the School of Pacific Studies at the Australian National University and later its vice-chancellor; A.F. Deer, later general manager of the MLC; Ivan Dougherty (later Sir Ian), who had a distinguished military career; and John Phillips (later Sir John), a banker who ended his career as Governor of the Reserve Bank. This was a truly brilliant cohort, making 1928 a vintage year for the faculty. Moreover, and demonstrating that romance was not necessarily banished from a faculty devoting itself to studying the 'dismal science', two of these faculty entrants found their wives among their fellow students: Sir John Phillips married Mary Debenham (an Arts student taking Economics who later worked as a secretary for the faculty for a brief period), while Syd Butlin married Dorothy Jean Conen (BEc, like her husband-to-be, in 1932).

The Sydney University Economics Society

The new faculty inspired a new faculty society. The Sydney University Economics Society was founded during 1920 and by 1921 had 150 members. Its objectives were more modest than those of its predecessor, the short-lived Economics and Commerce Association of New South Wales. Given its existence until 1943, the new society's objectives may be quoted in full:

> To encourage and develop the discussion from all points of view, of economic and applied questions by way of debate or by such other means as may be considered expedient.
>
> To foster and maintain a Faculty esprit de corps by arranging as far as possible for the economic and social welfare of members in so far as their mutual relations as students may be concerned.
>
> To co-operate, whenever possible, with other societies with a view to furthering that recent commendable movement for the propagation and maintenance of a community spirit within the University. (Annual Report 1921–22, University Archives)

Irvine, whose ideas are clearly visible in the objectives of the new society, was its foundation president ex officio. In 1921, he continued in office, together with three vice-presidents (Flora Eldershaw, author, high school teacher, public servant and industrial consultant; Portus and Taylor), J.M. Wilcox (BEc 1921) was honorary secretary and there was a small student committee. To finance its activities, it charged a modest, voluntary fee of half a crown (two shillings and sixpence). It proposed monthly meetings for debates and talks, social events, and later also organised faculty teams for inter-faculty sports competitions. No such activities were reported in its Annual Reports for 1920–21 and 1921–22, though the first of these proudly proclaimed that the faculty debating team consisting of McKay, Moore and Martin won the inter-faculty debating competition in 1921, a success repeated in 1922 and 1923. *Hermes* (November 1920), however, reported a well-attended meeting to debate the merits of a Profiteering prevention bill while four meetings in 1921 debated 'industrial control', 'unemployment', 'the social justification of the leisure class' and the principles espoused in Keynes' 1919 *Economic Consequences of the Peace* (*Hermes*, August 1921, p. 150).

The 1922–23 Annual Report mentioned that R.C. Mills had replaced Irvine as president. Phoebe Miller was now honorary secretary, and Benham vice-president. A membership of 80 was reported. The annual membership fee was now a compulsory 2s. 6d., but opportunities for life membership were provided on the payment of half a guinea. From 1923, the society systematically arranged the types of activities for which it had been founded. These continued over the two decades of its existence. There were social functions in the form of an annual dance, participation in inter-faculty, and occasionally inter-varsity, sports, debating competitions and meetings at which speakers presented papers. Speakers included Benham on 'the Foreign Exchanges' in May 1923, a talk which attracted 75 persons, and Miss D.M. Rivett (a 1918 BA who had studied Economics for her degree) on

'Psychology in Economics' to an audience of 65 in July 1923. In August 1923, 70 members and visitors debated the topic 'whether capitalism has failed' while for the final meeting for the year in September 1923, Duncan-Hall addressed 55 members on 'Imperial Preference'. That year, the society's debating team (comprising Melville, Jarvie and Heathwood) was University champion (*Union Recorder*, 18 October 1923, p. 2). All in all, 1922–23 was a successful year for the Society.

Hermes likewise recorded some of the 1923–24 society activities in glowing terms. At the 1923 annual meeting the secretary reported that Mills 'informed us of the economic history of tobacco from the humorous and romantic points of view. Many of us felt that this was the ideal method of teaching economic subjects. Mr Portus, not be out-romanced, recounted some amazing personal experiences of hair breath escapes on the dust-bitten plains of wildest Australia' (*Hermes*, September 1923, p. 131). At the 1924 welcome to freshers, Mills' presidential address mentioned the story of 'an old gentleman who mistook him for the venerable John Stuart Mill' and the whole occasion was considered a grand success. 'The ghost of Carlyle, who damned economics as a "dismal science", must have fled incontinent from the Union Bevery had it seen the gaiety and the lightheartedness of the Economists gathered therein to hear the Dean welcome the newcomers,' reported R.B. Modlin and Hermann Black (*Hermes*, Lent 1924, p. 55).

The society continued to be active over the next five years. Membership rose from 44 in 1924–25 to 75 in 1928–29. Five general meetings were usually held each year of which the first, in April, was a social occasion for welcoming 'freshers', and the time when the outgoing president gave the address. Mills continued as president for several years, to be replaced in 1926–27 by Benham, by Walker in 1927–28, and by Portus in 1928–29. Other formal meetings followed, with a variety of topics and speakers. Speakers came from student members, faculty teaching staff, university teaching staff and outside visitors, including academics from other universities. Topics were mainly economic in nature, but also included topics in public administration, history and economic history, and social and political issues.

For example, 1924 topics included 'Our Foreign Neighbours' by Professor Griffith Taylor (Economic Geography), 'Economics of Motherhood Endowment' by Bradley Goodwin, an MEc student, 'Immigration' by Miss Campbell and 'Fatigue from Factors affecting Production' by Professor B. Muscio (Logic and Mental Philosophy, that is, Psychology). The following year, Hermann Black led a debate on 'Protection and Australia's Secondary Industries', with Joseph Wilcox, Allan McConnell, Robert Madgwick and Owen Parry as the other speakers, an event attracting only 25 listeners. Subsequently that year, Dr McKenna (Zoology) spoke on 'Some Biological Factors of Interest to the Economist'; there was a public debate on strikes led by Madgwick, and Professor Browne lectured on 'The Future of Australia's Primary Industries'. During 1926, only three papers were given: one by the venerable Archdeacon Woodthorpe on the 'Nature and Functions of the State', one by Ronald Walker on 'the Economic Motive' and one by Stacy Atkin, a fourth-year student. For 1927, Professor Alfred Radcliffe-Brown (Anthropology) spoke on 'Primitive Economics'; a United States visitor, Professor Carter Goodrich, spoke on 'Labour Movements in Australia and America'; R.C. Mills spoke on 'The New Financial Agreement Between the States and the Commonwealth', while the year closed with a general discussion on 'The Relation of Industrialisation to Craftsmanship and Beauty of Environment'. Only two meetings were held in 1928 and in 1929. Portus spoke on 'Some Thoughts on Distribution' and Professor John Anderson (Philosophy) on the 'Economic Interpretation of History' in 1928 while during 1929 Professor James Brigden (Tasmania) discussed 'The Economist in Business' and Bland 'Some Problems in the Civil Service'.

The society's other activities are more quickly summarised. After its initial failure, the 'freshers' welcomes' attracted substantial numbers (about 70 on average with a maximum of 100) as did the annual dance, which usually made a handsome profit for the society. These helped to defray its quite substantial expenses, sufficiently onerous to force an increase in the annual membership fee to 3 shillings. Black recalled a typical Economics Society dance from the 1920s:

> Female students were few, and therefore favoured. At a Faculty Dance, you danced with the lot; and when Freddy Benham (textbook Freddy) came, he gave us a superb demonstration with one student, now alas, long dead, cut down in frailest youth, of how to cover the floor with grace. He helped with the decorations, until he fell off a ladder, and waltzed the evening with a plaster bandage from ear to ear, across his nose; and until it healed, he always seemed to enter the lecture room nose first, a sight too comic for most of us, and we roared him in. (1970, p. 15)

The society enjoyed many sporting successes. In 1925, the faculty team (including Hermann Black and Robert Madgwick) won the inter-varsity rifle match. Faculty tennis, athletics, cricket and football teams also competed, sometimes in combination with Architecture students, the faculty teams winning cups for inter-faculty cricket and athletics in 1926. The previous year, a staff–student tennis match featured staff doubles Mills and Benham, Cleary and Dale, Portus and Bland, who managed to defeat the students narrowly by a margin of fourteen games over sixteen sets (*Union Recorder*, 16 July 1925, p. 142). However, in the 1928 Annual Report, retiring president Ronald Walker requested more support for sport as no successes on the field had been achieved by the faculty over the previous two years. The faculty fielded its first rugby league team during Portus' presidency, appropriately given his former proclivities on the football field. Finally, the initial successes in debating of 1921, 1922 and 1923 as University champions were not repeated and the faculty debating teams were generally eliminated from the competition at the semi-final stage. An exception was when the 1928 team reached the finals.

The Evening Students Association also conducted social evenings, which 'day students' of the 1920s such as Hermann Black attended:

> Nowhere did this [the presence of ex-serviceman students] display itself more than at the Evening Students' Smokos. These revels in the old Union Hall were riotously noisy affairs, the floor being covered with saw-dust, like a bar room of yore; vast quantities of plain old fashioned beer were consumed (this was the pre-wine-bibbing era), and a few viands only floated on the fluid base. Lusty singing roared up to the rafters, but a student artist, like Russell Rix with his

robust baritone gave us the traditional song to elevate the evening. And all this attested one thing … we were students and it was a superbly pleasant thing to be. (Black 1970, p. 14)

An individual student's experience: Stacy Atkin's lecture notes

In 1923, Stacy Atkin entered the University of Sydney as a student in the Faculty of Economics. He did so as one of eleven recipients of a Public Exhibition in Economics, which exempted him from student fees (SM: 5 March 1923), a considerable achievement given their small number. His progress through the degree courses was satisfactory without achieving the results gained by his fellow students, Madgwick and Black. He maintained contact with the faculty by becoming a life member of the Sydney University Economics Society, and as a fourth-year student addressed one of its meetings on the topic, 'Equal Pay for Equal Work', a subject on which he had been lectured in first year. Atkin had a distinguished career in insurance, rising to the position of assistant general manager at the MLC.

Atkin passed Economics I, English I and Psychology I in his first year; Economics II and the four half courses in Statistics, Business Principles, Accountancy IA and Economic Geography for his second year; Economics III, Commercial and Industrial Law and Economic History in his third year; and he completed the requirements for the degree in his fourth year (1926) by taking Accountancy II, Public Administration and History of Economic Thought. Being placed second and fifth in the pass order of merit list for History of Economic Thought and Economic History were his major academic distinctions as an undergraduate. Having commenced his studies in 1923, his degree followed the curriculum laid down in the 1918 by-laws. His lecture timetable was presented earlier to illustrate the study task faced by the evening students (then predominant in the faculty) from necessity rather than choice.

The reason for devoting a special section to this student of the 1920s is that he preserved his lecture notes for the first three years of his studies (presented in 1989 to the author by Atkin's son, and now in the University Archives). These notes provide a unique insight of the type of material taught for the degree in the mid-1920s but only a brief impression of their rich contents can be given, with an occasional quote of some selected snippets.

In Economics I, the lectures provided an introduction to the principles of economics covering scope and method, production, exchange and distribution; the state and industry; and elements of the theory of taxation. Mills, who was the lecturer, showed himself critical of the textbooks (which more than likely had been selected the year before by Irvine). At one stage Mills stated about two of the authors of these texts on a topic in distribution, that 'Clay is of course wrong, as he follows Hobson'. Atkin took down this brief description of inflation as experienced during Germany in 1923: 'Before the war [1914–18], I went to the market with my money in my pocket and brought my goods back in a basket; but now I take my money in the basket and bring my goods back in my pocket'. Unemployment was explained in terms of inflexible wage rates (what Keynes was to call the classical supply and demand theory), an explanation which persisted in the more detailed treatment of this topic offered in Economics II and III. Finally, feminists in his class could not have been too annoyed with the analysis of why women's wages were lower than men's wages 'in the same occupation'. Atkin took this down as, 'Women are not inefficient as would be imagined. Are they physically weaker? Probably, but this is not the cause. Many occupations are shut to women. They work in a narrow area.' Hence excess supply of women workers in the jobs in which they could be employed explained why their wages were lower than those paid to men in the same occupation. Atkin's English I course covered language, Chaucer and Shakespeare. A World War I anecdote was recorded to illustrate one of the many vagaries of that phrase, 'English language': 'prominent sign on shop near the front: English spoken, American understood'. Atkin's Psychology I course concentrated on logic and scientific method, the lectures were illustrated by many military metaphors, but also contained a great deal of material on heredity and on the nature and working of the brain.

In second year, the Economics II notes covered the syllabus on value, money, credit and banking, foreign exchange and international trade and trade policy, and the organisation of industry including trusts. It ended with a discussion of industrial fluctuations. The last lectures inspired Atkin to record 'that the chief evil of the Trade Cycle is perhaps the unemployment in times of depression'. The other lecture topics were competently presented with quite a few illustrations from the history of the subject. They seem to have been given by Benham, constituting thereby useful preparation for his book with Mills mentioned earlier (Mills and Benham 1925). Atkin's notes for the four half courses he took to complete his second year convey some interesting insights into their contents. Few notes were taken for Business Principles, which largely followed Braddon's textbook, even though the course was by then taught by his successor, Cleary. Elementary statistics involved much graphing and arithmetical calculations, as Butlin recalled from a half decade later. Accounting lectures commenced with a historical introduction to affirm its long lineage as a practical art, and then covered the elements of bookkeeping, the major accounts and statements including the balance sheet, profit and loss account, and illustrated from the practice relevant to particular industries. Finally, Economic Geography covered climate and patterns of land use, focusing on resource use in rural activity and mining by giving an overview of these together with population data for many countries arranged by continents. Their substantial final segment on Australia dealt with similar topics together with trade, irrigation, and the use of water resources more generally, including hydro-electricity.

Economics III dealt with problems of distribution such as poverty and inequality; alternative economic systems (that is, capitalism versus socialism including a lecture on developments in Soviet Russia, the notions of syndicalism and workers' control) ending with a strong attack on Douglas social credit. Third term was completely devoted to public finance topics, that is, government revenue (a great deal on taxes and their incidence, a little on public borrowing including some comment on the forced taxation implied in financing government activity through the printing press) followed by a review of public expenditures (containing much discussion on the relationship between education, economic growth and income distribution). Surprisingly, they said nothing about fiscal federalism problems. The Economic History lectures by Portus frequently bordered on social and political history, particularly the Australian material. Ancient history and a critical discussion of the economic determination of history (particularly with respect to Marx's historical materialism) together with an overview of British history covering the middle ages, occupied the first term. The Tudor period and the Industrial Revolution followed in second term, with much discussion of mercantilism versus free trade and strong emphasis on the importance of freedom for economic growth as well as labour and industrial history, Owenite socialism and liberal reform. Australian history dwelled on Henry George, unions and strikes, the myth of Australia as a 'workingman's paradise', ALP history and federal Labor politics, hence justifying the earlier judgement that Portus' economic history was often indistinguishable from labour and political history. Atkin's final subject, Commercial and Industrial Law taught by Bradley, systematically covered the major issues: contracts, negotiable instruments, bankruptcy, worker's compensation, arbitration and conciliation, goodwill, patents, laws of agency, partnerships, banks, insurance, and in conclusion a substantial dose of company law. Unfortunately, Atkin's fourth-year lecture notes were not preserved.

Some general observations can be made on the economics courses taken by Atkin as presented by his lecture notes. First, economics lectures had become more conservative than those Irvine had given as Professor of Economics. Parts of Portus' economic history, for example, were highly critical of Marxism and aspects of labour and trade union politics. Second, economics lectures were largely devoid of mathematics, including diagrams, with Elementary Statistics a partial exception. Instead, there was much emphasis on factual, descriptive material and applied topics, not only in Economics but also in the more business oriented courses such as Accountancy, Business Principles, and Commercial and Industrial Law.

Research and publications by teaching staff during the 1920s

Although some of the publications by Mills and Benham for the 1920s have already been mentioned, work by other teaching members of the faculty should not be ignored even if only a few teachers actively published at this time. For 1920, the 'bibliographic record of the University', then regularly published in the *University Calendars*, lists several articles on city government in the *Australian Highway* by Bland, together with an Anglican pamphlet on 'Class Consciousness'; *American Impressions*, a book of essays on a recent American visit by Sir Henry Braddon; a series of articles on 'the roots of our discontent' published by Irvine in the *Chemical Engineering and Mining Record*, together with a self portrait by Irvine as 'the Scot we know' for the *Scottish Australasian*. Guthrie, the lecturer in Technology and Industrial Products, listed six short articles in the *Agricultural Gazette N.S.W.* on wheat types, superphosphate, French potash salts, licks for different classes of country and a one-page note 'on rotted manure'.

For 1921, Bland listed a conference paper on 'The Organisation and Control of the Public Service', a five-page section on the 'Economic Effects of raising the school age' in a booklet on *Adolescent Education* and various articles (unlisted this time) for the *Australian Highway*. Guthrie reported five articles on agricultural topics connected with wheat, fertiliser, soil analysis and the saltbush; Mills listed an article on 'the Study of Australian history' for the *N.S.W. Education Gazette*; Portus a booklet on *Marx and Modern Thought* together with a newspaper article, 'The University and the Worker' for Holman's *Sunday Times*. Finally, Russell, the lecturer in Commercial and Industrial Law, listed a 28-page pamphlet on 'Cheques, special and non-negotiable crossings and their effects'.

No fewer than ten items were mentioned by Bland in 1922. They included four articles in the *Church Record*, one in the *Sydney Morning Herald*, two in the *New Outlook* (including an 'Appreciation of Irvine as a great Public Servant'), the sketch of Irvine in *Hermes* mentioned previously in this chapter, and a number of articles in the *Australian Highway*. The only other faculty publication was by Sir Henry Braddon, a pamphlet on European finance.

The following two years continued as meagre ones in faculty publication. For 1923, Bland included two publications: a 300 page book on *Shadows and Realities of Government* and an article on examinations for the *Public Service Journal of New South Wales*. Mills listed articles on 'advertising' and on 'immigration' for non-academic periodicals (though it should be remembered that the *Economic Record*, the major place for academic publication by Australian economists before 1960, was not established until 1925). In 1924, Bland was the only publisher in the faculty with a series of articles on William Lane for the *Australian Highway*.

For 1925, Benham and Mills reported the two editions in that year of their joint book on *Money, Banking and Foreign Exchange*, with Mills in addition mentioning his contribution to an official report on the Queensland basic wage, a pamphlet on 'the general problems of economics' and a short article on economic aspects of population. Bland listed an article for the public service journal on 'Government, Enterprises and Administration', a short piece on 'Areas, Agencies and Administration' for the *Shire and Municipal Record*, and he and Portus contributed chapters to the six-volume *The Story of Australia* (edited by J. Colwell) on 'Commerce and Industry', 'Land and the Water Problems' (Bland) and 'Labour, Trade Unions, the political Labour Movement, Arbitration and Wage Regulation' (Portus).

During 1926, Benham published two articles in the *Economic Record* on 'the Australian Tariff and the Standard of Living' and 'the efficiency of Australian manufacturing'; Mills also had two articles in the *Record*, both on the Tariff Board; and he contributed an entry on Edward Gibbon Wakefield to the *Australian Encyclopaedia*. Portus mentioned a very short (two-page) article on 'Marx and Hegel' he had contributed to the *Australasian Journal of Psychology and Philosophy*. This was the first year, it may be noted, when all publications recorded for members of the Faculty of Economics were 'academic' in the modern sense of the word, being published either in Australian academic journals or in a major reference work.

The 1927 publication list again featured Benham with two *Economic Record* articles (one on the national dividend, that is, national income; the other a restatement of his position on the tariff and the standard of living); in addition he contributed a chapter on wages and Australian wage regulation to the *festschrift* for Edwin Cannan. Bland published two articles for the *Australian Highway* on the Australian constitution, while Portus published another article in the *Australasian Journal of Psychology and Philosophy* on 'Some Difficulties in the Social Sciences'.

During 1928, Benham made his final contribution to faculty publications in the form of his important book, *The Prosperity of Australia*, a chapter on the optimum size of population for *The Peopling of Australia*, and a paper on Australian trade in the Pacific for the journal *Pacific Affairs*. Bland once again published ten pieces: 'Civil and Civic Services in England' and 'Public Administration' for *Red Tape*, one on 'The City and its Government' for the *Economic Record*, 'Unification and Self-Government' for the *Australasian Journal of Psychology and Philosophy*, essays on 'Training Public Servants' for both *On Service* and the *Journal of Public Administration* and articles on the 'University's Tutorial Classes Movement', 'City Government and Commissions', 'the Australian Constitution' and 'Development and Migration' for *Hesper*, a meeting of the Australian Historical Society, the Royal Commission on the Constitution of the Commonwealth and a book, *Studies in Australian Affairs*. Mills produced eight pieces including an article on federal financial relations for the *Economic Record*, a pamphlet on *Economics and Commerce*, an article on 'the Study of Australian History' for *Schooling*, material on the public debt and Australian loan policy for the Institute of Pacific Relations and *Studies in Australian Affairs*, a piece on the New South Wales income tax for the *Melbourne Stock Exchange Official Record* as well as a *Sydney Morning Herald* article on 'Britain's Industrial Future' and one for *Australia Today* on 'Australia's Credit'.

The detailed summary of the faculty's publication record in its early years is interesting for several reasons. In the light of Atkin's lecture notes, it explains some of Portus' specific emphases when teaching Economic History. Moreover, its relative shortness makes it possible at this stage to reproduce the complete record. Some specific characteristics of these faculty publications for the 1920s may be noted. Almost all of it was published in Australia, and much of its content was designed to address Australian issues in economics, politics and public administration (exceptions are the material on Marx published by Portus, and that on British industry by Mills). Secondly, relatively little of the listed material appeared in what would now be called academic publications, though some of it did (the *Economic Record* articles by Bland, Benham and Mills, the papers in the *Australasian Journal of Psychology and Philosophy* by Bland and Portus, and the paper by Bland for the [British] *Journal of Public Administration*). The authors of these articles all occupied or subsequently occupied chairs (Mills and Bland at the University of Sydney, Benham at London University in 1945, and Portus at the University of Adelaide in 1934). Braddon, Guthrie and Russell were the 'commerce' teachers whose publications were only reported during the early years of the faculty. As yet there were no publications in Accounting and Statistics.

Further initiatives in public administration and marketing

To emphasise the practical origins of the Faculty of Economics, the chapter closes by looking at two academic initiatives in public administration and in marketing which occupied the faculty at the end of the decade. The second suggestion, which initially came from outside the faculty, was not implemented. The first, on public administration, was initiated within the faculty and considerably stimulated the development of what in the late 1930s became the Department of Government and Public Administration.

At its meeting of 13 September 1928, the faculty set up a committee consisting of the Dean (R.C. Mills), Bland, Benham, Portus and Walker to investigate the feasibility of introducing a course on marketing and salesmanship. This had been requested by the United Commercial Travellers Association of Australia, with a view to introducing a diploma of marketing and salesmanship. A suggestion from Bland for the introduction of a diploma of public administration was referred to the same committee, which reported to the subsequent faculty meeting (16 November 1928) on both these proposals.

After debate, the faculty recommended the possibility of introducing a diploma of marketing and salesmanship on the following terms and conditions. It would entail a two-year course of two full courses of study per year. For first year, the course requirements were specified as Philosophy I or Accountancy I(A + B) and the existing two half courses, Business Principles and English (for Diploma of Commerce students). For their second year, these students had to take Economics I and the existing half course Commercial and Industrial Law Part I and a new half course, Marketing and Salesmanship. The diploma for students successfully completing these courses would be awarded by the Commercial Travellers Association and not by the University of Sydney, a decision probably based on a perceived lack of rigour of the two-year curriculum just described (relative to the required three years study for both the Diploma of Commerce and the proposed Diploma of Public Administration). The faculty stressed that introduction of a diploma of marketing and salesmanship would not entail new expenditure by the University. The cost of the new half course, Marketing and Salesmanship, estimated at £200, was to be met by the Commercial Travellers Association. If accepted by the University, the course was to commence in 1929 and students taking it would have to abide by the general University rule of compulsory attendance at lectures.

At its adjourned meeting of 17 December 1928, Senate referred the diploma of marketing and salesmanship proposal back to the Faculty of Economics, noting in its deliberations that the University of Melbourne had already agreed to establish such a course. This was duly reported to the next faculty meeting (21 March 1929). Faculty, however, decided that before going further with the proposal, a definite offer from the Commercial Travellers Association was required, so that the ball was firmly placed in that association's court. This proved to be the end of the matter, as Senate at its meeting of May 1929 confirmed. Marketing as a course of study had to wait for over half a century before it entered the faculty's syllabus as a specific discipline. Aspects of marketing were of course addressed in various parts of the Economics syllabus.

The diploma of public administration proposal fared considerably better. The faculty committee established in September 1928 stressed the desirability of introducing such a diploma for matriculated and unmatriculated students, placing it on a par with the Diploma of Commerce. In addition, it indicated that it would be a course of at least three years. The proposed curriculum was outlined as follows. In first year, students were to take Economics I and one optional subject; for second year, they were to take Public Administration and Economics III (with its high public finance contents) or an optional course; for third year, students had to take the two half courses Modern Political Institutions and (Advanced) Public Administration, together with Economics III (if not already taken in second year) or an optional course. Satisfactory optional courses for the new diploma could be chosen from those offered by the Faculty of Arts, or from combining two half courses available to Diploma of Commerce students. The proposal therefore required an additional Public Administration half course, that is, the (Advanced) Public Administration required for its third year. The cost of the additional lecturing salary a new public administration course entailed was optimistically expected to be recoverable fully from the fees of new students the diploma would attract. Bland, the chief proponent of the course, suggested that enrolments would be strong if the Public Service Board was persuaded to accept the diploma as an alternative to its own examinations. Bland also thought that the diploma would have the clear possibility of becoming a postgraduate course for graduates in Arts or Law desirous to enter the public service. On 21 March 1929, Bland reported to faculty that the Public Service Board of New South Wales now required the diploma instead of the subjects for examination formerly needed for promotion to higher grades. Earlier, Senate (at its 4 March meeting) had approved the new by-laws for the new diploma, with the proviso that if taken by diploma of Commerce students they must, if possible, take courses different from those already completed. In the end, the Diploma of Public Administration did not commence until 1930. It is interesting to note that the third-year compulsory combination of half courses in Political Institutions and (Advanced) Public Administration foreshadowed the mixture of disciplines from which the Department of Government and Public Administration was later constituted.

By the end of 1928, the faculty was therefore well established. It was attracting sizeable enrolments for the courses it offered, it had graduated some brilliant students, it had increased its full-time teaching staff by a considerably proportion when compared with the Board of Studies days of 1918. It also had gained better accommodation for its staff in the Arts quadrangle. Moreover, faculty had tightened its four-year curriculum for the degree with the 1924 by-law changes and had started postgraduate studies in earnest by graduating four MEc students by the end of 1928. Finally, it had also surmounted several crises, of which the damage done by the forced resignation of its foundation professor and dean was the major one.

By the late 1920s, the faculty's teaching staff included three persons with substantial publication records, to the benefit of the quality of their teaching for the students enrolled in their courses. Moreover, these students were also able to gain from the extra-curricular activities offered by the Sydney University Economics Society, with its opportunities for public speaking and debating, competitive sport and listening to addresses of relevance to the specialisations offered by the faculty. The last, as just shown, were also growing, by adding a Diploma of Public Administration to the existing Diploma of Commerce and, more importantly, by the degree studies for the BEc and the opportunity for postgraduate research which the MEc degree offered. By 1928, the Faculty of Economics showed itself to be an energetic and stimulating body of scholars, well prepared for implementing new initiatives when the opportunity arose. In the words of a 1920s undergraduate writing in *Hermes* (Lent 1927, p. 78), 'Economics is a young Faculty, but quite a virile infant'.

F.A. Bland, Professor of Public Administration

Sir Hermann Black, Senior Lecturer in Economics, Chancellor of the University

Sir Ronald Walker, Lecturer in Economics

Heinz Arndt, Senior Lecturer in Economics

Henry Mayer, Professor of Political Science

Ray Chambers, Professor of Accounting

Hugh McCredie, Lecturer in Accounting, Registrar of the University

Ted Wheelwright, Associate Professor of Economics

Carole Pateman, Professor of Political Science

Nine eminent faculty members: 1920–1999.

CHAPTER 2

The faculty in Depression and war, 1929–45

Two major traumatic world events of the twentieth century form the background to the decade and a half of faculty history told in this chapter. Both left their mark on aspects of faculty's development. The first was the Great Depression of the 1930s, which had commenced in 1929. The fiscal prudence and balancing of budgets it was believed to entail for state governments meant that university funding, and hence faculty funding, was significantly reduced. The brunt of this fiscal stringency was not felt until late in 1931 when the university (SM: 12 October 1931) imposed a 10 per cent cut in staff salaries, equal to the percentage reduction in the state government grant to the university. The Senate saw this as only temporary, to be reversed when the university's financial situation improved.

The Faculty of Economics was more widely affected by the Depression than the 1931 financial cuts. Despite the financial hardship it induced in the wider community, enrolments were surprisingly not adversely affected. The contrary occurred. As Butlin (1970, p. 10), himself a student at this time, put it, the Depression 'trebled the number of Economics students in three years'. Many of these enrolled because they wished to learn more about the phenomenon that was afflicting them so deeply, including the rationale for the policy remedies then extensively debated in the community. In addition, the demand from government for sound economic advice during the Depression called Mills to various official appointments. This started in the 1930s and, following similar demands for economist's services during the war, led ultimately to Mills' full-time employment in the Commonwealth Public Service and to his resignation as dean and professor. Like the war service of other faculty members as economic advisers and administrators, this is discussed later in this chapter.

Experience with wrong economic policy advice during the depression also brought syllabus changes, most importantly the introduction of Keynesian economics and the macro-economics edifice subsequently built thereon. These include alterations in course contents not really implemented until the post-war period (and therefore discussed in Chapter 3). However, some of Keynes' developing views were imbibed by the young Syd Butlin at Cambridge, where he completed Part II of the Economics Tripos during the mid-1930s. They therefore came quickly to Sydney economics. One 1930s student and graduate, Bruce Allen, recalls that two of his fellow students (Donald Kerr and Brian Fleming) who were doing honours, were Butlin's students when he presented Keynes' *General Theory* to them in 1936 (letter to the author, 13 September 2002). The 1936 *University Calendar* (p. 369) in fact included Keynes' major work (Keynes, 1936) as a recommended book for distinction students in Economics II, while a study of Australian Depression policy since 1929 was an important part of the 1938 Economics IV syllabus (1938 UC: p. 1015). By then, admittedly, the worst was over, and Australia's Great Depression experience was rapidly passing into economic history. It may also be noted that

Australian Depression experience was the subject for the first PhD dissertation completed within the faculty by Boris Schedvin in 1963 (conferred 1964). It was later published as a book (Schedvin, 1970) by Sydney University Press (faculty's neighbour for a brief period in its premises of the Institute Building on City Road).

The war affected the faculty considerably, though not, as Butlin (1970, p. 11) recalled, 'during the first eighteen months'. At that stage, active military service only involved volunteers and these were invariably given the privilege of completing their year's university studies through sitting special, frequently oral, examinations, before they were sent overseas. Staff also went off on government war work, despite the fact that university teaching was made a reserved occupation provided there was no salary increase for the duration of the war (Passmore 1997, pp. 185, 195). First to go was Madgwick to the Army Education Service, then Butlin as deputy director of the newly created Commonwealth Department of War Organisation of Industry, and ultimately Mills in 1942 as chairman of the Universities Commission. This allowed Butlin to return to the university, to be replaced by Trevor Swan at War Organisation and Industry. Swan, a distinguished graduate of the faculty, had been employed on its teaching staff since November 1941, initially in an emergency training course on industrial welfare (SM: 3 November 1941).

In his new appointment, Mills was responsible for the introduction of Commonwealth University Scholarships giving financial assistance to gifted students in the 1950s and 1960s, as well as for various training schemes for servicemen during the war and in the immediate post-war period. However, once conscription was introduced in 1941 in the face of the Japanese military threat to Australia, university enrolments began to fall drastically. As a consequence, '[s]tudent numbers in the Faculty were down to very low levels' during the last three years of the war' (Butlin 1970, p. 11).

The war induced a major bibliographical product from faculty teaching staff, albeit not published until some decades later. Butlin, later assisted by Boris Schedvin, prepared the two volumes on the war economy as part of the *Official History of Australia in the War of 1939–1945* (Butlin 1955; Butlin and Schedvin 1977). The changes for the faculty wrought by Depression and war are examined in detail in what follows.

Staff, enrolments and course timetable, 1929–39

At the start of 1929, the staff of the Faculty of Economics numbered eleven. Only two of these were permanent, full-time staff, both employed in the Department of Economics, that is, Mills as sole professor in the faculty and Benham as lecturer. While on leave that year, Benham resigned to take up a position in London. Walker was a temporary (three-year) full-time lecturer in Economics, financed by Frank Albert. Madgwick was appointed an acting lecturer in Economics in 1929. For other subjects, teaching staff stayed as in 1928: all were part-time, temporary lecturers. This changed during the 1930s. Despite the financial stringency imposed by the Depression, some additional staff were employed in these dark years, even if only on short-term contracts. This is what happened to Hermann Black, as he recounted in 1988:

> I was rescued by Professor Mills [from life as a high school teacher, often at schools where no economics was taught]. Beginning 1932, I marked term essays for him and addressed

> the classes involved; and then with Madgwick ... I lectured in the evening to third-year students on international trade ... and in the same year read a paper for the Australian Association for the Advancement of Science on Gold ... [Mills] sent for me later in the year [1932] and said: 'We have acquired some additional funds permitting the appointment of a Temporary Assistant Lecturer for four years. I want to improve the quality of the lecturing in the Faculty. The money will run out in four years, and then we must kick you out. Will you come?'
>
> I resigned the Department of Education without trauma, began lecturing in 1933, and as a result of the sheer incompetence of the University Administration I was still lecturing in three Faculties on invitation over five decades later ... I took the commission to lecture as Mills envisaged as a life-commitment. (Black 1988, § 4–6)

By the start of 1939, the financial situation for the university and the faculty had improved considerably. Faculty teaching staff had grown to twelve. There were now two professors in the faculty—Mills in Economics and Bland in Public Administration. Sawkins was still teaching Statistics but now as reader, a position to which he had been promoted in 1937. There were in addition nine lecturers, of whom five were full-time, permanent appointments. Black and Butlin were full-time lecturers in Economics; Madgwick was now lecturer in Economic History. J.G (Jack) Crawford was lecturer in Rural Economics, but as he was on leave in 1939 he was replaced by Ira Butler as acting lecturer. In the other faculty degree subjects, associate professor McDonald Holmes was teaching Economic Geography; J.A.L. Gunn replaced Burt as teacher of Business Principles and Practice in 1938; and Ashburner had replaced Bradley in 1936 as part-time lecturer in Industrial and Commercial Law. During 1939, temporary teaching staff included H.C. ('Nugget') Coombs for a couple of terms, as well as R.S. Parker and K.F. Walker, partly replacing members of the permanent teaching staff seconded to war work.

Enrolments rose sharply over the period. Between 1929 and 1939, those for the BEc almost trebled, for the Diploma of Public Administration they more than trebled (from the small base of fifteen in its first year of operation in 1930). For the Diploma of Commerce, however, they steadily declined, halving between 1930 (146 students) and 1938 (70 students) with a slight recovery to 93 in 1939. During the 1930s the BEc was increasingly seen as the more desirable goal for students wanting a broad commercial education. The vast majority of faculty students were still de facto evening students. This was not always by choice because day and evening lectures were only provided in Economics I, II and III; in every other course, lectures were only held in the evening.

Over the 1930s, enrolments became even more skewed to male students than they were for the previous decade. Conditions of employment in the New South Wales Public Service ensured that the proportion of women taking the Diploma of Public Administration averaged only 3.5 per cent for the 1930s; the comparable proportion for the Diploma of Commerce was 3.3 per cent. For the BEc it had dropped to 14.9 per cent during the 1930s as compared to the 25 per cent averaged over 1920–28. The Depression was probably a major factor in this as employment opportunities for women were greatly curtailed during the 1930s when a large proportion of men, the traditional bread winners, could not be assured of work.

A second professor for the faculty

At its meeting of 4 May 1935, Senate was informed that an additional state government grant for the Economics Faculty enabled the establishment of a chair in Public Administration. In fact, Bertram Stevens as premier had expressly arranged this increase to create such a chair because he greatly valued both the teaching and the teacher of Public Administration at Sydney University for lifting standards and quality in the public service. In response to the Senate announcement of this new funding, Mills moved, and Cleary seconded, that a chair in public administration be established forthwith. Later during this meeting, Mills as dean of the faculty proposed that F.A. Bland be appointed to the chair as 'the best candidate available'. He added that 'no good purpose would be served in advertising the position in Australia or Great Britain', where the field was not nearly as well established as at the University of Sydney, if it was established at all. Bland accordingly was appointed Professor of Public Administration as from 1 May 1935 (SM: 4 May 1935). On 13 May, he was introduced to Fellows of the Senate who congratulated him on his appointment, a virtually unique occurrence in Senate practice at this time (SM: 13 May 1935). Bland stayed on the faculty until he retired in 1947, aged 65.

Bland pioneered the study of public administration in Australia, and had enjoyed a long association with the Faculty of Economics and the University of Sydney before his appointment to the chair. He had graduated BA in 1909 in Economics and History, completed an LLB with honours in 1912, and gained an MA in Economics in 1914. That year he was appointed lecturer in Tutorial Classes, and after two years (1916–17) of postgraduate studies at the London School of Economics with Graham Wallas he became assistant director of Tutorial Classes. From then on he maintained a close association with Adult Education in various official capacities, an association he treasured for the whole of his life. Bland became a part-time lecturer in Public Administration in 1916, the position he held when appointed to the chair in 1935. He also lectured on municipal administration (Curnow 1993, pp. 202–04).

Bland's outstanding qualities as a public administration teacher developed from his earlier employment as a public servant. This commenced in the New South Wales Taxation Department in 1901, and continued as examiner in the Public Service Board from 1903 and as a member of the Public Service Board of Examiners from 1919. Early on in his work for the Public Service Board he had encountered Irvine, who in 1909 strongly supported Bland's application for the position of Clerk of Examinations. Irvine's reference described Bland as 'absolutely sober in his habits … industrious, intelligent and painstaking in his work'. The other referee was John S. D'Arcy, Bland's earlier boss in the Department of Taxation (Bland File, university Archives G3/159). At the time of his appointment to the chair, Bland was already well published with half a dozen books to his credit, the position as editor of the *Australian Highway*, and contributions to the *New York Law Journal*, the (London) *Journal of Public Administration*, the *International Labour Review*, the *Economic Record* and the *New South Wales Quarterly*.

Bland was greatly admired by his students. He had, as Mills and Butlin described it, 'a style of lecturing all his own' (1948, p. 132). He prepared his lectures with tremendous care and each year revised, 'to the despair of the Faculty office, what was called the "synopsis" of his course'. Bland's synopsis was not the brief course outline then customary in most faculty subjects, it 'was a complete text of full book length, in which Bland did his formal teaching duty by his students, and equipped them with a formidable array of references for reading'. Mills and Butlin add in parentheses that Bland could not have expected 'that even his most industrious student could consult more than a small part of them'. Their tribute to Bland the teacher continued as follows:

> His lecture began with the characteristic 'Well, peoples' and was delivered—more than one student has coined the phrase—in machine-gun staccato, an outpouring of ideas, critical comment, anecdotes, and factual record. After the first lecture or two, the student realised that Bland meant it when he said that the 'synopsis' was meant to obviate note-taking, but that, unlike similar systems used in some other University departments, this did not mean that everything in the lectures was already in the typescript. In a sense, nothing in one way was in the other; the lecture was comment on, extension of, digression from the condensed material of the typescript, to which one could listen with close attention and interest.
>
> Bland was a great success with students, inspired them in their work and sometimes influenced them in their outlook. He had always held strong political and social views, and was not afraid to disclose them to his students … The student felt always that here was a man who knew the material of his subject, who was widely read in its theory, and who held his views with a passionate, even religious conviction. (Mills and Butlin 1948, pp. 132–23)

David Wood (letter to the author, 9 September 2002) recalled that Bland 'could speak more words in a minute than anyone else I have met' and that 'he was knowledgeable about his subject'.

Bland was an active participant in faculty business, rarely missing a meeting and contributing extensively to its various committees. For twenty years (1944–64), he was also a Fellow of Senate, regularly attending its monthly meetings and serving on many of its committees. He greatly enjoyed taking part in the social and sporting activities of the university and participated in many a staff cricket and tennis match. (Mills and Butlin, 1948, p. 133).

Bland combined his university work with much activity in the community, giving advice and assisting in the work of government and public administration. His energy in this was boundless and it was no surprise to those who knew him that during his retirement he entered active politics as Liberal Party MHR for Warringah for a decade (1951–61). During his period in federal parliament, Bland both re-established and actively worked on the Joint Committee of Public Accounts, that powerful instrument for ensuring that funds from the public purse were properly expended.

Deliberations at faculty meetings, 1929–39

Faculty met regularly during the 1930s, at least once a term or three times a year. Attendance at its meeting was growing as a consequence of the increased teaching staff. Average attendance for the 1930s was 6.2, with a maximum attendance of nine for this decade recorded on three occasions. These included a 1939 meeting to discuss a new curriculum for the BEc.

Faculty business was frequently routine. It dealt with special cases of student admissions or exemptions from lectures or examinations, and with pleas for deferred examinations from students who had failed. It gave views on more general university matters referred to it by Professorial Board or Senate such as the rules for matriculation and, more importantly, amending by-laws, regulations and curriculum for its degree and diplomas, occasionally on a massive scale.

Thus faculty did not favour setting a minimum age limit on entry to university (FM: 30 July 1936). It accepted a request from the Evening Students Association to have only day examinations as from 1940 (FM: 23 October 1936). However, it altered this two years later (FM: 14 October 1938) to starting day examinations only from November 1942, gradually phased in for first-year examinations from 1939, second-year examinations from 1940 and third-year examinations from 1941, provided that students in these years accepted the new arrangements by voting for them. Moreover, after much debate (FM: 15 June 1938), faculty opened admission to the MEc for graduates from other universities (at the prompting of the Professorial Board), the first such students being admitted at the start of 1939 (FM: 23 March 1939). However, faculty also decided in 1938 that the time had not yet come to offer students a chance to attempt a PhD (FM: 14 October 1938).

Faculty recorded with pride the successive awards of the Walter and Eliza Hall Research Fellowship in Economics to some of its first rate graduates: Jack Crawford in 1933, S.H. Wolstenholme in 1936 (whose premature death was commemorated in the naming of the faculty library, the establishment of which was made possible by a substantial contribution from his parents), to K.F. Walker in 1938 and, on his early resignation from the Fellowship, to F.B. Horner, a future Deputy Commonwealth Statistician, in 1939. The faculty also continued to accept donations for the establishment of academic prizes from bodies like the Public Service Board, the Chamber of Commerce, the New South Wales Branch of the Economic Society and from individual donors. It was therefore not surprising that in March 1931 it accepted a special prize for accounting performance, with rather highly restrictive conditions. The prize in question was to be a one year only prize for Diploma of Commerce students, the conditions for its award stating that the winner had to have scored the highest marks in Accountancy II and, in addition, distinction results for Accountancy I (A+B) and Accountancy II (FM: 19 March 1931). At the subsequent faculty meeting, it was reported that the Accountancy Prize accepted at the previous meeting was not in fact *bona fide*: the offer of the prize had been 'made by the only student of Accountancy who had fulfilled all the conditions of award and was eligible for the prize'. The minutes (3 July 1931) also record that the prize was therefore not awarded and that its student donor had been 'reprimanded'.

The most important business of faculty concerned changes it made to course syllabus and degree curriculum. At its March 1931 meeting, it set up a committee (consisting of the dean, Professor Lovell [Psychology], McDonald Holmes [Economic Geography], Martin [Psychology], Portus, Bland, and Madgwick) to examine the faculty's Accountancy courses in a comparative way. However, any action on changing the Accountancy courses was delayed to the next meeting when Mills returned from a trip to Europe and North America, during which he visited various business schools to investigate the nature of their business courses, including accountancy.

Nothing appears to have come of this. Not until 1939 did faculty debate a drastically revised curriculum which, as part of the changes, was to add substantially to the opportunities for students to specialise in Accounting studies.

In 1934, Bland introduced a proposal for a Public Administration II course intended solely for students taking the Diploma of Public Administration. However, Public Administration II in conjunction with the existing half course in Public Administration on offer would become a full course in Public Administration. This proposal was accepted by faculty (FM: 15 March 1934) and with some minor amendments adopted by Senate (SM: 8 October 1934).

In July 1937, faculty altered the curriculum for the fourth year of the BEc degree. This eliminated the overload in the fourth year by separating Advanced Economic Theory and the History of Economic Thought. To achieve this, History of Economic Thought was once again (as it had been before 1926) made a subject in its own right, compulsory for all BEc degree students. Fourth-year requirements for Group A degree students now included Economics IV and History of Economic Thought as compulsory subjects, while for their third subject Group A students could choose either an Arts course not yet taken or Public Administration II. Group B students (those specialising in Accounting and Business Studies) were required in their fourth year to take Economics IV, History of Economic Thought and Accountancy II.

In October 1939, in the presence of Professor Robert Wallace, the vice-Chancellor, faculty deliberated on an extensive set of amendments to Chapter XVIII of the by-laws governing the Faculty of Economics, its degrees and diplomas. It amended section 1 defining membership of the faculty as follows: 'The Professors of Economics, Law, History, Public Administration, Psychology, Philosophy, Political and Moral Philosophy, the associate professor of Economic Geography, the Reader of Statistics, and lecturers in the subjects primarily prescribed for degrees in the Faculty'. Some of these changes reflected promotions of staff, others the introduction of new courses such as Political Theory to be given by A.K. Stout as newly appointed Professor of Moral and Political Philosophy. This replaced the Modern Political Institutions course taught for so long in the faculty by P.R. Watts, who had retired that year.

The Diploma of Commerce changes removed its English, Economic Geography, Modern Political Institutions and Business Principles components and replaced them with the following three-year course structure. For first-year, students completed Accountancy I, Law I and Economics I; for second year, Accountancy II and Law II; and for third year, Accountancy III and Law III. It was explained that Accountancy I was the former Accountancy I (A + B) course; that Accountancy II added new material to the existing Accountancy II course; that Accountancy III was a completely new advanced course; that Law I was the former Commercial and Industrial Law course, that Law II was a completely new course, and that Law III, another new course, would deal with federal income tax law. There would be three lectures each week for the Law courses, the Accountancy courses would be taught in two lectures a week together with a 90 minute tutorial for groups of 25 students (incidentally, the first reference to such a form for organising teaching in the faculty's history). The additional cost was steep. Accountancy II and III both required an additional lecturer at £200 each, Accountancy I required two tutors, and Accountancy II and III one tutor each at £100. Two additional lecturers would also be required for Law II and III and for Economics I at £300 each. Total cost was therefore estimated at a massive £1800, to be met from fees at 45 guineas plus a charge of 3 guineas for the diploma, that is, a total of £50 8s. Enrolments from 36 students per annum were needed to cover the additional costs from these extended Accounting and Commercial Law offerings. The restructuring of the diploma in this way had the advantage of making it acceptable as a qualification for membership of the Commonwealth Institute of Accountants.

The course and teaching requirements of this revised Diploma of Commerce syllabus opened up new possibilities for an additional way of completing the BEc degree. This would require the compulsory core of Economics I, II, III and IV; together with Accountancy I, II and III and Law I, II and III as the two other subjects for the first three years; with Economic History and one subject chosen from Psychology I, Philosophy I, History I, Mathematics I and Statistics for the other two fourth-year subjects needed to complete the twelve courses for the degree.

More generally, the new curriculum for the BEc can be described as follows. For first year, Economics I, Business Principles and one course from either Psychology I, Philosophy I, Mathematics I or History I; for second year, Economics II, Economic History together with Economic Geography and Political Theory; for third year, Economics III, Statistics, Public Administration I or a second-year Arts subject; and for fourth-year, Economics IV, History of Economic Thought and either Public Administration II or an Arts subject. This included the compulsory core of the degree in the form of the five economics courses, Economics I–IV and History of Economic Thought; the possibility of an additional major in Political Institutions, Public Administration I and II, or in an Arts sequence (from Psychology I, Philosophy I, Mathematics I or History I). It was therefore a degree structure largely reflecting the fields of the two chairs in the faculty: Economics and, to a much smaller extent, [Government]/Public Administration.

Finally, alterations for the Diploma of Public Administration were proposed. Its first year would require Economics I and one subject chosen from Philosophy I, Psychology I, History I, Mathematics I, Accountancy I or Economic History; for second year, the required subjects were Economic II, Public Administration I and Political Theory; while for third year, students had to take Public Administration II and one subject from the following three groups: (1) Psychology I, Philosophy I, History I, Mathematics I, Law I, or Accountancy I if not already taken; (2) Psychology II, Philosophy II, History II, Mathematics II, Accountancy II, Law II if eligible to do so by having passed the appropriate first-year course; or (3) Economics III, with its strong public finance component.

Faculty approved these changes in principle. However, as the dean had warned at the close of the meeting, 'the only difficulty in bringing in the new curriculum was that of finance' and this made it impossible to make the changes effective in the foreseeable future. In fact, they were never implemented and were replaced by a far more ambitious scheme of curriculum change introduced by the faculty after much debate during the final years of the war.

Notable students and graduates, 1929–39

The subsequently famous first-year students who had entered the faculty in 1928 generally performed very well during the course of their studies. Jock Phillips won the Frank Albert Prize for proficiency in first-year Economics with a pass in Economics I, a high distinction in Business Principles and a solid pass in Economic Geography. Surprisingly, he decided not to pursue honours in his later years, so his results on graduation were not spectacular. Jack Crawford won the Economic Society Prize for distinction at the first-year examinations (high distinction in Economics I, a pass in Business Principles and a distinction in Economic Geography). Syd Butlin began his initial year of economic studies with a distinction in Economics I, a high distinction in Economic Geography, and a pass in Business Principles. On the other hand, Fred Deer only managed last in the merit list for Economics I, while Ivan Dougherty simply had passes recorded in Economics I, Economic Geography and Business Principles. Jean Conen (Mrs Butlin to be) passed with credit in Economics and Economic Geography. Jean Debenham had high results recorded in Statistics. In their final year, both Butlin and Crawford graduated with first-class honours, to which Butlin added the medal, the Frank Albert Prize and the Chamber of Commerce Prize as the best graduate in Economics for 1932. Butlin obtained high distinctions in Economics IV and Economic History to secure this result. Crawford topped the pass order of merit lists in both Economics IV and Public Administration II. Phillips and Dougherty in 1932 obtained pass degrees while Deer in the end did not graduate until 1936, having had to suspend his studies for some years during the early 1930s.

The 1930s produced many other graduates later famous for their endeavours. In alphabetical order they include: Ruth Atkins (political scientist), Ira Butler (a manager of the Reserve Bank's Research Department), Noel Butlin (lecturer in Economic History at Sydney and later Professor of Economic History at the Australian National University), John Carrick (Liberal Senator, secretary of the New South Wales Liberal Party and Minister for National Development), Ray Chambers (foundation Professor of Accounting), Roden (later Sir Roden) Cutler (insurance, distinguished war service and Governor of New South Wales), Kevin Ellis (MLA for Coogee, Speaker in the Legislative Assembly), Tom Fitzgerald (financial editor, *Sydney Morning Herald*), Bruce Fleming (Australian Treasury and Australian representative in the IMF and the International Bank of Reconstruction and Development), Alan Greenhalgh (principal, Balmain Teachers College), F.B. Horner (Deputy Commonwealth Statistician), Tom Kewley (senior lecturer in Public Administration, University of Sydney), Harry Lancaster (Professor of Mathematical Statistics, University of Sydney), G.D.B. Maunder (Deputy Director of Works, Victoria), Ron Mendelsohn (assistant secretary, Prime Minister's Department, first assistant secretary, Department of Housing), Bruce Miller (Professor of International Relations, Australian National University); Pat Mills (reader, Commercial and Industrial Law and later dean for some years of the Faculty of Economics, University of Sydney); Ron Parker (Professor of Political Science, Australian National University); John Passmore (philosopher and historian of ideas, University of Sydney and professor, Australian National University); W.H. Pawley (statistician), J. (later Sir James) Plimsoll (Permanent Secretary External Affairs, Australian delegate, United Nations), Richard (later Sir Richard) Randall (deputy secretary,

Commonwealth Treasury), Cyril Renwick (senior lecturer in economics, University of Sydney; Director Hunter Valley Research Association), M.S. Ruddock (MLA for the Hills), Bob Scott (Research Department, Reserve Bank of Australia and secretary, Economic Society of Australia for many years), Tom Williams (long-term secretary of the University Union) and Trevor Swan (senior lecturer in Economics, University of Sydney; later Professor of Economics, Australian National University). This is an outstanding list indeed of students and graduates in the Faculty of Economics during the 1930s.

A number of other, less well known, students from the 1930s left written impressions of their experience as students in the faculty. Portia Mortimer (Hickey), the first of a distinguished line of Mortimer economics graduates, recalled Mills as 'a gentleman and a scholar', taking fourth-year economics classes in which he practised a tutorial system where students presented papers discussed under his supervision. She also recalled Sawkins as a 'dreadful lecturer', whose one and a half hour Statistics class was 'absolute misery'. Black, Madgwick and Walker were all described as 'good lecturers'. As one of the few women students taking Economics at this time, she also recalled having to participate in nearly every inter-faculty sports event to make up the numbers but she did not participate in activities organised by the Evening Students Association or in non-sport events organised by the Sydney University Economics Society.

Several male evening students recalled their student days from the 1930s. One specifically mentioned Hermann Black's approach to essay marking. Given a mark of 8 out of 20, Black 'explained to students that they were not to despair—the low marks given were to cater for the brilliance of the top students and to give a true measure of their ability in relation to the rest of the group.' (letter to the author, 11 September 2002). Another recalled Black's lectures as 'occasions we all looked forward to … [because of] his dynamic style, rich language and his warm personality'. His lectures in the second half of the 1930s covered Economics I and Economics IV, the last partly devoted to discussion of Roosevelt's New Deal and other anti-Depression policies (J.E. Linton to the author, 7 September 2002).

Another student, Warren Perry, more generally recollected:

> The Faculty of Economics in my time in the 1930s was an evening faculty. So the students, generally speaking, were a more mature group than the day students. These evening students were drawn largely from the State and Federal public services, from school teachers and from Banks. When I began my degree course in Economics, I had already been working in a Trading Bank, the Union Bank of Australia Limited, for the previous ten years …
>
> In the 1930s students no longer wore academic dress to lectures. But the staff continued to lecture in black gowns. The part-time staff may not have worn gowns as, like students, they probably came straight from their daily work.
>
> Again, the location of the Faculty of Economics in the 1930s was different from its present location. In the 1930s it was part of that original segment of the University built around the edges of the quadrangle and the entrance to the Faculty of Economics was up a stairway between the Office of the vice-Chancellor and the offices of the Registrar …

> Another feature of student life in the Faculty of Economics of the 1930s was the Faculty's Economics Society. Its membership was made up of Faculty staff and students. Professor Mills, I remember, attended the meetings regularly. Some good speakers addressed the Society. Professor Shann, Professor of Economics in Perth, was a speaker on one occasion. On another occasion, Professor Sir Robert Wallace [the vice-chancellor] spoke at a meeting ... Professor Mills himself addressed the Society ... Earlier in the 1930s he had made a prolonged visit to the USA on some academic business the nature of which I cannot now remember. Nevertheless, this lecture was full of dry and subtle wit ... Incidentally, I believe Professor Mills did write under a Pen Name on non-economic subjects. But I have not been able to ascertain what this Pen Name was. (letter to the author, 30 September 2002)

Colleen McCullough in her biography of Sir Roden Cutler writes that he 'enrolled in the Faculty of Economics as a night student ... he would be able to afford the minimal fees, buy his textbooks—second hand of course—pay the fares ... There was no difference between the day and night course; both had to be completed in four years, both involved exactly the same number of lectures and assignments per week, and both kinds of student sat for the same examination at the same time ... In the examinations at the end of 1935, his first year of Economics, he did well ... (McCullough 1998, pp. 36, 39–40, 46). John Passmore recalled in his autobiography:

> If I took only one course in economics this, once more, was for geographical [he was living in Manly at the time and the ferries stopped running early in the evening] rather than intellectual reasons. After first year, economics was only taught in the evening; it was presumed that it would only be of interest to those who were in business employment. With a staff of three, this limitation was also a way of economising on lecturing resources ... The three members of the economic staff at this time were ... R.C. Mills, E.R. Walker and R.B. Madgwick ... I cannot say that Madgwick's lectures particularly excited me ... The course left me with a reasonable, but not mathematically refined, knowledge of the basic principles of classical economics ... Two features of the economics course were particularly noticeable. First, it was the only [university undergraduate] course in which there was a limited amount of class discussion. That was principally because the class contained a few ardent exponents of the teaching of Major Douglas, the prophet of social credit. They, among other things, supported a measure of inflation, whereas the monetary policy in 1931 was one of sharp deflation. [Secondly], we had been taught about trade cycles, but as we watched the world beginning to tumble to pieces it was hard to believe that market forces, the economist's version of divine grace, would eventually solve our problems ... we [therefore] sought a rational economics that recognised its own limits. (Passmore, 1997, pp. 86, 87, 88)

Sadly, there are few recollections for this period of faculty teachers in subjects other than Economics, except for the comments on Bland's and Sawkins' teaching already quoted. However, in a letter to the author, J.E. Linton spoke of Ivo Kerr's Accountancy teaching as that of 'a dynamic teacher who imbued us with his enthusiasm', while Portus occasionally sent his evening students asleep during his lectures, to their rather than to his embarrassment (Maureen Hedley, née Deer, to the author, 6 September 2002).

The effects of war on staffing and enrolments

Faculty lost a substantial portion of its teaching staff to war work. Until early 1943, Syd Butlin worked for the Department of War Organisation and Industry, where Trevor Swan joined him in 1942. In 1939, Hermann Black gained the position of part-time adviser to the New South Wales premier and treasurer, Sir Bertram Stephens. Robert Madgwick went to Army education at the start of the war. From December 1942, R.C. Mills went to work full-time for the Commonwealth Public Service, though he did not resign his position as dean and Professor of Economics until 1945. By way of replacement, John La Nauze was appointed lecturer in Economics from the beginning of 1940, and Ira Butler in April 1941. Pawley was asked to lecture in Rural Economics during 1941 and Torleiv Hytten gave sixteen lectures on International Trade filling in during Mills' absence. In February 1944, Kingsley Laffer, J.S.G. Wilson and Cyril Renwick were appointed as temporary lecturers in Economics, their positions made permanent after 1945. In 1945, Noel Butlin became a lecturer in Economic History, and Trevor Swan briefly returned as senior lecturer in Economics before departing in 1946 for a chair in Economics at the Australian National University.

In April 1941, Tom Kewley was appointed lecturer in Public Administration, and in November 1941 he joined K.F. Walker and Trevor Swan to give a special emergency training course in industrial welfare covering industrial history, industrial law and industrial relations (SM: 7 April, 3 November 1941). Previously in November 1939, Gunn had resigned as teacher of Business Principles and Practice, to be replaced by A. Clunies Ross, the lecturer involved in its teaching before the course was abolished in the new by-laws proposed during the final years of the war to take effect during the post-war period.

As Butlin recalled in 1970, the war years adversely affected enrolments in the faculty only really from 1943 onwards. If 1939 is taken as the pre-war bench mark, 408 students enrolled that year for the degree, 93 for the Diploma of Commerce and 49 for that of Public Administration. In 1940 enrolments held their own with 408 degree students, 97 Diploma of Commerce students and 52 for the Diploma of Public Administration. The following year enrolments declined slightly: 358 degree students, 69 for the Diploma of Commerce and 49 for the Diploma of Public Administration. Enrolments were substantially lower in 1942, 1943, 1944 and 1945. The number of women degree students increased in relative terms during the war, the proportion rising to a peak of 47.5 per cent in 1944.

The departure of R.C. Mills (1943) and his replacement by S.J. Butlin

During the 1930s and 1940s, Mills was increasingly called away from administering the faculty and his department to serve on government and university committees. From 1934 to 1941 he served as chairman of the university's Professorial Board, hence also as an ex officio member of the Senate. In addition he served, often in the capacity of chairman, on the Joint Committee of Tutorial Classes, the university Extension Board, the Board of Social Studies, the Appointments Board and the Bursary Endowment Board. Mills tended to play an active part in the proceedings of these committees, as demonstrated by the frequent references to his work there in Senate Minutes. On the occasion of his retirement from the university at the end of 1945, Senate's tribute to Mills indicated that 'he has exerted a profound influence on all phases of staff and student life … he rendered signal services to the cause of university education … [and he made] extensive contributions to government and community' (SM: 17 December 1945).

Mills' government services had started just before the 1920s. They continued during the 1930s with the advice he (and other economists) gave to state governments when preparing the Premiers' Plan, his consultancy to the (New South Wales) Bureau of Statistics in 1933, his membership of the influential Royal Commission into Money and Banking during 1936–37, his chairmanship of the Commonwealth Grants Commission (1941–46) and of the (Commonwealth) Committee on Uniform Taxation in 1942, his 'outside' membership of the Finance and Economics Committee (of Treasury) and his (full-time) chairmanship of the Universities Commission from November (Butlin 1953, pp. 182–83). The last appointment implied complete withdrawal from his various university responsibilities. However, the vice-chancellor was only willing to let Mills go to full-time Commonwealth service if Butlin was released from his war work, so that he could replace Mills in the faculty as acting dean and in the Department of Economics as acting professor (J.J. Dedman to Sir Robert Wallace, vice-Chancellor, 23 November 1942; Mills File, university Archives). It is no exaggeration to claim that Mills' work for the Commonwealth during, and after, World War II was far more important to the university's future development than his labours on the Professorial Board and in other university committee work during the 1930s. His reforms to intergovernmental financial relations following the introduction of uniform income taxation arrangements, and the changes to financing universities and students made under his direction in the post-war period, greatly influenced university operations for decades to come.

Mills' activities as university teacher and administrator, as well as his increasing role as government adviser, did leave some time for academic publication. During the 1930s, these included a number of important articles on federal–state financial relations following on from his important 1928 *Economic Record* article on this subject (see Groenewegen, 2002). One of these, written jointly with Bland, commented on the relationship between state finances and recovery from the Depression. Undoubtedly, his most important publication of this period, and the one on which he himself set the greatest store, was the textbook, *Money*, written jointly with E.R. Walker, which went through many editions (the twelfth being published in 1952). He also wrote some pieces on Wakefield and immigration schemes, an obituary of his former teacher, Edwin Cannan, and a number of book reviews (Butlin 1953, pp. 187–88).

On Mills' death in 1952, Senate recorded by way of obituary that he had made the Faculty of Economics at the University of Sydney into 'the leading school in Australia' and that in his university decision making at all levels, he employed 'mature wisdom and disinterested devotion to academic principles' combined with 'great personal charm and wit. The tribute concluded that 'his last and greatest achievement were the securing of University Scholarships which effectively remove financial barriers to University education' (Mills File, university Archives). On the occasion of Mills' retirement as dean and professor, the Faculty of Economics drew attention to the fact that Mills never saw 'himself as the Head of Department controlling a subordinate staff, but as one among a band of fellow teachers' (FM: 16 November 1945).

Many decades on, Mills' life and work continued to draw accolades from colleagues and former students. John Passmore (1997 p. 144), a former student, albeit only for one year, mentioned that R.C. Mills was for him 'the academic to whom I should most naturally apply the epithet "gentleman" in the best of its senses', a judgement made on the basis of a single experience with Mills' behaviour at a specific faculty meeting. Ronald Walker characterised Mills as 'quiet and unassuming' and as a person who literally 'spent himself in the service of his university and country (letter to the author, 21 December 1984). Hermann Black remarked that Mills' 'lectures possessed clarity, precision, organisation, and could be followed by his students since he (as was the general faculty practice) provided detailed structures of the lecturers in synopses … This was an immensely helpful practice, of value to the student, and compelling the lecturer to prepare his lectures in a structured and organised form, with reading listed to pursue each point beyond the prescribed texts'. However, Black diluted this praise of Mills as lecturer by adding that his lectures were exceedingly 'dry' and that his lecture-tutorial type classes in fourth year tended to be far more inspirational (letter to the author, 4 December 1984).

A dissenting voice to this extensive praise for R.C. Mills was R.H. Mathews. He graduated BEc in 1930, and claimed to have been Mills' 'white-haired boy' when he was his student in the late 1920s, having many private conversations with Mills and assisting him in his office with much clerical work. However, he intensely disliked his final-year studies in Economics, particularly the high history of economic thought content of Mills' seminar classes. On the basis of this experience, Mathews regarded Mills 'in many ways [as] a phoney. He was more a historian than an economist as such. The rapidity with which he left Sydney Uni to go to Commonwealth Education …. is symptomatic to his approach to academic life' (letter to the author, undated but received in June 1982). The last part of this quoted opinion is somewhat dubious; it is difficult to describe Mills' departure from the university in the 1940s as particularly rapid given the fact that he had been appointed in 1921 and had served the university well over the subsequent two decades as Professor of Economics and Dean of the Faculty of Economics. However, it is true that Mills was more historian than economist, a quality reflected in much of his published work and clearly visible in at least some of his teaching.

From 1943, Mills was replaced by S.J. Butlin, initially as acting professor and dean. Butlin had been an outstanding student, a medallist at graduation, with postgraduate studies completed at Cambridge and a faculty teacher from the mid-1930s. Butlin's war time initiatives as acting dean are discussed below.

External service students, internal students and graduates during the war

Enrolment figures for the war years given previously indicate the decline in student numbers in the faculty from 1942 onwards. Following conscription of many males of student age for war service from 1943, a considerable rise in the proportion of women taking economic studies was also noted. The fall in students is even more strikingly reflected in the number of Economics graduates recorded between 1940 and 1945. Graduate numbers fell steadily from 89 in 1940 to only 16 in 1945. Diploma of Commerce students likewise declined sharply, but this was due to faculty's intention to abolish this course of study from December 1943. Fourteen Diplomas of Commerce were awarded in 1940, seven in 1945. From 1943 enrolments in the Diploma of Public Administration also declined substantially, with none whatsoever in 1945. (*University Annual Reports*, 1940–46).

Some of these fluctuations are explicable from students deciding to interrupt studies started before the war in order to resume them in the immediate post-war period. One of these was John Linton, an employee of the Bank of New South Wales (now Westpac). He had started his degree studies in 1938 and completed his second-year studies before enlisting in the AIF in 1940. He resumed his studies as a third-year student in 1945, completing fourth year in 1946 and graduating in 1947. He was therefore also part of the 'flood of ex-servicemen' entering the university from 1945, whose relative maturity gave them a completely different outlook on university life and who, if they had shared Linton's experience of several years of pre-war studies, found a completely new Keynesian world in economics when they resumed their studies (letter to the author, 7 September 2002).

Another student, Ernest Lloyd Sommerlad, first completed an Arts degree with three years Economics, then commenced a BEc in 1940. He completed six out of the nine additional subjects required for his second degree, having been exempted from taking Economics I, II and III. He then studied Economic History as an external serviceman student (without attending lectures) and completed his last two subjects, Economics IV and History of Economic Thought, in 1946, enabling him to graduate in 1947. He was appointed in 1954 to the New South Wales Legislative Council for twelve years, having previously been active in student politics and union affairs, and serving as editor of *Honi Soit* while still an Arts student. He recalled Bland's lectures as particularly useful for him as a member of the Upper House but unfortunately could no longer remember whether his pass in Economic History as an external student was achieved with or without having to sit an examination (letter to the author, 12 September 2002).

Bruce Miller's degree studies, commenced in 1940, were not interrupted by the war. He graduated BEc in 1944 and gained his MEc in 1951. He was an evening student, initially employed by the Bank of New South Wales (now Westpac), then by the ABC and the Department of Tutorial Classes at the university. He recalled the high vocational tone of the degree in these days, with students largely drawn from the banks, the public service and education. Miller, who confirmed he was not a good student by any stretch of the imagination, strongly disliked the compulsory studies in Business Principles and Practice, Accountancy and Statistics. However, he greatly enjoyed Bland's course on Public Administration, describing Bland as a 'hypnotic lecturer and in many ways a great teacher'. Bland indirectly inspired the topic for Miller's masters thesis—a critique of some of Bland's views of parliamentary government—and was recalled by Miller as the person to whom he owed most during his undergraduate education.

Miller also recalled doing quite well in History of Economic Thought, then taught by John La Nauze, whom he describes as another 'fascinating personality'. Butlin (1970, pp. 10–11), it may be noted here, mentioned La Nauze's 'waspish lectures' on the history of economic thought as treating the subject 'as if it were a peculiar branch of English literature'. Miller recalled that La Nauze had set an essay, 'John Stuart Mill—His Father's Son', which he had attempted largely on the basis of Mill's autobiography, with its detailed account of Mill's strict and arduous education regime from his father, which had effectively robbed him of a real childhood (Mill, 1873, Chapters I, II). La Nauze returned the essay with a good mark and the comment, 'you had better find out about their economics' (letter to the author, 20 September 2002). Miller did not do honours, and gathered no laurels on the way to his degree in the form of credits, distinctions or high distinctions. He later enjoyed a distinguished academic career in international relations and politics, with chairs initially at Leicester and then for many years at the Australian National University.

Six persons obtained their MEc during the war years. They included distinguished graduates from the 1930s, Jack Crawford, Alan Greenhalgh and Ron Parker (all in 1940), Walter Ives in 1942, Arthur Kidd in 1944, and Fred Larcombe, a future historian of New South Wales local government, in 1945.

There were other distinguished graduates during the war years. In 1940, Trevor Swan graduated with first-class honours and the medal, joining the faculty's economic staff in January 1940, initially as an assistant lecturer. In 1941, W.T. Dowsett graduated with first-class honours, but there were no firsts awarded in 1942. In 1943, Noel Butlin followed in his older brother's footsteps by graduating with first-class honours and the medal, just beating Cyril Renwick. Both joined the teaching staff almost immediately: Renwick as a temporary lecturer in December 1944, and Noel Butlin as a lecturer in Economic History in March 1945. A future dean of the faculty and member of the economics teaching staff, Geelum Simpson-Lee graduated in 1944 with second-class honours. He started his subsequent teaching career as a full-time tutor for serviceman students, initially on a one-year appointment. Ruth Atkins, who also graduated with honours in 1945, subsequently did much research on local government, ending her career as an associate professor in Politics at the University of New South Wales.

Relatively few of the war graduates stand out for subsequent fame in their non-academic occupations. One of them, E.J. Walder, who graduated with honours in 1945, became chairman of the Sydney Water Board in 1966; another, David Wood, a graduate of 1940, entered on a career in university administration, culminating as senior adviser to vice-chancellors at the University of Sydney; a third, A.W.B. Coady, became chairman of the Electricity Commission of New South Wales in 1959.

A new degree structure and curriculum for the post-war period

Faculty meetings continued during the war years on a regular basis, with attendances ranging from a minimum of five to a maximum of sixteen (at the meeting which considered drastic revisions to the faculty's teaching programs), and an average of 8.8. The last reflected the effective increase in teaching staff despite the war, together with the practice, introduced at this time, of regularly inviting temporary teaching staff to meetings, without giving them voting rights. The reconstitution of faculty membership approved at the end of 1939 aided attendance figures, since John Anderson (Philosophy) and J. McDonald Holmes (Geography) attended Economics Faculty meetings far more frequently than previous academics outside the faculty who were ex officio faculty members.

At the July 1940 meeting, faculty was informed of war time stringencies announced by the vice-chancellor as university policy for the duration of the war. These included syllabus curtailment and the cessation of courses not absolutely necessary for a degree; limitations on practical work and on research unrelated to the war effort; while anything else which reduced expenditure was to be encouraged. As faculty response, Mills proposed reduction in the faculty's typing staff, a discontinuation of the *Faculty Handbook* and maximum savings in essay marking (FM: 29 July 1940).

In early April 1941, Bland proposed that honours candidates for the BEc should be able to specialise in subjects other than Economics. This was contrary to the vice-chancellor's war policy, and therefore deferred. Bland later successfully amended the regulations for the Diploma of Public Administration by allowing Political Institutions to be taken in first year, as a prerequisite for Public Administration I, hence creating a distinct three-year sequence in a subject other than Economics (FM: 9 April 1941). At the next meetings, Bland successfully moved for a change in honours regulations to require three instead of four courses from Economics I, II, III and IV and History of Economic Thought This gave students greater opportunities for specialising in Public Administration I and II, and for work in the other three subjects to be completed at distinction level for an honours result. This amendment was approved (FM: 15 August, 17 November, 1941).

In May 1942, faculty decided to give students in army camps exemption from lectures, providing for special deferred examinations for soldiers (FM: 1 May 1942). Following the reduction of Michaelmas term in 1942 to seven weeks from the customary eight, the university introduced a four terms teaching year from 1943 for the duration of the war (FM: 15 August 1941, 28 September 1942). The second of these meetings was the final one chaired by Mills as dean and the minutes were signed as a true record on 16 April 1943 by Syd Butlin, in his new role as acting dean. At a special faculty meeting chaired by Bland, faculty disagreed with the new four-term teaching year, claiming that like the Faculty of Arts, a three-term teaching year was the only feasible option for the Faculty of Economics (FM: 29 October 1942). Special examinations for army personnel were approved in principle in 1943 for the duration of the war (FM: 16 April, 1943).

Formal and informal discussions on major revisions to the courses and qualifications offered by the faculty also took place in 1943. The faculty meeting of 15 October 1943 debated the two diploma courses it was then offering, deciding in general that 'the attitude of the Faculty towards Diplomas in future should be to work for their abolition or conversion into post-graduate diplomas'. This principle was to be immediately applied to the Diploma of Commerce. The BEc degree had effectively made it redundant, as was demonstrated by both its small enrolments and their declining quality. Suitable provision was to be made for students who had enrolled for the diploma prior to 31 December 1943, the date which faculty proposed for its abolition.

On the Diploma of Public Administration, faculty accepted that this differed from the Diploma of Commerce because it was largely designed for public servants. Hence the full BEc degree could not be described as a good substitute. As the Diploma of Public Administration accepted unmatriculated students, very significant changes would have to be made to turn it into a postgraduate qualification. It was proposed to keep the diploma for public servants who had suitable qualifications for entering the course, deemed by faculty as equivalent to passing the Leaving Certificate (FM: 15 October 1943). A subsequent faculty meeting (10 November 1943) adopted three criteria for admission: being a graduate, having matriculation qualifications or being a public servant. However, the joint award of a BEc and a Diploma of Public Administration was not permitted; graduate entry implied that students could not repeat courses for the diploma already taken elsewhere, while candidates for admission had to show the direct benefit to their work of the course, a criterion designed to facilitate entry of public servants. By eliminating entry by Intermediate Certificate, the new entry criteria considerably lifted the educational standards for admission to the diploma.

The 5 April 1944 faculty meeting discussed a proposal from the university Appointments Board for courses in business administration. Given the faculty's declared position on diplomas, business administration courses were not acceptable as an outside diploma course but acceptable in principle as a postgraduate qualification. However, new BEc regulations then under discussion made separate business administration courses redundant. It is interesting to note that on this subject the faculty distanced itself from Mills' 'speculative and controversial' remarks in favour of a one-year Diploma of Business Administration during a public university lecture on 'The University and Business' (Mills 1940, pp. 20–23). A Master of Business Administration was not introduced into the faculty until 1974, though there was an earlier, unsuccessful, attempt to do so in 1961.

Drastic revisions of the by-laws applying to the BEc degree were put to faculty on 18 May 1944. They were based on broad guiding principles of maintaining the general structure of a four-year degree with three subjects per annum in which Economics I, II, III, IV and History of Economic Thought provided the compulsory core for all degree students. Additional principles approved by faculty were a common first-year course, the introduction of a second major sequence of courses, and the extension of honours to subjects other than Economics.

The new degree structure was defined as follows. The common first year would contain Economics I, Scientific Method (continuing to be taught by a member of the Philosophy Department) and a new course, Descriptive Economics. In the three subsequent years, students would complete Economics II, III and IV, History of Economic Thought (in fourth year); a sequence of three courses from a specified list of approved subjects; and two other courses in second and third year, again from a specified list.

The sequences in addition to Economics approved by faculty were as follows: Political Theory, Public Administration I and II; History I, Economic History I and II; Accountancy I, II and III; Statistics I, II and III; and Business Administration I, II and III. Faculty was given the power to add to this list after gaining approval from the Professorial Board. The two optional courses in second and third year could be selected from the second list of major sequence courses if not already taken, Commercial Law I and II, or appropriate Arts subjects. Courses selected by students for the degree had to be approved by a faculty officer prior to enrolment in second year, and no qualified accountant was permitted to take the Accounting sequence.

The rationale for these changes was as follows. The existing BEc structure was too business orientated and failed to provide opportunities for specialisation in related non-business subjects. The compulsory first year was described as essential to all students taking the degree, particularly when Descriptive Economics was depicted as an amalgam of parts of Business Principles and Practice, Accountancy IA, Commercial Law I and, especially, Economic Geography. The new degree proposal, above all, allowed additional specialisation in Economic History and Statistics, and rationalised existing Accounting/Commercial Law sequences. New specialisations such as Business Administration and Pacific Studies were also contemplated as future developments. Practical classes designed to give students advice on how to study, the use of libraries and some grounding in mathematics for economists and in statistical method were envisaged as parts of the compulsory first-year courses. These classes could also provide opportunities for practical work. Finally, the new faculty structure completely eliminated half courses.

Other factors were stressed during the debate. All courses for the new degree were to be 'properly provided for by a full-time lecturing staff and tutorials'. The proposed Statistics sequence was described as a first for Australian universities and a unique opportunity for training 'real statisticians'. An admitted weakness of the new structure was that some students could obtain their degree 'without taking up history'. This provided the rationale for a compulsory History of Economic Thought which paid adequate attention to the social, political and economic institutional background influencing economic doctrines.

The new structure created a major distinction between pass and honours students. Special honours classes would commence in all schools from the start of second year. Results in examinations would reflect this difference: pass students at best could obtain a pass with credit; honours students had their results recorded as either a pass, credit, distinction or high distinction. Honours schools specified for the new degree structure were Economics, Public Administration, Economic History, Statistics and, probably as substitute for the proposed sequence in Pacific Studies, Anthropology. Accounting was a noticeable omission at this stage, a real shortage of suitably qualified teachers being the most likely explanation.

The faculty proposals likewise addressed the 'problem' of evening students. Since most evening students were not on a par with full-time students in terms of hours devoted to their studies, it was proposed that genuine evening students could complete their degree over six years, progressing by way of two subjects per annum. There was a precedent for this in the practice of the universities of Melbourne and Western Australia. Moreover, completing a degree in a much shorter period created a powerful incentive for students to be full-time day students. The Education Department strongly opposed this aspect of the proposal, because it meant that future economics teachers, if taking the BEc rather than a BA with three years of Economics, would need several additional years to get their degree if, as frequently was the case, they were studying part-time in the evening.

Alterations were also made to the MEc regulations. Its examinations were now explicitly designated as qualifying ones, with an exemption for students with a first-class honours BEc. Emphasis was on thesis and research, and the examination subjects for those qualifying for entry in this way had to match the specialisation (Economics, Public Administration, Economic

History, etc.) chosen for the research. Honours results for the MEc were abandoned. The changed emphasis towards research and thesis was recalled by Bruce Miller, who had graduated MEc in 1951. He described the standards set for the thesis and its examination (three examiners of whom two were external) as very close to a PhD if not, at least in some cases, more arduous (letter to the author, 20 September 2002). This matches the author's own experience when he completed his MEc by thesis in 1961–63. It was examined by Syd Butlin (internal examiner), Graham Tucker (Australian National University) and John La Nauze (University of Melbourne).

The remaining faculty meetings of the war years revised, or attempted to revise, specific aspects of the new degree structure proposal. Alan Clunies Ross and Ivo Kerr unsuccessfully tried for an honours school in Business Administration (FM: 10 August 1944). The proposed new by-laws also foreshadowed abolition of the Diploma of Public Administration because faculty no longer wanted diploma courses for unmatriculated students. Senate meetings (9 October, 1944, 6 November 1944, 4 December 1944) approved the new degree structure, though they were not finalised until the end of 1945 (FM: 6 October 1945).

When Sawkins (Reader in Statistics) retired in May 1945 after 22 years of service, faculty argued for his replacement at senior level, given the proposed sequence of Statistics courses. In August 1945 Senate approved the creation of a general chair of Statistics as a special appointment in Economics and Agricultural Science. Senate also noted faculty's request for additional staff in Statistics, since 300 students were expected to enrol in first year in 1946, of whom 200 were in the services. Moreover, 150 senior students still had to complete Statistics for degrees they had started (SM: 13 August 1945). It proved difficult to find adequate staff for statistics teaching, and for this and other staffing reasons faculty announced transitional arrangements for Accounting I, Law I, Statistics I and Political Theory based on existing courses from the old degree structure (FM: 10 October, 1945). The last faculty meeting in 1945, apart from marking the formal resignation of Mills and the election of Butlin as dean, also gratefully accepted the offer of an annual lecture in Advanced Accounting from the Commonwealth Institute of Accountants.

The University of Sydney Economics Society in Depression and war

In line with Butlin's (1970) comments that interest in economic issues was especially strong during the Depression of the 1930s, the Economics Society thrived over those years, only to collapse during the final war years when, from 1943 onwards, student numbers plummeted. Society membership, therefore, fluctuated considerably with 75 members in 1928–29, 35 in 1942–43, a maximum of 101 in 1936–37, a minimum of 18 in 1941–42 and an average membership of 67 (Sydney University Economics Society, Annual Reports, university Archives).

Meetings with speakers, including the traditional freshers' welcome at which the presidential address was customarily given, continued to be the major activities of the society during the 1930s and the early war years. There was also an annual dance, the profits of which financed a greater part of the society's activities, as well as the organisation of faculty debating and sporting teams for inter-faculty competitions.

In 1929–30, the society's year started with Madgwick's presidential address at the April freshers' welcome, attended by 130 persons. In July, Professor Robert Firth (an anthropologist) addressed an audience of 70 on 'the economic life of savage peoples'; in August, Curry spoke to 70 people on his 'Impressions From a Recent Tour of Japan and the East Indies' while at the final (September) meeting for the year, Bland addressed 'Some Aspects of American Government'. In 1930–31, Mills gave his presidential address to the freshers' welcome attended by 240 persons; in May, Mills talked on American student life to an audience of 124; a talk on 'The Russian Revolution as I Saw It' given by A.A. Faminsky drew a record crowd of 350 in July; the then leader of the opposition in New South Wales, Bertram Stevens (a close friend and associate of Bland, Black and Mills), drew 85 in August with a talk on 'Prominent Problems in Public Finance'; and Edward Shann (Professor of Economics at Western Australia) closed the year in September on the topic, 'Can Silver Do It?' (that is, replace the abandoned Gold Standard) to 114 persons.

In 1931–32, Bland gave the presidential address to the freshers' welcome, attracting 220 persons; Mills had an audience of 130 in May for a talk on 'Economic Reconstruction in Australia'; in July, 70 members listened to C.W.D. Conagher on 'The Northern Territory'; in August, the same number heard E.S. Spooner, then assistant state treasurer, on 'The Premiers' Conferences', while the German Vice-Consul closed the year, speaking to an audience of 65 on 'The Economic Situation in Germany'. In 1932–33, the April freshers' welcome attracted 180; while in May, July and August, T. Hytten spoke on 'Road and Rail Transport', Hermann Black on the 'International Economic Conference' and 1931 graduate Mary Debenham, BA, spoke on 'Recent Central Bank Action Towards Raising the Price Level', drawing audiences of 65, 120 and 110.

Under Hermann Black's presidency in 1933–34, audiences ranging from 60 to 68 listened to D.A. Nicholson on 'Douglas Social Credit' (May), A.G.B. Fisher, from the Bank of New South Wales on 'Autarkie' (July), Bland on 'The Administrative Difficulties of a Nationalised Banking System' (August) and W.G.K. Duncan (Tutorial Classes and temporary Economic History lecturer) on 'The Prospects of Liberty in a Planned Economy'. E.R. Walker gave the presidential address at the freshers' welcome in 1934–35. In that year international affairs was the major crowd puller. For example, an audience of 140 listened to Frank Albert's talk on 'Russia Revisited', and 120 to R.M. Crawford (Modern History) on 'Abyssinia' (in the spotlight as under active consideration for enlarging Mussolini's new 'Roman Empire'). The economists, by contrast, only drew an average audience of 30 for R.C. Wilson's address on 'Wool and its Competitors', S.J. Butlin on 'An Economist in Cambridge' and R. Randerson (BEc 1935) on 'Gold Standards: Old and New?' Butlin was president in 1935–36, giving his presidential address to 250 students at the March freshers' welcome; in May, Madgwick addressed 100 on 'Life at Oxford', W.E.H. Stanner drew 110 on 'Australian Aboriginal life' (June) and S.A. Maddocks (Commissioner for Road Transport) drew an audience of 30 for a discussion of 'Transport Abroad'.

For subsequent years, topics discussed at meetings were no longer recorded in the society's Annual Reports, though names of speakers and the size of their audiences continued to be. Thus in 1939, Black twice attracted audiences of well over 100, recent graduates Henry Randerson and James Plimsoll and newly appointed lecturer, John La Nauze, spoke in 1940; La Nauze as president in 1940–41 organised Black, Ian Clunies Ross, Jack Crawford and what look like three Burmese speakers (Mo Myit, Ba Neyin and Kyan Nyun). The first women president, Margaret

Barry (BA 1943), assisted by Noel Butlin as honorary secretary for 1941–42, organised talks by Roden Cutler, Mills, Sir Bertram Stevens and J.S. Collings in which Cutler with his newly acquired Victoria Cross probably discussed military matters and the others issues of war economy and plans for post-war reconstruction. Attendances of 150 for Roden Cutler and 100 for Mills and Stevens were very satisfactory. Finally, in 1942–43 (with Tom Kewley as president and Geelum Simpson-Lee as secretary), five meetings were organised with Professor Ian Clunies Ross, Dr E. Allen Peterson, J.D. Holmes, Dr A.H. McDonald and Mr S.D. McPhee as speakers. In addition, the society organised a weekly discussion group on Wednesday evenings 'during term', with a membership of twenty, for which Harold Levien (BA 1952) was the organising secretary and Tom Kewley a frequent discussion leader on social security issues (twice), post-war reconstruction, and the ABC.

On the social front, annual dances were held continuously during the 1930s, with fluctuating profits as well as occasional losses. During the war years, dances were sometimes replaced by parties and once (1940) with a Society Ball. The profits of this ball, amounting to just over ten guineas, were donated to the Vice-Chancellor's Patriotic Fund. Graduand members in May 1933 hosted a dinner for the academic staff in the faculty, but this failed to set a precedent and was not repeated. Another apparent oncer was the 'Economics Tableau' as the society's float for the Annual Commemoration Day Parade in 1929. No photographs of this 'Tableau' are extant and what this float presented to make economics intelligible to the citizens of Sydney on the eve of the Depression unfortunately remains a mystery.

Successes on the sporting field were rather mixed, and presidents of the society frequently had to plead for greater participation. In 1929–30, the Fishman Cup was secured in inter-faculty athletics and unspecified successes were reaped by the faculty rugby league team, while the faculty team won the tennis A competition. The following year faculty teams participated unsuccessfully in rowing, athletics, boxing and cricket, came third in the swimming relay championships and, in combination with Arts, won the inter-faculty rugby union. The Annual Reports of the later 1930s either omitted sporting achievements or reported poor performances. An exception was 1940, when faculty enjoyed successes in athletics, boxing and swimming, while in 1943 faculty teams participated in tennis and boxing competitions and, with assistance from Arts, fielded an inter-faculty cricket team.

Faculty's record in inter-faculty debating was very uneven. In 1930–31, the faculty debating team reached the semi-finals; in 1933–34, it lost the final. In 1934–35, it failed once again to survive the semi-finals, and in 1936–37 it once more lost in the finals. However, a team consisting of Bruce Miller, John Watson and Albert Kent won the inter-faculty competition in 1940 and repeated this success in 1941 (with Miller also leading the university debating team). For the last two war years (1941–42, 1942–43) over which the society was active, it unsuccessfully fielded debating teams in the normal inter-faculty competition.

Although not strictly related to the Sydney University Economics Society, this section concludes with two excerpts from student writings on economics in *Hermes*, the university's literary magazine, at both the beginning and the end of the 1930s. The first is a presentation of Economics III as either a dream or a nightmare by M.E.B. (probably Michael E. Breen, BA 1930, who gained first place in Economics III for that year). In this discussion, faculty teachers of the time play a significant but anonymous role in what resembles a Dantesque journey:

> We eventually reached the tenth floor and found the place a veritable hive of economic industry. Nowhere was the division of labour more thoroughly developed. Adam Smith was there, busily engaged in conducting 'An Enquiry into the Nature and Causes of the Wealth of Nation' and Cannan was amassing his 'Wealth', Brown was engaged in 'International Trade', Bastable was organising "The Commerce of Nations" and the infamous Pigou was creating the notorious 'Unemployment' with which his name is connected. The local faculty was well represented.
>
> In one corner, a tall and somewhat serious-looking gentleman was discussing problems of sovereignty, another was feeling 'very worried' over the problems of reconciling popular control on various 'Boards' with the use of administrative experts, 'wondering' all the while 'where this was going to lead us'. A third was carrying out manoeuvres with mean average population, curves of normal distribution, skewed curves, chest measurements of goldfish, etc. in the presence of an audience admiring but bewildered. (*Hermes*, Trinity Term 1931, pp. 32–33)

In 1939, 'Canopus' addressed 'Salvationism and Economics', partly on Robbinsian lines (Robbins' *Nature and Significance of Economic Science* had been published in 1934 and for many years thereafter was used as an Economics IV textbook for pass students). Canopus represented the economist as a diligent seeker after truth, interested only in seeing 'how things are objectively interrelated', and strongly rejected the popular view of 'the economist as a sort of witchdoctor, concerned with "remaking the world"'. However, Robbins' individualistic approach to economics, which envisaged 'society as an agglomeration of individuals', was described as 'too naïve'. This, according to Canopus, was because it, and the associated subjective (utility) theory of value, unduly neglected 'the general social structure, and its influence on economic values, price formation and production', a much more institutionalist approach (*Hermes*, June 1939, pp. 25–26). The last approach was then also an important part of the University of Sydney's economics syllabus, particularly in the first-year exposition of its basic principles by Mills, Black and Madgwick. These emphasised the practical utility of economics as well as its scientific qualities and singled out economic problems such as protection and unemployment, emphasising the economic role of the state in this context. Canopus showed himself a good student of Sydney University's economic methodology perspective, which he was willing to share with the wider university community in his *Hermes* article.

The faculty's bibliographical record in Depression and war

As was the case during the 1920s, Bland was the major publisher in the faculty during the 1930s and early 1940s, publishing over 75 articles in these fifteen years. Although many of these were printed lectures and addresses in local government, public service and adult education periodicals, a significant number appeared in academic journals (*Economic Record*, *Australian Journal of Public Administration* and *Australasian Journal of Psychology and Philosophy*). In addition, Bland published an important book, *Planning and the Modern State*, in 1945. It went through many editions and undoubtedly was very influential in Australia's post-war debate on these issues. Bland's range of subject matter was wide, embracing not only government and public administration but also constitutional issues, budgetary policy and accountability, natural resource problems, hospital administration, post-war reconstruction and foreign affairs. (A full bibliography of Bland's major published writings is in the *Australian Journal of Public Administration*, September 1948, pp. 93–120).

R.C. Mills and E.R. Walker also had distinguished publication records over this period. Mills' published work during the 1930s was mentioned earlier; that published during the war years included further editions of *Money*, several government reports for the writing of which he was largely responsible (one on uniform income taxation and four Grants Commission Annual Reports), two pamphlets in 1940 (one on *The Real Costs of the War*, the other on *The University and Business*) and a long chapter in a book on *Repatriation* published in 1945 (Butlin 1953, pp. 186–88, provides a Mills bibliography, which unfortunately is incomplete).

Ronald Walker published no fewer than 36 items between 1930 and 1939, when he held his lectureship in Economics: 12 as articles in the *Economic Record*, two in the *Australian Journal of Public Administration*, one in the Chicago *Journal of Political Economy* and one in the *Weltwirtschaftliche Archiv*. In addition, he published four books, of which two were texts. These included the highly successful *Money* (written with R.C. Mills), an *Outline of Australian Economics* (written with Madgwick), his important and original book on *Unemployment Policy* and a book on *War-Time Economics with Special Reference to Australia*. He also published chapters in several books including *Marketing Australia's Primary Products*, edited by Walter Duncan, a one-time colleague.

Other members of the economics teaching staff were far less productive publishers, though this is often explicable by the fact that they were relatively recent appointments. Black published three items in the *Australian Journal of Public Administration*, all during the war years. Butlin published articles on banking, taxation and the war economy in the *Economic Record* and the *Australian Quarterly*. Jack Crawford published a chapter in a book on trade in the Netherlands East Indies and Malaysia as well as an *Economic Record* article on the Australian tariff with S.H. Wolstenholme. John La Nauze in the 1940s published five items in the *Economic Record*, three of them on the history of economic thought; J.S.G. Wilson published four *Economic Record* articles during the war, one on the basic wage in Western Australia and three on the war economy; Kingsley Laffer published an article on taxation in the *Economic Record* while Wolstenholme during his short life recorded two publications, the article on the Australian tariff with Crawford, and one in the *Australian Quarterly* on the falling birth rate.

Faculty's teachers of Economic History also published. Portus (who lectured on Economic History until his departure for Adelaide in 1934) published a book on *Communism and Christianity* in 1931 and one on *Australia Since 1906* for Oxford University Press in 1932, an article on trade unions in the *Economic Record* in 1934, and one on 'The Emergence of Australia' for *Australia Today* in the same year. W.G.K. Duncan, Portus' successor as teacher of Economic History during 1934 and 1935, published two edited books and four journal articles over these two years, none of them devoted to his temporary field of teaching. Madgwick, who taught

Economic History for the remainder of the 1930s, published the *Outline of Australian Economics* with Walker already mentioned, an important study on *Immigration in Australia* in 1937 and an article on the Australian economy for the *Swedish–Australian Trade Journal* in 1933.

As part of the Public Administration staff, Tom Kewley published two articles on aspects of social security in the *Australian Journal of Public Administration*. Sawkins (Statistics) listed nine publications in the bibliographical summary for 1930, including a 1930 *Economic Record* article on wage setting. Before his retirement in 1945 he published two further articles in the *Economic Record* and one in the *Australian Quarterly*. Ivo Kerr, who taught Accounting for the whole of the period, in 1930 published a book on company liquidations, an elementary text on bookkeeping in two parts (published in 1933 and 1934), an article on 'Company Liquidations' for the *Chartered Accountant in Australia* in 1935, and a book on company accounts in 1936. J.A.L. Gunn, who taught Business Principles and Practice from 1938 until its abolition, published a book on Australian income tax in 1938 while finally, P.R. Watts, the lawyer who until 1939 lectured on political institutions, published a number of legal articles on conveyancing during the 1930s, as well as a topical book on the defaulting purchaser in 1934.

The bibliographical record of the faculty between 1929 and 1945 shows a considerable improvement on that of the 1920s. The number of teaching staff actually publishing increased considerably and the quality of the destinations for the listed publications greatly improved. In particular, the younger full-time teaching staff appointed from the second half of the 1930s were all inclined to publish. Bland, Walker and Mills were the leading publishers in the faculty, though Mills' publication record virtually ceased when his Commonwealth government responsibilities grew during the war.

Preparing for peace and post-war reconstruction

In the final years of the war, the faculty actively prepared for the influx of students expected to come from ex-servicemen on the cessation of hostilities. It did so by abolishing the diploma courses, while other remnants of its beginnings, such as Business Principles and Practice, were also swept away. The new degree structure adopted remained in force until the end of the 1950s as the basis for a rigorous economics, social science and business education for many generations of students. This was a significant and courageous step, given the additional staff requirements the new degree structure entailed.

These growing staff requirements implied abandonment of the strategy to recruit only from amongst the university's own quality graduates. This policy had been justified by Mills on the ground he had become thoroughly contemptuous of English referees ('who think anything is good enough for the colonies') and believed sending his own young men abroad was a better way to build his department. But this was in large measure making a virtue of necessity since the enforced reliance on assistant lecturers in the 1930s 'virtually ruled out oversea[s] recruitment' (Butlin, 1970, p. 10) Only Benham and John La Nauze were exceptions to this policy, though the appointments of Kingsley Laffer and J.S.G. Wilson in the early 1940s heralded the changes to come in recruitment. Whether the necessity of the 1930s, to use Butlin's own words, resulted in bad appointments from the faculty's own graduates seems highly debatable given the undoubted quality of Walker, Crawford, Butlin, Swan, Kewley and Parker, who commenced their academic careers at this time.

Another preparatory step, only briefly mentioned so far, was the foundation of the Wolstenholme Library as a real study aid for students in the faculty.

As Butlin concisely put it:

> One other development stemming from the last part of the war was the real as distinct from nominal creation of the Wolstenholme Library. In 1943 it consisted of a few books, about two dozen in all, no room, no librarian, no income. Steel, of the Fisher Library, overruled doubts as to the wisdom of developing it; harassed for lack of space, books, staff, money, he was keen to see any kind of additional library facilities. The first move was to badger all likely donors of material. S.R. Carver, then acting Commonwealth Statistician, was very generous with files of statistical serials and other material. Various banks and others gave material, or, modestly, money. Space was made by installing lockable bookshelves in a small class room, whose seminar-type furniture enabled it to double as a reading room. The Vice-Chancellor was prepared to concede a Librarian, disguised as 'clerical assistant'. (Butlin 1970, p. 11)

It may be noted that Carver's support for the new library was also visible on the general journal shelves. For instance, he donated a large number of past copies of the *Economic Record*, then particularly useful to Economics students. Relevant scientific journals were at that stage circulated to academic staff in order of seniority, frequently staying for a long time on the desks of at least some of them, thereby hindering their effective circulation and availability to more junior members of staff and students. A sample of this system from 1940 in the form of the 25 May issue of *The Economist* came fortuitously into my hands during 1989. It indicated that Mills, who was the first on the circulation list to receive it, had read it by 15 July; Bland, next on the list, finished it by 20 July; La Nauze finished with it on 24 July, Swan and Walker appear to have read it next but failed to note the date when they passed it on; Kewley passed it on by 22 August; it went then either to Black or Madgwick, and last at this stage, to Syd Butlin. The injunction, 'Please pass it on as quickly as possible, and immediately if you do not intend to read it' was therefore widely interpreted on the evidence from this isolated sample. This system made multiple copies of journals and periodicals a boon to students and staff low on the circulation list.

Depression and war imposed no enduring detrimental effects for faculty development. The opposite was in fact the case. Enrolments grew, course availability and variety greatly expanded, and full-time faculty teaching staff grew at an enormous rate when compared to the 1920s. Moreover, developments in Public Administration, largely inspired by Bland as its first professor, began a gradual decline in the hegemony of the Economics Department within the faculty structure. The post-war period accelerated progress to establishing a multi-department Faculty of Economics

Final year Economics students in 1930 in the Great Hall.

Staff and final-year students in the final decade of the 'old' by-laws: the classes of 1950 on the steps of the R.C. Mills Building.

Staff and final-year students in the final decade of the 'old' by-laws: the classes of 1951 and 1953 on the steps of the R.C. Mills Building.

Staff and final-year students in the final decade of the 'old' by-laws: the classes of 1954 and 1955 on the steps of the R.C. Mills Building.

CHAPTER 3

Post-war reconstruction and shortening the BEc degree (1945–62)

The nearly two decades of faculty history of this chapter deal with the rapid growth of enrolments in the immediate post-war period as a result of the special provisions made for university studies of ex-servicemen and the pressures on staff growth this generated. In 1949 this made the University of Sydney the third largest university in the 'Empire'. Other problems arose as well. Butlin recalled, 'One of the minor handicaps … was the effect on evening lectures of the frequent blackouts caused by chronic power shortage. Faculty equipment included a number of "Aladdin" lamps which were lit at dusk and distributed around lecture rooms just in case. Too often they were needed, with disastrous effects on any lecture which depended on blackboard work' (1970, p. 12). With evening students still the vast majority, this was a serious problem, raised at two Senate meetings (SM: 4 July 1949, 5 February 1951). A letter to Harold Maze (22 March, 1950) from Butlin as dean survives in the archives (File 1372) requesting ten blackout lamps, plus four for staff giving evening classes, and six hurricane lamps.

By the mid-1950s, growth in university education was accelerating more generally, not only at the University of Sydney and its Faculty of Economics but also through the establishment of new universities. In Sydney, these were the University of Technology (from 1948 the University of New South Wales), and Macquarie University from the mid-1960s. Outside Sydney, the University College at Newcastle was established in 1948 and the pre-war (1938) University College of New England at Armidale became a full university in 1954.

The late 1940s also witnessed a move towards a formal departmental system to replace the monolithic structure of single-department faculties, as the Faculty of Economics had been from its inception. After all, it had been the product of simply converting its Department of Economics and Commerce into a Faculty of Economics. Departments of Government and Public Administration, of Accounting, and of Economic Statistics were created in 1947, 1960 and 1962; those of Economic History and Industrial Relations followed in 1969 and 1975. Separate Finance and Marketing departments only came in the 1990s. New initiatives in postgraduate education by the faculty included masters degrees by coursework and thesis (or long essay), and the PhD as (initially a full-time) research degree in 1958.

In 1951, the faculty moved into its own building. This enabled the Wolstenholme Library to become a genuine faculty library, with its own reading room and part-time librarian. Housing the expanding staff in the one building, and having its own lecture and seminar rooms for most of the courses offered by the faculty, enhanced the *esprit de corps* for its members. This faculty home was not abandoned until the middle of 1965. By then, it was far too small to accommodate steadily growing staff and student numbers. The subsequent move to the Merewether Building, on the other side of City Road, is discussed in Chapter 4.

Finally, and as indicated in its title, Chapter 3 reviews the demise of the twelve-subject, four-year, full-time BEc degree and its replacement by a ten-subject, three-year pass degree with an additional year added for honours. Discussions of this major change dominated debate at faculty meetings in the mid-1950s. This explains 1962 as the cut-off year for this chapter. It was the year of graduation for the last cohort of what were by then known as 'old by-laws' students, who had completed their final, fourth year of the degree in 1961. Growth in faculty numbers of academic staff and students also saw considerable expansion of non-academic staff. The appointment of departmental secretaries and from 1945 a graduate assistant to the dean, initially the formidable Joyce Fisher, of research staff and of professional librarians for the Wolstenholme Library are key examples. Wolstenholme Library benefited greatly from specific donations it received during the general appeal for funds launched by the university as part of its centenary celebrations in 1952–53. The teaching of accounting did likewise, as did economics research through the then very substantial donation of £1000 from the Commonwealth Bank in 1953.

Enrolments, curriculum and staffing: an overview, 1945–55

In the decade following World War II, enrolments in the Faculty of Economics initially fluctuated widely. Only from the mid-1950s did the university and faculty experience the steady growth in student numbers which marked large segments of the remaining period of this history. In 1945, enrolments in the faculty were 290, made up of 183 men and 107 women students, accounting for 6.6 per cent of total university enrolments. Over the next four years, faculty enrolments more than doubled, but rose more modestly relative to total university enrolments. Many new students were ex-servicemen, making the general ratio of women to men students in the faculty plummet.

The alteration in the nature of enrolments may have had something to do with the changed degree structure which came into effect in 1946, and the details of which were presented in chapter 2. These changes more tightly structured the type of studies offered by the bachelor's degree. In particular, the new structure considerably reduced choice of subjects in the degree for students by adding a second, three-year specialisation which students had to choose from Government and Public Administration, Accounting and its adjunct, Commercial Law, Statistics, Economic History and the in fact never offered Business Administration— all considered of special relevance to those studying economics for a career in business or the public service. It also provided for a common first year and compulsory History of Economic Thought in the fourth year. Hence, when the second sequence had been selected at the time of enrolment for second year, students were effectively left with a free choice of subjects (albeit from a limited list) for only one subject in both their second and third years of study. In addition, students could seek admission to honours studies if their first-year results warranted this. Honours could be attempted in the major faculty subjects, although Accounting did not begin to offer studies at honours level until 1955. Increasing students' freedom of choice over the selection of courses of study for the degree was one issue featuring strongly in the debates of the mid-1950s over the three-year degree structure.

The absolute growth in student numbers over the decade 1945–54, combined with the new degree structure, implied substantial additions to academic staff. The 1945–46 *University Calendar* recorded eight full-time teaching staff in the faculty (including two professors) and half a dozen temporary and part-time staff. Ten years later, the faculty still had only two professors: Syd Butlin (dean) and Dick Spann (appointed in 1954) in Government. There were eight senior lecturers, of whom five were in Economics (Hermann Black, Ron Gates, Kingsley Laffer, Cyril Renwick and Geelum Simpson-Lee) and one each in Accounting (Ray Chambers), Government (Tom Kewley) and Economic Statistics (Stuart Rutherford); eight permanent lecturers of whom three were in Economic History (Alan Birch, Ken Buckley and Jules Ginswick), four in Economics (Noel Drane, Harry Edwards, Ted Wheelright and Jim Wilson) and one in Government (Henry Mayer). Kurt Singer was a temporary lecturer in Economics, Alan Bridge and R.F. Cross were part-time lecturers in Commercial (and Industrial) Law, N.F. Stevens was part-time lecturer in Accounting, while Accounting also had two part-time tutors, Ron Brown and Hugh McCredie. By way of support staff, there were two graduate assistants for the professors.

These staff changes largely reflected the changed curriculum of the four-year, old by-law degree, enshrined in the changes approved in 1944 by Senate. These required the teaching of six compulsory courses in Economics (Economics I–IV, Descriptive Economics and History of Economic Thought) and in principle, but not fully implemented until the early 1950s, three courses in either Government and Public Administration, or Economic Statistics, or Economic History or Accounting, the last invariably combined with two Commercial Law courses. The part-time staff in Accounting (Ray Chambers as senior lecturer was the only full-time Accounting staff member) meant that for the whole of the 1950s, Accounting and Commercial Law lectures were given only in the evening. The more generously staffed Economics, Economic History and Government courses were offered at both day and evening slots. Economic Statistics, with its one full-time staff member and small number of students, only provided lectures during the day aided by part-time or temporary staff. These included W.F. Nichols, a part-time teaching fellow in Statistics and Harry Edwards, a temporary lecturer in 1948, while A.H. Pollard was a part-time lecturer for some years in the mid-1950s. Even when additional full-time staff was hired later in the 1950s, only Economic Statistics I lectures (by 1957) were given at day and evening times.

Compared with the staffing position in 1955, that in 1945–46 highlights the pressure for additional faculty staff to deal with the massive influx of returned ex-servicemen students, which began in earnest in 1946. To remedy this shortage, the Faculty of Economics (together with Dentistry and Physics) sought leave to pay higher salaries than elsewhere in the university. In the light of this request, the Senate (SM: 1 April 1946) established a committee (including Bland and former graduate, Clarey Martin) to examine urgently the state of the Faculty of Economics in general, with special reference to 'the numbers and grades of staff, salary scales and accommodation'. It reported at the next Senate meeting (6 May 1946). Recommendations were based on four considerations: the need to strengthen staff in the light of student numbers, the lower Australian academic salary scale relative to that in the United Kingdom and other Commonwealth countries, the need to raise salaries sufficiently to ensure adequate recruitment and the fact that advertisements so far had failed to attract suitable applicants.

The committee proposed a second Economics chair in Applied Economics (intended to embrace fields like Statistics, Commercial Law and Accounting, then formally still within the Economics Department), readerships in the History of Economic Thought and in Statistics, two vacant senior lectureships, a vacant lectureship and an additional lectureship for immediate advertisement, a higher salary for Heinz Arndt, appointed earlier in 1946 as senior lecturer, and the need to improve university accommodation for staff. The adjourned Senate meeting (20 May 1946) approved all these recommendations except for the readership in Statistics. At its 1 July 1946 meeting, the Senate approved salary increases for Arndt, Kewley, Laffer, Noel Butlin and Renwick. On 12 August 1946 it appointed John La Nauze as Reader in the History of Economic Thought.

The Senate meeting (2 September 1946) re-emphasised the urgency of providing better staff and teaching rooms, but nothing was done for some years. Staff accommodation was in fact not improved until 1951, when the faculty moved into the new R.C. Mills Building. A chair of Applied Economics was, however, advertised. Ronald Walker was offered the position, but when he declined (SM: 4 November 1946), the chair was not re-advertised. At the final Senate meeting in 1946 (23 December), Senate approved Bland's request for an additional lectureship in Public Administration. Six years later, but without the benefit of a special report, Senate converted a part-time lectureship in Accounting into a senior lectureship (to which Ray Chambers was appointed), provided an additional part-time lecturer in Commercial Law, an additional lectureship in Economics and converted two part-time lectureships in Economics and one in Economic History into permanent, full-time positions.

Considerable changes in actual staff are apparent from the previously supplied snapshots of faculty staff for 1945–46 and 1955. Many of these, as already mentioned, came from departure of staff to the new Canberra University College, that is, Heinz Arndt, Trevor Swan, Noel Butlin and, after a stint in Melbourne followed by a return to Sydney as Professor of Political Theory and dean, Percy Partridge. Stuart Wilson went to a chair in Economics at Hull; Eric Russell, who had joined the Economics staff as a lecturer in 1951, resigned in 1952 to go to Adelaide; Bland and Sawkins both retired, aged 65; R.B. Madgwick departed to head New England University College at Armidale; A.H. Martin left for unspecified other fields. Among the temporary Accounting teaching staff, Ivo Kerr had retired and Clunies Ross had died in 1946.

Much of the new staff was internally recruited from the faculty's, or the university's, own graduates. However, as the Senate had reported in 1946, a growing number of academic staff had to be recruited 'overseas'—that is, either from Great Britain or from other Australian universities. Thus, of the 1955 academic staff, Butlin, Black, Renwick, Simpson-Lee, Chambers, Kewley, Drane, Edwards and Jim Wilson were all Sydney University graduates and, with the exception of Edwards (an Arts graduate with a major in Economics), all graduates from the Faculty of Economics. Henry Mayer had degrees from the University of Melbourne, Ron Gates from the University of Tasmania and Kingsley Laffer from Western Australia. Of the British recruits, Spann and Rutherford both had Oxford degrees, while Wheelwright, Birch, Buckley and Ginswick had graduated from St Andrews, Manchester and London (for the last two). Only Kurt Singer, who had arrived in Australia as a displaced person from central Europe, had German qualifications. In Accounting, Bridge, Cross and McCredie were Sydney law graduates, Brown had a BEc degree, while Stevens, Brown and McCredie also had Australian accounting qualifications. Arndt, although by then no longer at the University of Sydney, had Oxford qualifications as well, even though he, like Singer, was born in Germany.

Two of faculty's immigrant academics left accounts of their years at Sydney in the 1940s and early 1950s. Arndt did so for his intellectual memoirs (Arndt 1985, chapter 2). These recalled his room in the faculty overlooking 'the pleasant central quadrangle'; Butlin as professor and dean 'only a few years older' and with an 'outstanding scholarly record at Sydney and Cambridge'; Hermann Black ('a Schumpetarian … and popular broadcaster'), John La Nauze ('the later biographer of Deakin'), Noel Butlin ('Syd's very much younger brother'); Kingsley Laffer ('who later built-up … a sub-department of Industrial Relations' and taught second-year micro-economics); Max Hartwell (economic historian of Van Diemen's Land and later professorial fellow in Economic History at Nuffield College, Oxford); and Kurt Singer (a pupil of Knapp, acquaintance of Keynes in the 1920s, and 'the epitome … and caricature of the German scholar' who taught History of Economic Thought with La Nauze in various academic positions over his half a dozen years on the faculty staff.

Arndt also recalled that there were 400–500 first-year students (one-third full-time, two-thirds part-time or evening students), and still some 350 students in third year, to whom Arndt taught macro-economics (basic income theory in first term, money and banking and fiscal policy in second term, and international monetary economics in third term). The text for the last with respect to Australia was the *Report* of the 1936 Royal Commission on Money and Banking in the writing of which R.C. Mills had participated, with standard international texts for the previous two terms.

Arndt also recorded his enjoyment of teaching. His 'non-rigorous' lectures avoided mathematics (apart from some diagrams and the simplest algebra, more than sufficient to strike 'terror into the hearts of nine-tenths of the students, a majority of whom suffered from obsessional maths-phobia'). Apart from lectures, Arndt organised voluntary tutorials for his classes in groups of ten to fifteen students, whom he 'encouraged to meet once a week'. He gave a weekly seminar as well to honours students (the last including Harry Edwards, Alan Hall, Don Lamberton, Noel Drane and Alan Barnard, all future academics, and Don Sanders, Jack Wright, Gordon Menzies, Jack Donovan, Ken Foreman and Roy Fernandez, future central bankers or high ranking public servants). Two noted, because 'articulate critics', from among Arndt's pass students were Alan Barton (the future transport tycoon and founder of the short-lived Australia Party) and Billy McMahon (future federal treasurer and prime minister). Arndt's academic publications while at Sydney are mentioned later; his semi-political writings of the time included the best-selling Fabian Society pamphlet, *The Case for Bank Nationalisation*, with appendixes by Noel Butlin and a then young barrister, later judge, Rae Else-Mitchell. It may be noted here that the Fabian Society at this stage had strong informal associations with the Faculty of Economics. The distinguished graduate, postgraduate, member of the university Senate and parliamentarian, Clarey Martin, was president, Noel Butlin, secretary and Kingsley Laffer, treasurer. In 1950, Arndt left Sydney to take up a professorship in Canberra, later to enjoy far greater research opportunities at the Research School of the Social Sciences at the Australian National University.

Other observations on Sydney University and its Faculty of Economics in the 1950s came in an article on Australian universities by Ken Buckley (Buckley 1957), then a new lecturer in Economic History. Written for the British academic thinking of emigrating to Australia, the article emphasised comparative aspects of the two university systems, but its observations about the Faculty of Economics on the basis of his three years experience is interesting in this context. Buckley noted that teaching loads were generally speaking lighter in Australia, but that large enrolments and evening studies meant that many lectures (especially in Economics and Arts) had to be repeated. Students in the larger classes tended to be 'a sea of faces', and only in honours classes became individuals. 'The best Australian students are every bit as good as the best in Britain, but many of them chose pass rather than honours studies (especially if they are evening students) and few go on to postgraduate work'. Evening students were, however, more mature than their day counterparts, generally fresh from school. Evening students therefore worked harder but were invariably pressed for time. Buckley also noted the 'appreciable number of students from Asian and Pacific countries', many of them scholars under the Colombo Plan, a 1950 British Commonwealth initiative to provide tertiary education opportunities as one form of technical assistance to persons from the developing world in Asia.

More generally, Buckley claimed that research assistance, both staff and financial, seemed easier to obtain in Australia, while important research topics in fields such as history were far more plentiful. This advantage was offset by the tyranny of distance, not only from Europe (requiring at least four weeks by ship each way) but also within Australia for the purpose of attending conferences (such as ANZAAS) or for simply meeting with inter-state colleagues. However, forecast and already realised growth in student numbers meant deteriorating staff-student ratios, room shortages for both classes and staff, and the wasteful practice of failing a high proportion of first-year students to make senior class sizes more manageable. The last was a marked feature of university experience from the 1950s and I recall being told by the chancellor at the Matriculation Ceremony at the start of my university studies in 1957 that only one in three of those present would enter second-year studies in 1958. This quip endured to at least 1970, as Graeme Dean informs me. A report to Senate (7 July 1958), however, gives somewhat lower failure rates for 1957 and 1958: Economics I failed 41 and 53 per cent, and Descriptive Economics 29 and 47 per cent.

Faculty deliberations and administration, 1945–55

The first faculty meeting in peacetime took place on 18 May 1945. R.C. Mills was in the chair and others present were Butlin, Bland, Anderson (Philosophy), Black, Kewley, La Nauze, Partridge and Renwick. The meeting recorded Sawkins' retirement after 22 years service to the faculty. Faculty immediately requested Sawkins' replacement at the readership level. Faculty's proposal for replacing him enabled Stuart Rutherford's appointment in 1947.

Faculty also recorded complaints from the New South Wales Department of Education about the effective lengthening of the degree for evening students (from four to six years) implied by the new faculty by-laws. Subsequent faculty meetings in 1945 reported transitional arrangements for commencing the new degree structure with respect to first-year courses, because Descriptive Economics could not be offered in 1946 and was in fact not offered until 1949. Faculty also accepted the formal resignation of R.C. Mills, recording that his 'assistance was constantly sought by the "City" and by Ministers of State' with respect to money and banking, special financial assistance to states, income taxation and post-war university development and finance. Butlin was then elected as dean, a position retained by him with only a few breaks until his departure from the university in 1971. At its September 1955 meeting, faculty was told that the establishment of an R.C. Mills Memorial Lecture was under discussion with the Economic Society of Australia (NSW Branch). In October 1951, the Commonwealth Institute of Accountants provided funds, initially £30 per annum, for an accounting research lecture. Such lectures were given from 1952 onwards, the first by S.R. Brown, while M.E. Murphy was appointed (a visiting) research professor in Accounting for that purpose in 1953. The first R.C. Mills Memorial Lecture was delivered in 1958.

Faculty meetings in subsequent years dwelt on other aspects of the implementation of the new degree structure, admissions to postgraduate courses, the appointment of new staff and the retirement or departure of others, and expanding opportunities for postgraduate study from the introduction of the PhD degree. Consideration of the last was deferred by faculty until 1955. However, it did approve rules about eligibility for doctoral studies in the form of an honours BEc degree or an MEc, then still by thesis only. It set a minimum completion time of two years, but academic staff could be admitted to part-time candidature and complete a PhD in four years. In 1947, Butlin was re-elected as dean but his absence on leave without pay during 1948 meant that Partridge was elected as dean in April 1948 to hold office until the end of 1949.

The April 1948 meeting also marked the retirement of Bland. Faculty recorded him as 'a pioneer in Australia in the academic study of Public Administration', a field in which he had also extensively published and where his students gratefully remembered that 'he brought the political controversies of the day into the class room'. Faculty also pointed out that Bland's 'highly personal method of combining lectures with discussions and questions' greatly stimulated his students and enabled them to learn 'by way of extempore illustration or anecdote, much that could never have been gained from official document or book'. It may not have been coincidental that this same meeting changed the field of Bland's chair to 'Government and Public Administration' and those of the courses over which he had presided to Government I, II and III. From 1951, these re-named courses became available to Arts students, as approved by Senate at its June 1950 meeting.

During 1949, faculty debated whether deferred examinations should be abolished, following a move in that direction by the Faculty of Arts. This was not approved but the regulations for awarding such examinations were greatly tightened. Faculty's last meeting for 1949 re-elected Butlin as dean and thanked Partridge for his services in that capacity over the previous twenty months. In December 1950 diploma courses in Commerce and Public Administration were finally abolished when Senate deleted sections 65–74 of Chapter XVIII of the by-laws.

In May 1951, faculty set up a travel fund for academic staff, and proposed appointment of a Research and Publication Committee to administer it. A first grant of £500 was allocated at its next meeting to assist Harry Edwards' 'research [of] statistics' in England, and in addition awarded him the Denison Miller Scholarship and a Walter and Eliza Hall Fellowship in Economics. Kingsley Laffer was given a staff travel grant of £500 in January 1953, Noel Drane in 1954 to supplement his Fulbright Fellowship at Harvard, while Jim Wilson was given one for doctoral studies at Cambridge. The committee administering the travel grant in the end was not the Publications Committee, but one including the professors of Economics and Government, Hermann Black and one other, unspecified, member of faculty. In November 1951, Butlin made his re-election as dean conditional on improved resources, especially staff, for the faculty. If this did not eventuate, he would have to resign (University Archives, File 1372).

Publications committees were on the agenda for several faculty meetings in 1952, the 13 January 1953 meeting electing the first such committee. It comprised the dean, Cyril Renwick, Geelum Simpson-Lee, Stuart Rutherford and Ted Wheelwright, and was to report regularly to faculty meetings. Its first report in July 1953 recommended that textbooks by staff members would not be eligible for funding, that 50 per cent of the scarce publication funds would go to finance the publication of 'original research work', and that the remainder would be used to finance a series of reprints of classics in the history of economic thought. The first of these, a reprint of the *Report on the High Price of Bullion*, was edited by Butlin and published in 1951 with assistance from the publication fund (which itself had been set up with a donation from the MLC Assurance Company). It was priced to produce a modest profit when all copies were sold. Further reprints were Malthus' review of the 'Controversy respecting the High Price of Bullion' from the *Edinburgh Review* (March/August 1811) in 1952 and his *Five Papers on Political Economy* in 1953, both edited by Renwick. Membership of the Publication Committee changed from time to time.

During its March 1955 meeting, faculty appointed two special committees. One was to report on the MEc degree (with Butlin as dean in the chair, and including Spann, Rutherford, Chambers, Birch, Ginswick and Wilson), the other to examine sections 16 and 26 of the by-laws prescribing the progression of evening students from one year to another. The MEc committee later (19 June) added consideration of the PhD 'as an urgent matter' to its terms of reference. It reported in September 1955, recommending that the PhD should be offered by the faculty as a full-time degree only, with special provisions for faculty's academic staff. Tighter regulations were proposed for administering the MEc, given the high incidence of non-enrolment by persons formally admitted to studies for the degree. Heads of departments were to approve thesis topics, appoint supervisors and exempt candidates from preliminary examinations where appropriate. Students were required to meet with their supervisors at least once a term, complete their theses within four years, be examined by external examiners if a member of staff or when the supervisor was appointed as the internal examiner. Students were permitted to re-submit (and be re-examined) if the thesis on first examination was of insufficient quality to pass, but deemed 'capable of improvement'. The Senate approved these new regulations at its November 1955 meeting. The faculty meeting that month also elected Spann as dean until December 1958, with Hermann Black acting dean during Spann's absence in January 1956.

The May 1955 faculty meeting heralded the start of a new faculty sequence of courses when Kingsley Laffer proposed a course in industrial relations, initially as an 'optional subject'. A committee elected to report on this proposal recommended to the 29 September 1955 meeting that industrial relations should if possible be available for the start of 1956 and that the appropriate sections of the by-laws should be amended accordingly. Faculty approved the report, and Industrial Relations lectures duly commenced in 1956. The last faculty meeting for 1955 agreed to make Accounting a full honours subject forthwith, and heard that a second chair in Economics would be established in 1957. The last did not eventuate and the second chair was not advertised and filled until 1962. By then, there were four chairs in the faculty, those of Accounting and Economic Statistics having joined the long-established chairs of Economics and Government.

Over the ten years just surveyed, the faculty met 38 times, that is, three or four times per calendar year, or at least once a term. Attendance at faculty meetings ranged from as few as six to the sixteen recorded as present at the last two in 1955. Rising staff numbers were therefore clearly reflected in attendance at the meetings. These were generally held in university meeting rooms; but from the early 1950s, when the faculty had moved into its own new premises, meetings generally took place in the seminar room the new building provided next to the dean's office.

At this stage, something should also be said on faculty administration. Growing student numbers, together with the tighter rules governing subject combinations which could be taken for the degree, implied scrutiny of all enrolments by a person acting on behalf of the dean, who was the *de jure* person deciding such matters. From 1945 onwards, deans were aided in this task by a graduate administrative assistant, initially Joyce Fisher, but in 1946 Mrs Audrey Horn (SM: 14 October 1946) and in 1947 Barbara Mann. Fisher was one of two separate appointments of graduate assistants in Economics and Government, then the only two departments in the faculty. In 1954 she returned to the faculty, first as graduate assistant to the Professor of Economics, then as graduate assistant, and from 1963 as administrative assistant, to the dean. She retired in 1972, but over nearly two decades scrutinised enrolments of students from second year in combination with her many other administrative duties within the faculty. Moreover, she provided valuable research assistance to Syd Butlin, accurate typing of his manuscripts and those of others, as well as preparing the indexes for his scholarly books. Although 'many students may recall Joyce as a rather strict, authoritarian figure … they did not know that, behind a strict exterior, lay a very warm and kind personality, who genuinely cared about the students and their problems' (J. Butlin, 1997). Be that as it may, in my undergraduate days in the late 1950s her nickname was 'The Dragon' because of her intimidating and abrupt manner to students. This sentiment was reflected concisely in a *Honi Soit* article (October 1967, p. 3). Her departure from the faculty in 1972 marked the end of an era, for reasons more fully explained in later chapters.

The new Dean and Professor of Economics: S.J. Butlin

At its February 1946 meeting, the university Senate appointed S.J. Butlin, who hade been elected dean the previous November, as Professor of Economics. From 1943 Butlin had been both acting Professor of Economics and acting dean while Mills was away on government duties. Butlin had graduated in 1932 with first-class honours and the medal, had completed postgraduate work at Cambridge, and had returned to the faculty as a full-time lecturer in 1937. Two years later he was promoted to senior lecturer. Initially, he taught Public Finance, the subject in which he published most of his early articles (a detailed bibliography is appended to N.G. Butlin 1978, pp. 115–18). He subsequently concentrated his research on the monetary history of Australia (his *Foundations of the Australian Monetary System, 1788–1851* gained him the DLitt from Cambridge) and published two volumes (the second jointly with C.B. Schedvin) of Australia's official history of World War II, devoted to its economic aspects. He published a *History of the Australia and New Zealand Bank* in 1961. His daughter Judith prepared the sequel to his *Foundations* for the press in 1983 with the title, *The Australian Monetary System, 1851–1914*, just as earlier she had done with her father's five chapters on *The History of Central Banking in Australia (1945–59)* published in the *Australian Economic History Review* (S.J. Butlin, 1983).

On his return to active duties in the faculty during the later war years, Butlin lectured in Economics I and Economics III to both day and evening classes, and took the evening Economic History honours courses. His growing responsibilities as dean gradually reduced the time he could devote to teaching. By the end of the 1950s, he only taught third term History of Economic Thought, giving both the lectures to pass students and the pass with credit seminar. In his obituary, brother Noel described Syd's teaching activities as follows:

> An economist could teach. Syd taught successively public finance, money and banking, and micro-economics. There was universal agreement (and my personal experience confirms) that the delivery was appalling and the contents superb. With fully prepared notes, Syd ignored them and prowled his dais, his eyes fixed firmly on his shoes (later, he preferred some distant horizon), precisely and lucidly explaining the intricacies of monetary theory and micro-economics. He hated public performances though he subsequently became an excellent

and witty after-dinner speaker. But the manner of lecturing address was lost in the quality of the content of his lectures. He came fully and personally alive in honours seminars when face-to-face confrontation with small groups provided an environment that better suited his temperament. (N. Butlin 1978, p. 106)

My own recollections of Butlin's 1960 teaching confirm his gazing at some distant horizon and his poor delivery. I also found him very unapproachable as an undergraduate student. However, when I was a teaching fellow in 1962 he became easier to talk to, particularly in the early afternoon when he had just returned from lunch and, as legend had it, was two whiskies over par.

Butlin devoted much time to wider university activities. For many years he served on the Proctorial Board and on the Appointments Board, of which he was chairman twice (in 1954–55, 1959–61). He was a member of the university Senate from 1963 to 1967. In 1945, Butlin advised the government over new banking legislation, but unlike younger brother Noel and Heinz Arndt, he stayed clear from the heated debates over bank nationalisation. He was active in the affairs of the Economic Society of Australia serving as its president in 1953–54, and was a member of the *Economic Record* editorial board for twenty years. He was a foundation member of the Social Science Committee of the Australian National Research Council through its casual transformation into the Social Science Research Council (of which he was chairman in 1961–62), later the Academy of Social Sciences. He was heavily involved in establishing Sydney University Press and served as its deputy chairman for fifteen years (1962–77). Schedvin (1993, p. 322) recalled that he was a 'good chairman', allowing committees and meetings 'a free rein, to pull the discussion together in a few, crisp sentences'. Finally, he was a staunch advocate and major planner of the two buildings which sequentially housed the faculty from 1951. He left the University of Sydney for a research professorship in Economic History at the Australian National University in 1971, a position he held over the last six years of his life.

Graduates and students, 1945–55

As is to be expected from the fluctuating enrolments in the post-war period ending 1955, graduate numbers changed considerably over these years. The war years had lowered the number of graduates in 1945 to twenty, including five students graduating with honours. In 1946, there were 30 graduates. They averaged 74 over the next decade, peaking at 108 in 1951. Honours graduates fluctuated less widely, averaging 19 per cent of all graduates over the decade ending 1955, with 24 per cent in 1955.

As Heinz Arndt recalled in his memoirs, some of these students from the 1940s were of high quality. They included Alan Hall and Harry Edwards in 1948; Don Lamberton in 1949; Jim Wilson and Alan Barnard in 1950, and Noel Drane, Neil Runcie, and John Donovan in 1951, the first with double honours in Economics and Statistics. In addition, N.L. McMullin and B.P. Sloan graduated with first-class honours in Government; in 1953, Hugh Hudson (future academic and deputy premier in South Australia) gained double honours in Economics and Government. Honours at graduation was conferred that year in every faculty honours school: Economics, Government, Statistics and Economic History. Future staff members Helmut Kolsen and Jan Kmenta gained first-class honours in Economics and Economic Statistics in 1954. Prominent 1955 honours graduates included Bob Scotton, Ken Turner, Stuart Harris and Barry Gordon.

The number of women graduates in Economics over these years fell drastically, from 1949 occasionally even in absolute numbers. The average number of women graduating in the four years including 1949 was sixteen; in the four years up to and including 1953, this fell to fewer than five. The number of female honours students declined even more and there were often no women honours graduates in Economics at all. Women did not start to enrol in the faculty in large numbers until the 1980s and 1990s, and the first woman medallists in Economics came only during the 1990s.

By 1955, evening students were still the majority of students enrolled in the faculty. This is not surprising when it is recalled that Accounting courses (including Commercial Law I and II) were only offered in the evening. Accounting continued to be taught exclusively in the evening until the mid-1960s. By then Accounting had become a separate department with its own professor (Ray Chambers).

Economics evening students declined from 669 in 1946 to 369 in 1954, even if the university's proximity to the city made it attractive for persons working in banks, other financial institutions, and more generally in business or the public service to study part-time for a degree by attending its evening lectures. Evening students therefore continued to provide close to three-quarters of Economics student numbers for most of the 1950s, and remained important until the faculty's 1966 decision to phase out evening classes, when the presence of such classes in economics at both the University of New South Wales and Macquarie University enabled it to do so.

Prominent graduates other than later academics should also be mentioned. For the 1940s, they include Don Sanders and Jack Wright (central banking), Gordon Menzies (banking), Jack Donovan, Ken Foreman (later Deputy Commonwealth Statistician), and Roy Fernandez (an outstanding career in external affairs), Gordon Barton (successful businessman and founder of the Australia Party), future prime minister William McMahon and Arthur Ford (secretary to the Advisory Council of Bond University). From the first half of the 1950s, M.A. Gleeson-White (a noted company director and businessman) and David Asimus (banking, insurance and chancellor at Charles Sturt University) need to be mentioned.

Some graduates from the 1945–55 period recorded their experiences as students. Harry Levy, a returned ex-serviceman from the RAAF in Britain, studied for the BEc from 1946 to 1949, majoring in Accountancy and taking Commercial Law. Levy mentioned Alan Bridge as a first-class exponent of the last mentioned subject, but in Economics found Heinz Arndt's 'Germanic accent' difficult to adjust to, though Arndt was an 'excellent lecturer'. He also recalled that 'no apology was made for the view … that the University did not regard Accountancy as a "true" university subject, relegated to part time study serviced by only two part time lecturers'. However, the first of these, Ivo Kerr, was well known in accountancy education; while 'his successor, Neil Stevens, was an excellent lecturer, whose practical knowledge of his craft, and skill at imparting it, was much appreciated'. This last view was not shared by John Holmes, a fellow veteran from the RAAF (and later Commonwealth trade commissioner in various countries), who completed his BEc degree from 1946 to 1949. He could not understand why 'Accountancy was admitted as a university subject' and found Ivo Kerr's lectures 'a tremendous bore'. Not surprisingly, he failed Accountancy I and by way of a concession from the dean (S.J. Butlin) was permitted to take four subjects the following year, all of which he passed. However, he greatly enjoyed Bland's Public Administration classes and found Partridge's lectures in Political Science 'highly stimulating'. He gained much from Kingsley Laffer's and Arndt's lectures on price theory and Keynesian economics, but described La Nauze's lectures as 'somewhat patronising' and Dr Singer on Plato in the History of Economic Thought as 'truly hilarious'. '[Singer] talked on and on … taking notes was out of the question, and I had to bluff my way through his question in the examination paper' sat, as was then so often the case, 'in the Great Hall'. His future career in the public service benefited greatly from his studies in economics.

James Tedder, an evening student from 1947 to 1950, recalled Kingsley Laffer lecturing on micro-economics with Stigler's *Theory of Price* as text; Heinz Arndt, then 'still very radical in his views' was a 'very concise, relatively easy to understand, and good teacher'; Renwick 'interesting and stimulating' in first-year Economics; Simpson-Lee and Hermann Black later on in 'international trade and lots of politics'. Tedder, however, greatly preferred his Government classes from Partridge and Bland, and his Geography courses, in which he was also able to major because Descriptive Economics was not available as part of the compulsory first-year course in 1947. How typical these three recollections are is difficult to say; they do indicate that those taking the BEc degree in the 1940s had quite different tastes.

Another student from the early 1950s, Gillian Lord, recalled aspects of the faculty during her time as student and later as research assistant in the Statistics 'Department'. First-year Economics was mainly Cyril Renwick, with a little bit of Hermann Black. Second-year Economics was largely Kingsley Laffer on micro-economics, and in third year Jim Wilson and Ted Wheelwright, then just arrived from England. She recalled that lectures in each subject were given twice a week and repeated in the evenings. Tutorials for pass students were non-existent, 'though students helped each other with problems'. Many library books were scarce, but some could be reserved for weekend borrowing: they had to be collected from Fisher Library at 9 pm on Friday and returned first thing on Monday morning. Photocopying had not been invented, and student notes were duplicated on a 'messy Gestetner machine'. She remembered Professor Butlin with respect, 'both for his war time work, and his book, *Foundations of the Australian Monetary System*'. The last she asked him to autograph, and 'he wrote my name in it. He looked at it, realised there was something wrong, and added SJB.' She also noted academic staff came predominantly from an English-speaking background with three European-born exceptions. These were Kurt Singer, Henry Mayer and Jan Kmenta, the last a brilliant young statistician both as student and staff member, who later moved to prestigious appointments at leading American universities. Gillian Lord did not identify the research project in Statistics for which she was employed as research assistant, but she noted that at this stage 'slide rules were still mainly used there for calculating'. However, 'the Department did own several calculating machines: a nice little Swedish Halda, and a couple of Marchants. They were extremely large and heavy and took a fair while to produce an answer'. Silliac, the first university computer, was not installed until 1956

Research and scholarship, 1945–55

Research activity in the faculty grew with expanded staff. All the major disciplines taught within the faculty now produced research, and several faculty members placed their articles in major international journals. Some research was funded from university research money, to finance the necessary research assistance, equipment and travel, and for which staff could apply. Non-academic articles or contributions to minor, non-academic journals were still listed by some staff members in official university reports on research and scholarship, but this was now a decreasing practice, discouraged by the university.

For the decade covered in this chapter, faculty staff published nine books, four chapters in books, 122 articles, contributed to official reports and produced a 'booklet', a monograph and some reprints of economic classics. Other than Butlin's two books in the early 1950s, in 1949 La Nauze published his *Political Economy in Australia* (which reprinted three previously published articles), Renwick and Simpson-Lee published their high-school and first-year university text, *The Economic Pattern*, and Buckley a *History of Trade Unionism in Aberdeen*. In Government and Public Administration, Bland listed second editions of his books on local government and planning, while Wills published a book on the growth and development of the Australian iron and steel industry. Chambers in Accounting published the first of many books on accounting theory and practice, *The Functions and Design of Company Annual Reports* (1953), as well as the second edition of the first Australian management education book, *Financial Management* (first published in 1947). A monograph on Australian taxation policy listed Ron Gates as one of its five authors, while Syd Butlin contributed to two government reports from the Papua-New Guinea Customs Inquiry.

Articles came from nearly every member of the academic staff. In his four years in the faculty, Arndt published thirteen articles on theoretical and applied macro-economics as well as on monetary theory and practice. Many were placed in major international journals including the *Economic Journal, Review of Economic Studies, Quarterly Journal of Economics,* and *Oxford Economic Papers*, but he also published in the *Economic Record* and other Australian journals. Kurt Singer published sixteen items in journals on topics ranging from his personal recollections of Keynes and an evaluation of Von Neumann's general equilibrium system to Japanese poetry and conflict resolution. Hermann Black claimed nine pieces for minor journals (such as *Rydge's Business Journal*, the *Australian Outlook* and the conference proceedings of the Brisbane Junior Chamber of Commerce) dwelling on European integration and general aspects of economic development. The *Economic Record* and other Australian journals also gained contributions from Drane (2), Edwards

(2), Gates (5), Laffer (6), Simpson-Lee (3) and Wheelwright (1), while Edwards in addition contributed articles to both the *Economic Journal* and *Oxford Economic Papers* that drew on his doctoral research on the theory of the firm.

In Government, Bland listed eight articles devoted to various aspects of public administration before leaving the faculty in 1948. Partridge, his successor, listed one on political theory. Kewley published six articles on public enterprises and on social security, largely in public administration journals; Wills published four articles, some devoted to the steel industry; McCallum published two article (one on oil policy and Iran); Joan Rydon three; and Henry Mayer six, on topics ranging from Marxist theory, Malaya, and Soviet Democracy to the Gwydir by-election. After his arrival in early 1954, Spann published four articles in his field of public administration. Chambers published three articles in accounting journals after his appointment in 1953. The faculty's economic historians published articles as well as books. Syd Butlin listed six, and Noel Butlin two before his departure to Canberra; Hartwell published articles on Tasmanian development and on the 1820s depression; Birch and Buckley published an article each, in the *Journal of Economic History* and in the *Economic Record*. Rutherford, still the only full-time teacher in Statistics, produced four articles, largely on technical aspects of statistical analysis.

The university's research reports also listed work in progress in the faculty, including several general research fields on which staff were working. Rutherford listed cycle and trend in Australia since 1860, with assistance from Edwards; Gates, history and analysis of uniform taxation in Australia; Edwards, Drane and Simpson-Lee, industry economics; Henry Mayer, the party system, and Ray Chambers, accounting theory. S.J. Butlin signalled a continuing interest in Australia's monetary and banking history, as well as his work on the war economy.

A new faculty building, 1951–65

Faculty required consolidated space for staff and students from the end of the war, and planning for this started in 1946. A site in Fisher Road occupied by the present R.C. Mills Building was in 1942 set aside for a Commonwealth Office of Education, and later to contain a building for both the Architecture and the Economics Faculties. This 'proved too ambitious a plan' (Connell *et al.*, 1995, II p. 205). In 1950, again from initiatives by the Commonwealth Office of Education, a building was finally constructed there. It was named the R.C. Mills Building in 1959 to honour Mills' work on Commonwealth contributions to university funding and Commonwealth education initiatives more generally. By agreement with the university in 1947, this building was to be taken over for exclusive university use when no longer required for Commonwealth purposes (SM :19 May 1947). Economics initially shared space there, the first floor of the building being put at its disposal from the beginning. By October 1953, other occupants still included the Appointments Board, Social Studies, the Department of Education and the Commonwealth Office of Education, taking up close to three-quarters of the available space (University Archives, R.C. Mills Building File; 1954 *Faculty Handbook*, p. 67, reproduced as fig. 3.1). When the faculty eventually occupied the whole of the building, this space proved inadequate by the early 1960s (Butlin 1970, p. 13). From 1955, for example, some staff had to be housed in temporary accommodation, while from 1959 the lecture rooms were too small for the rapidly growing student numbers in Accounting. When faculty moved to the Merewether Building in 1965, only 44 members of staff departed the R.C. Mills Building, eighteen came from temporary accommodation in the 'lecturers' hut' and ten from the Institute Building (University Archives, File 1373B).

The R.C. Mills Building initially provided adequate faculty accommodation. By the end of the 1950s it contained two seminar rooms (for use by honours students and staff) and four lecture rooms of various sizes (the largest providing seating for 148 students). This was then more than sufficient for housing the smallish classes in Economics and associated subjects the faculty was then offering, Economics I with nearly 200 faculty enrolments being the single exception. Economics I lectures were therefore given in larger lecture theatres: from 1954, that for Organic Chemistry, and later on, the Wallace Theatre. In 1957, no classes (apart from the compulsory first-year courses of Descriptive Economics and Scientific Method with enrolments of 122 and 155) exceeded 100. Faculty students in Economics II, III and IV numbered 72, 69 and 75; in Government I, II and III 22, 14 and 17 (to both of which Arts enrolments should be added to give actual class sizes); Accounting I, II and III had 68, 51 and 32 students; Commercial Law I and II 69 and 36; Economic History I, II and III 14, 7 and 7 and Statistics I, II and III 5, 4 and 3 (an exceptionally small year). The new Industrial Relations course numbered 8 and compulsory History of Economic Thought 65. It should not be forgotten that students for most courses (Accounting, Law and Statistics excepted) were spread over day and evening lecture time slots.

Apart from a large professorial room assigned to Butlin, the administrative offices for departmental secretarial staff and the dean's graduate assistant on the top floor, staff accommodation was in smallish rooms on the ground floor. The last were created occasionally by subdividing large rooms. More substantial rooms on that floor were, however, assigned to Dick Spann as Professor of Government and to Hermann Black, presumably marking his seniority in appointment. Only full-time, permanent academic staff had a room to themselves. Research students, research assistants and junior teaching staff like temporary lecturers or teaching fellows shared accommodation. By the early 1960s, some of that accommodation was distinctly below standard. From 1960, for example, Boris Schedvin, as the faculty's only PhD student, shared a former storeroom without adequate ventilation with temporary lecturers, teaching fellows and research students (Igor Gordijew, Bruce McFarlane and myself). This room also housed a chemical apparatus used by the Wolstenholme librarian for making copies of journal articles. Not surprisingly, it became known to its many occupants as the 'Black Hole of Calcutta'.

For a while, the Mills Building provided faculty with more adequate space for its Wolstenholme Library. It had the use of a sizeable room, with a central table accommodating no more than a dozen users, a librarian's desk, and economical metal shelving for various periodicals, government reports, statistical yearbooks, and books. The library was only open during the five afternoons of the working week, and for two nights a week to cater for evening students. It was extremely useful for those keen to acquaint themselves with current journal literature in a quiet environment (unlike the noisy Fisher Library reading room) while its lending policy favoured those wishing to read beyond the immediate demands of reading lists and course outlines. I for one was a regular user from my second year onwards. Part-time librarians in the Wolstenholme included Mrs Barbara Gates and Miss Robin Marsden.

As a departmental library, the presence of the Wolstenholme Library soon conflicted with Fisher's centralising tendencies (see, for example, SM: 8 October 1957), but as a memorial library it could not be easily touched. Wolstenholme Library in fact survived until 1998 as a valuable facility for students in both the Mills and the Merewether Building, its greatly enlarged premises making it also a more attractive target for donors. For example, it benefited substantially from the university's centenary appeal in 1952–53. The Economic Society of Australia and New Zealand (as it then was) for several years donated £20 to the Wolstenholme on an annual basis; the newly formed Economics Graduates Association donated £100 in 1961, and again in 1962; the Public Accountants Registration Board donated £250 in 1962 and 1963 for the purchase of accounting books. In December 1961, Emeritus Professor Bland donated many of his papers, documents, books, journals and reports to form part of the Wolstenholme's collection. However, as Butlin wrote to Ken McInnes (Buildings and Grounds) on 27 December 1961, this gift could not be adequately housed in the Wolstenholme, unless more storage space was found. For many years it was therefore housed in hastily acquired storage boxes provided by the university.

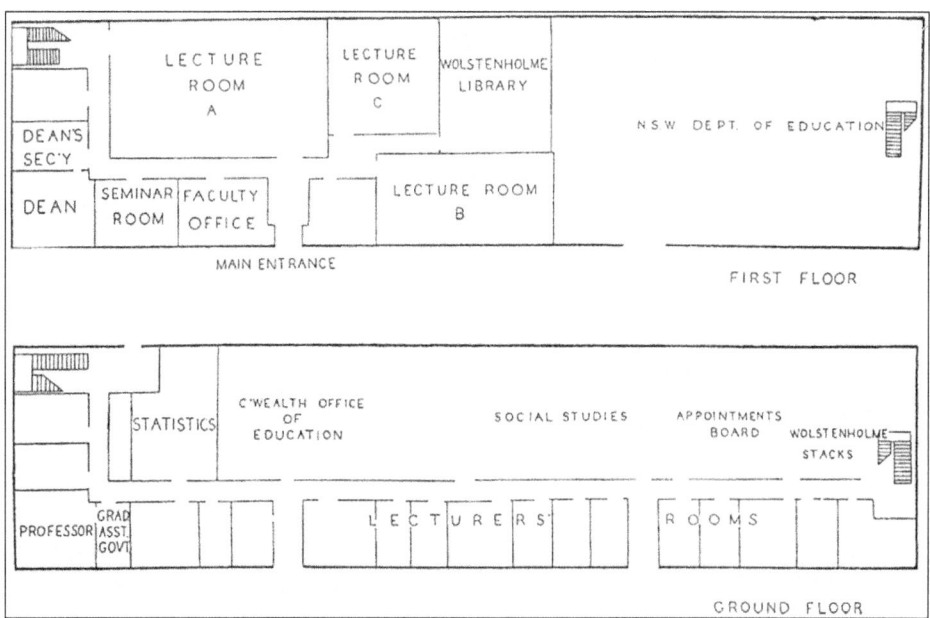

R.C. Mills Building Floor Plan 1953.

Staff changes and appointments, 1955–62

The 1963 *Faculty Handbook* (prepared at the end of 1962) listed vastly increased faculty teaching staff as compared with 1955, subdivided into separate departmental groupings. Economics now had two professors (Syd Butlin and Harry Edwards, appointed to a chair in 1962). In addition, Economics employed six senior lecturers (Hermann Black, Noel Drane, Ron Gates, Geelum Simpson-Lee, Ted Wheelwright and Jim Wilson), four lecturers (Vic Argy, Neil Conn, Derek Horner and Ted Kolsen), two senior tutors (Gordon Patterson and Hugh Pritchard) and nine part-time tutors (R.J. Adams, A.F. Agafonoff, D.A. Archbold, F. Argy, Mrs R. Goth, J. Herbertson, R.V. Horn, H.I. Stebbins and J.G. Willis). In 1962, I joined the temporary teaching staff as a teaching fellow in Economics. Still formally within the Economics Department, Economic History had three senior lecturers (Alan Birch, Ken Buckley and Jules Ginswick) and one lecturer (John McCarthy), while Industrial Relations had one senior lecturer (Kingsley Laffer) and one lecturer (Maxine Bucklow).

Government had one Professor (Dick Spann), two senior lecturers (Tom Kewley and Henry Mayer), three lecturers (Coral Bell, Peter Loveday and Peter Westerway), a part-time lecturer (Ken Turner), and two part-time tutors (Thelma Hunter and Bob Scotton).

Growth in academic staff was particularly marked in the newly created departments of Accounting (1960) and of Economic Statistics (1962), both headed by professors. The Accounting Department included Ray Chambers as its professor, two senior lecturers (Pat Mills in Commercial Law and Alec Shaw), two lecturers (Ron Brown and Peter Standish), a part-time lecturer in Commercial Law (Barry O'Keefe) and four part-time tutors (C.L. Heaton, H.A.L. McGregor, K.J.M. Ross and A.C. Smith). The Department of Economic Statistics had Stuart Rutherford as its professor, one senior lecturer (Jan Kmenta), a part-time lecturer (R.A. Layton) and three part-time tutors (Michael Bush, John Goodhew and J.G. Willis).

As compared with 1955, in 1962 the faculty had five professors, with Economics the only multi-professorial department. It now formally had four departments instead of the two in 1955 and employed a large number of part-time tutors as well as two senior tutors, both in Economics. The expanded staff reflected the growth in student numbers under the new by-laws for the three-year BEc degree and the introduction of a tutorial system to supplement teaching by lectures. By 1962, there were also four women on the teaching staff (two lecturers and two tutors).

The faculty continued to rely heavily on part-time teaching staff, particularly in Accounting. McCredie, Brown, Thomas and Young were continually reappointed as part-time lecturers in Accounting, joined in that role by Peter Standish in 1958. However, in November 1960, Ron Brown and Peter Standish both became full-time lecturers in Accounting, thereby doubling the department's full-time teaching staff. Barry O'Keefe continued his part-time teaching in Commercial Law II. In Government, D.M. McCallum, O.G. Benjafield, O. Herries, Ken Turner and Ron May provided part-time lectures when necessary, Ian Campbell (an honours graduate) became a teaching fellow in 1961. T.W. Goodyer provided part-time lectures in Economic Statistics. Industrial Relations employed specialists (for example, Dr Lloyd Ross) to give lectures on a special topic, and did not gain a second fulltime permanent staff member until the appointment of Maxine Bucklow in 1962.

Faculty deliberations, 1956–62

The first faculty meeting for 1956 (held on 28 February) was chaired by a new dean, Dick Spann, elected at the end of 1955. Fourteen faculty members were in attendance. It noted that Senate had approved Accounting as an honours school, admitted three future academics (Mike Bernasek, Robert Scotton and Barry Gordon) as candidates for the MEc, noted an annual donation of £150 from CSR for at least three years to be used for the new Industrial Relations course, and formed a subcommittee (consisting of the dean, Hermann Black, Stuart Rutherford, Keith Campbell, the Professor of Agricultural Economics, and Jim Wilson) to consider Agricultural Economics as a suitable optional course for students in the faculty. The committee reported favourably (13 April 1956) and from 1957 Agricultural Economics was listed as an optional faculty course. That meeting also set up a time table subcommittee (consisting of Black, Chambers, Rutherford, Ginswick and Laffer). It reported (27 September) recommending that (1) classes not be excessively spread over the week; (2) day and evening lectures be held on the same day; (3) avoidance of classes on Mondays because of the high incidence of public holidays; (4) one or two time slots (that is, mornings or afternoons) to be kept free of classes to give time for meetings; (5) avoid 8.15 pm lectures whenever possible; (6) hold courses which cannot clash, such as Economics I–IV, Government I–III, at the same time; and (7) cater adequately for honours classes and special pass with credit courses. The committee also argued that day and evening classes should be available whenever possible, and that approved sequences had priority over optional courses in timetabling. The 1957 timetable incorporated most of these principles. The compulsory Scientific Method course gave its second lecture for the week on Tuesday at 4 pm (day class) and on Wednesday at 6.15 pm (evening), as did one of the Industrial Relations lectures (Wednesday at 11 am, repeated on Monday or Friday at 5.15 pm). Accounting and Commercial Law lectures were still offered only in the evening, as was the case for Statistics I and II.

During 1957, faculty quarrelled with Agriculture over the use of 'economics' in the names of some of its courses (meetings of 8 April and 1 August); such quarrels over nomenclature were not infrequently repeated in later years. This embraced titles like 'management' and later 'information systems'. More importantly, faculty standardised the recording of marks for honours courses (80+ for high distinction, 70–79 for distinction, 60–69 for credit), with the pass mark set at 50–59 and a deferred examination permitted for those gaining marks in the range of 45–49. The meeting of 11 October announced a major curriculum revision in the form of a three-year degree course to replace the existing four-year degree. As the dean reported, this had already been informally discussed over several years. Despite this preparation, getting agreement for this major change took a further ten faculty meetings (including at least five special ones) and the new by-laws were not approved by faculty until August 1958.

By November 1958, faculty meetings were able to concentrate once again on 'normal' business, even if course changes continued to be frequently on the agenda. For example, Kingsley Laffer (7 November 1958) proposed that Industrial Relations become a two-year sequence, the second-year course designed to provide relevant economic, legal, psychological and sociological material. This was approved (FM: 6 March 1959) for introduction in the third year of the degree as Industrial Relations II.

The 6 March 1959 meeting discussed a new third-year course, Mathematical Economics, making Mathematics I a prerequisite for Economic Statistics II, and heard reports about the expected rapid growth of the university during the 1960s and beyond. The last induced faculty support (FM: 5 August 1959) for restricted first-year entry, the encouragement of new universities (especially Macquarie), modification of the existing staff structure to enable employment of more secretarial staff, and the prospects of reorganised university governance particularly with respect to faculties and the Professorial Board. Faculty was also informed that Senate had approved the recently acquired Royal Institute Building for the Deaf, Dumb and Blind as the future location of the Faculty of Economics, a most appropriate choice according to some wags. To oversee these developments, faculty re-elected Butlin as dean for a further two-year term.

In August 1960, faculty appointed a committee (Butlin, Chambers and Wheelwright) to investigate relevant aspects of the proposed new university for Sydney (FM: 5 August 1960). It recommended that the new university when established needed to teach at least one major sequence (Economics, Accounting, Government or Statistics) offered by the faculty (FM: 23 November 1960). That meeting also heard that borrowing of periodicals was to be abandoned by the library, that Chinese was to be dropped as a faculty subject, and that three independent examiners would be required for PhD examinations. A proposal for a graduate diploma in public administration was sent to a committee (consisting of the dean, Chambers and Spann) for preliminary investigation. Other meetings (4 March 1960, 6 April 1961) introduced 'show cause' regulations for failure in a course, with automatic exclusion after two failures.

The committee investigating the Graduate Diploma in Public Administration reported in May 1961 in favour of a more general, two-year Diploma of Administrative Science, to cover both business and public administration. Its subject matter was to be theoretical rather than practical, and to be taught in seminar format over three afternoons per week. First-year prerequisites were drawn from Economics, Economic Development, Government and Public Policy, Industrial Relations, Accounting and Finance, Statistics, Law and Legal Institutions. Second-year courses covered Organisation Theory, Computing, Decision Making and Human Relations. Control of the diploma was to be vested in a committee consisting of the dean, the heads of Economics, Government, Accounting and Economic Statistics, together with three others members of the faculty including one from Industrial Relations and one representative each from the Science and Engineering Faculties. The committee subsequently (24 July 1961) refined and proposed courses. Course outlines were attached to the report and by-laws for submission to faculty for its approval. This was given on 13 October 1961. Senate approved the courses on 4 December 1961, and at its October

1962 meeting approved a chair in Business Administration. In the end, the courses were never introduced in this form, but masters courses in Public Administration and Business Administration became part of the faculty curriculum at a later stage.

The 24 July 1961 meeting also set up a committee to reconsider provisions for the MEc (then still essentially a research degree) in the light of faculty's adoption of the PhD as part of its academic offerings It reported (30 July 1962) in favour of introducing a two-year coursework and thesis MEc. Successful candidates could not be given an honours grade, as was the case with the old MEc by thesis. Coursework examinations were to be annual, while the thesis was to be submitted within two years of completing coursework. Henceforth only honours graduates were permitted to attempt an MEc by thesis only. The new coursework degree was designed as a part-time degree, with classes to be given at appropriate evening slots.

Other issues were discussed. Double honours under the new by-laws for the three-years degree were proposed, to be completed over two consecutive honours years, part-time honours was accepted on a trial basis for the second year but continuation after third year was made dependent on prospects for success. History of Economic Thought became compulsory for all honours students, and was to be completed as part of the final honours year (FM: 4 May and 30 July 1962). A proposal to institute a faculty standing committee on which all departments were to be represented but without executive powers was rejected at this stage. On 30 July 1962, faculty was also told that sketch plans were available for the new Merewether Building on the site adjoining the Institute Building and that a contract for its construction had been approved by Senate. Earlier, Butlin had wisely rejected faculty's use of the existing Institute Building as not really suitable for teaching and staff accommodation. At the end of 1962 he was re-elected as dean for yet another term.

Creating a three-year BEc

At its 11 October 1957 meeting, faculty had decided to investigate a new three-year degree structure, comprising ten courses. The courses proposed at this stage included compulsory Economics I, II and III, Descriptive Economics in first, and History of Economic Thought in third year; a second major sequence to be chosen from either Government, Accounting, Economic History or Economic Statistics, leaving two optional courses to be taken in first and in second year. Economics IV and compulsory Scientific Method were therefore dropped, though the latter course could still be taken as an optional one. The new degree would contain five recognised honours schools. Earliest starting date for the new degree was set at 1959. The proposal created much debate in faculty.

The inadequate degree of choice in the proposed new structure drew criticism from at least six members of faculty (FM: 22 October 1957). An adjourned meeting (30 October) debated an alternative proposal containing a compulsory first year designed to give students a taste of the four sequences from which they had to select a second major, the historical emphasis of which reduced the need for a compulsory History of Economic Thought in third year. A new faculty committee (Spann, Chambers, Rutherford, Buckley and Simpson-Lee) was established to report back to faculty, which it did on 12 November 1957.

Following the report, a special faculty meeting (16 January 1958) agreed on the principle of a three-year pass degree for day students, a five-year pass degree for evening students, ten subjects in total for the degree, an additional honours year for all schools, but failed to agree on whether a 'common' first year was necessary. Another meeting (29 January 1958) decided to make only Economics I compulsory in first year, leaving the other first-year courses open to choice. Less than a week later, further meetings (2, 3 February 1958) settled first year as comprising Economics I, the Australian Economy and two options of which at least one was from a faculty sequence. Second year was to consist of Economics II, the second of the chosen faculty sequence plus an optional course, while third year was left undecided because no agreement could be reached on a compulsory History of Economic Thought. Butlin's compromise of a compulsory History of Economic Thought for all faculty honours students, taken in their fourth year, plus an optional History of Economic Thought for pass students in third year, broke the deadlock. The final *pass* degree structure was then accepted without compulsory History of Economic Thought (cf. Laffer 1981, pp. 11–12).

The honours degree regulations were finalised over two meetings (27 February, 30 June 1958). Honours study was to commence in second year. Students could attempt double honours from the five agreed faculty honours schools. The final honours year would constitute a fourth year, with compulsory History of Economic Thought as the only common element. Subsequently, faculty approved the possibility of admission to honours at the start of third year, and automatic approval for postponing the final honours year for one year after pass requirements were completed. Longer postponement of honours would need faculty permission. By-laws for the new degree were passed (8 August 1958) providing for a three-year pass BEc degree, a four-year honours BEc degree, an MEc degree and a PhD as the four degrees of the faculty. Senate then approved the by-laws to take effect from the start of 1959 (SM: 7 October 1958).

The growth of departments in the faculty

For the first 27 years of its existence, the Faculty of Economics was a one department faculty. Initially, this was the Department of Economics and Commerce (with its wide range of teaching responsibilities in economic and commercial subjects), later simply the Department of Economics. Although Public Administration had gained its own professor as early as 1937, it did not become a separate department in the faculty until Bland's retirement in 1947, perhaps because Bland had been far too busy with his writing and other activities to take responsibility for administering a department as a separate unit in the faculty. Another explanation may be the small number of teachers in Public Administration, rarely more than two, but in this context it should not be forgotten that the Department of Economics for a long time had consisted of only one full-time teacher, assisted by a large part-time teaching staff. On becoming a department in 1947, it was called Government and Public Administration, a mouthful later condensed to Government.

Thereafter, creation of further faculty departments largely followed the appointment of a professor in its area of study. Thus Accounting became a separate department in 1960, not long after Ray Chambers' appointment to the chair of Accounting in 1959. Economic Statistics became a separate department in 1962 when Stuart Rutherford became a full professor. Economic History, the other three-year faculty sequence, remained part of Economics until 1969, and Industrial Relations until 1975. If a generalisation is possible from this experience, a prerequisite for becoming a separate department in the faculty was the establishment of a chair, and the existence of a sequence of three courses as the core of its teaching responsibilities.

The creation of departments became indispensable with the growth of staff and the range of courses offered. It enabled more efficient academic decision making on teaching and research by a smaller group of staff members all devoted to a closely related area of study. By the end of 1962, Economics, the largest department in the faculty, had two professors, six senior lecturers, four lecturers, two senior tutors, a teaching fellow and nine part-time tutors to teach the four compulsory Economics courses for the degree (Economics I was then subdivided into Economics IA, the start of the sequence, and IB, a survey course intended for those not wishing to pursue further study in Economics), the three honours courses in Economics, the optional subjects of the Australian Economy, Mathematical Economics and History of Economic Thought as well as teaching and supervision of postgraduate students for the MEc and the PhD.

Government, the next largest department, had one professor, two senior lecturers, three lecturers, a part-time lecturer and two part-time tutors to teach its sequence of three courses for pass and honours students, and for supervising its postgraduate students. Accounting, next in size, had one professor, two senior lecturers, two lecturers, a part-time lecturer, a senior tutor, and four part-time tutors to teach its sequences of three pass and honours Accounting courses together with the two courses in Commercial Law. Economic Statistics, the smallest department, had one professor, one senior lecturer, one part-time lecturer and three part-time tutors to teach its sequence of pass and honours courses. Although still *de jure* sub-groups of the Economics Department, Economic History had three senior lecturers and one lecturer, while Industrial Relations had one senior lecturer and one lecturer. Departments provided a level of decision making below that of the faculty. In principle, this saved it much time in formulating new courses or re-designing existing syllabuses, planning staffing needs and carrying out the teaching and research appropriate to their subject area under the auspices of the faculty.

Graduates and students, 1956–62

Enrolments in the Faculty of Economics sharply increased over the seven years from 1956 to 1962, particularly after the introduction of the three-year degree in 1959. The new degree structure especially boosted enrolments by day students, until then very much the minority in faculty student numbers. They almost doubled in absolute terms from 493 in 1956 to 933 in 1962, but, reflecting the overall growth in student numbers, relative to overall university enrolments grew only from 6.2 per cent in 1956 to 6.6 per cent in 1962.

Postgraduate numbers likewise rose, stimulated by revisions in the postgraduate program already discussed. Four postgraduate students were enrolled in 1956, 22 in 1962. Postgraduate students continued to be only a very small proportion of total faculty enrolments, but trebled in relative terms from 0.8 per cent in 1956 to 2.4 per cent in 1962.

The gender balance in faculty enrolments remained poor. Enrolments by women on aggregate rose from 23 in 1956 to 68 in 1962 or, in relative terms to total enrolments, from 4.7 per cent to 7.3 per cent.

The trend in the number of graduates matched the growth in enrolments. Interpretation of these data is made difficult by the effects of the introduction of the three-year degree, in which students could first complete their courses for the degree at the end of 1961 for graduation in April 1962. BEc graduates rose from 53 in 1956 to 92 in 1962. Of these totals, women graduates rarely made up 5 per cent, keeping the Economics Faculty as essentially a male preserve. This was even more marked at the postgraduate level. All twelve MEc degrees awarded from 1957 (there were none in 1956) were to male students. Given the nature of the MEc degree, graduate numbers fluctuated from one in 1957 to five in 1961, with an average close to two.

Faculty honours results likewise remained a male preserve. For the seven years covered by this section, only five women gained honours at graduation, one awarded first-class honours in Statistics in 1956, three second-class honours, division I (in Statistics in 1956, in Economic History in 1959 and in Economics in 1960), and one a third-class honours in Government in 1956. There were no women honours graduates in four of these years. Male students on the other hand gained the two medals (one in Government, one in Statistics), while a further eighteen men gained first-class honours (eight in Economics, three in Government, six in Statistics, one in Economic History and none in Accounting). There were thirteen upper seconds: eight men in Economics, two in Government, two in Economic History, two in Economic Statistics and one in Accounting. Total honours graduates averaged twelve over these years, or over a fifth of all graduates.

The honours classes from 1956 to 1962 produced a number of persons who later made outstanding careers for themselves. Not surprisingly, given rapid growth of university education during the 1960s, many honours students initially went into academic positions. Stuart Harris (first-class honours in Economics in 1956) became Professor of International Relations at the Australian National University after a distinguished public service career in Foreign Affairs and External Trade. Bruce McFarlane (first-class honours graduate in Economics in 1956) spent several years as research fellow at the Australian National University, became Professor of Politics at Adelaide, and then in Economics at Newcastle. Peter Westerway, a first-class honours graduate in Government in 1956, taught first at Sydney University, then worked in broadcasting and television and was chairman of the Australian Broadcasting Tribunal from 1991 to 1995. Roger Layton, a first-class honours Statistics graduate in 1956 became professor at the Australian Graduate School of Management. George Palmer, likewise a first-class honours Statistics graduate in 1956, held chairs in statistics at Queensland and in Hospital Administration at the University of New South

Wales. Among 1957 honours graduates, Igor Gordijew (first-class honours in Economics) held academic teaching posts at Sydney, New South Wales and Macquarie universities; Neil Conn, first-class honours in Statistics, taught Economics at Sydney for some years, then moved to the Northern Territory to head its Treasury department, followed by two terms as Chief Administrator of the Territory; Gordon Patterson (second-class honours in Economic History) was senior tutor in Economics at Sydney before joining the business sector.

Honours students in 1959 included Victor Argy (first-class honours in Economics), who started an academic career at Sydney then went to the International Monetary Fund and the OECD, ending his career as Professor of Economics at Macquarie. Boris Schedvin, first-class honours in Economic History, completed the first PhD awarded by the faculty in 1964, then followed an academic career which took him from Sydney to Professor of Economic History, and later deputy vice-chancellor (Research) at Melbourne. In 1960, Peter Groenewegen (first-class honours in Economics) had a Sydney University academic career continuing after his retirement in 2002 as Emeritus Professor in Economics with research work as a faculty honorary associate; Ron May (first-class honours and medal in Government and second-class honours in Economics) after part-time teaching at Sydney and a research position in the Reserve Bank moved to full-time academic work at the Australian National University; J.G. Willis (first-class honours in Statistics) built a distinguished career first in Sydney and then in the United States; John Goodhew (second-class honours in Statistics) taught the subject at Sydney as lecturer and senior lecturer; Michael Hudson (second-class honours in Economic History) taught economic history at the University of New South Wales and in New Zealand universities before moving to the University of Leeds.

Louis Haddad, first-class honours in economics in 1961, became an Economics academic at Sydney, as did his brother Maurice, who later moved to the Canberra public service (initially on the Restrictive Trade Practices Commission and then as director of the Bureau of Transport Economics and Communications); Trevor Mathews (first-class honours in Government) taught Government at Sydney University, eventually as one of its professors; Nigel Nettheim (first-class honours in Statistics) obtained a chair in Melbourne; William Birkett (upper second in Accounting) started an academic career in Accounting at Sydney ending up as dean of Business Studies at James Cook University; and George Dowcra, (upper second in Economics) became associate professor of Economics at the University of Queensland. In 1962, Margaret Power (upper second in Economics) held academic positions at Sydney in Economics; M.W.T. Layard (first-class honours and the medal in Economic Statistics) completed his PhD at Stanford after a short period as lecturer at Sydney; B.T. Phillips (upper second in Economic Statistics) enjoyed an academic career in Statistics at Sydney for some time, then moved to the University of New England. D.S. Clarke (third-class honours in Accounting) completed an MBA at Harvard before commencing a business career culminating as executive chairman of Macquarie Bank Limited.

Other faculty honours students went into non-academic careers, even if initially they did some part-time university teaching. Ian Parker (upper second in Economic History in 1956) had a brief central banking career; Fred Argy (an upper second in economics in 1957) entered the Commonwealth Public Service, and later worked with CEDA, the Australian Industries Development Corporation and the OECD; P.P. (Paddy) McGuinness (upper second in Economics in 1960) had a distinguished career in banking and journalism, including many years as chief editor of the *Australian Financial Review*, and subsequently of *Quadrant*; Alan May (first-class honours in Government in 1961) had a career in banking; John Walton (upper second in Accounting and thirds in Economics in 1960) had a business career in retailing, for some time chairing Walton Enterprises; Ken Nugan (upper second in Economics in 1962) was involved in citrus growing and associated with the finance company, Nugan Hand.

Many pass graduates built distinguished careers in business and government. Prominent business graduates include Ian Angus, managing director of NCR (Australia) Pty Ltd; Ian McNair, managing director, McNair Surveys Pty Ltd and chairman, McNair-Anderson Associates Pty Ltd; Brian Scott, a distinguished management consultant; G.F. Heeley (BHP); David Lane, executive positions in many companies and deputy chancellor at UTS; Norm Bevan, banking; Michael McGrath, executive director of Wardley Australia Pty Ltd and a partner in Patrick Partners; Edward Dunne, IBM, the Reserve Bank, the Schools Commission and one-time chairman of the South Australian Chamber of Commerce; Warwick Kent, banking and insurance, including directorships in Colonial Limited and the Perpetual Trustees Company; Barrie Martin, banking, finance and insurance; Bruce Robertson, managing partner in Touche Ross and Co.; Ian Muir, AGB Research Australia; John A. Illife, many company directorships including ABN Amro Australia Limited, AWA, Charter Cruise Air Limited, Direct Trade Indemnities Australia Limited, GIO Australia Holdings, Woolworths Limited and Pacific Limited; Robert Paterson, vice-president and division manager Coca-Cola Export Corporation; William George Hunter, financial management BHP, Director Bank Tokyo Australia Limited and chairman of many other companies; M.J. Sharpe, 1994 Accountant of the Year, chairman Cooper and Lybrand; Neil Anderson, chairman, Energy Resources Australia Limited; John P. Bragg, management consultant including as managing director of Cooper and Lybrand and W.D. Scott; Warren Heynes, managing director and chief executive officer of ICI Australia; Walter Kommer, News Limited; Ian Stanwell, insurance including chairman of AMP; Graeme W. McGregor, 1992 Accountant of the Year, directorships in the Foster's Brewing group; Laurie J. Gluskie, insurance including director, Permanent Trustee Limited; Gordon J. Howell, vice-president and general manager, Asia Pacific Avis Corporation; and Brian J. Wright, who had a career in finance and banking, including as director, AISIC Development Corporation.

Prominent public servants who were graduates at this time include Peter Dixon, Treasury, Foreign affairs and Trade; Alan Barclay, Immigration and Defence; Richard Manning, World Bank, United Nations and the Australian National University; Robert Adams, theatre and the arts; Rae Taylor, various branches of public service; Phillip Flood, diplomatic service; Malcolm Dan, diplomatic service; John Wilcox, Foreign Trade; Michael Sellway, Prime Minister's Department; Fred Bennett, Defence, Tourist Commission; and Donald Whiteford, Foreign Affairs. There was also a politician, Robert Brown (MHR, MLA, Mayor of Greater Cessnock and Minister for Lands in the Hawke and Keating governments), a university administrator, David Williams (New England), a judge, Peter Grogan, and Malcolm Mackerras, teacher of politics at the Australian Defence Force Academy and noted election commentator.

Only one student from these years recorded some memories of his experience. Robert de Viana was a one-year, part-time student of Economics at Sydney in 1958 (he finished his degree at the Australian National University):

> With hindsight, I often feel that I came at the tail end of a golden era at the University … I only have a vague memory of the actual courses [I took at Sydney]. Descriptive Economics … was boring [so] that most of us made a big show of reading the newspapers. [Then there was] Gates with his incredibly convoluted income and expenditure flows which resembled the ravings of a mad plumber. Chambers was teaching Accountancy, so dapper! Also I fondly recall the Faculty Secretary, but her name escapes me [Joyce Fisher?]; she was so considerate to us callow youths. Finally, there was Miss Walker, 'Nightmare Alice' with her peculiar logic. However, to be fair, I often mention to young students how much they will miss out if they fail to grasp the elements of logic and scientific method. (letter to the author, 9 October 2002).

Having myself attended these classes in 1957, I can only add that Alice Walker's presentation of scientific method consisted largely of extensive readings from John Stuart Mill's *System of Logic* on the nature of the syllogism, a very dull way of teaching an intrinsically boring but very important subject, and that at least some of the other classes I attended were not always of high standard.

Sydney University Economics Society and the Economic Review

The student economics society revived after the war, partly because Economics day students could no longer obtain free membership of the university's Evening Students Association. Records of its activities are scarce after the *University Calendar* stopped providing regular information on this type of university society.

Tantalising glimpses of its 1949 activities are available in the university archives. John Donovan was elected the society's representative on the Union Board in April and meetings of the society in that year shared the inconvenience of frequent electricity blackouts, but whether with or without the assistance of the 'Aladdin' lamps which came to the rescue at evening classes is not recorded. At the end of April, Melbourne University's Commerce Society proposed 'to start an Australia wide commerce magazine to be called *Margin*' but if this name was inspired by the method of the dominant economic theory or by aspects of stock trading practice is not known. Dr Frank Horner, a 1939 graduate and in 1949 employed at the Bureau of Economics and Statistics, addressed the 5 May meeting on 'My Experiences Overseas and Work at the London School of Economics'. The only other speaker recorded was Douglas Darby, Liberal MLA for Manly (1945–62), a 1938 graduate and author of the book, *Lenin: Master or Monster?*

The society adopted a new constitution in 1955. This stated its objective as the 'promotion of social and intellectual intercourse between the members and generally to further the collective interests of the members'. All undergraduate day students were admitted to membership, academic staff received life memberships, and individual staff members often served as society presidents, and provided speakers for its meetings. Publication of the society's journal, the *Economic Review*, also began in 1955. The *Review* survived into the 1970s, producing nearly twenty issues, to the pleasant surprise of the various deans who wrote messages to its readers. Thus Dick Spann in 1956 mentioned how nice it was to introduce the *second* issue of the *Economic Review*, and though this did not quite make it an 'established' journal, it enabled the 'safe prediction that the *Review* will continue'. He also praised the brevity of its articles and applauded the fact that it failed to resemble, 'the Lord be praised, *Econometrica*'. Finally, to ensure fulfilment of his wish that 'there be many more', he urged future contributors to record their 'bright ideas … Get a friend to correct the spelling, and send it to the editor' (*Economic Review*, Vol. 2, 1956, p. 3).

Occasionally, the *Economic Review* provided snippets of the society's history over the next few years. Doug McCallum (Government) was president in 1956; Alan Birch (Economic History) in 1957; Ron Gates (Economics) in 1958, Ted Kolsen (Economics) in 1959, Jan Kmenta (Statistics) in 1960 and M.K.H. Powell in 1961 and 1962. Gates, in his published presidential address, recounted amusing examination howlers under the heading, 'Examination Blues'. Examples included 'Tariff barriers are also a detergent to international trade', 'the birth rate is higher than the immortality rate' and the succinct but primitive social observation in an answer to a question on male and female wage differentiation, 'most girls between the ages of fifteen and twenty go to work in the banks, but around the age of twenty they meet up with men and get married'. In that year, Butlin was society patron as dean and Peter Westerway was its life member representative. Vice-president Eugene Baikovsky and honorary treasurer Vladimir Kiklhorn were editors of the 1958 *Economic Review*. Its editorial compared Sydney's economics degree favourably with that of 'Kensington's commerce graduate', because of its greater 'intangible [and unspecified] services' conducive to 'the good life'. Student articles dealt with Oscar Lange's views on the socialist economy, surveyed the various theories of profit, lamented the neglect of industrial relations studies, and discussed freedom from want, marketing, the development of the ALP, and accounting rationale and practice. Society meetings in 1958 included a talk by Black on 'An Economist Abroad', Gates on Australian family household budgets, a student symposium on Indonesia, and student talks on Soviet agriculture and the motor car population of Australia. A successful cocktail party at Manning House was also reported, as were several sport and debating team successes.

The fifth issue of the *Review* (1959) contained Kolsen's presidential address, Kewley's impression of American universities, Professor D.C. Rowan's defence of the University of New South Wales Commerce degree in response to the 1958 editorial, and articles on federalism (P.J. Clim), direct overseas investment (Ted Wheelwright), the future of the Democratic Labor Party (D. Miles-Connolly), automation and revolution (G. Robinson) and aspects of the market in South-East Asia (F.Vohralik).

Issues 6 (1960) and 7 (1961) continued the mix of student and staff articles. Thus issue 6 included Chambers on the study of accounting, Bruce McFarlane on market socialism, Kolsen on 'studentmanship', Hermann Black on Britain and Europe, as well as students Tom Jilek on accounting profits, John Walton on Australia's real economic problem, Alan May on the birth of a women's movement against socialisation and Ron May on fiscal federalism. Issue 7, edited by Maurice and Louis Haddad, had articles by Jan Kmenta on the growth of student numbers, Peter Groenewegen on Josiah Tucker as a neglected economist, Kingsley Laffer on industrial relations, Noel Drane on mathematical economics and Syd Butlin on graduate studies, with student contributions on political philosophy (R.W.Butler), Soviet agricultural policy (Tom Connors), objectives in accounting (A.I.R. McFarlane), federal financial relations (Ron May), accounting objectivity (H. Moenting) and articles by the editors on capital intensity in developing countries (Louis Haddad) and the population problem (Maurice Haddad). By then the *Economic Review* was fully established. Its seventh issue, Louis Haddad informed me, was even ordered by the Lenin Library in Moscow.

Records also survive for the other 1961–62 activities of the society. Boris Schedvin was president and the society maintained its by now traditional annual routine including the welcome to freshers, the annual dinner dance at the Pickwick Club and talks, among which was one by Hermann Black on the European Common Market. Most surprising was the report that the society had made Digby Wolfe, a TV personality of the early 1960s, an honorary life member, despite his total lack of any visible connection with the faculty.

Sydney University Economics Graduates Association

A Sydney University Graduates Association was established in 1953, the foundation president being A.F. Deer, vice-president Barry Chaffer and secretary Gerard d'A. Chislett. Its aim was to maintain contacts between the faculty and its graduates, and between the graduates themselves. It did so by organising social functions, and occasionally promoting talks to graduates by notable persons in the field of economics or associated subjects. From the late 1950s, it organised annual dinners for members, a Christmas party, an annual general meeting, where speakers sometimes featured, and gatherings for new graduates. All graduates were eligible to join on payment of £1, raised to £2 in 1959. Office bearers had, unfortunately, to be frequently reminded by the registrar to fulfil their obligations as a recognised university society by annually submitting both an audited financial statement and a list of office bearers. The association's first auditor was Ivo Kerr, faculty's part-time Accounting teacher from the 1940s and early 1950s.

To assist its establishment, the initial mailout to prospective members (cost £14 18s. 6d.) was defrayed by Butlin as dean of the faculty. Over the following years, presidents included graduates William McMahon (1955) A.C. Gray (1956), Ivan Dougherty (1957), Claude Schoffel (1959) and J.S. Leplastrier (1960–62). Association membership fluctuated considerably: from 69 in 1955 to 21 in 1956, 15 in 1957, 203 in 1958, 148 in 1959, 74 in 1960 and 43 in 1962.

The association seems to have made few financial contributions to the faculty during the first decade of its existence, though it occasionally presented books to the Wolstenholme Library. In any case, Butlin as dean was anxious to ensure the association's continuation, as he wrote to the registrar in 1957 during one of its periodic losses of official recognition because it had failed to file the requisite documents (University of Sydney Economics Graduates Association, File 42/019). Nevertheless, as shown in subsequent chapters, a graduate society continued to be part of faculty organisation over subsequent decades, albeit with some discontinuities and the attendant resurrections.

Faculty research and scholarship

Over the seven years from 1956 to 1962, members of the faculty published eight books, including two edited books; one monograph, one report, five chapters in book and 110 articles. Government department staff were the most prolific publishers, with 54 articles, two books and two edited books to their credit; Economics was next with fifteen articles and two books. For the other two departments, published work was largely produced by one person. Thus the twelve articles and one book produced by the Accounting Department were with three exceptions (two articles by Peter Standish, and one item by Pat Mills) all produced by Ray Chambers, the book being his important, *Accounting and Action*, while he also published many chapters in books. The sixteen articles published from Statistics were, with the exception of an article by Jan Kmenta, all written by Henk Konijn. Economic History was responsible for seven articles and one book (by Alan Birch jointly with David Macmillan, the first university Archivist) and Industrial Relations for six articles, all by Kingsley Laffer.

The rather disappointing publishing performance by the large Economics Department is partly explicable by the substantial research effort invested in a four-volume report on the economics of the dairy industry (1959), funded by the Australian Dairy Industry Council. Seven members of staff were involved in its production (Black, Drane, Edwards, Gates, Rutherford, Simpson-Lee and Wilson) and a summary of the research was subsequently reproduced as a book. Other books from the Economics Department were Butlin's *History of the Australia and New Zealand Bank* and Edwards' Oxford DPhil thesis on *Competition and Monopoly in the British Soap Industry*, the fruits of the large travel grant faculty had given him to enable his work at Oxford with P.W.S. Andrews. Among published articles were Gates' surveys of Australian public finance for the *Handbuch der Finanzwissenschaft* (1957) and the Harvard Law School (1958), Edwards' articles drawn from his DPhil thesis for *Oxford Economic Papers* and *Kyklos*, and on the dairy industry (jointly with Drane) for the *Economic Record*; two items by new recruits Kolsen and one by Victor Argy, and three papers by Wheelwright. Hermann Black reported seven items in non-academic journals, as did Simpson-Lee for his one publication.

The economic historians reported two articles in the *Economic Record* by Ken Buckley, three by Alan Birch, and one by new staff member, John McCartey, who also reported completion of his Cambridge PhD thesis. Industrial Relations' six articles all came from Kingsley

Laffer and were published in the *International Labour Review* and the newly established *Journal of Industrial Relations*. In Statistics, Henk Konijn's fifteen articles appeared in both international (including *Metroeconomica*) and Australian journals (*Australian Journal of Statistics*, *Economic Record* and *Statistical Society of New South Wales Bulletin*), while Kmenta's sole piece appeared in the *Economic Record*. The Accounting Department's publishing record of one book and twelve articles has already been mentioned.

The Government Department's extensive publication list was also led by its senior staff. Spann's edited book on *Public Administration in Australia* contained chapters by himself and Tom Kewley. In addition, Spann published eight articles, two for the English, and three for the Australian *Journal of Public Administration*, one for *Social Service*, one for *Quadrant* and one for the *Australian Quarterly*. Kewley also published three pieces in the *Australian Journal of Public Administration*. Henry Mayer published nine articles and one joint article (with colleagues Peter Westerway and Peter Loveday). They included continuing work on Marxist theory (two articles for *Etudes de Marxologie* and a bibliographical study of Marx's works for *Les Temps Modernes*); the others appeared in *Historical Studies*, *APSA News*, *Australian Outlook*, *Australian Journal of Politics and History*, the *Journal of Industrial Relations* and the *Australian Journal of Public Administration*. In addition, Mayer edited a book on *Catholics and the Free Society*, to which both he and Spann contributed chapters. Among the lecturers, McCallum wrote two articles for the *Australian Journal of Politics and History*, as well as a joint piece with Peter Westerway for *APSA News*; R.M. Martin wrote two pieces for the *Journal of Industrial Relations* on trade unions, one for *APSA News* and one for *Political Science*; Peter Westerway wrote two articles for the *Australian Journal of Politics and History* in addition to the two joint pieces already mentioned; Coral Bell published a book, *Negotiations from Strength: A Study in the Politics of Power*, an article for the *Australian Quarterly* and two encyclopaedia articles (on 'International Organisation' and on 'New Age and New Problems'). Temporary staff in the department published widely. Ian Campbell wrote articles on industrial groups (a movement of the 1950s and 1960s set up within the Labor Party to combat Communist influence in the trade unions) for the *Australian Journal of Politics and History*, on parties and the referendum process for the *Australian Quarterly* and a chapter for *Sydney Studies in Politics* I on group theory and practice. In addition, he contributed half a dozen two-page surveys of the New South Wales political scene for the *Australian Journal of Politics and History*. Thelma Hunter wrote on women's labour and wages for the *Journal of Industrial Relations* and the *Economic Record*; Ron May produced a political survey for the *Australian Quarterly* and an article on the Commonwealth Grants Commission for the *Australian Journal of Public Administration*; Joan Rydon wrote on the 1958 federal elections for the *Australian Journal of Politics and History* and a study of 'New South Wales Politics, 1901–1910', as the second in the series of *Sydney Studies in Politics*. J.E. Bromley, a research assistant in the department, reported writing the New South Wales political chronicle for the *Australian Journal of Politics and History* in 1956.

Editorial initiatives from the faculty may also be mentioned in this context, another activity in which the Government Department led the way. The long-established *Australian Journal of Public Administration* was edited by Dick Spann; *Sydney Studies in Politics* was a Henry Mayer initiative as was the formation of the Australian Political Science Association's *APSA News*. In 1961, Kingsley Laffer became editor of the *Journal of Industrial Relations*, in the establishment of which he had been the driving force. Alan Birch, in conjunction with David Macmillan and the Business Archives Council of Australia, established the *Australian Journal of Archives and History* in 1961, which from 1967 became the *Australian Economic History Review*.

Group research was a feature of that conducted in the Department of Economics. The dairy industry study already mentioned is one instance; Gates' research work on household budgets (later assisted by Drane and Edwards) generated important data for Australian household income distribution analysis, forming the basis for the important statistical tax incidence analysis conducted with Drane's assistance at Macquarie University in the 1960s.

The R.C. Mills Memorial Lectures and other research lectures

The first R.C. Mills Memorial Lecture was given to a large audience on 29 April 1958 in the Great Hall of the university. This public lecture, and many subsequent Mills Memorial lectures, had been funded by public subscription organised by the Economic Society of Australia and New Zealand (New South Wales Branch) in conjunction with the Faculty of Economics. It was given by Dr H.C. Coombs, Governor of the Commonwealth Bank and a distinguished Commonwealth public servant, who in the late 1930s had also taught Economics at the University of Sydney under the direction of Mills. He was therefore a particularly suitable choice to present the first Mills lecture. Coombs' topic was 'Conditions of Monetary Policy in Australia', a subject on which as head of Australia's central bank he had much to contribute. Subsequent Mills lectures included three given by Coombs' successors as head of the central bank, many distinguished academic economists from Australia and abroad (including two Nobel Prize winners in economics, Sir John Hicks and Friedrich von Hayek). The texts of the nineteen Mills Memorial lectures given by 2003 were collected and published by the Faculty of Economics in 2004 to commemorate the fiftieth anniversary of Mills' death (Groenewegen, ed., 2004).

A number of other research lectures were held under the auspices of the faculty over these years. A 1952 Research Lecture in Accounting, sponsored by the Commonwealth Institute of Accountants, has already been mentioned. On 16 August 1962, Sir Alexander Fitzgerald gave the Ninth Annual Lecture of the Society of Accountants in the Great Hall on the topic, 'The Search for a Definition of Income', partly under the auspices of the Department of Accounting and the Faculty of Economics.

Towards a new phase in the faculty

This chapter has chronicled the rapid growth which the faculty experienced in terms of staff and students over both the immediate post-war period and the decade ending 1962. It stressed the increasing problem of inadequate space in the R.C. Mills Building as one consequence of this growth. Building plans therefore dominated the early 1960s. The new departmental structure of the faculty likewise developed more vigorously and gradually expanded, so that the decade became an important consolidation phase for faculty activities in teaching and research. Much of this was achieved under the continuing leadership of S.J. Butlin as dean, and that of Professors Chambers, Spann and Rutherford as heads of the then other three departments within the faculty.

CHAPTER 4

The Merewether Building (1965) and a Golden Jubilee (1970): the faculty (1963–72)

The decade of the faculty's development discussed in this chapter marks an important period of transition in its operations and staff. Without exaggeration, these changes constituted the end of an era. Replacing Leaving Certificate results in 1968 by results from the new Higher School Certificate as the main vehicle for entry into the university can be noted at the outset. Furthermore, faculty undergraduate growth was curtailed from 1964 by the imposition of quotas on first-year enrolments, lowered from an initial 450 (in 1964 and 1965) to 400 in 1966 and to 350 from 1967 onwards. Declining undergraduate numbers were partly offset by growth in postgraduate student numbers. This came mainly from part-time, coursework masters students, but also through a gradual increase in doctoral students. This growth was from a very small base. The first faculty PhD was conferred in 1964 on Boris Schedvin (see Chapter 3); the second was awarded to Sol Kim in Economic Statistics in 1970; the third, fourth and fifth to Yew Kwang Ng in Economics, Robert Jackson in Economic History and Kenneth Chan in Government, all in 1971; and the sixth in 1972 to Ernie Houghton in Economic Statistics. In 1971, the faculty introduced a higher doctorate, the DSc (Econ), approved by Senate in the previous year (SM: 6 October 1970). The first such was conferred on Ray Chambers, Professor of Accounting, in May 1973. In June 1972, the first honorary DSc (Econ) was conferred on Sir John Crawford, vice-chancellor of the Australian National University and a former faculty graduate.

Faculty organisation also experienced much change. The gradual adoption of a committee system to expedite the rapidly growing volume of business conducted at faculty meetings was a major alteration in procedures. By the end of 1972, faculty operated a Staff/Student Liaison Committee, a Wolstenholme Library Committee, a Curriculum Committee, a Planning Committee and a Graduate Studies Committee. All committees reported directly to general faculty meetings, still held at least once a term. At this stage, committees were expressly forbidden to take on an executive role, with the exception of the Graduate Studies Committee. More surprisingly, and a response to the growing student unrest at the university as part of the wider, international youth protest movement, direct student participation in faculty meetings was also gradually introduced from 1968. At the end of 1972, faculty had approved three elected student members. Admission of student representatives to faculty meetings was a first in the university, as was the formation of formal faculty machinery for staff/student liaison.

From 1967, faculty started to phase out evening lectures. This did not mean the end of part-time students. The last were still able to complete their degree over five years. However, from the late 1960s, part-time enrolments began to fall steadily, partly reflecting the growing opportunities elsewhere in Sydney for part-time university economics studies. In addition, foreign students in this period became subject to a small, separate quota (set initially at ten but increased to 25 by 1972), thereby starting an increasingly important trend in enrolments for the subsequent development of the faculty.

Staffing also grew, though some departments had so much difficulty in attracting suitable staff that they continued to rely heavily on temporary and part-time teachers. Multi-professorial departments in the faculty increased. By the end of the 1960s, the Economics Department had three professors; and by 1970 the Government Department had two. Moreover, with tutorials increasingly used as a vital supplement to lectures, tutorial staff grew rapidly, often through recruiting honours students as temporary, part-time tutors. Finally, the growing importance assigned to research as part of the duties of a university academic induced substantial increases in the number of research assistants employed in the faculty by every department, financed either from within the university or by outside bodies like the Australian Research Grants Commission (the forerunner of the ARC) and the Reserve Bank.

This growth in staff meant that the new Merewether Building (completed during 1965) had by that time become an urgent necessity. For well over a decade, Merewether provided adequate room for permanent as well as temporary faculty staff and, initially, for members of the newly created Fine Arts Department and the Department of Ancient History. Moreover, it enabled most faculty teaching to be carried out in its own lecture theatres, seminar and tutorial rooms. The greatly increased space allocated in the Merewether to the Wolstenholme Library also allowed it to serve effectively for several decades as a faculty library. In this it was assisted by the large amount of money (well over $22,000) raised by a special library appeal, superbly coordinated by Jules Ginswick for the Economics Graduates Association. Even then, the amount raised fell well short of its $40,000 target.

When the faculty celebrated its golden jubilee in 1970, it had much of which to be proud. It was by then well established as an important part of commercial and social science instruction within the university and the wider community. It produced graduates who gained important positions in private and public enterprise as well as in academe. It generated a growing numbers of publications in its own journals, in other refereed periodicals and in books. However, this anniversary year was also marked by the retirement of the faculty's longest serving member of staff, Hermann Black, followed in 1971 by that of Syd Butlin, when he resigned his position as Professor of Economics to go to the Australian National University. Other senior academic staff left to join the new Macquarie University or other Australian universities, or sought employment elsewhere. Replacements, particularly from the late 1960s, had to be increasingly recruited from other universities, not only in Australia but in New Zealand, Great Britain and North America.

Course changes by the early 1970s, particularly in the compulsory Economics I and II courses offered by the Economics Department, generated considerable student unrest in a climate when student demonstrations and political activism were already on the increase, partly a result of Australia's participation in the Vietnam War. Student protest against the new professors of Economics was generated by the refusal of the Economics Department to reappoint two tutors, Bill Waters and David Hill, who had been among the more ardent critics of the new course content of Economics I and II. The subsequent Political Economy dispute and the associated campaign for greater staff and student participation in departmental government are left to Chapter 5.

Enrolment, curriculum and staffing, 1963–72

As mentioned above, quotas were applied to enrolments in the faculty from the beginning of 1963. These helped to stabilise total faculty enrolments at the 1000–1100 student level. Most faculty students were undergraduates, whose numbers fluctuated between 930 and 1080. Postgraduates were a small minority, never exceeding double figures over the ten years ending 1972. Most postgraduate students were part-time masters students, who occasionally, as in 1965, made up over 90 per cent of all postgraduates. However, PhD student numbers were rising, They reached double figures after 1968, a substantial number when it is recalled that by 1972 the faculty had awarded only six PhDs in total.

Other features of faculty enrolments need to be mentioned. Although part-time students predominated in the postgraduate program, the number of part-time undergraduate students declined rapidly with the abolition of evening classes. This policy was initiated by the faculty and approved by the Senate during 1966 (its one opponent on Senate being student senator, Michael Kirby, who was completing a BEc in the evening during the mid-1960s and passed Government III in 1966). Although part-time students generally constituted the majority of undergraduate enrolments for most of the early 1960s, by 1972 they had fallen to 12.8 per cent. The phasing out of evening students from 1967 was a major watershed in the faculty's history, reversing as it did its initial practice (from 1920) of only providing evening tuition (even to full-time students)—a practice preserved in the teaching of Accounting and associated Law courses until the early 1960s. This drastic change, initiated by Syd Butlin as one of his last major actions as dean, was strongly supported by the vast majority of academic teaching staff. Lecturers at the time invariably resented the very long working day when the last course for the day could be scheduled as late as 8.15 pm (to end at 9.15 pm), even if few day lectures were given in the faculty before 11 am. The implementation of this major change in teaching was perfectly timed. By the mid-1960s evening classes in Economics and many commercial subjects were offered by both the University of New South Wales and the then newly established Macquarie University. Moreover, demand for student places in first year would be reduced in 1967 as this was the transitional year between the end of the five-year Leaving Certificate course and the start of the new, six-year Higher School Certificate course.

Furthermore, there was a marked increase in faculty enrolments by women students. At the PhD level, the first woman did not enrol in the faculty until 1967; there were three women PhD students in 1970 and 1971. The first PhD to a woman in the faculty was awarded to Elaine Thompson from Government, but this was not conferred until 1973. The masters program regularly attracted some women. These never rose to double figures during the

1960s, the highest enrolment being nine in 1967. Women undergraduate enrolments in the faculty more than doubled in the ten years ending 1972, and in relative terms rose from a minimum of 7.1 per cent to 22.8 per cent in 1972, or a three fold increase in percentage terms. Nevertheless, the faculty remained a predominantly male enclave. Ninety per cent of postgraduate students and over three-quarters of undergraduate students were male. However, the times in this, as in other things, were definitely 'a-changing', as a popular protest song of the period could have put it.

Over 1963–72, faculty's traditional subjects—Economics, Accounting, Economic History, Economic Statistics and Government and Public Administration, all with honours courses—continued to be offered. Optional courses included Law I and II, Industrial Relations I and II (by 1970 a designated major faculty sequence and honours course by making either Law I or Government I its first-year course), Agricultural Economics, History of Economic Thought, Mathematical Economics, Descriptive Economics, and a new course offered by the Economic Statistics Department, Econometric Methods.

Economics remained the compulsory core of the degree, but by the early 1970s a substantial optional element had been introduced into Economics II and Economics III, partly the result of student pressure. In Economics II, one weekly lecture class out of three was devoted to an optional segment (where students could choose from Industry Economics, Public Finance or Mathematical Economics, the last being compulsory for honours students). In Economics III, half the lecturing time was devoted to a compulsory International Economics course, while for the other half students chose two from seven options. In 1972 these options included Advanced Economic Theory, Economic Development, Economics of Socialism, Managerial Economics, Monetary Economics, the Political Economy of Modern Capitalism and Quantitative Economics I (the last was compulsory for third-year honours students, as were Advanced Economic Theory, International Economics and one option from the remaining five).

The final honours year (Economics IV) also contained much choice by the early 1970s. Students could either proceed by thesis and four options (each consisting of two hours of formal teaching per week) or they could take six options from a list of seven (Advanced Micro-Economic Theory, Advanced Macro-Economic Theory, Applied Economic Development, Economic Planning, Economic Classics, Quantitative Economics II and Welfare Economics). The quantitative element offered in the options, and the compulsory nature of this type of course for honours students in Economics, reflected the substantial mathematisation of the first-year micro-economics and second-year macro-economic syllabus which started from 1969 under the two newly appointed professors of Economics.

By the early 1970s, Government and Public Administration had also adopted a course menu with much internal choice in the face of student demand for such a program. Government I consisted of a compulsory first two terms providing an overview of main forms of modern government as well as models of contemporary democracy. Third term consisted of optional courses (Australian Class Structure, Current Australian Political and Public Policy Issues, Democratic Theory and Modern Political Thought) from which students had to chose one. Government II used the same framework of a compulsory core for the first two terms of Political Thought (one lecture per week in both terms), American Politics (first term) and Russian and East European Politics (second term). Third term comprised options developed out of work from the first two terms, that is, Political Thought, and American Politics and that of East European Communist countries. Government III was completely optional. Four options were offered for first and second terms (Public Policy and Administration, South-East Asian Politics, International Politics and Approaches to the Study of Power) while in third term students could choose between Development Administration and Approaches to Political Change. The final honours year (Government IV) was devoted to research for a thesis and coursework to be arranged for individual students by the Professor of Government.

No internal choice was offered in the Accounting courses. Accounting I provided an introduction to accounting theory and business finance. Accounting II was devoted to anticipatory calculation, financial decision making and criteria of choice, as well as to organisational theory and management structures. Special attention was given to the impact of inflation on financial decision making. Accounting III dealt with advanced accounting problems, including those relating to amalgamations, reconstructions and liquidations, as well as financial statement analysis (term 1), comparative accounting systems, such as those based on historical cost, inflation adjusted costs, present values, and continuous contemporary costs (second term) and auditing theory and practice (third term). The final honours year included coursework on accounting and cognate fields, as well as a thesis. In combination with its Accounting courses, the department also offered two courses on law. Law I gave an introduction to legal studies together with issues in constitutional law, law of contract and regulatory law (including employment law and law on restraint of trade); Law II covered bankruptcy law, company law (and practice) and taxation law (and practice). Together, these courses went a substantial way to providing Accounting majors with full accreditation to the professional accounting bodies.

Economic History courses by the early 1970s likewise offered little choice. Its first-year course was devoted to the industrialisation of Europe from 1750 up to the post-World War II period. Economic History II dealt with Australian economic history in three stages: the initial development stage (1796–1850); the gold rushes, economic development and the 1890s depression (1851–1900); and development issues for a small, industrialising economy in the twentieth century (1900–60). Economic History III covered economic development in Japan from the feudal era to modern times, as well as the economic history of the most advanced capitalist nation, the United States, from the middle of the seventeenth century to the 1960s. The final honours year in Economic History contained seminars on historical method, development and instability of the capitalist system, as well as aspects of Australian history, together with an undergraduate thesis.

The Economic statistics curriculum only provided choice for students in its final honours year. Economic Statistics I introduced a variety of issues from estimation theory to data collection, descriptive statistics, sampling distributions, hypothesis testing and decision theory, time series and demographic issues. Economic Statistics II enabled further study of the mathematical basis of general statistical theory, but in addition dealt with fields of economic application such as statistical inference, classical regression theory and economic modelling and estimation problems including simple stochastic process models for economics and sociology. Economic Statistics III devoted its first term to the purpose, design, evaluation and interpretation of sample surveys, and to experimental design with reference to computer simulation. Second and third terms were used for studying research methodology, operations research, business decision theory and computer simulation models. The final honours year required a thesis based on supervised statistical research as well as a number of courses. Some of these were compulsory (Advanced Time Series Analysis, Multivariate Analysis Theory, Operations Research and Macro-Economic Planning, and Australian Macro-Economic Modelling). Others were optional, and some courses were to be drawn from other departments (that is, from those of Pure Mathematics, Mathematical Statistics, Computing, Economic History, Economics and Accounting). Final honours-year students were also expected to participate in the Department's Research and Current Literature seminars.

At the start of 1967, Industrial Relations had become a full three-year sequence with either Law I or Government I as its first-year course. Industrial Relations I (a second-year course) provided an outline of industrial relations systems in the world, topics in personnel management, legal issues and the development of trade unionism. Industrial Relations II dealt at a more advanced level with the arbitration and industrial relations system, personnel management, legal issues (employment liability, factory legislation, workers' compensation and award structures) as well as the practice of trade unionism. The final honours year (also approved in principle in 1967 but not started until 1971) was designed to include comparative industrial relations systems in advanced and developing countries, issues in motivational and organisational theory, industrial democracy, trade union law and strike law, trade union organisation and administration, and methodology. There was also provision for completing a thesis.

Staffing, needless to say, had to match this faculty syllabus. By the end of 1972, the faculty's five departments and one sub-departmental unit (Industrial Relations), had seven professors, one reader, five associate professors, twenty senior lecturers, 26 lecturers as well as two teaching fellows, two assistant lecturers, three senior tutors, eight full-time tutors, and several dozens of part-time tutors and guest lecturers. Total teaching staff in the faculty amounted to 70 persons, virtually double the 37 at the start of 1963. Economics and Government remained the largest departments in terms of staff and students, and were the only ones at this stage with more than one professor. Accounting, Economic History and Economic Statistics had one professor each, but Industrial Relations, not yet a full department, was headed by an associate professor.

With 28 full-time staff members by the end of 1972, the Economics Department remained the largest in the faculty. Two new professors, Warren Hogan and Colin Simkin, additional to Syd Butlin, were appointed in 1967 and in 1968. Two staff members appointed in the early 1950s, Ted Wheelwright and Jim Wilson, were promoted to associate professor in 1965 and 1970. Of the five senior lecturers, Geelum Simpson-Lee's first appointment dated also from the early 1950s while the other four were more recent appointments. Neil Conn was lecturer in 1962, promoted to senior lecturer in 1966; Sol Kim, one of the faculty's early PhDs, was teaching fellow in Economic Statistics from 1966, lecturer in Economics in 1969 and promoted to senior lecturer in 1972; Peter Groenewegen was appointed lecturer in 1965 and senior lecturer in 1967; D.M. Kannangara was appointed as senior lecturer in 1971. All eleven lecturers in Economics were appointed after 1963. In alphabetical order, Debesh Bhattacharya and Gavin Butler were both appointed in 1970, Maurice Haddad in 1965, Louis Haddad in 1967 after holding a temporary lectureship from 1965, Evan Jones and Bill Merrilees were both appointed in 1972, Tony Phipps in 1970, Bruce Ross in 1972, Ian Sharpe in 1971 and Frank Stilwell in 1970. Judy Yates, a teaching fellow in 1972, became a temporary Economics lecturer in 1967–68, before completing her doctorate at Amsterdam. The three senior tutors—Margaret Power, Hugh Pritchard and Surrinder Singh (later Joson)—were appointed in 1967, 1963 and 1970. Of the four full-time tutors, Patricia Woodhouse was appointed in 1971, the other three—Jock Collins, William Hickson and Paul Roberts—in 1972.

Some Economics staff departed. Hermann Black, retired in 1970. From 1971, he continued to teach in the department for some years as a senior fellow, before his duties as chancellor of the university (to which he was elected in May 1970) prevented such activities. In 1965, Harry Edwards resigned to take up a chair at Macquarie University; he was followed there a year later by Noel Drane. Ron Gates, after promotion to an associate professorship in 1964, resigned in 1965 to take up a chair at the University of Queensland. He was followed there in 1968 by Helmut Kolsen, a senior lecturer from 1963 and associate professor from 1965. Victor Argy, promoted to senior lecturer in 1965, departed in 1967 to take up a position with the International Monetary Fund; Gordon Patterson resigned in 1968 for employment in the private sector; Paul Wooding, a senior tutor in 1966 and lecturer in 1968, left in 1970 to return to New Zealand; John Zerby resigned as lecturer in 1971 to take up a position at the University of New South Wales; Nigel Stokes, a distinguished 1966 graduate, resigned as lecturer in 1972 to join the New South Wales Treasury; Bill Horrigan, resigned as senior lecturer in 1970. Undoubtedly, the most dramatic departure from the Economics Department was Derek Horner's suicide. He hanged himself in one of the Union's shower rooms on 22 March 1965 (*The Australian*, 23 March 1965; *Sydney Morning Herald*, 23 March 1965), partly because of the rough treatment he received from his students in class. This high staff turnover in the department was not unrelated to the student unrest over new course curriculum (discussed later in this chapter).

The Government Department had 22 full-time academic staff members at the end of 1972. Dick Spann, one of its two professors, had been appointed in 1953; Henry Mayer was appointed Professor of Political Theory in 1970. Jim Richardson was the department's only associate professor, promoted in 1972. Government's seven senior lecturers included Tom Kewley (whose association with the faculty preceded World War II), Ian Grosart, Ross Curnow, Peter King, Rex Mortimer, John Power and Ken Turner. Government's six lecturers were all appointed after 1963: Trevor Mathews in 1964, Dennis Altman in 1968, Michael Leigh in 1970 while Des Ball, Peter Nelson, Carole Pateman and assistant lecturer

Lex Watson were appointed in 1972. A teaching fellow (A.P. McIntyre) and tutors Warren Osmond, Elaine Thompson and Judith Walker had joined the teaching staff in 1971 or 1972. Departures from the Government staff included Carol Bell, who in 1966 went to the London School of Economics; Peter Westerway resigned in 1964 to join Channel 7; Peter Loveday went in 1963 to the Australian National University, as did Ian Campbell in 1966; Robert Scott left in 1967, while Bob Connell resigned to go to Flinders University in 1972.

Accounting, with thirteen full-time teaching staff, was the third largest department in the faculty. Its one professor, Ray Chambers, had been in that position since 1960. Pat Mills was reader, the position to which he had been promoted in 1965. Its five senior lecturers were Alec Shaw, Ron Bowra, Ron Brown, Bill Birkett and Murray Wells. Of its four lecturers, Frank Clarke had been appointed in 1970, John Staunton in 1968, Alan Craswell in 1972 and Bob Walker in 1967. T.R. Sappideen was appointed as assistant lecturer in Law in 1972, as was the department's only full-time tutor, P.I. Carter. Departures included Peter Standish, Bob Brooker, Bob Baxt and Barry O'Keefe. J.G. Davies, a teaching fellow in 1964, and R.K.A. Chaudari, a temporary lecturer in 1966, were employed in the department for only one year.

There were five permanent staff members in Economic Statistics by the end of 1972: Stuart Rutherford, its only professor appointed in 1962, and four lecturers. These were John Goodhew, Steve Harrison, Ernie Houghton and T.A. Ramasubban (lecturer from 1971). Bob Layard and Jan Kmenta both resigned in 1963, B.J. Phillips in 1967, and Ernie Treloar in 1968.

Economic History, a department in its own right from 1970, had Derek Aldcroft as its first professor (appointed in 1972). Jules Ginswick was its one associate professor. Its two senior lecturers were Ken Buckley and Boris Schedvin. Peter Hall and Barbara Tucker were the two lecturers. A number of staff resigned from the department: John McCarthy left to take up a chair at Monash University in 1968; Alan Birch, a senior lecturer, resigned in 1967 to go to Hong Kong; while Sybil Jack, a senior tutor in 1963, left for the university's Department of History during 1971. Barbara Little, a first-class honours graduate of 1969, was assistant lecturer in 1971.

The Industrial Relations staff of five included Kingsley Laffer, its creator and only associate professor. Maxine Bucklow and Geoff Sorrell were its two senior lecturers, Malcolm Rimmer its only lecturer, and Phillip Bentley its one part-time lecturer.

Faculty deliberations and administration, 1963–72

In the decade under consideration, the Faculty of Economics held 54 meetings, of which three were special meetings and one an adjourned meeting. This was an average of close to two meetings per term, only a slight increase over the seven years ending 1962 when the faculty had met frequently to finalise the new by-laws for the three-year pass degree. With increased staffing and expansion of faculty membership (senior tutors were given faculty membership in 1969, tutors and teaching fellows in 1972, while three student members were elected annually from 1973 onwards), average attendance rose to 24.8. A maximum attendance of 43 was recorded for the September 1971 meeting, the minimum attendance of fifteen for that of July 1965. Most faculty meetings over the decade were held in the Senate Room of the university, which provided more space and facilities for the growing faculty, but increasingly during the 1970s, meetings were also held in the Professorial Board Room.

Butlin resigned as Professor of Economics and dean of the faculty during 1971. He had held this position continuously from the end of World War II, except for 1957–58 and 1968–69 (both periods for part of which Butlin was away on study leave) when Dick Spann was dean. The faculty elected Geelum Simpson-Lee in September 1971 to take Butlin's place, the reason for the very high attendance at this faculty meeting. Simpson-Lee's election was controversial, partly because non-professorial deans at that time were still quite rare within the university. As Stilwell (2001) stated in his obituary of Simpson-Lee, his election as dean was assisted by the fact that he was known to support the dissident views on economics which were held by the self-styled 'political economists' group' within the Economics Department (see Chapter 5) and because his election in itself was seen as diminishing traditional professorial powers in the running of departmental and faculty affairs. Simpson-Lee had graduated BEc in 1944 and joined the teaching staff not long thereafter, initially as a teaching fellow.

The February 1963 faculty meeting was informed that Economic Statistics had become a separate department from the end of 1962, and that Harry Edwards and Stuart Rutherford were now (as professors) both ex officio members of the Diploma of Administrative Science Committee. Faculty approved the new by-laws for the revised MEc with few amendments. These finalised the introduction of a coursework masters program, a step which considerably increased Masters degree enrolments. This, and other faculty meetings in 1963, also discussed individual MEc results including examiners' reports and reviewed admissions of new postgraduate students. The time devoted to this often routine business at faculty meetings induced the establishment of a Board of Graduate Studies.

A proposal by Stuart Rutherford to establish a faculty research institute was discussed at the July 1963 faculty meeting. This was to be given powers to raise funds from outside the university in order to finance research staff, equipment and accommodation. Its governing council was to contain both non-university (one-third) and university members (two-thirds). Among other things, it would organise sample surveys for commercial customers and university clients from within or without the faculty (potential clients to include Agricultural Economics, Psychology, Social Studies, Town and Country Planning). It would regularly publish a (quarterly or monthly) bulletin, award postgraduate scholarships to the tune of £15,000, and appoint senior lecturers to its staff. A committee of professors set up to investigate the proposal further reported in-principle support, but nothing eventuated.

In 1966, the faculty introduced 'show cause' provisions for the re-enrolment of failed students. By deciding to restrict deferred examinations ('posts') to special cases of illness and misadventure, it encouraged the use of 'further tests' in this context as already permitted by existing by-laws. More importantly, faculty unanimously approved measures to eliminate evening studies from the beginning of 1967, with no further evening students to be admitted from that year. Hence by 1968 Descriptive Economics became a day course only, while details for phasing out Economics I, II and III as evening courses were announced in July 1967.

In July 1967, faculty was also told that the dean would consult with the Dean of Law to establish a combined BEc/LLB degree as quickly as possible. At its June 1968 meeting, faculty approved a course structure for the new combined degree. First year would consist of Economics I, Descriptive Economics, the first of a faculty sequence and Legal History; second year of Economics II, the second year of the sequence and Constitutional Law I; and third year of Economics III, the third year of the sequence and Constitutional Law II. All courses were to be given on campus, including the required law ones. The Law Faculty only approved the BEc/LLB in September 1972, and the combined degree course did not commence until 1974.

In 1968, the faculty appointed a committee to review faculty structure in response to a general request from the Professorial Board for all faculties and other university bodies to do so. Two months later, its first report supported transformation of the faculty into a faculty of economics and social sciences, to be achieved by adding Sociology and Social Anthropology to the major sequences offered by the faculty. The report also proposed formalising the relationship between heads of department and other departmental members, including the powers of sub-professorial staff to initiate department meetings. A departmental committee to consult with, and advise, the head of department was to be established in every department, to meet at least once a term. As a minimum, it had to include every person who was a member of faculty. The committee also recommended that these changes in departmental administration were to apply to the then sub-departments of Economic History and Industrial Relations (FM: 5 September 1968).

At its September 1968 meeting, the faculty discussed staff–student relations and established a faculty–student subcommittee. That same meeting proposed a staff/student liaison committee, the procedures and constitution of which were to be discussed with students, drawn largely from Students Economic Society (SUES) office bearers. Its powers were to be broad, enabling it to raise any matter of interest to students for discussion, to make recommendations to faculty or other pertinent bodies, and to organise general student meetings of the faculty or any specific part of it. Its standing committee was to comprise the dean and the vice-president of SUES, with each major course unit represented by one staff member and one student. Subcommittees could be established from persons representing individual classes in each unit, the appropriate staff member taking the chair. Formal recognition of these committees was to be given in all classes, which also had to set aside time for electing student representatives.

Inspiration for this institutional change came from student complaints: the need for greater student–staff interaction, better access to and feedback from academic staff, improved teaching, legible comments on class assignments, opportunities for students to comment on particular classes, improved reading guides, and better course organisation. The last required greater choice within courses, bridging courses, better access to books on reading lists, and additional tutors for more difficult courses. These demands reflected the results of a student survey. This had recorded majority support for introducing more current economic topics in lectures, organised general interest lectures at lunch times, provision of an official question time during lectures, slower delivery of lectures, lecturers' participation in the tutorial program, term examinations, classwork to count explicitly in the final result and lower failure rates. The survey also rated most faculty teaching staff highly, claimed at least half the staff showed interest in seeing their students, while two-thirds of staff regularly allowed time for answering questions after their lectures had finished.

Data on failure rates were provided in conjunction with the report on the findings of the students survey. These showed that first-year failure rates were highest, particularly in Economics I and Accounting I where more than 40 per cent of students failed. By third year, less than 15 per cent were failed in Economics and Accounting, and less than 5 per cent in Economic History and Government.

A special meeting of faculty (13 September 1968) discussed these proposals, including formal student representation on faculty. The last was rejected as too radical a change. Faculty did agree to a limited form of student participation in March 1969: three student representatives were able to present submissions in person at faculty meetings on items of the agenda they had selected, implying previous consultation with the dean on the faculty agenda. Subsequent student submissions proposed making 'passes with merit' more widely applicable (implemented from the end of 1970); a faculty committee to inquire into the assumed level of knowledge and the general first-year load for students; greater student representation on the Staff/Student Liaison Committee, and a mathematics prerequisite for Statistics I but not for Economics I. A faculty committee to examine prerequisites for Economics I proposed both Higher School Certificate Economics Level 2 and Mathematics Level 2 Short. The last was amended by students on the Committee to Mathematics Level 2 Full, because that, and not the Level 2 Short course, contained calculus, essential for grasping modern mainstream micro-economics. At this meeting (20 July 1970), faculty also decided to make its decisions formally available to students by publishing them after each meeting in a statement prepared by the dean. In June 1971, students proposed direct student representation on faculty, a proposal which gained unanimous support from SUES (reported 9 September 1971). A subsequent meeting (28 October 1971) approved the presence of three elected student representatives at all faculty meetings, details of election procedures were approved by faculty (9 March 1972) and by Senate (29 June 1972). On 5 July 1972, Dennis Mortimer and Eric de Haas were elected as student representatives until the end of 1972 since only two nominations were received (*University News*, 26 July 1972, p. 6). Henceforth, faculty sat formally as a board of examiners at the end of the year for the purpose of discussing final examination results and not as a faculty, to legally prevent attendance by student members of faculty.

Some other items of faculty business can be mentioned. Faculty congratulated Ray Chambers on receiving a Gold Medal from the American Institute of Certified Public Accountants for his book, *Accounting, Evaluation and Economic Behavior* (FM: 7 November 1967). It did likewise when Chambers became the first recipient of the faculty's new higher doctorate, the DSc (Econ), in early 1972 (FM: 4 May 1972). On his retirement from the university in 1971, Butlin was praised for his 29 years as Professor of Economics, of which 22 years were served as dean (1946–49, 1950–53, 1955–67 and 1970–71). Butlin's curriculum vitae were formally included in the minutes. The recorded appreciation from students 'for all he had done in our Faculty' would have been particularly gratifying to Butlin. Specifically mentioned were his staunch support for the *Economic Review* as an annual student publication and his generous provision of space for students in the new Merewether Building, including an office for SUES and a general students common room. Many members of faculty saw his departure as the end of an era (FM: 9 September 1971), particularly when his resignation was followed less than a year later by Joyce Fisher's retirement as administrative assistant to the dean.

The faculty committee system introduced during this decade needs also to be mentioned. This was a reflection of both the growing routine business of the faculty, as noted when discussing the establishment of the Graduate Studies Committee, and of faculty's growth in size. A faculty standing committee, consisting of the dean, three professors and three sub-professorial staff, was recommended by the Committee on Faculty Organisation (FM: 14 March 1969). Every faculty member would have the right to attend its meetings, to be held one week before the faculty meeting. The Standing Committee would star items for discussion at faculty meetings a week later, all other items to be confirmed en bloc at the start of meetings. Every member of faculty had the right to star items for discussion if not starred by the Standing Committee, which would also set the dates and times of all faculty meetings at the start of each year. The first faculty standing committee was elected on 12 May 1969, with Dick Spann in the chair as dean, Warren Hogan, Syd Butlin and Ray Chambers as the professorial members, and Maurice Haddad, Ron Bowra and John Goodhew as non-professorial members.

Given the library's increased size and importance in the Merewether Building, a Wolstenholme Library committee had been in existence from 1965 (FM: 17 June 1965). Its first convenor was Syd Butlin, who was succeeded in this role by Jules Ginswick (1968), Boris Schedvin (1969) and Peter Groenewegen (1971). Every department and sub-department was represented on the committee, while the Wolstenholme Librarian was present at meetings ex officio.

A faculty committee to review the MEc program recommended the establishment of a Post Graduate Committee, with the dean as chair and at least one representative from every department (FM: 16 March 1970). It was given executive functions on admission of new candidates, change of supervisors, titles of theses and other matters referred to it by the Professorial Board relating to the MEc and PhD degrees offered by the faculty (FM: 16 March 1970). In 1972 it changed its name to Board of Post Graduate Studies (FM: 29 June 1972) to accommodate the expansion envisaged for the faculty's postgraduate program.

Faculty established two further committees in early 1972. The Curriculum Committee—consisting of the dean, heads of departments and five other faculty members elected for two years—was designed to deal with aspects relating to the undergraduate curriculum, including its periodic review. The Planning Committee with a similar composition was designed to examine matters referred to it by the faculty of a longer-term nature. The subject of examination procedures became the first item of business for the newly created Planning Committee, a reference undoubtedly inspired by the publication of recent data on faculty pass rates indicating considerable improvement in the past five years (FM: 4 May 1972) As another reflection of changing standards, the faculty examined data on the 1972 quota of 350 first-year entrants and investigated the consequences of its variation.

The penultimate report of the faculty's Economics/Social Sciences Committee (presented to faculty at its last meeting for 1971) proposed that the requirements for a pass Economics/Social Science degree entail ten subjects to be completed over three years; of which only Economics I and II and one faculty sequence would be compulsory. In addition, it would be possible to complete an Arts sequence. Finally, no more than five 'first-year courses' and only four courses per subject group would be counted towards the degree.

For the honours degree, the committee recommended that honours work could commence in either the second or the third year of studies in the honours subject; the third-year distinction course would count as two courses towards the degree; and a thesis was not considered essential for final honours-year students. Implementation of this change was delayed until after presentation of a final report in 1973.

One further major faculty meeting outcome needs to be mentioned in this chapter. In May 1972 faculty decided to appoint a working party to review proposals for an MBA (FM: 4 May 1972). A subsequent meeting (12 September 1972) was informed that the possibility of introducing a master of public administration was also under consideration and would be reported on in the near future. Hence, two years after its golden jubilee in 1970, faculty considerably expanded both its graduate and undergraduate program to widen its appeal to potential students.

The new Merewether Building, 1962–66

By the early 1960s, the R.C. Mills Building could no longer pretend to meet the needs of the Faculty of Economics for both lecture rooms and staff accommodation. A new building therefore had to be found. The Senate had initially proposed to meet this need by converting the Institute Building on City Road. However, pressure from Syd Butlin, together with the Institute Building's unsuitability for faculty purposes, caused this strategy to be abandoned in favour of erecting a new building on a site adjoining the Institute Building, on part of its grounds. At the second faculty meeting for 1963, Butlin as dean reported that a contract for the new building was to be approved in July 1963 (FM: 13 May 1963). At the end of 1963, he announced that Senate at its 4 November meeting had approved J.G. Pettigrew as builder, that costs were estimated at £525,000, and that construction was to be completed within 65 weeks (FM: 8 November 1963; SM: 4 November 1963, give £425,764 as the cost declared in Pettigrew's successful tender). In 1964 Butlin expressed the hope that the new building would be ready for occupation during Lent term 1965. This date was uncertain,

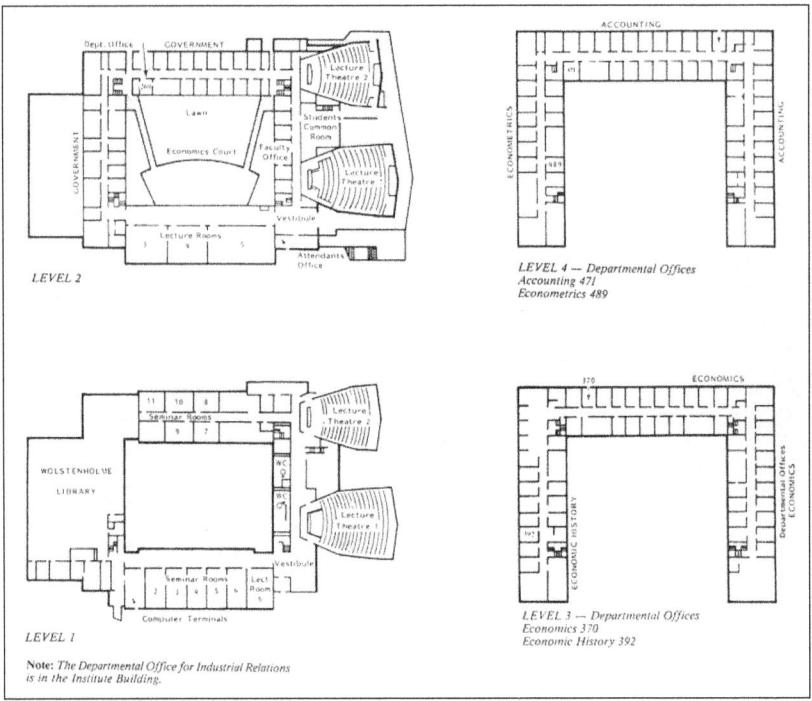

Merewether Building Floor Plan 1992.

however, though the contracted completion time of 65 weeks had expired by then (FM: 28 September 1964). The fact that South Sydney Council consent for the plans was not given until 11 December 1963 (University Archives: Merewether Building File) was one cause for this delay, while Pettigrew advised other unavoidable delays in construction during the building process, which were not helped by quarrels over concreting between builder and architects during October and November 1964.

The plans provided for four floors for most parts of the building, but for a single floor in that part where the two large lecture theatres were to be located. Lecture rooms 1 and 2 provided seating for 320 and for 200 students. A small lecture room (No. 6) provided seating for 56 students, and adjoined six seminar or tutorial rooms of similar size. The second floor, facing the courtyard, provided a further three adjoining lecture rooms (Nos 3, 4, and 5, designed to seat 150, 120 and 90 students). The second floor in addition provided two professorial rooms and 30 ordinary staff rooms, some of which could be used as departmental offices. The third floor provided a large staff common room for morning and afternoon tea as well as for small faculty functions. The third floor also provided four professorial rooms (each with attached but separate secretarial accommodation), two seminar rooms (which could also serve as 'machine rooms') and 44 staff rooms. The fourth floor provided three professorial rooms (again, with separate but attached secretarial rooms), 44 staff rooms, four seminar rooms and what was described as 'considerable storage space'. The ground floor at the southern end of the building provided a great deal of space for the Wolstenholme Library, enough for a reading room with seating for 150 students, book stacks to house 60,000 volumes, and three special use rooms (for photocopying, staff rooms and meetings). This was an immense improvement on the very limited library space in the R.C. Mills Building, and undoubtedly provided the impetus for the library appeal mentioned at the start of this chapter.

Although construction was not fully completed, faculty nevertheless moved into its new building during August 1965, because lectures were to be given there from the commencement of Michaelmas term (6 September 1965). The September faculty meeting congratulated Syd Butlin, and thanked him, Joyce Fisher and Mr L. McGregor for their hard work in seeing the task successfully concluded. The move itself was a major undertaking. Forty-four staff (including the then five professors) were shifted from the R.C. Mills Building, eighteen staff from the wooden, temporary 'lecturers' hut' and ten staff from the Institute Building where overflow staff had been On 14 June 1966, the Merewether Building was officially opened by Senator John Gorton, then Commonwealth Minister for Works and Housing. He unveiled a bronze commemorative plaque, explaining that the building had been named after Francis Lewis Shaw Merewether (1811–98), a Fellow of Senate (1850–75), vice-chancellor in 1854 and chancellor in 1862. His nickname was 'Futurity', if only because his enthusiastic foresight procured 130 acres for university purposes when the University of Sydney was established in 1850. This was a very tangible sign of Merewether's faith in the new institution, and of the great social value he placed on higher education. Use of his name for the new Faculty of Economics building was therefore very appropriate, since in 1965 its size also appeared very generous for meeting future space needs the faculty could conceivably have until at least the beginning of the 21st century. That, in any case, was what Syd Butlin told me when in September 1965 I moved into the Merewether Building as a newly appointed lecturer, in a staff room on the third floor overlooking the courtyard and in between the two professorial suites. I might add that Butlin's optimistic expectation was given considerable support from the fact that every staff room on the other side of that corridor, in between the economics departmental office and the corner seminar room (Room 350) was then used by Butlin for housing his massive private library.

Alas, circumstances change rapidly. On 7 November 1969, the faculty was told that it was proposed to extend the Merewether Building as part of the 1973–75 Triennium Plans. This extension was required to meet additional staff accommodation and to create the additional teaching rooms needed for the late 1970s (FM: 7 November 1969). Within five years from its first occupation, space in the Merewether Building proved to be insufficient. What better proof is there of the growth in staff, teaching program and student numbers during this period? Over the next 30 years, faculty had to rely increasingly on space for housing staff and teaching in the adjoining Institute Building (FM: 7 November 1969).

Merewether under construction.

The official opening of Merewether (14 June 1966).

The creation of the Department of Economic History, 1970

The appointment of two new professors of Economics in 1968 and 1969 was largely responsible for the creation of a separate Department of Economic History. By 1970, considerable friction existed among the three professors of Economics over the changes to economics teaching the two new professors wished to introduce, as earlier there had been disagreements between Hogan and Butlin over Simkin's appointment. The vice-chancellor clearly saw advantages in moving Butlin to Economic History, which after all was Butlin's major area of research, to head a newly created Department of Economic History. At its first meeting for 1970, Senate noted that Professor Butlin, still designated Professor of Economics, had been appointed head of the Department of Economic History, now legally separated from the Department of Economics of which it had been a part for so long. At the same time, Senate was told that the vice-chancellor had appointed Professor Warren Hogan head of the Department of Economics (SM: 2 February 1970). A week later, the faculty noted the same information (FM: 10 February 1970). This change was effected too quickly for inclusion in the *1970 Faculty Handbook* staff list. However, the *1971 Faculty Handbook* included Butlin as the most senior member of the Economic History staff, which in addition comprised three senior lecturers (Ken Buckley, Jules Ginswick, Boris Schedvin), one lecturer (Peter Hall), one senior tutor (Sybil Jack) and one tutor (Gary Wotherspoon). This information remained correct for only part of 1971. In August, Butlin resigned. He was replaced by Jules Ginswick as acting head of the Economic History Department until the appointment of the university's first Professor of Economic History, Derek Aldcroft, in 1972.

Graduates and students, 1963–72

The number of graduates produced by the faculty between 1963 and 1972 more than doubled, from 88 in May 1963 to 218 in April 1972. In 1972, faculty graduates were a sufficiently large group to warrant two graduation ceremonies, particularly since in that year fifteen MEc students received their degree and one PhD was conferred. Over the decade as a whole, 1560 BEc degrees were conferred, of which 169 (or 10.8 per cent) were honours degrees. In addition, 91 MEc degrees were awarded, the majority of them over the six years starting in 1967 when the first coursework and thesis masters students graduated. Six PhD degrees were also conferred. By 1972, 16 per cent of the graduates were women (as compared with an average of 9.3 per cent for the decade and a minimum of 4 per cent in 1965). No PhDs were conferred on women by 1972 (though one had completed her PhD thesis by that time), and only six women received an MEc degree (or 6.6 per cent of the total). Ten women graduated with honours over the decade (5.9 per cent). They included one medallist (Diane Osborn in Government), one additional first-class honours graduate (Barbara Little in Economic History), six with upper seconds and two with lower seconds.

The 169 honours degrees conferred over the decade included fourteen university medallists, 34 first-class honours graduates (of whom nine, including three medallists, graduated in

1970), 60 upper second honours graduates, 36 lower second honours graduates and 26 third-class honours graduates. Honours graduates remained a small proportion of students completing the degree, accounting for 14.7 per cent of all graduates in 1963, and for 13.8 per cent in 1972. The average for the decade was 9.9 per cent. Absolute numbers therefore fluctuated widely from a minimum of ten in 1966 to a maximum of 30 in 1972. Only one student, Hyam Gold, achieved double honours over the decade: his result in Government was recorded as first-class honours; that in Economics as an upper second.

By departments, the award of honours varied considerably, as did the grade of honours awarded. For the decade as a whole, Economics, with by far the largest number of students, awarded 39.4 per cent of honours degrees, Economic Statistics awarded 18.8 per cent, Government 14.4 per cent, Economic History 13.8 per cent and Accounting 13.1 per cent. In 1972 Industrial Relations awarded a third-class honours as its first honours degree. Awards of honours by grade for individual departments did not fully match the data for aggregate honours awards by department. For example, with respect to university medals, Economic Statistics awarded five (35.7 per cent), Economics and Accounting three each (21.4 per cent), Government two (14.3 per cent) and Economic History one (7.1 per cent). Medallists by departments depended on the first-class honours degrees they awarded: Economics awarded 41.9 per cent of the total, Economic Statistics 25.9, Economic History and Government both 11.6 per cent, and Accounting 9.3 per cent. Not surprisingly, honours graduates featured prominently among faculty graduates who distinguished themselves in their later careers.

Take first the medallists. Three of the 1964 medallists pursued academic careers. Tom Valentine became Professor of Banking and Finance at the University of Western Sydney in 1995 after several decades of teaching at Macquarie University; Ted Sieper went to the Australian National University, while Jeremy Davis became Professor of Management at the Australian Graduate School of Management after being its dean (1979–89) and holding several company directorships. Careers of the two medallists of 1966, A. Eames (Economic Statistics) and John Pearson (Accounting) were not easily identifiable. The sole 1968 medallist, Grahame Cocks, worked as an economic consultant, building up his own business. The careers of two of the three 1970 medallists—George Foster (Accounting), Michael Hinchy (Economic History) and Diane Osborn (Government)—are not fully available from the public record, though George Foster was on the teaching staff of the Accounting Department for some time. Foster went to the United States to gain his PhD from Stanford. He returned to Sydney in 2005 to deliver the R.J. Chambers Lecture for that year. A similar lack of information applies to the later careers of two of the three medallists for 1972, Peter Bryant (Government) and Piet de Jong (Statistics). The third 1972 medallist, John Laker (Economics), followed a career in economic research at the Reserve Bank to become chairman of the Australian Prudential Regulation Authority in 2003.

Other first-class honours graduates from this decade likewise enjoyed good careers, in so far as these were ascertainable. The subsequent careers of the three firsts in Economics additional to the medallist in 1964, that is, R.A.C. Keene, Tom Lyle and Owen Stanley, were not recovered. The subsequent career of the one 1965 first-class honours graduate

(Economic Statistics), Stephen Grenville, embodied Foreign Affairs, the Organisation for Economic Cooperation and Development, the International Monetary Fund, and deputy governor of the Reserve Bank. Of the four first-class honours graduates in 1967, three entered academic life and one followed a career in business. William Ferris held many company appointments after a stint on the Australian Trade Commission; Peter Forsyth became Professor of Economics at Monash after holding positions at Macquarie, New England and the Australian National University; Nigel Stokes, after teaching in the faculty for some years, entered the NSW Public Service, initially in Treasury; while Barbara Little taught Economic History for a year in the faculty. In 1968, the three first-class honours graduates from Economics, Economic History and Government went respectively into banking and finance (André Cohen), academic life at the University of New South Wales and financial journalism (David Clark) and business (A.G. Kaldor). The career of the one first-class honours graduate of 1969, C.B. Williams, was not identified. Of the six first-class honours graduates from 1970 additional to the medallists, Frank Clarke went into academic life to become Professor of Accounting at Newcastle; David Mortimer (Economics) became deputy director of Australia Post and held many company directorships; Jack Frisch (Economics) initially entered banking, while the careers of David Chodkowiecz (Economics) and of the two first-class honours graduates from Economic Statistics, R.J. Shields and L.R. Wiggins, were not traced. The only first-class honours graduate of 1971, Hyam Gold (Government), started an academic career in America after completing postgraduate studies there. Apart from the three medallists in 1972, the only other person gaining first-class honours was Richard Shepherd (Economics), for a short time adviser to the then leader of the opposition (Billie Snedden) before starting a career in the finance sector.

Other graduates of the decade, with or without honours on graduation, and frequently with additional degrees, made careers in politics, in public administration, the law, in academe and in business, often blending two or more of these broad classes of employment in their subsequent careers.

Seven faculty graduates from these years followed successful political careers for part of their lives. John Tierney, after an academic career in education at Newcastle University, was elected Liberal Senator for New South Wales in 1991. Nick Greiner combined a distinguished career in New South Wales politics (1988–92) as Premier, Treasurer and Minister for Ethnic and Aboriginal Affairs, with five years as director of Price Waterhouse Coopers, director of the Sydney Organising Committee for the Olympic Games and directorships in many companies and consultancy roles. John Hewson was leader of the federal Liberal Opposition (1990–94) in between an academic career at the University of New South Wales and Macquarie University and work in the financial sector (including the International Monetary Fund and the Macquarie Bank). John Bradford, after a career in TAFE teaching and in the army, became Liberal MHR for McPherson. Phillip Smiles was state Liberal member for North Shore (1984–91). Kerry Bartlett was Liberal MHR for Macquarie from 1996 to 2007; and Charles Blunt was a federal National Party MHR for Richmond (1984–90) and leader of the party (1989–90) before becoming national director in Australia of the American Chamber of Commerce from 1990.

Many graduates entered the public service at either state or federal level, with five embarking on diplomatic careers. Richard Butler held ambassadorial posts at Singapore and the United Nations (including that of weapons inspector in Iraq) before becoming Governor of Tasmania for a brief period; Ian Hutchins (in External Affairs from 1968) was ambassador in Egypt from 1987; Peter Grey held ambassadorial posts in Japan (1998–2001) and in Belgium, Luxembourg and the European Community from 2003; Tony Hely had diplomatic positions in Jakarta, Tokyo and Geneva, was ambassador to Korea (1998–2001) and High Commissioner to Canada and Bermuda from 2001; while Stephen Sedgwick was executive director of the Asian Development Bank and senior economic adviser to the Office of the Prime Minister (1985–88). Other Commonwealth public servants among faculty graduates included John Limbrick with careers in Education and Training, Labour and Manpower; Tony Cole who held senior positions with Treasury, Prime Minister and Cabinet, Health, Housing, Local Government and Community Services. Philippa Smith was Commonwealth Tax Ombudsman (1993–98) and director of corporate policy and planning at the ABC (1989–90) after serving in senior positions at ACOSS (1977–83), the Australian Consumers' Association (1985–89), the Law Reform Commission (1982–84). In 1998 she became CEO of the Association of Superannuation Funds of Australia.

State public servants among graduates include Gary Wilmott (New South Wales Department of Education and Training); Percy Allen as financial adviser to the premier (1981–85) and director State Bank of New South Wales (1987–90) before becoming a private consultant in Percy Allen and Associates; Warwick McDonald, New South Wales Department of Industrial Relations, and manager of Workcover; David Richmond, as director general Olympic Coordination Authority in the Department of Public Works, head of the Department of Health and director, Graduate School of Government from 2003; David Hill, as chief executive of the New South Wales Railways (1980–86), managing director ABC (1986–95), chairman of the Australian Soccer Federation from 1995 and back at the university studying archaeology for an Arts degree in 2005; George Jepson in public health and hospital administration; Michael Lambert in Treasury and Finance; and Stephen Rochester as chief of the Queensland Treasury Corporation. Hylda Rolfe, after a distinguished career in consultancy and local government (mayor of Woollahra 1985-6, 1989–90) was a member of the Commonwealth Grants Commission from 1999 to 2004.

Four graduates had very distinguished legal careers. Michael Kirby, after practising as a solicitor (1962–67) and barrister (1967–74) was subsequently appointed to the judiciary, first on the New South Wales Supreme Court, and as Justice on the High Court of Australia from 1996 to 2009; Nigel Cotman, Ian Johnston and Frank Lever had distinguished careers at the bar, becoming either a New South Wales Senior Counsel or a QC.

Many graduates enjoyed academic careers, sometimes in combination with work in business. Leonie Still was director of the Centre for Women and Business at the School of Management, University of Western Australia, after teaching at the University of New England, UTS, the University of New South Wales and work in personnel management and training positions with Waltons, Unilever and other private firms; Neil Radford had a lecturing and librarian career with the University of Sydney and was Fisher Librarian

1980–96; Stephen D'Alton enjoyed an academic career in sociology at the University of New South Wales; David Neilson was vice-principal at La Trobe University (1988–94) and held other administrative positions in the tertiary education and health sectors; Phillip Maxwell was Professor of Mineral Economics and Mine Management at Curtin University; Steve Harrison, after teaching in Economic Statistics, held senior Sydney University administrative positions including those of deputy principal and bursar, before becoming CEO of the Institute of Chartered Accountants in Australia in 1991; Maxwell Aiken became Professor of Commerce at La Trobe University; Bob Walker and Bill Birkett became professors of Accounting at the University of New South Wales; Michael Berry became Professor of Urban Studies and Planning at RMIT; Yew Kwang Ng became Professor of Economics at Monash University; and Sidney Gray Professor and head of the School of Business at the University of Sydney from 2003 after an academic career in Australia, New Zealand and Great Britain.

Not surprisingly, many graduates built major careers within the private sector, in banking and finance, in management and industry, as well as in financial and other forms of journalism. The names of various distinguished graduates follow, commencing with those who mainly found employment in the financial sector.

From the 1963 graduates, David Clarke became executive chairman of Macquarie Bank in 1985; Leigh Hall worked in various finance and investment companies until becoming general manager of investment operations for the AMP Society from 1988; Colin Baxter became manager of the New South Wales National Mutual group from 1984 after roles in similar companies over the previous two decades. Ian Payne, a 1965 graduate, rose in his career in the Commonwealth Bank to executive director (1992–97) and was chairman of the Export Finance and Insurance Corporation from 1997. Amongst 1967 graduates Tony Berg held a variety of management positions in business including that of managing director of the Macquarie Bank (1984–93) and William Buttrose was director of ING Investment Management Limited (1995–2001) and general manager of Invest Ahead Limited from 2001. John Austin, another 1967 graduate, after a distinguished career in the Reserve Bank including Chief Economist in its Research Department, entered the private sector with a number of chairmanships in financial institutions. Peter Burrows, a 1968 graduate, had a distinguished business career including that of stockbroker (Bell Potter Securities Limited) from 2001, in addition to holding various honorary positions at the University of Sydney including fellow of the Senate, and president of the Medical Foundation and of the Power Foundation for Fine Arts; Graham Lenzner, also a 1968 graduate with employment as stockbroker, added a number of management positions and directorships to a distinguished business finance career. Robert Ferguson and David King, both 1969 graduates, also enjoyed distinguished careers in business. Ferguson became managing director of Bankers Trust in 1994, and King, following an earlier accounting career, as deputy general manager of the Australian office of the Banque Nationale de Paris and Directorships in Peko-Wallsend and Peko Oil. A 1971 graduate, Paul Biancardi, followed a partnership in Price Waterhouse Coopers with a directorship for Cashcard Australia Limited (from 2003) and various other chairman and directorship positions. Brian Johnson, a 1972 graduate, became a partner in

Arthur Andersen (1983–94) and managing partner in various consulting groups including EDS Management Consultants, Andersen Consulting, and Asia Pacific PA Consulting Group.

In the business sector more generally, many graduates of this period filled prominent management positions. John Campbell, a 1965 graduate, enjoyed a long career with CSR (including as its executive director of financial operations) before becoming CEO and managing director of the Australian Stock Exchange (1988–93) and chairman of the Victorian Power Exchange (from 1994). From the many 1967 graduates, Captain John Spiers, had a distinguished career in the shipping industry and in general marine consultancy; Bill Ferris held many company directorships and chairmanships; John Leaver did likewise, including CVC Limited from 1994; Fergus McDonald combined consultancy with many directorship positions; Anthony Sherlock, after many years as a partner in Coopers and Lybrand (1976–96), became company director in a wide array of business; Geoff Kells built a major career in CSR including that of managing director from 1993; Phillip Chandler followed a career with Dalgety by entering the field of management and marketing consultancy; while Roy Lawrence became executive director of the Retail Trades Association of New South Wales from 1985. Among the 1968 graduates, Robert Dalziel held directorships and managing directorships in various enterprises ranging from the retail sector to Cable and Wireless Optus; and Robert Whyte held directorships and other managing positions in Thomas Cook Travel (Australia and New Zealand), Advance Bank, Publishing and Broadcasting Limited and Trafalgar Properties Limited. Of the 1969 graduates, Glenn Dudley held management positions in several companies including Metal Manufacturers (1988–2000), Hudson Timber and Hardware and Vinidex; Gregory Gardiner did likewise with Hitachi, media organisations including Channel 7, and in private health insurance; while Geoffrey Hill had an extensive career in merchant banking and as company director in a wide range of industries. Amongst 1970 graduates, Phillip Scanlan held management positions in Hallmark Asia Pacific and Reflex Holdings, and Joseph Skrzynskie (Fellow of Senate from 2008) in Castle Harlan, Sheridan Global Holdings, MIA Group, Rogen International and the Opera House Trust, the Film Commission and the National Capital Planning Authority. Bob Wicht, a 1971 graduate, became a managing partner with Coopers and Lybrand from 1994; while 1972 graduate, Gregory Andrews, held various positions in the arts and cultural sector, including the Australian National Gallery, the Queensland Cultural Central Trust, the Helpmann Academy and the National Museum of Australia, after an initial career with the New South Wales Auditor General's Department.

Three graduates from this decade had distinguished careers in the world of journalism and the media more generally. Max Walsh, a 1966 graduate, edited the *Australian Financial Review* (1974–81), was editor in chief of the *Bulletin* (from 1998) after a career with the *Sydney Morning Herald* and interspersed with work on television, including the *Carleton-Walsh Report* on the ABC (1985–87). Chris Anderson, a 1967 graduate, worked as managing editor for various media companies including the ABC (1993–95), as editor in chief for the *Sydney Morning Herald* and as editor of the *Sun-Herald* before becoming CEO of Optus in

1997. Another 1967 graduate, Clem Lloyd, became foundation Professor of Journalism at the University of Wollongong after an academic research career in the Australian National University and a political career as adviser to the leader of the opposition (1978–80), press secretary to the Minister for Urban and Regional Development (1974–75) and a formative decade as sub-editor and journalist in Sydney and Canberra (1955–66).

In short, the BEc continued to be either a starting point or a mature-age qualification for many interesting careers in business, finance, government and the universities, and undoubtedly assisted many graduates to gain distinction and leadership in their chosen fields.

Only a few students provided reminiscences of their student years during the 1960s. Colin Dennett, who graduated in 1966, recalled his lonely existence as an undergraduate from semi-rural Castle Hill, who failed to make friends easily despite his attempts to do so at the Union Refectory or at Manning House. In those years, he recalled that conservative dress for students (Bermuda jacket, collar and tie) was for him still the order of the day, as indeed it was for most students in the professional faculties. He failed Accounting I and Economic Statistics I, a victim of the high first-year failure rates then in operation. Given the long distance between university and place of residence, he also detested the late evening lectures in Law I and II, especially when the Law II lecturer, Barry O'Keefe, failed to turn up, as apparently was then all too often the case. His one-line recollections of various lecturers are worth quoting: Hermann Black; 'likeable, interesting and a good teacher'; Ron Gates: 'studious and deadly boring'; Harry Edwards: 'always enjoyed his lectures'. Derek Horner: 'A real tragedy. He should probably have been advised never to lecture. Treated very badly by many students'; Peter Standish: 'pompous but good lecturer'; Peter Westerway: 'excellent lecturer who made his subject interesting'; Ted Wheelwright: 'hated the elite but gave the impression he was one'; Ray Chambers: 'down to earth with his general theory of accounting'; Victor Argy: 'excellent lecturer and good with students'. However, in his four years as undergraduate student in the faculty, Dennett could not recall ever having encountered Butlin as dean. Nevertheless, he appreciated the experience on the whole, particularly because it steered him into a career with the Trade Practices Commission, in which he rose to assistant commissioner.

Donna Lance, who graduated in 1972, completed her degree over five years as a part-time student. She especially recalled her enjoyment of John Goodhew as teacher in Economic Statistics, undoubtedly 'my favourite lecturer'. Goodhew 'always enjoyed a joke, even at his own expense, which they often were due to the nature of students … In a time when it was "cool" to be brash and crude and liberated, he was a gentleman who made the few girls in the course feel welcome and comfortable. He was only a young man … but very considerate.' She also did some debating with the Economics Faculty team, 'and it was great fun, particularly the staff/student debates with people like Sir Hermann Black in the opposition. Sir Hermann was also a very approachable man … And he always greeted me in the "corridors of power" as if I were a great friend.' Her tutor, David Hill, was also fondly remembered. He had persuaded her to enter the Economics debating team, and she recalled his weekly budgeting from his tutor's salary as an exercise in perpetual indebtedness, necessitating debt repayment on pay days which, after a drinking bout 'at the White Horse' that evening, started a similar cycle of indebtedness until the following pay day.

A third student, who wishes to remain anonymous, started studies in Merewether in 1968 (the last year of the *ancien régime*, as she put it). She completed her honours year in Government in 1971. Hermann Black taught Economics I either in Lecture Theatre 1 or in the Wallace, with his 'own idiosyncratic idea of economic theory … My second year was the first Hogan year, when equations ruled and people failed in droves.' However, 'Ted Wheelwright's course on the history of economic thought taught me that economics was not necessarily all about the ruling class.' Your class on public finance taught me that "economic theory did not rule out humanity".' On her Industrial Relations classes she recalls they had to be 'shared with engineers, who were completely out of control and lived up to every engineering stereotype'. However, she realised later from talking with two women students in Engineering at that time that her experience was as nothing compared to theirs. Ken Turner lectured in Government I, but Henry Mayer persuaded her to attempt honours during his second-year classes. She 'found him quite inspiring. I can recall him saying that you should always be suspicious when someone tells you that something is "just common sense", because common sense is always not to be trusted … I have found that advice always worth following. He was also a very nice man, who was very kind to me when I was having a hard time in third year.' Bob Connell, who supervised her honours thesis, 'was quite a hero of the times, having recently returned from Berkeley and being a participant in the anti-Vietnam movement, and the Prince Val haircut and combat boots added a romantic aura'. She greatly enjoyed a seminar run by Terry Irving and Denis Altman on Crisis and Conflict in American Politics. 'I also did Military Politics with Peter King, who spent a lot of time gazing reflectively at a corner of the ceiling. John Power did pretty much the same reflective gazing, combined with pipe cleaning, in Community Politics.'

Overall, her university experience was mixed. She found it was not an easy environment to enter from a working-class background and a state school education. Students 'were very conservative'. Moreover, in her tutorials she was often the only girl, and found that 'everyone else either lived on the North Shore or in the eastern suburbs'. Economics Society parties brought her 'first contact with the boat race', a 'fairly degraded [form] of drinking behaviour' fortunately confined to the male students present. She preferred an occasional trip to the Lalla Rookh and the White Horse. Nor was her economics degree an immediate entrée into a banking career as she had initially thought; the Commonwealth Bank stated they preferred girls with psychology degrees so that they could work in personnel; at the Reserve Bank she was the only female applicant with a degree, all the rest were school leavers. 'Yet having an Economics degree was a good thing for me in just about every way', even if she did not think that university had become more egalitarian and that, in her final year, she had been disappointed because Australian Politics was not on offer.

A student's lecture notes from the new era

The lecture notes reviewed in this section were taken by Robert Brown, a student for the BEc from 1971 to 1974, his final honours year. He graduated with first-class honours in Economics in 1975. On graduation he worked as a research officer for the Commonwealth Bank and tutored for some years (1976–78) in the faculty. He then went to Monash University where he rose from lecturer to National Australia Bank Professor of Finance in 1996. In 2001, he moved to the University of Melbourne as its Professor of Finance. His student record was very distinguished: no examination mark below 70 and high distinctions in his honours subject in 1973 and 1974. He won the Frank Albert Proficiency Prize for first and third year of the degree, and four other prizes. His first-year subjects in 1971 were Economics I, Descriptive Economics, Government I and Law I; he took Economics II honours, Industrial Relations I and General Pure Mathematics in 1972; Economics III honours, Industrial Relations II and Econometric Methods in 1973, and completed his final honours year in 1974 by coursework, taking Advanced Micro-Economics, Advanced Macro-Economics, Applied Economic Development, Quantitative Economics II and Welfare Economics. He subsequently completed an MEc.

In 1971, Economics I had a micro-economics and quantitative economics component, consisting of two and one lectures per week. In the A course then compulsory for all Economics Faculty students, lectures were given by Neil Conn, Frank Stilwell and John Zerby. The lecture notes and course outlines indicate the contents of the course was a strictly conventional, theoretical exposition of mainstream micro-economics (fundamental propositions, consumer theory, production theory, price and output theory under different market forms, distribution theory and elementary welfare economics). The quantitative component consisted of basic mathematics for economists (first term), and issues in statistical inference (second and third terms). Descriptive Economics dealt with growth, stability and resource allocation in first term (Geelum Simpson-Lee), the corporate sector in second term (Ted Wheelwright) and issues of economic policy (Nigel Stokes) and the labour market (Louis Haddad) in third term. In Government I, Trevor Matthews in Lent term gave an introduction to political thought (democracy, pressure groups, public opinion, pluralism), Ken Turner lectured on the Australian political system in second term; while in third term Warren Osmond, Terry Irving, Henry Mayer and Peter King lectured on political alternatives, liberty, the media and foreign policy issues. Law I was given by Pat Mills as a general introduction to the law. His lectures covered aspects of constitutional law, legal concepts in general, and topics in commercial law (sale of goods, contracts, agency, damages and so on). Exercises set in the last two subjects were interesting and designed to foster individual student initiative: for example, the study of a local political party branch in Government I; the analysis of a self-selected 'law report' in Law I.

Economics II consisted of two lectures a week on macro-economics (taught by D.M. Kannangara, Colin Simkin and Tony Phipps) covering finance and national income accounting (first term), elementary spending functions and multiplier analysis (second term) and macro-economic policy including fiscal, monetary and incomes policies (third term). The lectures all had a high mathematical and statistical content, incorporating lots of equations (Brown's lecture notes literally overflowed with them). Honours students in addition needed to do two options. As an honours student, Brown had to take Mathematical Economics (taught by Neil Conn) and chose Current Economic Problems (taught by Hermann Black and Gavin Butler) as the other option. The last dealt with economic growth, demographic issues, planning, health and education economics (Black), environmental issues and agricultural policy (Butler). Economics II honours seminars provided in depth coverage of economic policy issues (often from highly technical perspectives, such as that of the Reserve Bank model). The Mathematical Economics option covered techniques for static and dynamic equilibrium analysis, comparative statics and optimisation theory. Industrial Relations I provided a broad introduction to industrial relations theory and practice including its connection with labour economics, industrialisation, conflict and bargaining (Kingsley Laffer), psychological and organisational aspects (Maxine Bucklow) and legal issues (Geoff Sorrell). Malcolm Rimmer gave an introduction to the history of trade unionism. The reading list for the last segment included a fascinating misprint: 'Trade Unions in the Repression' (instead of Depression, as the context required), an interesting slip. As a non-faculty course, the contents of the General Pure Mathematics course, clearly invaluable for Brown's type of course selection, need not be summarised in detail.

Economics III consisted of a compulsory component (International Economics) and two options (three for honours students, for whom Advanced Economic Theory and Quantitative Economics I were compulsory). In 1973, International Economics was taught by Tony Phipps, Jim Wilson and Gavin Butler, who lectured on pure theory, on monetary aspects and on policy issues. Advanced Economic Theory had a micro-economics component with topics in methodology, conflict and cooperation, consumer theory, equilibrium analysis, and welfare economics (Evan Jones), and economic growth models from Smith, Ricardo and Marx to Kaldor, Solow, Leontief and von Neumann (Colin Simkin). Both courses were very mathematical, particularly the second, so that the compulsory Quantitative Economics I course was clearly required, given its emphasis on advanced mathematical methods for analysing economic issues in optimisation, stability and growth (Geoff Lewis). For his one, genuine third-year option, Brown chose the Political Economy of Modern Capitalism (taught by Ted Wheelwright) as an obvious antidote to this heavy mathematical fare: Wheelwright's course discussed the views of Veblen, Hobson, Marx, Schumpeter, Galbraith and issues associated with the state, globalisation and underdevelopment. Seminars for Economics III were devoted to growth theory (Debesh Bhattacharya) and international trade (Geelum Simpson-Lee, who warned students that his duties as dean would mean frequent alterations of the meeting times set down for the course in the timetable). Industrial Relations II included topics in the rule of law, arbitration, new industrial arrangements for the waterfront, and industrial democracy (Maxine Bucklow), arbitration and wage theory (Kingsley Laffer) and industrial law (Geoff Sorrell). Brown's third course, Econometric Methods, was taught by Steve Harrison, Stuart Rutherford and Ernie Houghton. The last course gave students a chance to assess the lectures and their presentation by way of a student questionnaire, which served as well as a means for testing the market for statistics courses. Given his mathematical preparation, Brown scored a good high distinction for the last course, and the highest mark he obtained for a degree course with the exception of Law I.

Five options, given as lectures and/or seminar courses, constituted Brown's choice for completing his honours course in Economics IV. Advanced Micro-Economics consisted of a critical examination of the theory of the firm (Frank Stilwell), and topics including methodology, competition and conflict (Evan Jones). Advanced Macro-Economics consisted of lectures and seminars on income distribution theory (Jim Wilson). Applied Economic Development was presented as lectures and seminars by Gavin Butler and René Cordoni, a visitor to the Economics Department for part of 1974. The Welfare Economics course was taught by Bill Merrilees and Evan Jones, and covered welfare maximisation, issues of social choice, and welfare economics as applied to the state. Finally, the Quantitative Economics II course (later called Macro-Econometric Model Building) consisted of lectures and seminars given by Viv Hall and by visitors from Treasury and the Reserve Bank, who discussed details of the models constructed within their organisations. Brown's experience reflects the quantitative and mathematical nature of a substantial segment of the faculty degree so characteristic of the early 1970s, and introduced substantially by Hogan and Simkin as the new professors of Economics. This played a major role in the 'political economy dispute', discussed in Chapter 5.

The faculty's Golden Jubilee, 1970

In 1970 the faculty had its fiftieth jubilee. Little was done to celebrate this milestone. A special supplement included with the 1970 *Economic Review*, however, published selected contributions on faculty history by Butlin as dean, Hermann Black as the longest serving staff member, and Geelum Simpson-Lee as another long-time member of faculty. The first two of these articles were cited earlier in this chapter; Simpson-Lee's brief article drew attention to what he called 'the Sydney tradition—an academic value system implanted by Mills, nurtured and grown to maturity by Butlin'. The article contained an implied critique of the drive to increased mathematisation and quantification in economics by the new professors, Hogan and Simkin, and an appeal for tolerance and permissiveness, especially in departmental teaching. Simpson-Lee demanded a broad scientific method for application to the social sciences including economics, with an emphasis on empiricism rather than on the economic history which constituted the major research work of Mills and Butlin. The Sydney tradition according to Simpson-Lee stood also in opposition to the emerging 'go-getting academic', and a growing 'publish or perish' syndrome, which he implicitly associated with the new wave sweeping the Economics Department. This last remark, ironically, came from a person who himself showed few signs of practising the Sydney tradition in his own published research, of which, in any case, nothing appeared during the 1960s. The 1970 jubilee supplement also contained brief pen portraits of the faculty's first two deans, Irvine and Mills.

It seems surprising that no mention of the jubilee was made at 1970 faculty meetings, or that no other celebrations of this event seems to have taken place. Several explanations can be offered for this omission. The first is that the starting year of the faculty was treated somewhat ambiguously during this period; the *Faculty Handbook* occasionally claiming that 1921 was the year it had all begun (for example, the *1973 Faculty Handbook*, p. 1). 1922, however, was the year (see chapter 1 above) when Irvine was forced to resign by the university Senate and Mills could start afresh as Professor of Economics and as Dean of the Faculty of Economics. Moreover, given the growing quarrels among the professors of Economics, and the 1969 transfer of Butlin as Professor of Economics to head of a freshly created Department of Economic History, Butlin was probably not in the mood to initiate official celebrations of this important faculty anniversary, particularly when Hogan and Simkin as the professors of the faculty's senior department would inevitably have had a substantial role in such festivities. The students and SUES were therefore left to organise their own celebrations in the form of the eleven-page supplement to the *Economic Review*, prefaced by their own editorial explanation as to why the celebrations had to be somewhat hushed:

> The year 1970 marks a significant turning point for the Faculty. In a somewhat quiet fashion we celebrated the fiftieth anniversary of its foundation. In the same year the world wide trend to exacuate [*sic*] the social sciences manifested itself in the unprecedented course changes in the department of economics. There was also a trend in 1970 which, though not as widespread, did find expression in the futile cries of too few academics for greater relevance in the social sciences, and almost by-passed our faculty completely.
>
> These two trends may at first appear contradictory. The introduction of Mathematics into the study of Economics was viewed by some as an attempt to 'scientificise' Economics and thereby alter the 'social' mask which disguised this field of study. The real danger lies in the adoption of mathematics as an end in itself; accuracy must be sought only as a means towards precise and careful analysis of social conditions and problems. Quantitative analysis complements the qualitative approach and only the latter can provide relevant analysis of real situations, only the latter can link theory to reality. In the field of humanities scientific analysis must remain only a sophisticated instrument.
>
> While it is readily recognised that mathematics is necessary for a full understanding of Economics, other fields have not received such recognition. Economics could well be supplemented by an integrated study of sociology, psychology and politics. 'Ceteris paribus' assumptions serve only to distort reality forcing Economics into a dreamworld of theory. (*Economic Review 1970*, p. 6)

Sydney University Economics Society and the Economic Review

The Sydney University Economics Society (SUES) was active for the whole of the period covered by this chapter, arranging faculty sports and debating teams, smokos and the annual ball, freshers' welcomes and farewells to final-year students, and producing the *Economic Review*. In 1963, a harbour cruise replaced the traditional freshers' welcome and Les Philpott (a 1933 Arts graduate) addressed a 'men's dinner' on 'His Times in the Faculty'. Attendance and support for these functions could vary tremendously from year to year. Thus the Economics Ball attracted 600 persons in 1964 and 450 in 1966, despite the introduction of a Miss Economics Quest that year as part of the entertainment provided at the start of the ball. Jenny Sahuza won this event in 1967, but that appears also to have been the last occasion such a quest was organised by SUES. Guest speakers featured on the program as well. Les Bury, then the federal Minister for Housing, and A.V. Loginov, the Soviet Ambassador, spoke at dinners held during 1966; Sir Roden Cutler, a former graduate, was a guest speaker in 1967.

The move to the Merewether Building in 1965 enabled the establishment of a student coffee shop, which for 1969–70 reported a profit of $457.90, the only recorded financial outcome of this entrepreneurial activity preserved in the university Archives. As discussed earlier in this chapter, staff/student liaison became a growing responsibility for SUES office bearers from the late 1960s onwards. At another level, staff and students interacted in debating. An example is the 1966 public debate between Nick Greiner, Max Wilson and Phil Chandler for the students, Hermann Black, Helmut Kolsen and Peter Groenewegen for the staff. Donna Lance recalled participating in similar debates arranged during subsequent years. However, the society's office bearers also complained in 1966–67 about the lack of support for society activities from such a large faculty.

Presidents of SUES for the decade were as follows. For 1962–64, M.K.H. Powell was in the chair; for 1964–65, Ian Hutchins; for 1965–66, Nick Greiner; for 1966–67, Phil Chandler; for 1968–69, David Scarf; for 1969–70, Sidney Gray; for 1970–71, Peter Wright; and for 1971–72, Eric de Haas. Although other office bearers of SUES undoubtedly played major roles in keeping SUES activities going, in what follows only the editors of the *Economic Review* can be individually named.

Regular publication of its journal was in fact the more permanent legacy of SUES over this decade, an achievement all the more valuable because the *Review* regretfully became a casualty of the intra-faculty struggles over 'political economy' which effectively ended this exercise in staff–student cooperation. A summary of the contents of its issues illustrates the flavour of student opinion as expressed over these years.

The 1965 issue was edited by Tony Berg and Greg Wood. It featured student articles on economic and accounting topics, reminiscences by student politicians from Student Representative Council and Union, practical dissertations including one on how to make money in the stock market, book reviews and a list of final-year students soon to disappear into the real world. Contributors included Nick Greiner, Peter Forsyth, Jim Spigelman, Max Wilson, Nigel Stokes, Cecily Small, George Braddock and Bill Ferris from the students, and Vic Argy as lone representative of the staff. The 1966 issue (edited by Wayne Lonergan and David McGrane) contained much of the same, and included many of the previous year's contributors (Nick Greiner, Max Wilson, Jim Spigelman and Bill Ferris). Michael Kirby was a new student contributor, while Ken Broadhead provided an epitaph for the evening student, whose existence was to be phased out by faculty decree from the following year onwards. Staff contributions, however, increased. Vic Argy was joined in this issue by Bill Birkett, Ron Brooker and Stuart Rutherford.

The 1967 *Review* (edited by Lyn Carroll and Ross Hutcheson) adopted a larger format but preserved a similar mix of content and some familiar authors (Nick Greiner, Nigel Stokes, Peter Forsyth, Bill Ferris and Ron Brooker). An Economics honours student (Robert Douglas) defended the use of mathematics in economics, Wheelwright made some observations on the Chinese economy, Bill Ferris queried the value of a BEc without accounting, Hermann Black reviewed the latest on Britain's entry into Europe and Bob Baxt looked at tougher legislative controls for company directors. There were also five book reviews including one by Bruce McFarlane of Wheelwright's *Anatomy of Australian Manufacturing Industry* and one by Joe Skrzynskie of Hylda Rolfe's *The Controllers*. The 1968 issue (edited by David Hill) was bound in a pink psychedelic cover (a picturesque ode to love, and very much a reflection of the times). It also contained lots of photographs by Chris Hall. There were long (as compared with previous issues) articles on economic growth (Russell Warnken), the cost of conscription (Jack Frish, David Mortimer and Jo Skrzynskie), the benefits of studying economics (Brian McLennan), the case for planning in Australia (Roy Bennett), capital and socialism (Brian McLennan again), the tariff (Charles Thomas), accounting and consolidated statements (Frank Clarke), and one on Winnie the Pooh and Ray Chambers (Chris Hall) which amusingly juxtaposed comparable passages drawn from A.A. Milne's children's classics and the writings of faculty's distinguished Professor of Accounting. Five book reviews brought the issue to a close.

The 1969 *Economic Review* was edited by David Mortimer and Joe Skrzynskie. It contained reminiscences of his student days from Hermann Black, Richard Ackland on tariffs, Kimberly St Mortske on 'Soviet Planning and Investment Criteria', Tom Perry with two articles, on 'Foreign Investment' and on 'Innovation and Research in Australian Industry', Mike Berry on the value of studying other men's ideas, Percy Allen on Australian student revolt, Warren Hogan on economic development, Nigel Stokes on congestion and pollution, and a note on the birth of the Sydney University Pacioli Society for Accounting staff and students, followed by Nick Greiner's recollections of his experiences as a Harvard MBA student.

The 1970 Jubilee issue was edited by Martin Indyk and Michael Milston, the first of whom later gained a major international reputation in international affairs as American Ambassador to Israel, and subsequently as adviser to President Clinton on the Middle East. The 1970 *Economic Review*'s articles contained student and staff contributions in almost equal numbers, as well as a single review of an economics text. To match its editorial on the 50-year jubilee already quoted, it started with Rutherford's article on 'the use and abuse of mathematics in economics', as well as a piece from Rutherford's colleague, T.A. Ramasubban, on 'data collection and analysis in economic investigation'. Debesh Bhattacharya raised the issue of 'starvation or plenty' for the developing world, while student contributions dealt with 'Accounting Information and United Kingdom Takeover Bids' (C.W.F. Beelaerts),

Economic Society Office bearers (1966–67).
Opp. page: changing covers for the *Economics Review* (1955–75).

racial issues in 'Cops + Niggers = Dynamite' (Dianne Johnstone), 'New Developments in Economic Theory' (D.H. Jacobs), 'The American Left in the Sixties' (Martin Indyk), 'Institutional Advertising' (Bob Loader) and 'Working Mothers—a Need for Research' (Michael Milston).

The final issue of the *Economic Review* for discussion in this chapter, that for 1971–72, was edited by Claus Cordes and Eric Forbes. Much of its contents were devoted to environmental and political issues, though Chambers contributed an interesting article on accounting reform to demonstrate the relevance of accounting theory on practice. Peter Hall discussed 'Revolution in Africa—Tanzania 1961-71', Bill Winning 'New Guinea-Trouble Ahead' and Richard Sappey 'The Black Australia Policy', while James Weaver examined 'the Consequences of Economic Growth', Frank Stilwell 'Reallocating Australian Growth', Paul Roberts 'The Destruction of the Myall Lakes' and Hermann Black reviewed the pollution versus growth debate under the title, 'Development and Doctrine'. This turned out to be the penultimate issue. The last *Economic Review* appeared in 1973 and is discussed in Chapter 5. The contents of the 1971–72 issue clearly reflected the demand for reform so characteristic of the years before Whitlam Laborism, which triumphed at the ballot box in 1972, ending 23 years of continuous Liberal–Country Party government begun in 1949 with Menzies defeat of Chifley. The *Review*, it may be reiterated, became an early victim of the growing antagonisms within the faculty which climaxed during the mid-seventies. Nor should it be forgotten that Butlin's strong encouragement of this venture departed with him when he left the university in 1971, so that the final two issues were far less lavishly produced than their predecessors in the 1960s.

The Sydney University Economics Graduates Association, 1963–72

The faculty's graduates association, founded in 1953, continued its activities over the decade from 1963 with dinners, a Christmas party and occasional attempts at fundraising activities for the faculty. In this context, its role in the Wolstenholme Library Appeal in 1964 has already been mentioned. This had been initiated under the presidency (1962–64) of Bruce Allen (a 1937 graduate, some of whose student reminiscences were presented in Chapter 2), when an official membership of 54 was reported. Sheila Chaffey (a 1939 graduate) took over as president in 1965, during which year membership more than doubled to 114, partly the result of a successful function to view the new Merewether Building and a Manning House Christmas party which attracted 100 members and friends. At its 1965 annual general meeting E.J. Eyers spoke on the implications of mortgage insurance for housing. During 1965–66, membership rose to a phenomenal 568 (which included 48 signed-up 1966 graduates) and a very successful annual meeting was held at the Weinkeller restaurant in August 1966. John Gadson (a 1949 graduate) was elected president for 1966–67, and membership once again declined to the one hundred mark. Gadson was succeeded as president in 1970–71 by Keith Bracken (a 1962 graduate). The annual general meeting (20 October 1970) attracted only 27, but the Christmas party at the Weinkeller did better (70 attended). The 1970 annual dinner at the Wentworth Hotel also drew a good crowd. It had invited Hermann Black as guest of honour (to mark his election as chancellor and retirement from the teaching staff) and featured Dr Robert Nielson (from the Area Transport Study) as guest speaker on 'Transport Problems in Australia and the United States'. The dinner also noted with regret Syd Butlin's imminent departure from the faculty as the end of a long era. Another 1970 function featured Mr Justice Le Gay Brereton as guest speaker. For 1971–73, the chair was taken by Ellis Setton (a 1964 graduate), during whose period in office membership rose from 49 to 61.

The graduates association clearly experienced fluctuating fortunes over the decade under discussion. A strong alumni tradition was not really part of the faculty's experience, despite the efforts by SUEGA committee members to achieve this end. Much later, the association decided to publish a regular newsletter under the title, *The Sydney Economist*, the first issue of which appeared in 1987.

Research and scholarship, 1963–72

For the greater part of this decade, details on research publications by department were published annually in the *University Calendar* after a two-year lag. The Government Department continued to be the faculty's most prolific publishers, closely followed by Accounting. Economics performed relatively poorly in the research area, even with its research output initially inflated by the inclusion of that from the economic historians (until 1969) and from Industrial Relations (until 1975). However, Economic Statistics was by far the poorest performer: it only listed a minor monograph in 1967, an ANZAAS paper in 1969, and three articles (all contributed by new staff) during 1971.

The most substantial individual publication record for the faculty was that of Ray Chambers. Over the decade in question, he reported three books, 63 articles and five chapters in books. Much of his work was also translated into Italian and Spanish, and many of his articles appeared in the international journal literature. Some of the honours he reaped for his research need to be mentioned. For example, in 1964 he was elected Fellow of the Academy of Social Sciences in Australia, one of the few faculty members with this distinction. The others were Syd Butlin (a foundation member), Henry Mayer (elected 1965) and Colin Simkin (1970).

For the ten years from 1963, the excellent Accounting publication record was also greatly assisted by Pat Mills, Ron Brooker, Bob Baxt, Ron Bowra and by the department's own graduates who had joined the staff, Bob Walker, Bill Birkett, George Foster, John Staunton and Frank Clarke, to name the more important. Chambers' magnificent example in research was clearly contagious and actively followed by his junior colleagues, many of whom considered themselves to be his devoted and loyal students.

The Government Department continued to produce a steady flow of publications from its members, all of whom did in fact publish over the period covered by this chapter. Thirty-seven individual members of the Government Department therefore reported publications over this period, even if they sometimes spent only a few years there as a staff member. Henry Mayer was the major departmental publisher, with six books (most of them edited), twenty articles and one chapter in a book. Dick Spann, his senior professorial colleague, had three books (all edited), nine articles and seven chapters in books to his credit. Jim Richardson, the single associate professor in Government by the end of 1972, recorded two books, sixteen articles and two chapters in books over the seven years he was a member of the department. Other strong publishers included Carol Bell, who during her four years with the department reported one book, nine articles and one book chapter; Ken Turner (eleven articles and three chapters); Peter King (one book, nine articles and two chapters); John Power (one book, eight articles and three chapters); Ian Grosart (one book, eight articles and three chapters); Bob Connell (in three years with the department, two books, fourteen articles and four chapters) while veteran Tom Kewley reported three books, five articles and one chapter. It would be tedious to list all the publication details for the other 27 Government Department members over this period, apart from noting they included five women and a number of subsequent key players in department and faculty, among whom were Rex Mortimer, Terry Irving, Michael Leigh and Ross Curnow.

Although Economic History did not become a separate department until 1969, its publications are separately recorded here. Ken Buckley (with one book, seven articles and one chapter) was the major publisher, while Boris Schedvin (with one book and five articles) and Sybil Jack (nine articles) were not far behind. Before his departure for Hong Kong in 1967, Alan Birch had published five articles while John McCarty and Barbara Little reported one article each during their short time in the department.

In Industrial Relations, here likewise treated as the separate department it did not become until 1975, Kingsley Laffer published eighteen articles and four chapters in books; Maxine

Bucklow, one article and four chapters, Geoff Sorrell, two books (one jointly) and one article, while Malcolm Rimmer published a book. The last two were then very much newcomers to the department, arriving during 1971 and 1972.

Despite its size, the Economics Department was outperformed in publications by the Government Department for virtually the whole of the second half of the century. Its professors, for a start, did not quite set the example in this regard provided by Ray Chambers in Accounting, or for that matter by Henry Mayer and Dick Spann in Government. Syd Butlin reissued one of his books with a new introduction, and published two articles; Harry Edwards, until his departure in 1965, reported five articles; Warren Hogan after 1968 reported seven articles, two book chapters and a two-page note in the prestigious *American Economic Review*; Colin Simkin from 1969 one book, four articles and five chapters. The two associate professors had completely opposite publication records: Ted Wheelwright reported five books (two of them joint), eleven articles, six chapters in books, two monographs and one report; Jim Wilson by contrast could only list five CEDA reports on development issues in the two years immediately preceding his promotion. Helmut Kolsen, before his departure to Brisbane in 1968, reported eight articles, two encyclopaedia entries and one book chapter. The senior lecturers likewise displayed an uneven publication performance. Vic Argy published four articles (three in international journals) before his departure for the International Monetary Fund in 1967; Neil Conn six articles and a book chapter, Sol Kim three articles and Peter Groenewegen eleven. Of the freshly appointed lecturers from 1970, Frank Stilwell and Debesh Bhattacharya each reported one book and seven articles, Gavin Butler one book (with two joint authors) and two articles; Judy Yates, Viv Hall and Geoff Lewis reported one publication each. As senior tutor, Hugh Pritchard published four articles and two book chapters, while tutor Bill Waters reported two articles in 1969.

No fewer than five journals were edited from within the faculty. *Abacus*, a journal of accounting and business, was edited by Ray Chambers; the *Australian Economic History Review* had Jules Ginswick as one of its three editors; the *Journal of Industrial Relations* was edited by Kingsley Laffer; *Public Administration* was edited by Dick Spann and *Politics* by Henry Mayer. In addition, the Department of Government published two series of monographs: Sydney Studies in Politics and Occasional Monographs. The Economics Department housed no regular economic publication, though it began publishing a series of working papers by staff members and visitors from 1975. The faculty continued to host and publish the R.C. Mills Memorial Lectures, of which three were presented between 1963 and 1972. 'The Vicissitudes of an Export Economy: Britain since 1880', was given by R.S. Sayers in March 1965; 'Indicative Economic Planning in the United Kingdom' by E.H. Phelps-Brown in July 1969; and 'Developments in Monetary Theory of Policy' by faculty graduate and Reserve Bank Governor, J.G. Phillips, in April 1971 (reprinted in Groenewegen 2004, chapters 3–5).

Faculty research during this period began to be supported by research money from university and other sources. In 1963, Economics received £200 from the ANZ Bank, £100 each from the Commonwealth Bank, the Commercial Banking Company of Sydney and the Bank of New South Wales, £50 from the Rural Bank and £35 from CSR a total of £585 for economic research (SM: 8 October 1963). In 1964, Anderson Analysis donated £200, Unilever £150 and the Reserve Bank £4200 for economic research, the second donation undoubtedly generated by Harry Edwards' research on the detergent industry (SM: 3 February 1964). In 1965, the Reserve Bank's research fund provided £1772 for Ted Wheelwright's work on ownership and control of Australian companies, and £2500 for research into liquidity, its significance and control (SM, 8 February 1965). Later that year, the ANZ Bank provided a further £100 for research, as did the Reserve Bank with an additional £2310 (SM, 6 November, 6 December 1965). During 1968, the Reserve Bank provided $1800 to assist preparation of an econometric model of financial interaction in Australia (SM: 5 February 1968), the Bank of New South Wales donated $200 for the *Australian Economic History Review* (SM: 4 March 1968). This was followed by donations for the same purpose of $200 from the Reserve Bank, $100 from the Commercial Banking Company of Sydney (SM: 6 May 1968) and $50 from the ANZ Bank (SM: 3 June 1968). The Reserve Bank also gave $2000 to assist publication of Boris Schedvin's book on the Great Depression in Australia, based on his PhD thesis (SM: 5 August 1969). In 1970, the Reserve Bank provided $3025 for Warren Hogan's research on foreign investment in Australian manufacturing, and $2900 to Neil Conn for research on technical progress in Australian manufacturing, with special reference to the impact of foreign capital inflow (SM: 2 February 1970). Later that year, Simkin received $240 to purchase a calculator for his research (SM: 4 August 1970). In December 1970, the Reserve Bank provided a further $2,550 for Neil Conn's research project, $2450 for Warren Hogan's and $4450 for research by Peter Groenewegen into Commonwealth budget making. T.M. Ramasubban gained $4000 from the Reserve Bank for statistical research. (SM: 7 December 1970). In 1971, Jim Wilson obtained $5000 from the Commonwealth Department of Immigration for a cost/benefit analysis of Australian immigration policy in the post-war period (SM, 6 December 1971). In total, Economics attracted over $54,000 in outside research money for the decade. This makes the department's poor research performance in terms of publications all the more disappointing.

Faculty research funding in 1969 totalled $53,160. This was made up from university funds ($30,504), Australian University Commission funding ($4859), ARGC funding ($7643), other government grants ($5761) and other funds from outside sources $4393 (*University of Sydney News*, 22 October 1970). Of the ARGC funding for 1970, $2350 went to Accounting and $13,242 to Government. Moreover, the Government Department in 1970 also obtained $2000 from the New South Wales government to prepare the yes/no case for a referendum on Sunday trading for hotels (SM: 1 December 1969). In 1970, ARGC was reported to have allocated $18,877 in grants for individual faculty members (SM: 2 November 1970), a statistic seemingly at odds with that provided by the *University News* during the previous month.

Towards the turbulent 1970s

Growing disquiet within the faculty and in the Economics Department was briefly reported in previous sections of this chapter. Contentious issues for the faculty included the nature and extent of student representation at faculty and at the departmental level; the election of Simpson-Lee as dean, the first time a non-professor had been elected; and the reform process in departments with respect to regular departmental meetings, an issue in which the faculty likewise involved itself. Scrutinising new course initiatives at the undergraduate level via the Curriculum Committee and reducing 'excessive' professorial powers (far more extensive in the 1970s than now) also became a perceived part of the faculty's reform agenda under its new, non-professorial dean. Moves to turn the faculty into a social sciences faculty were likewise not well received by all faculty members.

It was also indicated that major syllabus changes in Economics were made by its two new professors. These generated much hostility in some staff and especially from large numbers of students. The exclusive concentration on micro-economics as the core of Economics I, and the macro-economic emphasis of Economics II, were mentioned in this context, as was the high International Economics component of Economics III. Stronger criticism was attracted by what was perceived as excessive mathematisation of the syllabus, particularly in its Economics I and II core, and in the compulsory quantitative requirements for Economics honours students. Although by the end of 1970, these changes had been sweetened through the introduction of a substantial degree of choice with respect to part of the Economics II and III courses, the remaining degree of compulsion in these courses and the mathematical manner in which they were taught attracted much criticism and resentment from some students and staff

Student demands, and demonstrations in support of them, also rapidly developed, assisted by the experience gained by militant left-wing students in the anti-Vietnam war campaigns conducted within and without the university. Teach-ins, a concept imported from the United States, could be applied not only to enlighten students on national or international political issues such as the Vietnam conflict, they could be used very effectively for examining the power structures in the university at various levels, including purely administrative ones. In March 1970, students had invaded the registrar's offices, and 'occupations' of other parts of the university followed suit.

Many of these issues became enmeshed at the end of 1970 in an argument over the failure to reappoint two popular tutors in the Economics Department. The tutors in question, David Hill and Bill Waters, had both been highly critical of the course changes in Economics, and of the manner in which Hogan and Simkin as professors controlled departmental affairs. The issue attracted much attention in the student newspaper, *Honi Soit*. It described non-reappointment of the two tutors as their effective 'dismissal' and complained that this had occurred during November when students were busy with their examinations, thereby making it difficult for them to protest. The issue was also linked to the unpopular course changes (described as the new 'economaths') and to what was called 'the Manchester conspiracy' in economics. The last drew on the fact that Bruce Williams, the vice-chancellor, had previously been Professor of Economics at Manchester University and that Warren Hogan had spent time there on leave, while it was (wrongly) alleged that Simkin also had strong connections with Manchester University. Even Bill Horrigan, a Manchester academic before his appointment in 1968 as senior lecturer in the department, became part of this conspiracy theory. *Honi Soit* used 'the Manchester conspiracy' to 'explain' Butlin's removal as head of the Economics Department in 1969 and the ease with which the new Economics courses were introduced by Professors Hogan and Simkin (*Honi Soit*, 10 September, 9 November 1970).

The Hill and Waters affair was also raised in a letter to the vice-chancellor (17 November 1970) from Ted Wheelwright (on leave in Chile). This letter requested Senate to investigate the 'dismissal' of Hill and Waters as part of a wider investigation 'into the conduct of the Department'. Such an investigation would need to seek reasons for the non-renewal of their contracts, and for the recent controversies in the department over course changes, as a consequence of which Wheelwright feared 'some staff could be penalised'. In reply, Bruce Williams stated there was no need whatsoever to investigate the department, and he severely criticised Wheelwright's other arguments. Tutors were appointed on a year-to-year basis, with a maximum appointment of five years. Strictly speaking, it was therefore not a case of dismissal, but one where the tutors in question did not have their contracts renewed. There could be very valid reasons for such non-renewal. The Senate therefore decided to take no action. During the discussion, Arthur Deer (a 1936 graduate and prominent businessman) expressed the wish that faculty reverse its decision to abandon evening classes, and reiterated his request for information about the need for mathematics to be a prerequisite for the new economics courses (SM: 7 December 1970).

Simkin, appointed as head of the Economics Department for 1971–72, also commented on the issue in the *University News* (24 March 1971). He dismissed remarks about a Manchester conspiracy, indicating he himself had never visited Manchester University in his life, while Hogan had been there briefly for his research on foreign investment in Australia. He stressed that the course changes had all been approved by the department and that nothing had been done to curb Wheelwright's teaching (as *Honi Soit* had also alleged). On the non-reappointment of Hill and Waters, he indicated that Waters had been a tutor for three years, Hill for two. 'Neither had the academic capacity suited to the development of our courses. There was the opportunity for making better appointments, and in the interest of students this was done.' Simkin concluded his article by showing that the controversy had had no effect on 1971 enrolments in Economics. This implicitly responded to the claim in *Honi Soit* that the student survey conducted by Hill and Waters was the real reason for their 'dismissal'. This survey had found a high degree of student dissatisfaction with the contents of Economics I and II, but not with Descriptive Economics in the teaching of which Wheelwright was heavily involved. A report of the new Economics courses made by Peter Wright as student representative on faculty made at its June 1970 meeting (and not mentioned in the official minutes) provoked Simkin into calling Wright 'mendacious', a remark which Butlin as dean forced Simkin to retract. This was yet another example of the poor relations between the professors of Economics at this time (*Honi Soit*, Vol. 43, No. 15, p. 1).

Simkin's reply did not end the debate over professorial powers and the new courses. The issue continued to be raised in *Honi Soit* during 1971. It carried headlines that Hogan had fled the country (he had in fact departed on a period of study leave), that Waters had exposed Hogan's 'lies' about the 'dismissal' of the tutors, and that staff in the Economics Department continued to be intimidated (*Honi Soit*, Vol. 44, No. 1, pp. 4, 6). More importantly, *Honi Soit* reported on 1 April 1971 that six members of the Economics staff (Maurice Haddad, Louis Haddad, Margaret Power, Nigel Stokes, John Zerby and Debesh Bhattacharya) had petitioned Senate to establish an inquiry into the affairs of the department, with special reference to its new courses. Such an inquiry was not initiated until 1973, and then by faculty committee rather than a Senate inquiry. This is discussed in the next chapter. It more generally raises faculty aspects of the growing turmoil within the university associated with the prolonged 'political economy' dispute, including the unrest and threatened strikes within the Government Department and elsewhere in the faculty. These events, by no stretch of the imagination, can only be associated exclusively with debate over course changes. Much of this faculty and university turmoil was designed to confront the basic issue of 'authoritarian departmental decision making', particularly by professors. It thereby sought to address the need for excessive powers vested in professors and heads of departments in the universities of a democratic society, and the rights of students and non-professorial staff in academic decision making. This chapter has shown that these troubles had origins in the preceding decade, but came to the fore during 1970 and after. In this sense as well, the 1960s can be described as the end of an era for the faculty.

CHAPTER 5

Turmoil in the cloisters: University governance, student participation, and the Political Economy dispute, 1973–1984

Over the twelve years covered by this chapter, the faculty shared much debate over university governance with the university. This included the role of student participation in the decision making process at the various levels of university government. Moreover, professorial powers were also effectively reduced over these years, as symbolised in 1975 when the Professorial Board was replaced by an Academic Board. The last included all professors ex officio, together with elected sub-professorial staff and student members. In addition, the university's by-laws formalised the functions of departments, heads of departments and professors for the first time in its 125 years history. Important in fostering debate over governance issues and student involvement for the faculty was the 'political economy' dispute within the Economics Department. This continued, sometimes hot, sometimes less hot, for the whole period covered by this chapter. It often overwhelmed faculty deliberations, and occupied much time for the new Academic Board, the vice-chancellor, the registrar's staff, and the Senate. In various respects the dispute was matched by similar disputes elsewhere in the university, affecting in particular the Philosophy Department, the Department of Social Work, and within the faculty but largely confined to matters of governance, the Department of Government. While emphasis in this chapter is on faculty involvement in these disputes and their consequences, the chapter cannot be seen merely as a history of the political economy dispute.

There were many other significant developments in the faculty over these years, especially in the postgraduate area. In 1973, the faculty introduced a Master of Business Administration, largely based within the Accounting Department. This over time generated significant developments during the 1980s and 1990s, including the Australian Graduate School of Management, an initiative discussed more fully in Chapter 6. A Master of Public Policy degree was introduced in 1981, after much preliminary discussion during the 1970s. It involved the Department of Government together with segments of the Accounting, Economic History, Economics and Industrial Relations departments. It did not really commence until the second half of the 1980s. The number of PhD and MEc candidates (and graduates) also rose significantly at this time. Five honorary DSc (Econ) were conferred: to graduate and former staff member Sir Ronald Walker in October 1973, to Australian National University demographer Mick Borrie in November 1978, to Sir Leslie Melville in April 1980, and to Fred Deer and James Plimsoll in 1984. At the undergraduate level, enrolments stabilised with the first-year quota of 350 (marginally adjusted during the early 1980s). However, over-filling of the first-year quota access of Arts students to faculty courses and the BEc/LLB combined degree implied larger student numbers than those suggested by the quota. Hence many faculty courses continued to operate with some of the highest student/staff ratios within the university.

Other major changes in the faculty came from its *de facto* transformation in 1974 into a Faculty of Economics and Social Sciences. Although not an official name change, this faculty decision effectively expanded from five to seven the number of majors students could count towards their degree, excluding the compulsory Economics component. Geography, Anthropology and Rural Economics majors were then added to the well-established list of Accounting, Economic History, Economic Statistics, Government and Industrial Relations course sequences. Computer Science became a further major course sequence in 1980, essential for meeting the increasing demands for such skills especially from students within the Accounting, Economic Statistics and Economics departments. By then, the compulsory element in the degree had been reduced to Economics I or Economics I(P), Economics II or Economics II(P) where Economics I(P) and II(P) were the alternative economics courses introduced in 1975 and 1976 as tangible consequences of the 'Political Economy' dispute. In June 1983, the Economic Statistics Department officially changed its name to Econometrics Department, reflecting changes in the subject matter of its courses and staff interests.

Rapid growth in university funding in the early 1970s was transformed by the second half of the 1970s to levels of financial resourcing barely sufficient for keeping expenditure constant in real terms. Growth in faculty staffing therefore also slowed. Seniority of staff, however, increased, despite university tightening of promotion opportunities to senior lecturer and associate professor. More significantly, the number of professors in the faculty rose, partly to accommodate the new Industrial Relations Department (formally established in 1975) and partly because the three largest faculty departments were by then very much multi-professorial. Economics had its full establishment of three professors from 1976 after Gordon Mills' appointment; Government had two professors at this stage, and Accounting gained two chairs when Murray Wells was appointed Professor of Accounting in 1975. Four professors — Ray Chambers, Henry Mayer, Stuart Rutherford and Colin Simkin — retired during the period covered by this chapter, and one, Dick Spann, died, aged 65, in 1981. Only some of the resulting vacancies had been filled by the end of 1984.

By that time, the Merewether Building was proving too small for adequately housing a growing faculty staff. It also failed to provide the necessary teaching rooms, given the growth in the number of courses, of tutorials and of other small-group teaching. In 1982, expansion of the Merewether Building was requested as an urgent necessity to provide the growing number of MBA students with more satisfactory facilities. Additional tutorial rooms were provided in 1977, and in 1978 the Wolstenholme Library was considerably altered and enlarged to create carrels and other private study rooms. This did not prevent continuing, and at this stage still unsuccessful, demands for private study space in the adjoining Institute Building.

The number of courses on offer increased, especially through the growth of optional courses, an expansion greatly encouraged by more forceful student demands for choice over what they were to be taught in their degrees. Students were also increasingly demanding more choice about the way their performance in a course was assessed. Hence the relative importance of the final examination to the final result fell drastically for many subjects.

This chapter therefore reviews much change for the faculty, including in the organisation of the way it transacted its business. Faculty increasingly began to rely on committees to effect its business more efficiently. This took its toll in terms of the dean's time, since deans chaired virtually all faculty committees ex officio. By 1980, therefore, faculty started to elect sub-deans for postgraduate and undergraduate studies in order to spread the expanding managerial and administrative tasks of the dean more widely. At the same time, the size of the faculty continued to increase. Staff growth was one cause; increasing membership to accommodate representatives from tutorial and temporary lecturing staff, staff representation for the new subjects added to the faculty, as well as more elected student representatives, were others. The Faculty of Economics led the way in the university in expanding its membership by adding student representatives and untenured staff members; and in the way it opened its business to the gaze of students. The last came from establishing an open faculty meeting with a public gallery for interested parties from non-member teachers and students, initially as an experiment condoned by Senate and Academic Board. At the end of 1978, Geelum Simpson-Lee resigned after more than four successive terms as dean; and in 1982 he retired from the university altogether. Simpson-Lee was replaced as dean first by Rex Mortimer, an associate professor in Government, who died in office in December 1979. Steve Salsbury, appointed in 1976 as Professor of Economic History, was elected dean in 1980, and re-elected in 1982 and 1984.

Enrolments, curriculum and staffing, 1973–84

Quotas on first-year enrolments, which remained in force for the whole of 1973–84, were marginally adjusted during the early 1980s from the 350 which prevailed for the 1970s. The quota was raised to 370 students in 1981 and 1982, and reduced to 330 and 320 in 1983 and 1984. In 1980, the faculty also introduced a separate Accounting quota, set initially at 300 but raised to 315 in 1984. This was needed to restrain demand for enrolments in what by then was the most popular faculty major, largely for future career reasons. Despite the relative stability of the quota for most of the period, faculty enrolments nevertheless rose from 1040 in 1974 to 1407 in 1984, a substantial increase. This kept student–staff ratios on the very high side for most of the period. The number of women students enrolled in the faculty also rose dramatically in these years. Constituting just under a quarter of faculty enrolments in 1974 (24.2 per cent), enrolments by women rose to well over a third of the total by 1984 (36.8 per cent), doubling over the period in absolute numbers from 252 to 518. Despite several unsuccessful attempts to reintroduce evening courses in the faculty, part-time student numbers fell from 220 (or 11.5 per cent of total undergraduate enrolments) in 1974 to 102 (or 7.2 per cent of total enrolments) in 1984.

Postgraduate numbers also increased, explained partly by the growth in the number of course offerings, most significantly when the MBA was added in 1973. Postgraduate students in the faculty in 1974 were made up as follows: eight PhD students (of whom one was a woman); 63 MEc students (of whom twelve were women and two-thirds were part-time), and 36 students enrolled for the MBA (of whom only one was a woman and the vast majority, 86.1 per cent, were part-time). For 1974, total postgraduate enrolment for the faculty was 107, less than 10 per cent of total enrolments. Ten years later in 1983, PhD enrolments had more than trebled to 28 (including four women), MEc students had risen to 115 (including 23 women) while the MBA was attracting 40 students (among whom there were no women enrolments whatsoever). Total postgraduate enrolments rose to 183 over these ten years, or to 13.0 per cent of undergraduate enrolments. This considerable increase implied quite a dramatic shift in faculty's teaching responsibilities. It constituted a significant compositional change in its student numbers as compared with teaching operations for its first half century. However, postgraduate enrolments were still considerably less than the growth in postgraduate numbers for the university as a whole.

Faculty curriculum also changed drastically, largely the result of expanding the major sequences which could be taken for the degree when it was decided in 1974 to enhance the social sciences status of the faculty. While Geography, Anthropology and Rural Economics became acceptable as major sequences in the faculty from 1975, Computer Science was added as a full three-year faculty sequence in 1980. Moreover, as a specific outcome of the political economy dispute in the faculty, the compulsory Economics component of the BEc degree from 1975 could be satisfied in alternative ways: Economics I or Economics I(P) for first year, Economics II or II(P) for second year from 1976, while a hybrid Economics II(P) conversion operated in 1975 for one year only to enable second-year students to take a (P) course when the first year of a two-year sequence of (P) courses was originally introduced. Economics III(P) was in operation *de facto* from 1977 but an Economics IV(P) at the fourth-year honours level did not eventuate until 1990. However, honours students in the (P) courses who commenced the necessary honours work in Economics III(P) could complete honours degree requirements by selecting a set of suitable options from those already offered in Economics IV.

The syllabus structures of the by now traditional faculty courses, Accounting, Economic History, Economic Statistics, Economics, Government and Industrial Relations, changed relatively little from those in the early 1970s described in Chapter 4. However, many new components were often introduced, generally in the form of additional options at the senior level. These frequently reflected the research interests of the teaching staff. Accounting remained the only faculty sequence which offered no internal choice in its course offerings; it was joined in this respect by the Rural Economics and Computer Science sequences. Economic History continued to offer choice only for third- and fourth-year students; Economic Statistics did likewise. Economics offered choice for a third of its second year, and for virtually the whole of its third- and fourth-year courses; although for Economics IV, a compulsory half course, Economic Policy Documents, became part of the syllabus from 1976. Economics I(P) and II(P) offered no internal choice at all. Government provided an optional third in both its first- and second-year courses, Government III offered choice for the whole of the year, while coursework in Government IV was selected by students from a number of course offerings on advice from the head of department. Industrial Relations still effectively started its sequence in second year with an Industrial Relations I syllabus devoid of internal choice. Industrial Relations II was half compulsory, half open to choice, students having to take two electives from the half dozen offered. Industrial Relations IV consisted of compulsory seminars on Research Techniques and Methodology, Contemporary Policy Issues, Social Philosophies of Industrial Relations: History and Theories and The Law and Industrial Society, together with a compulsory thesis requirement.

Anthropology and Geography, the new faculty majors, both had a high degree of choice within their syllabus structure. Anthropology I was taught in three unequal parts: Social Anthropology (half the course), covering four types of societies from hunter-gatherers to industrial society; Pre-History (one-third of the course) and Linguistics (approximately one-sixth of the course). For Anthropology II, students completed six core units (History of Anthropology, Anthropological Theory, Kinship, Religion, Economic Anthropology and Law) and three from eight optional units, six of which enabled specialisation by geographical area while the other two were the first of a sub-sequence: Community Studies I and Human Physical Evolution I. Likewise, Anthropology III offered three options (General Anthropology, Social Anthropology and Pre-History) each of which consisted of a mix of compulsory core units and optional units. Anthropology IV consisted of one option to be chosen from three (Social Anthropology, Pre-History or Linguistics), together with a thesis.

In 1975 Geography I, dealing with Weather, Water and Man, Landforms and Soils and the Geography of Land Use, offered no internal choice. Geography II comprised three parts, of which Geomorphology and Cold Climate Landforms were compulsory while the third was chosen from Introduction to Coastal Geography and Human Geography. Geography III involved choosing between Geography IIIP (Physical) and Geography IIIE (Economic). Geography IV offered specialisation in either Physical Geography or Economic Geography, together with satisfactory completion of a thesis. Although details of Geography and Anthropology courses altered, their structure remained largely the same.

An outline of the contents of the two Economics (P) courses introduced in 1975 and 1976 can be conveniently presented here. Economics I(P) was composed of four parts. By way of general introduction, the first examined types and functions of economic systems. Part two then discussed four different approaches to the analysis of the capitalist system, that is, those of neo-classical, Keynesian, institutionalist and Marxist economics. Thirdly, the course presented analyses of selected political economy problems including inflation, unemployment, environmental issues, and inequality and poverty. A segment reappraising economic methodology concluded the course. Economics II(P) was likewise subdivided into four parts. It commenced with a discussion of the process of economic growth and development. Part two covered the national economy and its sectors, with special reference to the role of the state and of the industrial system. The final two parts of Economics II(P) addressed issues of international economics and its institutions, and underdevelopment and imperialism. As already mentioned, Economics III(P) and final-year honours students from the (P) courses initially drew on existing options offered for Economics III and IV.

The Master of Business Administration (MBA) was the most significant curriculum addition at the postgraduate level. Initially, it was essentially an Accounting degree, requiring entrants to have satisfactorily completed three years of accounting studies at the tertiary level. By the end of the 1970s, its teachers encompassed members from the Economics and Economic Statistics departments as well as from Accounting. Its first year comprised three compulsory courses: The Structure, Management and Regulation of the Modern Corporation, The Theory and Practice of Decision Making and Financial Institutions and Sources of Finance. In second year, students were required to take three from the following five courses: The Securities Market and its Regulation, Corporate Dilemmas, Difficulties and Disasters, Corporate Finance, Operations Research, and International Business and Finance Institutions. In addition, all students had to complete a 15,000 words essay. Full-time, the MBA took two years; for part-time students, it took three. Students were admitted on satisfactory completion of the Graduate Management Admission Tests administered by Princeton's Education Testing Service, in addition to the other entry requirements already mentioned. Only a small proportion of the many applicants were admitted to this new and prestigious faculty postgraduate course. By the end of 1979, its 43 alumni included half a dozen academics and three public servants, with the remainder employed in middle and upper management positions within the private sector. In addition, Accounting for the first time offered courses for students taking an MEc degree in 1972.

Staffing in the faculty also changed considerably, and growth of staff between 1973 and 1984 enabled slight reductions in the officially estimated faculty student–staff ratios. However, irrespective of this, Faculty of Economics student–staff ratios remained the worst within the university after those for the Law Faculty. Per equivalent full-time student, costs were estimated in 1983 at $1315 in the Law Faculty and $1485 in the Economics Faculty (SM: 5 December 1983). By the early 1970s, student–staff ratios were 20:1 for the faculty; by the early 1980s they had dropped to 17.2: 1 (1981) and 18.5:1 (1982).

By the end of 1984, total permanent academic staff in the faculty numbered 84. In addition the faculty employed thirteen secretaries, one departmental administrative assistant, three full-time research assistants and several computer programmers. For the faculty's six departments, academic staff was divided into ten professorial positions, of which only eight were filled (three in Economics, one each in Accounting, Government, Economic History, Econometrics and Industrial Relations); two readers (both in Government), ten associate professors (four in Economics, three in Government, two in Accounting and one in Economic History); 41 senior lecturers (fourteen in Government, twelve in Economics, seven in Accounting, five in Economic History, two in Econometrics and one in Industrial Relations); 23 lecturers (nine in Economics, six in Accounting, three in Econometrics, two in Government, none in Economic History and three in Industrial Relations) as well as one assistant lecturer in Government. The only senior tutor was in Accounting, while Accounting and Economic History employed two tutors each. Tutoring in other departments was conducted by staff members and by temporary tutors recruited from final honours year and postgraduate students. Most departments in the faculty by the end of 1984 had converted their establishment senior tutor and/or tutor positions into lecturing staff when this option was presented by the university. Economics had gained its highly valued administrative assistant position by way of converting a tutorship.

As compared to 1972 (when it employed three senior tutors and four full-time tutors), full-time academic staff in the Economics Department in 1984 (without senior tutors or full-time tutors) had declined from 28 to 25. In terms of lecturers and above, Economics staff had, however, increased from 21 to 25. The department still had three professors of whom Warren Hogan (appointed in 1967) was the senior appointment, while Gordon Mills and Peter Groenewegen were appointed as professors in 1976 and 1980. Of its four associate professors by the end of 1984, Frank Stilwell had been promoted to that position in 1983 and Viv Hall in 1984. Moreover, in 1983, the vice-chancellor had appointed Frank Stilwell director of (P) courses to administer organisation of their teaching, following a recommendation to the Academic Board from the Wilkes Committee on Political Economy. (Stilwell had been appointed lecturer in 1970 and was promoted to senior lecturer in 1974.) The two other associate professors in 1984, Ted Wheelwright and Jim Wilson, had been in this position from 1965 and 1970.

By 1984, only one of the five senior lecturers on the Economics staff in 1972 (Sol Kim) remained a senior lecturer. The other ten senior lecturers (Debesh Bhattacharya, Michael Blad, Flora Gill, Louis Haddad, Bill Merrilees, Tony Phipps, Margaret Power, Peter Saunders, John Stuckey and Judy Yates) had been promoted to that position in the intervening years after initial appointment to the teaching staff from 1965; John Piggott was appointed as senior lecturer in Economics in December 1984. Of the nine lecturers in the department by 1984, two had been appointed before 1973 (Gavan Butler and Evan Jones) and the other seven (Joseph Halevi, Surinder Joson, Eric Kiernan, Geoffrey Kingston, Murray Milgate, Bruce Ross and Russell Ross) were appointed after 1973. By 1984, the department also employed a computer programmer (Maurice Peat), secretaries for its three professors (Sophie Jans, Valerie Jones and Swee Kuen Pan), two secretaries in the departmental office (Helen Marner and Jennifer Scott) and a full-time administrative assistant (Peter Clarke) who was a major support for its successive heads and for departmental administration in general. No distinction was made between what were called 'designated (P) teachers' in the department and the other Economics teaching staff in the staff lists recorded in the *Faculty Handbook* and *University Calendars*. However, in June 1982, Stuart Rosewarne was appointed as an Economics (P) tutor, and in May 1984 Dick Bryan became a full-time lecturer (probationary) for the Economics (P) courses. These were consequences of the Academic Board's Wilkes Committee, which reported on the political economy dispute during 1982 and 1983, as discussed later in this chapter.

The Department of Economics also recorded retirements and resignations. Colin Simkin retired in 1980, aged 65, after eleven years as Professor of Economics; and Geelum Simpson-Lee retired as senior lecturer in May 1982 after almost 40 years service on the Department of Economics teaching staff. There were also many resignations. Maurice Haddad resigned in 1975 to join the Trades Practices Commission in Canberra; Ian Sharpe, promoted to senior lecturer in 1974, left in 1978 to take up a chair at the University of Newcastle; Hugh Pritchard, a senior tutor, resigned in February 1975 to take up a position at Kuring-gai College of Advanced Education; Neil Conn, a member of staff since 1962, resigned in April 1977 to join the New South Wales Treasury; Ulrich Kohli, appointed lecturer in 1978 and promoted to senior lecturer in 1980, resigned in August 1981 to take up an appointment at the University of Colorado; Nick Oulton, appointed senior lecturer in 1982, resigned at the end of 1983 to return to the United Kingdom, and Murray Milgate, appointed lecturer in 1983, resigned as from January 1985 to take up an associate professorship at Harvard.

Academic visitors and honorary staff may also be mentioned, since they often participated in departmental teaching. Bill Norton, from the Research Department of the Reserve Bank, was appointed an honorary associate in the department in November 1973 to assist in teaching an honours course on econometric model building. René Cordoni from Zurich Technical University was a visitor in 1975, as was Dennis Lees, an English micro-economist from Nottingham University. Professor Paolo Sylos Labini, from the University of Rome, visited the department during September and October 1980; Professor Ivor Pearce, an international trade economists and general theorist from Southampton University, was visitor for six months from July 1981, while John Harsanyi, a University of Sydney graduate from the 1950s and a Nobel Laureate in 1994, visited the department for three months from mid-August 1982.

With 22 permanent teaching staff as reported in the 1984 *Faculty Handbook*, the Government Department likewise experienced little net growth in staff. However, this reflected a vacant professorship following Dick Spann's death in 1981, which had still not been filled. During February 1983, Giovanni Poggi was appointed to this vacancy, which in practice became a visiting professorship for the whole of 1984. The department had two readers: Carole Pateman, from the beginning of 1980 and Fred Teiwes, promoted to that position in February 1981. There were three associate professors: Terry Irving, Trevor Matthews and Ken Turner. By 1984, there were thirteen senior lecturers in Government. With two exceptions, they had all been promoted to that position between 1973 and 1984. In alphabetical order, they were Ernie Chaples, Ross Curnow, Graeme Gill, Ian Grosart, Michael Hogan, Bob Howard, Michael Jackson, Peter King, Michael Leigh, Helen Nelson, Martin Painter, Patricia Springborg and Rodney Tiffen. By the end of 1984, the two Government lecturers were Peter Nelson and Lex Watson. The one assistant lecturer was Christine Jennett. In addition, the department had two professorial secretaries (Sandra Donnelly and Betty Johnston) and two administrative assistants in the departmental office (Debbie Hurd and Nancy van Duren).

Dick Spann, whose death in July 1981 was mentioned earlier, was in June 1977 recommended by the New South Wales government for the award of an OBE for his extensive services to public administration. A dinner to launch an appeal for establishing a Spann Scholarship was organised in May 1982. Henry Mayer, Professor of Political Theory, retired in December 1984. He was awarded an AM in the Queen's Birthday honours list in June 1980 for services to education. Tom Kewley, at that stage the longest serving member of the Government Department, retired as senior lecturer in 1974. Rex Mortimer, promoted to associate professor from 1977, died in December 1979. There were also resignations. Jim Richardson resigned in 1976 to take up a chair in politics at the Australian National University; Denis Altman (first appointed in 1968 as a lecturer, and promoted to senior lecturer in 1974) resigned in 1980 to go to Monash University; Robert Taylor (appointed lecturer in 1975) resigned during 1979 to join the University of London.

The department welcomed three visiting professors. Professor Harry Albinski was appointed visiting professor in 1974 until February 1975; Professor Fukui visited for three months in 1977; Giovanni Poggi's visiting professorship in 1984 has already been mentioned. As in the 1960s and early 1970s, staff turnover in the Government Department was very small and a great deal less than that in Economics, suggesting yet another cost inflicted by the political economy dispute on the Economics Department.

With seventeen academic staff including two tutors, Accounting remained the third largest department in the faculty by the end of 1984. Murray Wells was the only professor; an attempt in 1983 to replace Ray Chambers, who had retired, was unsuccessful. Ron Bowra and Frank Clarke were the department's two associate professors. Its seven senior lecturers were Alan Craswell, Graeme Dean, Michael Gaffikin, Geoffrey Hart, T. Sri Ramanathan, Anne Riches and Peter Wolnizer. There were five lecturers, all appointed in 1981 and 1982: Roger Burritt, Mrs Wai Fong Chua, Cynthia Coleman, Stephanie Rees, and Trevor Wise. The two tutors in 1984 were Cecilia Spence and Michael Walsh, the senior tutor Leslie Szekely. The Accounting Department employed three secretaries: in 1984 they were Swee-Eng Chia, Susanne Donato and Sheilah Markham.

Four longstanding members of the Accounting staff retired during the period. Ray Chambers, its foundation professor since 1960, initially appointed senior lecturer in 1953 as the one full-time member of the Accounting teaching staff within the Faculty of Economics, retired during 1982 after three decades in the faculty as one of its most distinguished scholars. He was promptly appointed an associate supervisor for many of the department's PhD students (SM: 7 November 1983). Alec Shaw, a senior lecturer in the department also from the 1950s, retired in 1977; Ron Brown, a part-time lecturer in Accounting from the second half of the 1950s and promoted to senior lecturer in 1968, retired from March 1980. Finally, Pat Mills, the Reader in Commercial Law in the faculty since 1965, and a very active participant in, and chair of, faculty committees (including the Political Economy Committee discussed later in this chapter) retired at the end of 1983.

Several Accounting Department teachers resigned to go elsewhere. John Staunton resigned in 1973 to take up a position at the University of New England; Bob Walker, who had joined the department as a teaching fellow in 1965, resigned in 1978 to take up a chair at the University of New South Wales; Harry Rappaport resigned in 1975 to join the staff at the Gippsland College of Advanced Education; Stewart Leech, appointed senior lecturer in 1978, resigned from end February 1980 to go to the University of Tasmania. Ken Hale, B.M. Lall Nigam, Peter Luckett and Jeffrey Richards either left to complete postgraduate studies or took up positions elsewhere. Victor New, a lecturer appointed in 1979, left by the end 1980; Roger Burritt and John Trowell, appointed to tenured lectureships in 1980, resigned during 1983 and 1980. Given the international prestige of Chambers (discussed in more detail later in this chapter), the department also attracted many visiting academics of stature. These included Sydney Davidson (March 1978), E. Stamp (March 1979), Robert Sterling (November 1982), S.J. Gray (June to August 1980), Michael Bromwich (June 1980) and London School of Economics Professor Bryan Carlsberg in August 1984.

Economic History in 1984 had seven members of full-time academic staff. Steve Salsbury, the professor, had joined the faculty in 1975; Ken Buckley, its associate professor, was by then the longest serving member in the department, having been appointed in the early 1950s. By the end of 1984, there were five senior lecturers — John Drabble, Gary Wotherspoon, Ben Tipton, Peter Hall and Robert Aldrich — and no lecturers. Secretary to the department was Toula Markos and the 1984 *Faculty Handbook* listed two tutors, Andrew Moore and Sandra Tweedie. Boris Schedvin resigned in 1973 to join Monash University. Derek Aldcroft, who had succeeded Butlin as professor in 1972, returned to the United Kingdom in 1975. Jules Ginswick, another member of the department from the early 1950s, retired, age 65, in 1980. Barbara Tucker, appointed lecturer in Economic History in 1975, resigned in 1979 to return to the United States.

By the end of 1984, the Econometrics Department (formerly Economic Statistics), consisted of one professor (Alan Woodland, appointed in 1980), two senior lecturers — Bob Bartels and Dilip Madan — and three lecturers: John Goodhew, Ernie Houghton and Denzil Fiebig. Stuart Rutherford retired from his chair in 1979 after occupying it for seventeen years. Allan Anderson, a lecturer in 1978 and senior lecturer from 1982, resigned in 1984 to return to the University of Queensland. Other persons appointed to the teaching staff of the department included W.J. Haley, appointed senior lecturer in 1974; Piet de Jong, appointed lecturer in 1977; and Ms A. Talunen, appointed lecturer in 1984. For 1982–83, the department also listed an honorary associate, Professor C.W.J. Granger, and more generally a programmer (George Defina in 1984). A professorial secretary, Yu Can Poon in 1984, and a research affiliate, Janet Rybak, complete the 1984 staff list.

The relatively new department of Industrial Relation had five people on its teaching staff at the end of 1984. It had gained a full professorship in 1975, but its first incumbent, Harry Turner, only took up the position as a visiting professor from June 1976 to October 1977. In 1978, John Corina succeeded him as professor. Richard Morris, the department's only senior lecturer in 1984, was promoted to that post in 1983 after joining the staff as a lecturer in 1977. The three lecturers were Ron Callus, Greg Patmore and Keith Whitfield, appointed in 1983, 1984 and 1981. Two members of the department retired as senior lecturers: Maxine Bucklow in 1976 and Geoff Sorrell in 1981. Malcolm Rimmer, a senior lecturer in 1981, resigned in May 1983 to go to Monash University; Michael Wright, a probationary lecturer in 1979, resigned during 1982; Peter Scherer, a lecturer in 1975, resigned during 1979. After his retirement in 1975, Kingsley Laffer, the founder of industrial relations teaching at the university and the effective creator of the department, became a honorary associate in Industrial Relations until 1982. He used this period partly to write a history of Industrial Relations education at the University of Sydney, 1953–75, the department's first published occasional paper (Laffer 1981).

A giant in accounting education: Raymond John Chambers, 1917–99

Ray Chambers, who in 1982 retired as foundation Professor of Accounting after joining the faculty as its only full-time teacher of Accounting in 1953, had become a true giant in the Accounting education world by the 1980s.

Chambers had graduated BEc in 1939 at the University of Sydney as a part-time student, after matriculating at Newcastle High School where his distinguished performance earned him a scholarship for university studies at Sydney. Ray Chambers was born in Newcastle in November 1917. His parents had never received a secondary education and, as he himself later put it, his family could in no way be described as 'bookish'. His parents earned their living in small business, in which their children had to assist them from an early age. Ray Chambers' opportunity to receive a good education was therefore especially prized, while his high school teachers at Newcastle imparted not only their own love of learning but an ambition in the young Ray Chambers to become a teacher. As a part-time university student, Chambers had been employed in the NSW Public Service as a clerk in the Attorney-General and Justice departments. After graduating, he joined Shell, followed by employment in the Electricity Meter and Allied Industries, before going to the Australian Prices Commission in Canberra in 1943 'for war work'. During these years, he was also employed as a part-time correspondence teacher of auditing at Sydney Technical College. From 1945, this became a full-time teaching job in its Department of Industrial Management. During the early years of his full-time teaching, Chambers wrote his first book, *Financial Management* (1947, fourth edition 1986), a 'highly innovative work' of over 400 pages and 'the only one of its kind to the present day'. He also published fifteen journal articles over the eight years he taught at Sydney Technical College.

In 1953, Chambers joined the Faculty of Economics as senior lecturer in Accounting, became an associate professor in 1955 and foundation Professor of Accounting in 1960. Until Murray Wells, his first PhD student in Accounting, became professor in 1975, Chambers was also head of a rapidly growing department, a task he then readily abandoned to concentrate on research and postgraduate teaching. Chambers' research focused on theory construction and analysis, and on the history and practice of accounting. These became the foundations of his conception of continuously contemporary accounting (CoCoA) and the development of accounting thought. The first of these topics was written up in many places; a noted version being the *Foundations of Accounting* (1991) produced at the request of Peter Wolnizer, his PhD student during the 1970s and subsequent colleague and collaborator.

At Sydney, Chambers not only built up a renowned Accounting course and department over the decades from 1953, he created its honours and postgraduate programs, MEc, PhD and MBA. His fame as theorist, combined with his supervisory talents, generated the largest PhD school in Accounting in Australia during the 1970s, the long-term outcome of which was more than a dozen graduates appointed to chairs in major universities in the United States, the United Kingdom and Australia. As noted previously, Chambers kept up this supervisory activity on retirement in 1982, and continued to enrich the accounting literature over the remaining seventeen years of his life. Major works included *Accounting, Evaluation and Economic Behavior* (1966), *Accounting, Finance and Management* (1969), *Price Variation and Inflation Accounting* (1980), *The Foundations of Accounting* (1991), and ended with the enormous (over a thousand pages, more than six thousand classified quotations) *An Accounting Thesaurus: 500 Years of Accounting* (1995). He also published five volumes of collected writings (co-edited with Graeme Dean) under the title *Chambers on Accounting*, drawn from thirteen monographs and pamphlets, nearly 200 articles and a similar number of reviews, many of them translated into Spanish, Japanese, Italian, French and German (a full bibliography is appended to the posthumous *festschrift* published in *Abacus* by former students and colleagues in October 2000).

Not surprisingly, Chambers gained many honours and awards. He was elected Fellow of the Academy of Social Sciences in Australia in 1964. In 1976, he was the American Accounting Association's distinguished International Lecturer in the United States. That year he was also awarded the degree of DSc (Econ) at the University of Sydney. In 1978, he was national president of the Australian Society of Chartered Public Accountants, and appointed Officer of the Order of Australia. He was national president of the Australian Society of Accountants in 1977–78. In 1991, he was inducted into the Accounting Hall of Fame at Ohio State University, the first non-American to be given that honour. He was made a life member of the Accounting Association of Australia and New Zealand and in 1996 received its inaugural outstanding contribution to research award. In 1967, Chambers received the American Institute of Chartered Public Accountants Gold Medal and was Leverhulme Fellow at Waseda University, Tokyo, in 1976. He held visiting professorships at the universities of Chicago (1962), California, Berkeley (1966), Washington (1967), Florida (1970), Kansas (1970), Illinois (1980), Cape Town (1982), Otago (1984) and Simon Fraser (1985). As a permanent memorial to his name and distinguished reputation, the university established the annual Chambers Memorial Lecture, the first of which was given in 1985 by his friend and colleague, Professor R.R. Sterling.

In 1965, Chambers founded the journal *Abacus*, and subsequently edited it until 1974, when he passed the editorship to Murray Wells. It was therefore highly appropriate that this journal published Chamber's last article in its October 1999 issue.

Chambers was a most inspirational teacher, and could be described as a renaissance man in the full sense of the word. Who else in Australian accounting would preface an article with an apt quote from Chaucer's *Canterbury Tales*, treat representations in financial statements as testable, empirical matter, quoting Carnap in support; and then cite Machiavelli's *Prince* on the 'dangers in wait' for reformers, whether in accounting or anything else, in the space of one article? On a personal note, as an Accounting student in the second half of the 1950s, I found his lectures in Accounting III by far the most interesting in an otherwise rather boring but nevertheless very useful course. His general conversation at morning tea in the early 1960s (which I experienced as a very young colleague in the faculty) was invariably both instructive and entertaining. As student, teacher and researcher, Ray Chambers was undoubtedly one of the faculty's greatest products.

Faculty deliberations and administration, 1973–84

No fewer than 58 faculty meetings were held during this period, four of them special meetings arising from the political economy dispute. This averaged to almost five meetings per annum, an average greatly exceeded during the mid-1970s when the political economy dispute and issues of governance more generally were developing at a furious pace. Thus, nine faculty meetings took place during 1973 when the governance debates in the university were at their zenith and the political economy dispute had begun in earnest. Five meetings followed in 1974, seven in 1976, five each in 1977 and 1978. The more normal four meetings per annum returned only from 1979. Only three meetings — one per term — were held in 1984, when Steve Salsbury began his third term of office as dean. Given the growth in staff and the expansion of faculty membership by the admission of temporary staff representatives, average attendance per meeting rose to 38.3 for 1973–84, an increase exceeding 50 per cent on average for 1963–72. Minimum attendance of sixteen was recorded at the February 1978 meeting; maximum attendance of 69 occurred in March 1984, while 68 persons were recorded as present at the October 1982 meeting. An earlier meeting (8 October 1976) was informed that only three faculty members (the dean, Ken Buckley and Ken Turner) had attended all previous eleven meetings, while eight faculty members had attended one or none, and 36 had attended fewer than six.

The first faculty meeting for 1973 attracted an attendance of 50, including eleven new appointments and three elected student members. In his report to faculty, the dean announced that filling the quota for first-year enrolments in 1973 had resulted in a reduced cut-off mark; that a large number of candidates for honours had been approved, including thirteen students who wished to attempt double honours, as well as many new candidates for the faculty's postgraduate degrees. The dean also announced liberalisation of the supplementary tests for students with near passes in the final examinations. Supplementary examinations were to be replaced as far as possible by 'further tests'. These could be administered on that part of the course in which the student had failed, while for 'last' subjects for the degree, it became permissible to convert marginal failures into pass results without resorting to further tests.

The most important agenda item for this meeting was transformation of the faculty into a Faculty of Economics and Social Sciences, a step agreed to in principle by faculty in 1968. A committee which had looked at the necessary changes for the degree this entailed, first of all recommended a reduction in the number of compulsory courses for the degree from four to two. Only Economics I and II were to continue as compulsory, with the compulsory status of Economics III and Descriptive Economics being abandoned. This change carried the danger of effectively converting the BEc into a BA, particularly when the proposed by-laws in the committee's report required completion of only one of the faculty's major sequences, even though two third-year courses were to be completed. Not surprisingly, Professors Colin Simkin and Warren Hogan opposed this reduction in compulsory Economics requirements for the degree, arguing that if the BEc was to continue as a professional degree, then at least three Economics subjects — that is, Economics I, II and

III — needed to be completed. However, the majority at the meeting rejected this view, arguing that two compulsory Economics courses were quite sufficient to distinguish the BEc from an Arts degree.

Faculty also proposed the introduction of a unit system, with a minimum of 70 units from ten subjects required for the award of a pass degree. Junior, intermediate and senior courses would have different unit values, and course requirements for pass and honours students were to be differentiated. Junior (that is, first-year) courses were to be valued at six units; intermediate and senior (that is, second- and third-year) courses at eight units. No more than four junior courses and two senior courses needed to be completed for the degree. With four subjects in first year, and three subjects each in second and third years, students on completion would have accumulated a unit score of 72, at the rate of 24 units per annum. This was described as the normal manner of proceeding towards a pass degree. (If a student attempted the maximum number of first-year courses, that is five, and therefore needed to complete only five intermediate and senior courses, the unit score obtained totalled the minimum of 70 required for a degree.) The unit system was argued to give greater flexibility to students and enhance their opportunities for specialisation. For example, students could complete two senior courses in Economics (or Government) if they selected four third-year Economics options instead of the two making up a single third-year Economics course. However, the degree could also be completed with the minimum requirement of Economics courses, together with a sequence in Government and Anthropology and two other permitted first-year courses, say from history and a language, an outcome only distinguishable from an Arts degree by the fact that it needed ten instead of nine subjects.

Other new nomenclature was introduced for the degree. Honours courses were to be called advanced courses, and honours studies had to commence by third year at the latest. Courses needed to specify their own prerequisites and corequisites. With an eye to the expected introduction of semesters, the new by-laws also talked of short courses (half-year subjects) and normal (full-year) courses. A student completing a sequence could therefore do so by attempting a combination of short and normal courses, provided they produced the required aggregate of course units. The proposal as a whole was passed 33 votes to 5, with a distinct lack of interest visible for re-opening the debate in a general way, largely because five years had already been devoted to achieving this outcome. A motion by Warren Hogan and Stuart Rutherford to have two separate undergraduate degrees, a BEc and a BSocSci (Social Sciences), received virtually no support. On aggregate, the changes were welcomed by the vast majority of faculty members because they gave greater choice and flexibility to students.

A special faculty meeting (15 June 1973) was informed about imminent changes in university governance. These included a more broadly based Academic Board to replace the Professorial Board; the existence of university departments to be formally recognised in the by-laws and Senate agreement for widening faculty membership by including elected untenured academic staff and student members.

On 28 June, faculty received details of the Geography courses approved at the previous meeting, new courses in Economic Statistics and a substantial number of new Government courses (particularly new short courses) as well as Rural Economics I and II as a new faculty sequence from the Faculty of Agriculture. At this meeting, Warren Hogan and Jules Ginswick unsuccessfully moved for the reintroduction of evening lectures. In September 1973, faculty accepted Taxation Law as a third Commercial Law subject; a new Industrial Relations course on Workers Control and Participation; and an inter-department faculty course, The Political Economy of Women, to be taught by members from the departments of Economics, Government, Economic History and Fine Arts (then temporarily housed in the Merewether Building).

On the motion of two student members, Michael Brezniak and Steven Keene, both heavily involved with the political economy movement, the September faculty meeting also appointed a committee to report on the Economics courses. The elected committee comprised three staff members (Pat Mills from Commercial Law as Convenor, Ken Buckley from Economic History and Rex Mortimer from Government) as well as two student members (Stephen Irons and Graham Kerridge). The committee received submissions, interviewed members of faculty and held many meetings. It reported in November 1973, recommending both the creation of a separate department of political economy and the introduction of a separate sequence of political economy courses.

The September 1973 meeting also discussed Ray Chambers' proposals for an MBA; introduced Anthropology I–IV as a faculty sequence; included Legal Institutions, Public Law, Contracts and Torts as faculty courses to shorten the minimum time for completing a combined BEc/LLB degree; and approved the resolution that no more than sixteen units for the degree could be taken in the form of short courses (that is, four short courses in all). The October faculty meeting expanded faculty membership to cater for appropriate representation from Anthropology, Agricultural Economics, Computing and Geography. It also debated a submission from the Evening Students Association for the reintroduction of evening courses (a proposal apparently supported by the Reserve Bank of Australia, the Commonwealth Bank, Ampol and BHP). It re-elected Simpson-Lee as dean for 1974–75 and elected new student and tutor representatives, the majority of whom were supporters of the political economy movement. The last meeting for the year (19 November 1973) received the Mills Report on Economics Courses, rejected evening classes for the foreseeable future, and approved a three-year Accounting prerequisite for the MBA.

The first meeting for 1974 (5 March) was informed that faculty enrolments had exceeded the quota by 50 and that the new BEc/LLB degree was the third most difficult university course to enter. After prolonged debate, discussion of the Mills Report was adjourned to a special meeting on 17 April, which attracted a record attendance of 64. The debate concentrated on the proposition to split the Department of Economics by creating a separate department of political economy as the only way in which course reform in Economics was possible. All five recommendations from the Mills Report were passed with substantial majorities; that for the immediate introduction of alternative (political economy) courses for Economics I–IV was passed 41 to 12; while the recommendation that only a separate department of political economy would be able to introduce such courses, was carried 34 votes to 19. Recommendations that adequate consultation was required before introducing the new courses, and that the Department of Economics, and not the faculty, should implement their introduction were carried on the voices.

The 7 May 1974 faculty meeting was told that the Professorial Board had accepted the two major resolutions from the Mills Report. The vice-chancellor had acknowledged their receipt and had indicated he was interviewing individual members from the Economics teaching staff on the matter (Williams 2005, pp. 104–05). Faculty also received reports from its committees and resolved that all full-time teachers in the faculty should be members of faculty. The next meeting (4 June) was advised that the Professorial Board had rejected the new (P) courses at its May meeting because no adequate details on their contents were presented. A proposal for new first- and second-year courses (Economics I(P), II(P) conversion) for 1975 was then submitted by several members of the Economics teaching staff (Gavan Butler, Jock Collins, Maurice Haddad, Evan Jones, Margaret Power, Paul Roberts, Geelum Simpson-Lee, Frank Stilwell and Ted Wheelwright). Faculty approved these with majority votes. New Government courses for 1975 were also introduced. These permitted students to complete two options every year to enable better access to the department's four sub-specialisations (Marxism and Political Theory, International Relations especially in South-East Asia, Public Policy including Public Administration, and International Relations including domestic political topics). At its July, August and October 1974 meetings, faculty devoted much time on the degree of overlap between the alternative economic streams for first and second year and noted that Accounting and Economic Statistics wanted Economics I and II as prerequisites; Economic History wanted more quantitative economics; and Government opted for the two Economics (P) courses. A motion for splitting the faculty (Faculty of Economics and Faculty of Political Studies) was narrowly defeated (12 to 13 against), but an MPP degree (to be mounted initially by the Government and Economics departments) was sent to a special advisory faculty committee, approved, and accepted by the Professorial Board at its July meeting. By late 1974, the Professorial Board accepted the new courses (Economics I(P), II(P) conversion) for 1975 with the proviso that their academic value still needed conclusive demonstration.

From early 1975, faculty meetings were able to concentrate on less contentious matters. The March meeting was told that a separate industrial relations department was now imminent, and that continuous assessment (consisting of both formal examinations and coursework) was now strongly supported by the Professorial Board. A review of faculty membership regulated representation for departments active in more than one faculty, and confirmed that Economics, Accounting, Economic Statistics, Economic History and Government were primarily located within the Faculty of Economics. At its May meeting, faculty was told that suitable naming of the new (P) courses had been hotly debated in the Economics Department, and voted on a suggestion from a staff/student forum to increase student membership of the faculty to five (carried 18 to 13). The May meeting established twelve as a quorum for faculty meetings and proposed official appointment of an editor for the *Faculty Handbook*. The 14 July faculty meeting passed a motion from Frank Stilwell and Ted Wheelwright proposing the introduction of Economics III(P) and IV(P) and a separate Department of Political Economy (46 votes to 12). Course changes in Government II and

III, Economic History and Industrial Relations II (pass and advanced) were also approved. In September, faculty was told that its motion favouring a sequence of four (P) courses and a separate department of political economy had been sent to Senate by the Academic Board. At its November meeting, Senate had asked the Academic Board to set up a Committee of Inquiry into Political Economy to consist of John Ward (chairman), Edward Davis, Les Hiatt, Michael Pitman and John Young. Its terms of reference were confined to investigate the possibility of teaching political economy within the Department of Economics, and ways of providing adequate progression for (P) students in senior years. Faculty's October meeting re-elected Simpson-Lee as dean for 1976 and 1977 with a large majority (42 for, 18 against).

Faculty's first 1976 meeting (20 March) noted that Ted Wheelwright had been elected to the Senate for 1976–77 and that the first-year enrolment quota had been exceeded by 44. At its June meeting, faculty members were told that the Ward Committee had issued its first report in early May. Faculty accepted a proposal for open faculty meetings, with a 'public gallery' for those interested in observing the proceedings, to be implemented on a trial basis after considerable Academic Board and Senate debate (SM: 5 July 1976, 6 December 1976).

Faculty's July and September meetings were more turbulent. Recommendations from the three Ward Reports (its second report was dated 15 June 1976, the third July 1976) placed the political economy dispute once more firmly on the agenda. Students associated with the political economy movement had invaded the offices of the vice-chancellor and the registrar on 7 July, breaking into confidential files and doing considerable damage. They had also assaulted deputy vice-chancellor, Professor Michael Taylor, registrar Hugh McCredie and the yeoman bedell when they intervened to stop the break-in. A special meeting of faculty (22 July) debated reports on political economy by the vice-chancellor. These rejected a separate department or unit, but supported the principle of adequate progression for Economics II(P) students into senior years. Their release undoubtedly triggered the 7 July student break-in of university administration offices. As dean, Simpson-Lee acknowledged the seriousness of these break-ins, but in his letter to the vice-chancellor he also mentioned that violence was occurring elsewhere in the university, and that it had been a long dispute. The July special meeting then passed a vote of confidence in the dean by a large majority. In September, faculty adopted a revised Economics III program to ensure satisfactory progression for Economics II(P) students in 1977. Academic Board intervention to ensure that the new Economics III courses would be introduced in 1977 was reported to faculty in October.

As in the previous year, 1977 brought many faculty meetings, including the first 'open' faculty meeting in April. The June meeting recommended desirable percentages for first-, second- and third-year pass results by grade. The July meeting narrowly approved (29 votes to 25) a Statistics I prerequisite for Accounting II and III, strongly opposed by the dean (who during the debate proposed that faculty should consider the introduction of a separate bachelor of accounting degree). In August, faculty approved new Economic History courses and revisions to the MBA, reported Academic Board support for regular student assessment of their teachers; listened to reports from departments on their student consultation practices and noted that the Government Department had decided to make its examination results count for not less than 30, and no more than 70 per cent in the final result. The last faculty meeting for 1977 (7 October) re-elected Simpson-Lee as dean for 1978–79.

In 1978, faculty meetings were uncontroversial. The 17 March meeting paid tribute to the memory of Syd Butlin who had died in 1977. A proposal to have different prerequisites for Economics (P) courses from those in Economics was defeated (17 votes to 22), and alterations in Economic History and Economics courses were approved. Faculty also noted an Academic Board report on university governance, outlining the existing pyramid of power (Senate on top, then Academic Board, faculties and departments), with powers to initiate new courses confined to professors and heads of departments. Later meetings for the year decreed the 1979 quota on first-year enrolments should not be exceeded (FM: 21 July), noted the inadequate computer facilities in the faculty, and a need for more (P) teachers if senior (P) courses were to be satisfactorily staffed. It also reported the resignation of Simpson-Lee as dean and the election of Rex Mortimer as his replacement. Ray Chambers moved a vote of thanks to the retiring dean. This paid tribute to his role in course changes for the MBA, MPP and the undergraduate degree, his 'consultative administration', and above all, the way in which he had conducted faculty business 'with equanimity, patience and tolerance which have moderated dissent and assisted the Faculty to pursue its proper interests' (FM: 20 October 1978).

Rex Mortimer's period as dean was cut short by the onset of cancer from which he died in December 1979. Under his deanship, honours examiners meetings were formalised, faculty membership was increased from additional representation of Anthropology, Computing, Geography and Rural Economics teachers, in principle support was given for maintaining opportunities for part-time PhD candidature (especially for staff members), the BSc degree with Economics was approved, and complaints were aired about grave accommodation shortages in the Merewether Building. In 1979, faculty also reintroduced honours grades for the award of the MEc, opened the MBA degree to all graduates provided they had at least two years of business experience, and requested additional funding for part-time MBA teaching. A special faculty meeting (9 September) elected Ken Turner as acting dean for the remainder of the year, provided for separate Economics (P) representation on all faculty committees, established a special PhD award committee, and elected Steve Salsbury as dean from 1 January 1980 to 31 December 1981.

Salsbury's period as dean confined faculty meetings to routine improvements in faculty facilities, courses and resources. Only four meetings per year were now required to transact business. During 1980, much time was devoted to problems of space in the Merewether Building and for the Wolstenholme Library. There were minor changes in postgraduate regulations, including tightening PhD supervision procedures. A quota of 300 was set for first-year Accounting enrolments. There was also a serious attempt to revive the Graduates Association, to which Ted Wheelwright was appointed as a faculty representative. Meetings in 1981 marked the retirement of Stuart Rutherford and his replacement by Allan

Woodland, the preparation of a weekly faculty *Newsletter*, more debate about the future of the Wolstenholme Library and the increasing inadequacy of Merewether facilities, demands for additional Economics (P) staff and the death of Dick Spann. They also approved various course changes.

Similar problems occupied faculty meetings in 1982. A committee chaired by Carole Pateman was appointed to investigate declining honours enrolments, the *Faculty Handbook* was revised under Michael Hogan's editorship, faculty responded to the Ralph Report on business education (MBA) and various course revisions were approved. The dilemma of examining short courses in a three-term academic year was discussed, sparking demands (initially from the Economic Statistics Department) for the introduction of a semester system. At the October meeting, Salsbury announced Chambers' retirement in December 1982; Ted Wheelwright proposed two new Economics III(P) courses, and the replacement of Simpson-Lee (who had resigned as staff member) by a designated (P) teacher. More controversially, the meeting was told about a proposal for an Economics Department working party to consist of four non (P) and two (P) teachers, to investigate the possibility of merging Economics I and I(P), II and II(P) and provide better third- and fourth-year opportunities for those interested in (P) studies.

Carole Pateman's committee on honours noted the sharp fluctuations in faculty honours numbers for all departments. For the faculty as a whole, it observed a marked decline for the five years ending 1982 (an average of 34.2 honours students as against 52.1 for the previous seven years). This decline was particularly significant in the Accounting and Economic Statistics departments (two and seven honours students, as against 17 and 28 for the previous five years starting 1973). The committee also mentioned diverse departmental practice with respect to honours. Three departments (Economics, Economic History and Government) started honours work in second year, the other three (Accounting, Economic Statistics and Industrial Relations) not until third year. There was no mandatory thesis work in Economics IV. However, it was difficult to explain the decline in honours numbers given the general satisfaction with courses and the quality of honours teaching. Unfortunately, the student sample for 1982 on which that information was based was very small (a total of 31 students).

There were four faculty meetings in 1983. At the first meeting (25 March), the dean mentioned that yet another committee on political economy, this time chaired by Professor G.A. Wilkes (English), had reported to the vice-chancellor. Moreover, faculty's Curriculum Committee had reported in favour of introducing a semester system and simplification of the degree structure. The June meeting noted that the vice-chancellor had approved the Department of Economic Statistics' name change to Econometrics and the establishment of centres for both European and Asian studies. It approved recommendations for expanding the Merewether Building, and new courses in Economic History and Government. The July meeting discussed a Curriculum Committee report proposing a new Economics I course, and the addition of two new Economics III(P) courses. Both were the result of direct Academic Board intervention following the report of the Wilkes Committee, signalling a renewal of the political economy dispute. The final faculty meeting for 1983 (7

Administering the Faculty as graduate assistant to the Dean: Joyce Fisher.

October) re-elected Salsbury as dean for a third consecutive term, reported on staff changes and appointments, elected new sub-deans (Ken Turner for postgraduates, Anne Riches for undergraduates) appointed a Computer Users Committee and a faculty programmer, and noted complaints about excessive noise in the Wolstenholme Library and the introduction of a new MBA course, Industrial Relations and Human Resources Development. In addition, faculty was given greater use of rooms in the adjoining Institute Building to alleviate the chronic space shortage in the Merewether Building. Four departments (Accounting, Economics, Econometrics and Government) were noted by faculty as seeking an additional chair to their current establishment.

Only three full faculty meetings were held in 1984. The first (23 March) in principle supported the vice-chancellor's proposal to alter the composition of the faculty. This proposal criticised the overlap between the Faculty of Economics and the Faculty of Arts, noted that faculty's second largest department, Government, drew as many of its students from Arts as from Economics, and that Economics from 1974 onwards was no longer compulsory at the senior level. Moreover, faculty's structure had also been responsible for a decade of futile strife within the Economics Department. Ward therefore urged the Economics Faculty to rethink its functions and composition. In addition, faculty considered new Economic History courses and their prerequisites, and noted that the Academic Board had introduced departmental quotas on enrolments for Accounting and Computer Science. The second faculty meeting for the year (8 June) indicated that some Darlington Road terrace houses would be made available as additional faculty accommodation, completed resolutions for the MPP for inclusion in the faculty by-laws, and approved proposals for new Government courses. The third 1984 faculty meeting (12 October) coincided with the renewed flare-up of the political economy dispute. This was sparked by more debate over the introduction of Economics IV(P) and dissatisfaction with the common Economics first-year course given as an experiment in 1984 following a recommendation from the Wilkes Reports and subsequent Academic Board intervention. For 1985 only, a new Economics I was unanimously approved by the Economics Department and endorsed by faculty, 32 votes to 16. Moreover, Murray Wells as head of the Accounting Department and Allan Woodland as head of Econometrics informed faculty that Economics II(P) was not a satisfactory co-requisite for Accounting II or Econometrics II, but their motion to make Economics II the only co-requisite for these courses was lost on a tied vote, 27 to 27. A special faculty meeting (12 December 1984) elected Michael Hogan as sub-dean (undergraduate studies) to replace Anne Riches who had resigned.

This lengthy section on faculty deliberations can be brought to a close by recording the changes in faculty administrative staff from 1973 to 1984. Given the turmoil in the faculty over these years, it is not surprising that turnover was somewhat high. Joyce Fisher retired in 1973 as administrative assistant to the dean after nearly two decades in the position. She was replaced by Stewart Adam, who resigned in 1975. Given the dean's greatly increased workload by then, two assistants to the dean, Arthur Mason and Liz Stephenson, were appointed to replace him. Arthur Mason resigned from the position in 1977 to return to the registrar's office, and was not replaced. Liz Stephenson resigned in 1979, to be replaced by Raymond Patman. He was replaced by Ann Bryant in 1980.

Adding to the Merewether Building and changes in the Wolstenholme Library

The Merewether Building, so auspiciously opened in 1966 as the fulfilment of Butlin's dream for securing suitable accommodation for the faculty for the foreseeable future, was within ten years viewed as inadequate for meeting faculty's needs for the final quarter of the twentieth century. In 1977, additional tutorial space was created in the basement, and during the early 1980s there was talk of further extending the building. Merewether Building space was increasingly rationed for tutorial staff and for students, with room sharing rapidly becoming the general rule for them. Moreover, teaching had to be increasingly conducted in other places: the Carslaw Building was, for example, heavily used for that purpose. Increasing use was also made of the neighbouring Institute Building, its former director's cottage and, from the early 1980s, of the terrace buildings in Darlington Road adjoining the Merewether Building on the Redfern side. For some time, the terraces were used as tutor and postgraduate student accommodation. As discussed in the next chapter, the Institute Building and the adjoining cottage housed a significant proportion of faculty staff by the early 1990s. Hence an additional new building for the faculty became an increasingly pressing item on the faculty's agenda.

The Wolstenholme Library space, another major source of pride when the Merewether Building was inaugurated, particularly with its book stock substantially enlarged from the financial appeal to that purpose organised by Jules Ginswick, also soon proved inadequate as a satisfactory faculty library.

Curtailment of university funding from the mid-1970s implied less money for the library. This ensured that maintenance of its initial substantial serials holding was no longer feasible. Moreover, a quiet atmosphere for study in the library was more difficult to achieve when it was used by so many students. A silent study space was not produced from enclosed group study rooms, or by the construction of carrels for individual researchers. Although Gloria Muir, the Wolstenholme Librarian for the whole of this period, tried valiantly to maintain both library services and an atmosphere conducive to study, her task became more and more difficult as resources tightened. Closed reserve, a facility experiencing rapid growth in demand from the enormous expansion of courses and their required reading, encountered major difficulties. Library shortcomings were invariably raised by students and staff at Wolstenholme Library Committee and Staff/Student Liaison Committee meetings. From the mid-1970s, Wolstenholme Library's services steadily deteriorated. Gradual curtailment of its serial holdings slowly eroded its value for senior undergraduate and postgraduate students, while increasing problems with closed reserve made longer waiting times for undergraduates inevitable. With diminishing financial resources for the university, the ability to maintain adequate decentralised library services began to be seriously questioned by successive university librarians. Hence, by the end of 1984 the days of the Wolstenholme Library as a useful source of books, journals and government reports appeared to be numbered for both students and staff. As is shown in the next chapter, Gloria Muir, appointed Wolstenholme Librarian in 1972, was the last to hold that post.

At last! A Department of Industrial Relations

As Kingsley Laffer (1981, pp. 38–40) suggests, growing problems in relations between the Industrial Relations teachers and the Economics Department sparked the creation of a Department of Industrial Relations. Friction between the two groups became very serious in 1973 when Industrial Relations academics were requested by the head of Department of Economics to attend Economics Department meetings, despite the fact that such teachers were totally uninterested in listening to prolonged debates about the minutiae of Economics course changes. The timing of this request indicates that it was closely related to the accelerating political economy dispute since an 'expansion' of the Economics Department through adding Industrial Relations staff would perhaps have provided more favourable voting outcomes at these meetings for its head of department. At this stage, Professor Bruce Williams as vice-chancellor intervened. He had heard of the dispute from the head of Economics and asked Kingsley Laffer to explain his side of the issue. As Laffer tells the story, he adroitly used the opportunity of the meeting to sing the praises of the small Industrial Relations group (Maxine Bucklow, Geoff Sorrell, Malcolm Rimmer and himself). In his own words, his meeting with Williams 'was a turning point in our progress towards becoming a separate Department of Industrial Relations' (Laffer 1981, p. 40).

Good reasons for this institutional change were in any case growing quickly. First, much burdensome paperwork and time was required to obtain additional resources for the Industrial Relations group because these needed to go via the head of the Economics Department. Secondly, the Economics Department's poor relationship with students during the early 1970s, arising from the political economy dispute and the general pressures from demands for more student participation in departmental governance, created difficulties within the Industrial Relations group itself. Some of the Industrial Relations staff actively supported the political economy movement (Malcolm Rimmer, Geoff Sorrell) even if Kingsley Laffer and Maxine Bucklow had more conservative attitudes to student demands. However, the problems caused within Industrial Relations by this difference in opinion were minute as compared with those already existing in the Economics Department. Moreover, the Industrial Relations group was fully united in being unhappy 'about being tied to the Economics Department at this time' (Laffer 1981, p. 41).

Laffer therefore decided to take the issue of a separate industrial relations department to the faculty. In June 1973, he sent the dean a 'Proposal for the Establishment of a Separate Industrial Relations Department' in order to have it placed on the agenda. Laffer's memorandum contained six reasons for a separate department. These included Industrial Relations' recognised status as a distinct discipline in the social sciences, and as one invariably housed in a separate school in the leading international universities which taught industrial relations as part of their curriculum. The memorandum requested faculty to give in principle support to a separate department, an objective Laffer hoped to achieve by the start of 1974. However, only vice-chancellors at the University of Sydney were able to create new departments, and despite securing faculty assistance in gaining additional resources (a new lecturer, Peter Scherer, appointed in 1975, and a full-time secretary for the Industrial Relations group), Laffer had to negotiate with Williams to achieve his main objective. In many respects, the time was far from propitious for such a step, given the fact that Williams was denying separate departmental status to the political economy group in the department at this time. Nevertheless, on 15 October 1974, the vice-chancellor wrote to Laffer informing him that he had decided to set up a separate Department of Industrial Relations with Laffer as its head and that a professorship in Industrial Relations would be created at the same time. This chair, as shown earlier, initially went to Harry Turner (who only took it as a temporary visiting professor for one year) and in 1978 to John Corina. From the beginning of 1975, Industrial Relations became a separate department in the

Faculty of Economics. Laffer was able to enjoy his triumph as a staff member and as its first head for six months until his retirement in June 1975. He stayed on until 1982 as his department's first honorary associate.

Governance problems in the Government Department, 1973

During June and July 1973, the Government Department engaged in a massive debate about departmental governance, a climax to the ongoing discussion of this subject over previous years. It concerned professorial power, the various powers of heads of departments including their right of veto (powers then being clarified by the Senate) and, on the other side of the coin, the rights of sub-professorial staff and students in proposing new courses and, more generally, departmental decision making. The timing of these events within the Government Department was closely related to the disputes in Philosophy and Economics and to the more general student demands in the university for greater control over their courses. Strong support for the proposed women's course to be taught in the Philosophy Department by Liz Jacka and Jean Curthoys widened the debate by introducing issues of women's rights and sexual liberation, including that for homosexuals. However, 'democratisation' of departmental decision making, and limiting the 'autocratic' powers of heads of departments and professors, were the major issues for debate over appropriate university governance within the Government Department.

Only the broad flavour of the events of June and July 1973 in the Government Department can be given to illustrate the extent to which these issues permeated university and faculty life in the early 1970s. The surviving pamphlet literature on this Government Department 'struggle' indicates that the issues raised were much wider than governance problems within the department. For instance, they often addressed university governance as a whole. Examples are the allegedly undemocratic and authoritarian role of the Professorial Board with respect to the introduction of the Women's Issues course in Philosophy, and the rights to be given to heads of departments in the proposed new by-laws on university departments and their administration. The events portrayed in this section therefore had wide implications going well beyond the concerns of the Government Department.

The Government professors at the time, Dick Spann and Henry Mayer, based their arguments in favour of continuation of their 'powers' on their staunch belief 'in intellectual excellence', high devotion 'to a subject … and knowing that subject better than most' (Henry Mayer, speech at staff–student workshop, reported 8 June 1973). Dick Spann reiterated his colleague's position on a university's inherent inequality, given its long-established hierarchical structures with its distinct grades of staff. Spann went on to defend Mayer as the then head of department because 'it [was] absurd to talk of [him] as a sort of Dictator … [because he] had showed the greatest reluctance ever to become Head', only acquiescing to the vice-chancellor's request because of Spann's illness. Mayer subsequently produced a long document commenting on the subject of greater student participation in departmental decision making, in which he defended his well-known pluralistic and anti-authoritarian stance, as well as his generally progressive attitude to teaching and course construction.

Much of his argument relied on the special hierarchical nature of the university, and the personal responsibility of a head of department for whose actions he, and he alone, 'carried the can'. More specifically, Mayer rejected the notion of 'the academic as a *tap* turned on by "customers" … [since] it would mean the end of the autonomy of learning as a *principle*' (Mayer, comment on a petition, 8 June 1973, italics in original).

Irrespective of this reasonable, and reasoned, professorial position, a sizable proportion (fourteen sub-professorial members) of the Government Department's staff went out on 'strike' towards the end of June 1973. One of the many strike bulletins declared that 'while on strike … [staff] would not be teaching the prescribed curriculum … [but] would continue to attend the university to discuss issues raised by the women's course controversy [in Philosophy] with the students' (Strike Bulletin, issued 27 June 1973). The strike lasted until mid-July, that is, until the Philosophy Department's women's course issue had been satisfactorily resolved by a suitable compromise. The Government Department strike therefore arose not from the 'democratisation' debate within the Government Department itself, but from the Philosophy Department's women's course issue. After all, the democratisation debate was being amicably resolved in growing agreement with Henry Mayer as departmental head (Strike Bulletin, 5 July 1973). For example, a detailed draft constitution went to the department later in July; an adaptation of its complex proposals for departmental consultation procedures was eventually agreed at a series of departmental meetings during 1974.

The Political Economy dispute, 1973–84

Faculty's role in the dispute, and some reactions thereto from the vice-chancellor and Senate were discussed earlier in this chapter in the section devoted to faculty deliberations and administration. Some of the origins of the dispute were briefly raised at the end of Chapter 4, particularly the exercise of professorial powers not to renew the contract of two tutors in 1971 (the Hill–Waters affair), the course changes to Economics I and II introduced by the then newly appointed professors of Economics, Warren Hogan and Colin Simkin (which were criticised as an excessive mathematisation of the economics syllabus), and more generally, the issue of departmental governance *vis-à-vis* what were portrayed as the highly authoritarian actions of the two Economics professors with the support of the new vice-chancellor. This section, to repeat an earlier warning, cannot be taken as a detailed history of this lengthy and complex dispute. Its more limited task is to outline detail of the dispute relevant to faculty's role therein as revealed at faculty meetings. It therefore provides a short chronology of the major events, outlining the contents of the various official reports on the subject prepared either for faculty or for the university's Academic Board.

In July 1973, in a particularly notable year in this dispute, an article appeared in *Honi Soit* posing 'the choice: "Simkin or Economics"' while reporting that the Economics I lectures (taught by Frank Stilwell) had been suspended, as had those by Ted Wheelwright on the Political Economy of Modern Capitalism and the Economics of Socialism. On 10 July, a meeting of staff and students in Economics voted that six resolutions, including one to make all Economics courses optional in the faculty, and one excluding compulsory mathematics in Economics except for third-year honours students, be put to the two Economics professors. These issues were reiterated during a 'Day of Protest' (25 July 1973). The day ended with a 'disappointing' meeting with the professors to discuss grievances, followed by a further meeting of students with Professor Hogan in September on course changes and increased student participation in departmental decision making. A survey of economics students conducted by the Sydney University Economics Society (reproduced in the Mills Report, 1973, Appendix A) conveyed strong support for the new courses as designed during the Day of Protest. As already mentioned, these events induced the appointment of a faculty committee on the Studies, Lectures, and Administration of Economics I–IV (the Mills Committee, 1973). Its report reviewed the background to the political economy dispute, which it summarised as 'professional economics versus political economy'. the administration of the department, the nature of the existing Economics I–IV courses, factors favouring change (such as the faculty's transition to a Faculty of Economics and Social Sciences from 1974), the relevance of the Economics courses to Arts students, and the relationship of the political economy dispute to debates on university governance. It recommended a separate department of political economy, both Economics departments offering courses from first to fourth year; staff to select which department they wished to join; optional courses to be divided between the departments by agreement, and avoidance of unnecessary duplication through consultation between the two heads of the departments. Faculty's support of these recommendations at meetings in 1974 was mentioned previously, as was the introduction of Economics I(P) in 1975 and Economics II(P) in 1976, administered from within a single Department of Economics in accordance with decisions by the Academic Board.

However, problems associated with providing 'adequate progression' for (P) students by way of an Economics III(P) and IV(P) prompted the appointment of an Academic Board committee to enquire into Political Economy in 1976, with Professor John Ward as chairman. Its terms of reference were to investigate and report on the status of political economy as a distinguishable academic discipline, to comment on a 1975 faculty report on the subject, and to address the 'adequate progression' for students issue. Its first report described the dispute as one of the 'most intractable' in the university's long history, caused by 'a mixture of intellectual, pedagogic and personal circumstances' (section 1.5). As a result of meeting with economists from within and without the university (the last including Keith Hancock and Geoff Harcourt from Adelaide University, John Neville from the University of New South Wales, David Throsby from Macquarie University and Roy Webb from the University of Melbourne), it decided that political economy was not a distinguishable discipline from economics (section 2.9) and that a separate department would only 'force polarisation of viewpoints on *all* members' of the Economics Department (section 2.11). Enrolment data on Economics I(P) and II(P) showed that political economy could be successfully taught within the Economics Department even if within a climate of hostility and without academic consensus. These last factors suggested a 'temporary separation' of the (P) teachers and their courses from the Economics Department by creating a unit of political economy within the Economics Department (section 3.13). On the issue of suitable progression, the committee expressed the concern that it was difficult to justify additional resources to teach senior courses which largely overlapped existing courses (section 4.3). At this stage, the Ward Committee therefore refused to adjudicate the various alternatives placed before it. The committee's third report indicated that a separate unit had been ruled out by the vice-chancellor, and in addition condemned the intervening violence (the July 1976 break-in of the vice-chancellor's and registrar's offices) which had done nothing to advance the political economy cause.

A final report from the committee (10 August 1976) stated that the Economics III proposals approved by the Department of Economics that month appeared to meet the requirements of its first report's recommendations. The third-year course adopted consisted of a completely optional third year for students coming from II(P). They could take either one long option (short course) from History of Economic Thought, Industry Economics, Post-Keynesian Economics or Urban and Regional Development and two short options from either Advanced Micro-Economics, Advanced Macro-Economics, Economic Development, Economics of Socialism, Issues of Marxist Economics, Managerial Economics, Monetary Economics, Quantitative Economics I or II, Transport Economics, Public Finance or Australian Public Policy Issues. Alternatively, they could select a second course from the long options already listed. This was, however, never accepted as a complete solution to the dispute over adequate progression and for the subsequent seven years (1977–84) the battle by the (P) supporters from staff and students continued intermittently for a separate stream consisting of Economics III(P) and IV(P) courses. In 1976, a large political economy conference was organised at the University of Sydney and one of the overseas participants, Professor Ed Nell (New York School of Social Research) met briefly with members of the Ward Committee.

During the early 1980s, the debate over political economy courses hotted up once more. A political economy meeting and march were organised during September 1981, five new Political Economy third-year courses were prepared later that year and in November 1981 the Academic Board set up a new committee to examine the matter. Its chair was Professor Gerry Wilkes (its other members comprised Dr John Booker, Mr Anthony Cahill, Professor Michael Pitman and a postgraduate student, Mr Peter Wormal). It reported in May 1982, noting that positions in the dispute had hardened considerably since 1976, and that 'this prolonged and bitter dispute has done little to enhance the reputation of the participants or the university' (§3). Likewise, the report noted that a joint first year had made little progress (§4). It also found 'integrated' third-year courses with both (P) and non(P) teachers had been unsuccessful and that after 1976 few provisions had been made for improving progression into senior years for (P) students (§5). The report recommended a general review by faculty and Department of Economics of its course structure, with special reference to the (P) courses, that free movement of students between courses should be encouraged, and that an Economics (P) teacher should be named as 'professor most concerned' for the designated (P) teachers. It added that the Academic Board should exercise its power over courses if no substantial progression on its first two recommendations was reported within a reasonable period.

On 16 June 1983 the Academic Board reported insufficient progress from the Economics Department. It did so via a committee comprising Salsbury as Dean of the Economics Faculty, Wilkes as chair of the earlier Wilkes Committee, with the chairman of the Academic Board, Professor Collis-George, as chair. It recommended the introduction of a combined first-year course by the start of 1984; revision during 1984 of Economics II and II(P) to take account of the new combined first-year course; and, if separate second-year courses were to remain, Economics Faculty students should be able to count both for their degree. Third-year options were to be increased from 1984 enabling students to proceed with courses exclusively taught by (P) teachers to constitute an Economics III(P) and sufficient fourth-years options to effectively create an Economics IV(P). The new courses had to be submitted to faculty's curriculum committee by 8 July 1983 (that is, in just over three weeks). The vice-chancellor was again requested to appoint a person with administrative responsibility for the (P) courses from the associate professors among the designated (P) teachers. He responded quickly to this last request by appointing Frank Stilwell as director of (P) courses on 29 June. In the end, implementation of the other recommendations pleased no one in the Department of Economics.

The Department of Economics in April 1983 voted to support in principle a move towards common first- and second-year courses, a vote from which the designated (P) teachers abstained. Working out the details proved more difficult. Moreover, while the Academic Board deliberations reported in the previous paragraph were going on, a demonstration by political economy supporters on the front lawn was taking place in conjunction with an occupation of the university Clock Tower. This occupation culminated in a rally on 15 June at which prominent ALP politicians (Ray Giezelt, Minister for Veteran Affairs; Gough Whitlam; Laurie Ferguson, acting New South Wales premier; and Rodney Cavalier, MLA) were reported as expressing strong support for the (P) courses (*University News*, 21 June 1983). Results from an Economics students' referendum provided in a special political economy issue of *Honi Soit* (6 June 1983) revealed that 76 per cent of the economics students who voted supported separate Economics courses in first and second year, as well as additional (P) courses for third and fourth year.

Parts of the Merewether Building were occupied by political economy supporters on 29 June. This occupation ended when the occupiers were speedily evicted by the police at the request of the vice-chancellor to allow a departmental meeting scheduled for 1 July to take place. Subsequently, in response to Economics Department approval of a new combined Economics I and new third-year courses, political economy supporters reoccupied part of the Merewether Building. However, the combined first-year course recommended by the Wilkes Committee was taught in 1984, despite Senate intervention early that year (SM: 6 February 1984) to force alterations in its contents because they did not conform to the letter of the Academic Board prescription.

The out-of-pocket expenses of the demonstrations and occupations to the university (estimated in SM: 1 August 1983, at close to $20,000 for necessary repairs to the occupied property, and to pay overtime to university security guards) probably stimulated the vice-chancellor's 1984 suggestion to separate political economy from the other courses in the

Faculty of Economics, as noted earlier in this chapter. The full costs attributable to the dispute were in fact enormous. In terms of staff turnover in the Department of Economics, this was noted previously. The biographer of Richard Downing, Professor of Economics at the University of Melbourne at this time (Brown 2001, p. 283), suggests the dispute was seen in university circles outside Sydney as the 'complete disintegration of the Faculty'. This judgement is somewhat exaggerated, but it cannot be denied that both faculty and department suffered enormously. Two designated (P) teachers, Evan Jones and Frank Stilwell (1986) described the dispute as a clear case of intellectual suppression and as a 'classic manifestation of academic conflict'. Bruce Williams, vice-chancellor for much of this period, discussed the issue in detail in his memoirs of university life (Williams 2005, pp. 103–21), among other things suggesting that 'decisions by exhaustion are seldom satisfactory and the political economy decision in July 1983 was not'. Nor can it be said that the involvement of non-faculty persons in generating solutions for an academic dispute on how best to teach economics to tertiary students was a satisfactory means to produce academically acceptable course outcomes.

Turmoil in the cloisters: advancing the cause of 'Political Economy' in the University.

Demonstration in the Quadrangle in the 1980s.

Graduates and students, 1973–84

The number of faculty graduates increased from 266 (including 41 honours graduates) in 1973 to 364 (24 honours graduates) in 1984, reflecting that decline in honours students over the period investigated by a faculty committee at the beginning of the 1980s. These graduates included a steadily increasing proportion of women (21.4 per cent in 1973 to 35.6 per cent in 1984) but this relative increase in women students for the faculty was not matched at honours or postgraduate level. No women were awarded the DSc (Econ), the faculty's higher doctorate; only two women (13.3 per cent) were included among the fifteen PhDs conferred by faculty from 1973 to 1984; only six women (8.5 per cent) were among the 77 MEcs conferred; and there was only one woman (1.5 per cent) among faculty's 69 MBA graduates. With respect to honours students, there were two women medallists (15.4 per cent) among the thirteen medals awarded in total, and 74 (or 23.3 per cent) of faculty's 333 honours graduates were women. However, when twelve women successfully completed their honours year in 1976, the largest number for the period covered by this chapter, they accounted for 37.5 per cent of the honours class, while the next highest number (ten in 1981) amounted to 32.2 per cent.

The fifteen faculty PhDs conferred between 1973 and 1984 came from all schools in the faculty except Economic History. Three were conferred in 1973 and 1983; two in 1977, 1981 and 1984; and one in 1974, 1975 and 1984. Five PhDs, or a third of the total, were awarded in Accounting, a tribute to Chambers' skills as supervisor. Two of these, Murray Wells and Bob Walker, subsequently gained chairs in Accounting at the universities of

Sydney and New South Wales. Of the four Economics PhDs, three went to staff members (Hugh Pritchard, Peter Saunders and Surinder Joson), the fourth to John Whiteman, a Commonwealth public servant. The two PhDs in Economic Statistics (Bob Bartels and George Babich) likewise were academics, with one a faculty staff member. The same applies to the two PhDs from Industrial Relations (Margaret Gardiner and Michael Quinlan) and from Government (Trevor Mathews and Elaine Thompson).

Master of Economics degrees conferred totalled 65, with considerable fluctuations for individual years. Eight were conferred in 1973, four in 1974, only one in 1975, eight in 1976 (among whom were two Accounting staff members, Graeme Dean and Peter Wolnizer), ten in 1977 (including later academics John Burgess, Michael Danes and Phil Raskall), eight in 1978 (including Brian Donovan, later a prominent economic consultant); three in 1979 (among whom were two future professors, Bob Brown and Jock Collins, and one academic historian, Helen Murphy); two in 1980, five in 1981 (of which two, to Barbara Page and Laraine Hayes, were awarded with first-class honours, three at pass level); six in 1982 (including one with first-class honours to Peter Kriesler, a future academic at the University of New South Wales), two in 1983 and six in 1984. A good third of the masters graduates came from the Economics Department, more than double the output of MEc graduates in Government, Economic Statistics (Econometrics) and Accounting, and three times that for Economic History and Industrial Relations. In 1981, an honorary MEc was conferred on David Wood for his services to the university as a long-time special adviser to the vice-chancellor.

The first eight Master of Business Administration degrees were conferred in 1975. Subsequently, five were conferred in 1976, nine in 1977 and 1978, eight in 1979, two in 1980, six in 1981, two in 1982, twelve in 1983 and eight in 1984. The numbers taking this business degree therefore fluctuated markedly over the ten years of its existence and, as noted previously, only attracted one successful woman candidate.

Of the honours graduates in 1973, medallist William Evans went into banking, as did John Rush at the Reserve Bank of Australia and Ian Shepherd (after a period as adviser to the then leader of the opposition, Billie Snedden). Murray Milgate built an academic career first at Sydney, then at Harvard and Cambridge, as did John Burgess, initially at Sydney. Graeme Bullivant went into New South Wales Treasury, Graeme Thompson became chief executive officer of the Australian Prudential Regulation Authority after holding positions with the Reserve Bank of Australia as deputy governor and assistant governor (Financial Institutions). Dennis Mortimer built a career in transport. Diane Johnstone joined the Department of Foreign Affairs and Trade, becoming Australian High Commissioner in Kenya (1980–82) and Ambassador to Nepal (1986–89). Several 1973 pass graduates also distinguished themselves in later life. Nicholas Barton-Taylor became managing director of Hillgrove Pastoral Company after founding M.D. Hays Accountancy Personnel (1976–89) and being director of the National Heart Foundation (1995–97); George Cujes became headmaster of Trinity Grammar School in 1996 and was a member of the university's Senate from 1998 to 2001; Colleen Ryan built a career in financial journalism with the *Australian Financial Review*, becoming its editor (1998–2001) and senior writer (2002) and was named journalist of the year in 1992. David Martin held various managerial positions in the Sydney Convention and Visitors Bureau, the Opera House and in the National Institute of Dramatic Art; Gail Hambly became company secretary in John Fairfax Holdings, while Stephen Rix built a trade union career.

In the class of 1974, at least three first-class honours graduates made prominent careers for themselves. Terry Dwyer (after completing an LLB and a PhD at Harvard) enjoyed a distinguished legal career in private practice, often contributing to the press on economic subjects; Bruce Hogan held various directorships including in Energy Australia, St Vincent's Hospital, Coles-Myer and the Adelaide Casino; while Brian Cassidy made a distinguished career in the Commonwealth Public Service in Treasury, Industry and Environment and as chief executive officer, Australian Competition and Consumer Commission. Frank Gelber moved into economic consulting, initially with B.S. Schrapnell and Sons; Graeme Smith (after completing a doctorate in theology) involved himself in disability assessment and assistance; while four pass graduates, Ian Boardman, John Henningham, Ian McNamara (Macca) and Mark Sullivan distinguished themselves in public service and the law, academia and journalism, popular music and public broadcasting, and Commonwealth Public Service (Department of Immigration and Multi-cultural Affairs) and public broadcasting (head, Corporate Affairs, SBS).

In 1975, MEc postgraduate Tony Gentile followed a distinguished Commonwealth Public Service career with one in private enterprise as executive director (Food Division), Australian Retailers Association, and national executive director, Australian Soft Drinks Association Limited; Bob Brown and Michael Danes built academic careers on their first-class honours results at Monash University and the University of the West Indies; Greg Crouch for a period worked as researcher of multinational corporations with Ted Wheelwright's Transnational Research Foundation at the Faculty of Economics. Among 1975 pass graduates Gregory Bondar was deputy mayor at Kogarah Council and held many chief executive officer positions in private enterprise; Ken Matthews enjoyed a distinguished Commonwealth Public Service career including secretary to the Commonwealth Department of Agriculture, Fisheries and Forestry; Kerry Smith held managing positions in finance and banking, including that of chief executive officer and managing director, Schroders Australian Holdings Limited; Janco (John) Spasojevic made a career in the Commonwealth Public Service including deputy chief executive officer, Department of Industry, Science and Resources; Kerry Flanagan ended her career in the Department of Prime Minister and Cabinet as first assistant secretary, Office of the Status of Women.

Politics and academic administration attracted some of the better 1976 graduates. Margaret Gardiner, a first-class honours graduate in Industrial Relations, obtained a chair in that field at Griffith University, was head of school for many years and deputy vice-chancellor (Academic) at the University of Queensland from 2004, and vice-chancellor at RMIT (Victoria) from 2005; Peter Booth, a pass graduate, followed an academic career including Professor of Management Accounting (University of New South Wales) with the position of deputy vice-chancellor (Academic) at Sydney's University of Technology; Peter Wolnizer, an MEc in 1976 (and subsequently a PhD) followed a teaching career in Accounting with

Dean of the Faculty of Economics and Business at the University of Sydney from 1999; Michael Quinlan became Professor of Organisational Behaviour and Industrial Relations (University of New South Wales); Graeme Dean, another 1976 Accounting MEc, became Professor of Accounting in the Economics and Business Faculty at the University of Sydney in 2001. Martin Ferguson, a 1976 Industrial Relations honours graduate, entered federal politics as Labor MHR for Batman in 1996 after being president of the ACTU (1990–96) and a lifetime involvement in Trade Union affairs, and became a minister in the Rudd government in 2007; Genia McCaffery, 1976 honours Government graduate, became mayor of North Sydney after initially serving as a councillor for many years, as well as well as president of the New South Wales Local Government Association for a term. Other 1976 graduates had distinguished careers in management and finance. Graeme Kerridge was chief executive officer, Launceston General Hospital; Alan Kincade was general manager, Concord Repatriation General Hospital; Russell Brown was managing partner, Douglas, Heck and Burrell Chartered Accountants; and Belinda Hutchinson worked in banking and communication, with positions at Citibank, Telstra and Macquarie Bank.

The 1977 graduate list produced two federal Labor politicians: Craig Emerson (MHR for Rankin, Queensland, and Minister for Small Business in the 2007 Rudd Government) and Daryl Melham (MHR for Banks, New South Wales). Both have also held shadow ministries. In addition, three other honours graduates followed careers in banking (Robert Rankin), New South Wales Treasury (Eric Groom), and the Bureau of Statistics (Kerry Hogan). Thomas Giles (an MBA graduate) worked in senior management in financial institutions (including the United Permanent Building Society and State Bank of New South Wales); Robert Deutsch combined economics with a legal career as barrister, a partner in Millesons Stephen Jacques and as professor in the Board of Studies in Taxation (University of New South Wales); Keith Rewell was a New South Wales Senior Counsel, and William Roche executive chairman of Nutrimetics International (Australia).

The 1978 honours list produced several future academics: first-class honours graduates Peter Kriesler and John Lodewijks became associate professor in Economics at the University of New South Wales and professor at the University of Western Sydney; Rod O'Donnell, as a pass graduate followed by a Cambridge PhD, became Professor of Economics at Macquarie University; David Pitman and Ron Callus (honours graduate and MEc in Industrial Relations respectively) both obtained academic positions in Industrial Relations at the University of Sydney; Stephen Finch and Anna Booth (both Industrial Relations honours graduates) became Senior Counsel in New South Wales (after a law degree) and, following senior trade union positions with the ACTU, vice-president of Sydney Harbour Casino Holdings and board member, Australian Preservation Trust. Among the pass graduates, John Anschau had an extensive business career as partner in Price Waterhouse; Mark Burrowes had a distinguished management career in Medibank Private, the Colonial Bank and in sales and marketing at Caltex (Australia) limited, Francesco Carsaro (after a law degree) became a barrister and Senior Counsel in 2000, as did Anthony Bannon in 1996 and Steven Finch in 1997.

In 1979, Chris Murphy, one of the three medallists for that year, initially worked for the Commonwealth Treasury, then as a private consultant; Clive Hamilton (first-class honours in Economics) after several research positions became director of the Australian Institute from 1993; Greg Patmore (second-class honours in Industrial Relations) entered academic life in Industrial Relations at the university, as did Michael John Walton before becoming judge and vice-president of the New South Wales Industrial Relations Commission. Pass graduate Peter Docherty went on to a career at Sydney's University of Technology after completing a PhD and a period of teaching finance at the University of New South Wales. Tony Abbott, another pass graduate, after a career in journalism, was elected Liberal MHR for Warringah and has held various ministerial posts in successive Howard governments from 2004 to 2007.

Given the time it takes to make a name for yourself in a chosen career, numbers of easily identifiable distinguished graduates started to diminish considerably from the start of the 1980s. For 1980, first-class honours Economics graduate Glenn Stevens enjoyed a distinguished Reserve Bank career, attaining the position of its governor in 2005; Jeremy Campbell, who followed his pass BEc with an LLB, held various management positions before becoming secretary of the Law Reform Commission and chief financial officer of T Data Pty Ltd. Among 1980 pass graduates, James Longley was Liberal MLA for Pittwater (1986–96) and head of Government Finance, Commonwealth Bank. Apart from John Carson, a first-class honours graduate, for some years an academic at the University of Sydney, four 1981 pass graduates distinguished themselves by the end of 2005. Paul Malliate held accounting positions with Sydney Electricity and Rothmans (Australia) before becoming national manager and partner of Baker and McKenzie; Gregory Martin became managing director of the Australian Gas Light Company; Iain Ross had a career with the ACTU and various industrial relations positions before becoming vice-president of the Australian Industrial Relations Commission; Neil Williams, after a legal career and one as ministerial adviser to the federal parliament, became Senior Counsel in New South Wales.

Several 1982 honours students have commenced making careers for themselves. William Coleman began his academic career in Tasmania and continued it at the Australian National University; Nigel Ray entered the Commonwealth Public Service before joining the private sector; Simon Hannes ended an initially promising stockbroking career in disgrace as a convicted insider trader. Among distinguished pass students were the Reverend Peter Laurence, with a career in private education leading to appointment as executive director for the Anglican School Commission in Western Australia; Patrick Fair, who followed a legal career as partner and senior associate with Phillips Fox and senior partner with Baker and McKenzie; while John Hatzistegos followed his Economics degree with legal studies and a political career as Labor MLC in New South Wales from 1994, Minister for Justice in 2003, Minister for Health from 2005, Attorney-General in 2007, and Industrial Relations in 2008.

Three 1983 graduates have so far distinguished themselves. Warren Eades, an MBA in that year, enjoyed a major career in management in companies including Portfolio Management

Henroth and Pacific Strategy Investment Limited; Mark Latham started a short-lived political career as mayor of Liverpool (1991–94), became Labor MHR for Werriwa (1994–2004), federal shadow treasurer (2003) and leader of the opposition (2004), resigning from that position and from politics altogether in January 2005; David Binns had a career in the Commonwealth Public Service with the Department of Trade and Foreign Affairs, becoming Ambassador to Sri Lanka and the Republic of the Maldives from 2002. Two 1984 graduates rank among distinguished graduates so far. Morris Iemma was elected MLA for Labor in Lakemba (from 1999) and Hurstville (1991–99), becoming New South Wales Minister for Health (from 2003) and Premier from 2005 until his resignation in 2008. Allaster Cox, after a career with Esso and Shell, transferred to the public sector (Department of Trade and Foreign Affairs) in 1987, becoming Australian High Commissioner in Brunei in 2001.

The information on future occupations from the more famous graduates just presented for 1973–84 bears little resemblance to graduate employment of students from the Faculty of Economics collected by the university's Appointments Board for 1980 and 1983. The 1980 report indicated that of 157 economics graduates, 62 were continuing their education with further study and 82 were in full-time employment. Of the latter, 23 (or 28 per cent) worked for the public sector, three (or 3.7 per cent) in the education sector, and 52 (63.4 per cent) were employed in the private sector. In sharp contrast, the 1983 report indicated that of the 163 graduates for that year, 30 were continuing their studies (less than half the number in 1980), 12 were employed in the public sector (again, less than half as compared with 1980), 44 (or 27 per cent) were working in the private sector, only one person had joined the education sector. The data also showed that three graduates had gone overseas, while 21 (12.8 per cent) were unemployed and seven not looking for full-time work. In 1980, accounting graduates were 85 per cent of the total, a similar proportion applied in 1983.

Three honours students, all from Economics, recorded their recollections of studying at Sydney's Economics Faculty during the 1970s. Terry Dwyer, a first-class honours graduate who finished his undergraduate studies in 1973, particularly recalled an ability to combine an interest in economics with economic history and the history of economic thought. Thus he greatly enjoyed Sybil Jack's lectures in Economic History 'on the medieval wool trade and the first industrial revolution', and each time he signs a cheque he recalls their origin as bills of exchange at wool fairs. For him, the best teacher in the faculty was John Goodhew in Economic Statistics. 'He was unfailingly helpful and kind and always trying to make the subject clear, and I did tell him years later that he was better than any teacher at Harvard — and Martin Feldstein was not bad.' Not that all statistics teaching was of that quality. Dwyer recalled an Indian lecturer who gave 'ten incomprehensible lectures ... which he had cribbed from two undisclosed articles in the *Journal of the American Statistical Association*'. Moreover, a seminar on monetary theory by Colin Simkin taught him 'always carefully to examine assumptions, then look at the conclusions and, if they don't gel, getting suspicious about what has gone on in the middle of the argument'.

Robert Brown, Professor of Finance at the University of Melbourne from 2001, followed first-class honours in Economics in 1974 with an MEc and a position as full-time Economics tutor. He particularly recalled 'the political economy debate' which, judging from his experience, had essentially three causes. A major cause for the dispute was a sincere belief of some students and staff that 'Economics as a discipline was a force for conservatism, dressed up as a value-free social science'. Secondly, he recalled there was genuine student dissatisfaction with the lack of relevance of much economics teaching, particularly to 'the world of business that they were all hoping to join on graduation'. This made Wheelwright's lectures on multinational corporations a major drawcard for many students. Personalities were a third major factor in the dispute. 'Frank Stilwell and Ted Wheelwright appeared much more student friendly than Colin Simkin and Warren Hogan.' More generally, Brown recalled from his student experience that faculty's courses as a whole made him 'learn fewer *things*' and 'more about *how* to think, learn and write'. Hence self-learning was a major by-product of the system, particularly when in the early 1970s he had to complete twenty major essays as compared with the one or two his students have to do 'today'.

John Lodewijks, who graduated with first-class honours in Economics in 1978, recalled that when he decided to study university economics on completing his Higher School Certificate in 1973, the University of Sydney was the only choice for him as the place to do this. In his first year (in 1974), he particularly liked the Australian Economy course, then taught by Ted Wheelwright, Louis Haddad and Warren Hogan. This was at the height of the political economy dispute, and he therefore also recalled the 'schizophrenic' experience of being taught indifference curves as an indispensable tool for economic analysis by one teacher and hearing them 'ridiculed as useless theoretical trivia by another'. Statistics I he enjoyed for the quality of the teaching, recalling Stephen Harrison 'as superb', an experience inducing him to take Economic Statistics II in his second year. He took this together with Economics II(P) Conversion, Economics II Advanced and Economics II Additional, where teaching varied from the 'inspiring to dreadful'. 'The second year Macro courses were excellently taught by Viv Hall, Tony Phipps and Ian Sharpe … Peter Groenewegen strongly influenced me (first in Public Finance and later (third year) in the History of Economic Thought)'. Lodewijks then topped third year and successfully completed his fourth year, 'the hardest of my life in terms of work effort', with first-class honours. More generally, he recalled the high degree of specialisation in Economics the faculty course structure then permitted, no longer possible in courses currently offered. However, on looking back, the Sydney economics experience was 'a bit backward-looking. But I got to see Joan Robinson and John Hicks give Mills' Lectures, studied in the middle of a long Political Economy dispute that featured a lot of gossip, innuendo and back-stabbing (that harmed the external reputation of the place for decades) and was able to immerse myself in the breadth of economics (if not always the depth).'

Sydney University Economics Society, 1973–84

The faculty's students society continued to operate during the 1970s and early 1980s, organising functions such as the annual ball, inter-faculty debating teams and sport teams, as well as various other meetings. It also occasionally raised funds for the faculty library.

Few details of these meetings are retrievable, but some were occasionally reported in the *University News*. Much student activity in the faculty was diverted to the political economy dispute, where students organised the occasional debate between the parties involved. An example is the debate of 3 April 1974 in Merewether Lecture Theatre 1 between Warren Hogan, Peter Groenewegen, Gavan Butler and Frank Stilwell on the topic, 'Professional Economics Versus Political Economy', reported to have attracted an audience of 400 staff and students (*University News*, No. 6, 1974, p. 17).

By the 1980s, the faculty students society was also split with the emergence of a separate Sydney University Political Economy Society. This organised its own speakers for a regular 'P.E. Hour', as well as social functions for its students and adherents. A further victim of the dispute may have been the *Economic Review*. Its last issue (No. 18) appeared in 1973, ostensibly devoted to issues of technology. It was edited by Alan Hargreaves and contained the usual mix of students and staff among the contributors. Frank Stilwell wrote on 'Technology and Ideology', Gavan Butler on 'Technology, Foreign Aid and Trade Concessions', Warren Osmond from Government debated 'A Critic of Australian Universities' while former tutor Bill Waters contributed a paper, 'Radical or Orthodox Economics', where the latter, on Galbraith's authority, was described as 'socially irrelevant'. Among the students, Mark Healey wrote on 'Technological Change and Democracy', Richard Fields on 'A Need for a Refocusing of Aims ... [in Economics]', Simon Grose addressed the environmental consequences of technological change under the title, 'See You at the Food Riots', Michael Militon wrote on 'Technology and Underdevelopment' and Peter Freebody on 'Technology, Vocationalism and the Academic Dogma', while an anonymous contributor provided an essay on 'Papua New Guinea. The Issue of Bank Nationalisation'. Finally, Dennis Ansdure reviewed the 1972 Penguin Modern Economics Readings Book, *A Critique of Economic Theory*. This issue ended what In its file on the students' Economics Society, the university Archives preserve a list of its presidents from 1960 to 1987. They were recorded as Lindy Pessley (1973–74), John McGrath (1974–75), Chris Smith (1975–76), Megan Morris (1977–78), Kim McGrath (1978–80), Jim McInery (1980–81), Nina High (1981–82), John Martin (1982–83) and John Kain (1983–84). Of the nine presidents included in this list, two served double terms. A third of these presidents were women, a further reflection of the growing number of women students in the Economics Faculty.

University of Sydney Economics Graduates Association, 1973–84

Although its membership fluctuated considerably, the graduates association was able to sustain limited activity. Membership fees totalling $528 in 1974–75, the maximum, represented 204 members, as against a minimum of 98 members in 1977–78. Low membership then induced a rise in membership fees to $4 per annum, with a subsequent rise to $5 in 1982–83. Association activities depended greatly on the zeal of the annually elected committee and frequently took the form of the annual meeting, an annual dinner and an annual Christmas party, generally involving guest speakers drawn from faculty or elsewhere. Regulations put in force in 1980 prescribed at least two meetings a year, to be held during first and second term. However, even this modest requirement was not always met.

Association Annual Reports from 1973 to 1977 recorded no specific functions organised by the association. That for 1978 mentioned that Sir Hermann Black (graduate and university chancellor) had addressed the annual general meeting with 56 persons present. The 1978 Christmas function at the Journalists Club was addressed by retiring dean, Geelum Simpson-Lee. A 1978 mid-year forum on prospects for the Australian Economy for 1979 was introduced by graduates Paddy McGuinness (as editor of the *Australian Financial Review*), Harry Edwards (former staff members and MHR for Berowra) and Phillip Schrapnell (the business forecaster). During 1979–80, four meetings were held. Ted Wheelwright addressed 44 graduates and their guests on the Political Economy of Australian Capitalism in October 1979; 32 members attended a social function in late November; Alan Renouf spoke on Foreign Policy and Trade to 52 members in April 1980; while in August 1980, C. Costello (from Cullen, Egan and Dell) spoke on a topic close to many economics graduates' hearts, their remuneration prospects. The following year 38 members attended the annual meeting and a subsequent talk by Debesh Bhattacharya on the new international economic order. Later meetings that year attracted 38 members in first term to hear Kevin Munro on tax reform, and 49 members in second term to meet the new dean, Professor Stephen Salsbury, and to hear him speak on the implications for Australia of United States economic policy. In October 1982, R. Lyons addressed 29 persons on the economics of the corporate food sector; Mr J. Holmes (Australian Trade Commissioner, Vienna) spoking on trading with communist block countries to an audience of 42; while actuarian J. Graham attracted an audience of 33 for a discourse on superannuation and economy. No details of meetings were preserved for 1982–83 and 1983–84.

The association on various occasions published a newsletter, to keep graduates informed of events at the faculty once or twice a year. The most enduring of these ventures, *The Sydney Economist*, was published for half a decade or so from 1987. Among its contents it included not only stories of overcrowding in lecture theatres and more generally about faculty resource needs with its growing student numbers, it occasionally looked to the past. A good example are the two sets of reminiscences about his early years as an economist from the chancellor, Sir Hermann Black, recorded not long before his 90th birthday, and quoted in Chapter 2. An earlier version of this newsletter was extant in the early 1980s, hence warranting a mention in this chapter.

The association's major office bearers for 1973 to 1984 may also be recorded. Its presidents were D.M. Butcher (1973–74), C.N. Turner (1974–75), Miss M.F.S. Donnelly (1975–77), Noel Baker (1978–83) and Mr P. Kreznaric (1983–84). Secretaries were C.N. Jenkins (1973–75), P.G. Menzies (1975–78), and Jim Noble (1978–84). Faculty representatives were not regularly appointed or reappointed and there were none on the association's committee for many years. Two faculty representatives for the late 1970s came from Accounting (Frank Clarke in 1976–77, Graeme Dean in 1977–78) but in 1980 Ted Wheelwright was elected by faculty as its Graduates Association representative on a more permanent basis. This was at the suggestion of the new dean, Stephen Salsbury, who had hopes (never to be realised)

Economic Statistics staff and Honours graduates (1973).

of transforming the Graduates Association into an United States style alumni organisation and a source of additional resources for faculty activities in teaching and research. Apart from an occasional contribution to the Wolstenholme Library, and the financing of an annual prize for outstanding academic performance by a final-year undergraduate student in the faculty, financial support from the Faculty Graduates Association was virtually non-existent.

Research and scholarship, 1973–84

From 1974, faculty research by department was reported in the university's *Research Reports*. Government remained by far the most published department in the faculty, averaging nearly 40 items per year. It was now followed by the Economics Department with an average of 28 items annually. Accounting averaged nineteen items while the three smaller departments of Economic History, Economic Statistics (from 1983, Econometrics) and Industrial Relations (from 1975) averaged five items per year. Economic Statistics, the least successful department in research under the academic leadership of Stuart Rutherford, greatly improved its research performance after Alan Woodland's appointment as his successor. The department's average publication rose to eight items per annum from 1981 (as compared to an average of 3.5 items during the 1970s).

The number of strong research performers in the faculty was also rising. Although Chambers in Accounting continued to be among the most active researchers in the faculty with 36 published items recorded in the university's research reports for these years, he was now quantitatively surpassed by Henry Mayer from Government, who published 48 items over the period of this chapter, and by Peter Groenewegen from Economics (who published 37). Closely following Ray Chambers, Warren Hogan (Economics) published 25 items, Carole Pateman (Government) and Frank Clarke (Accounting) both published 24, Murray Wells (Accounting) listed 23 and Ted Wheelwright (Economics) reported 21 published items. Groenewegen's and Pateman's research productivity was recognised by the Academy of Social Sciences in Australia when it elected them as Fellows in 1980 and 1982.

The Accounting Department's research continued to focus on the development of a general financial accounting system for business firms. It addressed specific problems of financial reporting such as inflation accounting, a very significant problem for the 1970s, and most other areas of accounting and financial management. Chambers' and Frank Clarke's outstanding research example was followed to a lesser degree by other members of the department (in particular, Murray Wells and Bob Walker), including those from Commercial and Industrial Law. Pat Mills continued to be an active and productive researcher until his retirement in 1983, while Ron Bowra produced much practical tax research partly associated with his important position with the Taxation Institute of Australia. Over these years, Accounting research output was also significantly supported by the research of its postgraduate students who joined the staff, initially Murray Wells and Bob Walker, and later Bill Birkett, Alan Craswell, Graeme Dean, Michael Gaffikin and Peter Wolnizer.

The Government Department continued to display an excellent research performance in which all its members participated. Henry Mayer set a magnificent example, as did Dick Spann, who produced fifteen items (including several books) before his death in 1981. Carole Pateman, promoted to reader in 1980, produced 24 items in her field of political theory, for which she received increasing international recognition. Major research areas for the department were public policy and administration (Dick Spann, Ross Curnow, Martin Painter), political theory (Carole Pateman, Michael Jackson, Patricia Springborg), international politics, Australian politics (Ken Turner), political sociology (Terry Irving, Bob Connell), media studies (Henry Mayer and later, Rod Tiffen) and subsequently, Asian studies and especially Chinese politics (Ian Grosart and from 1978, Fred Teiwes), as well as Soviet studies (from 1981, Graeme Gill).

Despite its many problems, the Economics Department improved its research performance. Research output from Economics is reported separately from that of the P-group. The former concentrated on macro-economic policy with special reference to inflation, Australian public finance, trade and industry studies (including housing), labour economics, development with special reference South-East Asia and the history of economic thought. The P-group focused on transnational corporations, as well as radical political economy approaches to urban and regional development, the environment, and issues of conflict and power including the state and their impact on political and social relations.

The leading researchers in Economics were Peter Groenewegen (37 publications of which eight were books, largely devoted to topics in Australian public finance and the history of economic thought) and Warren Hogan (22 publications of which one was a book on the Euro-dollar, jointly written with Ivor Pearce, addressing issues of monetary theory, practice and policy as well as economic and industrial policy more generally). Next best published in Economics was Peter Saunders (eighteen items including one book, addressing labour issues, macro-economic policy, social security and poverty), Judy Yates (fourteen items largely devoted to housing economics); Colin Simkin (ten items recorded up to his retirement in 1980, largely devoted to South-East Asian development and trade); Joseph Halevi, Murray Milgate, Bill Merrilees and Gordon Mills (with eight items each devoted to political economy for the first two, and to micro-economic policy for the others). Louis Haddad recorded four items (devoted to socialist economies and the history of economics) as did Ulrich Kohli on theoretical economics and Flora Gill on labour economics. For the remainder of the department, Ian Sharpe recorded three items until his departure to Newcastle, as did Viv Hall (on econometric modelling), Eric Kiernan and Russell Ross (with three items each on labour economics). Surinder Joson reported two items (on industry policy and protection) as did Tony Phipps on inflation and macro-economic policy responses. This gives an average of 9.1 research publications per annum for the Economics Department.

Ted Wheelwright was by far the best published person in the P-group (with 21 publications of which nine were books, nearly all of them edited volumes of readings edited jointly with Ken Buckley from Economic History. Next was Frank Stilwell (with nineteen items of which one was a book, most of them devoted to issues of urban and regional development), Debesh Bhattacharya (with sixteen items dealing mainly with development issues in the Asian subcontinent) and Evan Jones (with nine publications, devoted to methodological issues and radical economics). Gavan Butler reported only one publication, while Simpson-Lee (until his retirement from the university in 1981), Margaret Power and Hugh Pritchard (until his move in 1975 to Kuring-gai College of Advanced Education) reported none. This gives an average of 8.3 publications per annum for the P-group, slightly below the average research performance in Economics.

Among the smaller departments, Economic History recorded twelve books (three by Derek Aldcroft as professor in 1974; six by Ken Buckley, mainly the books of readings jointly edited with Ted Wheelwright; and one each by Steve Salsbury, Gary Wotherspoon and Robert Aldrich). Thirty-two other publications were reported as chapters in books or articles. Of these, Richard Aldcroft reported one; Ken Buckley and John Drabble, six each; Steve Salsbury, Ben Tipton and Gary Wotherspoon, four each; Robert Aldrich seven; and Peter Hall, who had replaced John Drabble in 1983, one article. Research interests in the department were Australian economic history (Ken Buckley and Gary Wotherspoon), transport history (Steve Salsbury), Malaysian economic history (John Drabble), European economic history (Robert Aldrich), American economic history (Ben Tipton) and African economic history (Peter Hall). Average publications per annum for the department were four.

Economic Statistics (from 1983, Econometrics) reported 48 publications, of which four were books: one by Allan Anderson, one (jointly with Theil) by Denzil Fiebig, and two by Alan Woodland. The other 44 publications were articles or chapters in books. Bob Bartels published twelve of these, Allan Anderson and Dilip Madan eight each, Alan Woodland five, Denzil Fiebig four, Sheila Rybak three, Piet de Jong and George Babich two each, while S. Ramasubban published one. The department's applied research focused on labour supply variables, fuel substitution, entropy methods, electricity demand, consumer demand and portfolio choice. Average publications for the department per annum amounted to 4.4 items.

Industrial Relations, the faculty's newest department, produced five books and 41 other publications. One of these books was by Geoff Sorrell on an aspect of industrial law, the other four were joint and reported by Harry Turner, Ron Callus, Malcolm Rimmer and by Stephen Frenkel and Alice Coolican. Of the 41 research papers, Richard Morris produced nine, Ron Callus seven, John Corina and Keith Whitfield six each, Malcolm Rimmer and Greg Patmore two each, and Geoff Sorrell and George Warburton reported one paper each. As the department noted in one of its research reports, its average rate of 4.6 publications per annum was good for a new department with no real research culture. By the early 1980s, the department recorded its major research interests as the structure of professional labour markets, industrial democracy at the organisational level, industrial relations in the building and metal industries, the restoration of trade unions in China, Australian waterfront labour and industrial relations in the New South Wales railways.

Two departments developed major working papers series: Economics, with no fewer than 80 working papers between 1973 and 1984, and Economic Statistics with 26 until the end of 1976. Other departments were active in the publication of journals. Accounting continued regular publication of *Abacus*, the Industrial Relations Department published the *Journal of Industrial Relations*, while Government was heavily involved with both the *Australian Journal of Public Administration* and *Media Information* and contributed editorial expertise to *Politics*, the *Australian Quarterly* and *Ethics*. In July 1975, the Transnational Research Project announced the publication of a journal devoted to the subject of transnational corporations.

Faculty members also successfully attracted research funds and research grants from outside bodies. In 1976, the *University News* reported that Denis Altman had gained a grant of $1140 to research the Australian Union of Students while Ken Turner had obtained $8275 to work on the history of the New South Wales Labor Party, 1920–70. In 1980, the *University News* reported Alan Craswell's grant of $8000 to investigate 'qualified auditing reports'. In 1981, research grants were announced for Ray Chambers to study 'criteria for redesign of accounting standards' ($5000), to Flora Gill for research on 'The Arbitration System in Australia, 1950–75' ($6700), Bill Merrilees to support research of 'Labour Substitution by Age in Australia' ($7000) and for Ted Wheelwright for research on 'the growth and impact of institutional investors' ($3000). The Australian Research Grants Council in 1981 announced the award of $5250 to Flora Gill for her Australian Arbitration System study and $6920 to Terry Irving to research the politics of New South Wales government business in the 1840s and 1850s, for which he gained an additional $7500 in 1982; Dick Spann obtained $18,321 for researching 'the structure and functions of New South Wales government agencies' and Rod Tiffen $15,711 for a study of news and power, a project for which he gained a further $17,595 in 1982. Russell Ross in 1981 received $3000 from the Bureau of Labour Market Research for studying the labour supply of married women. For 1982, the Australian Research Council approved grants of $5000 for John Corina and Ron Callus to research Australian full-time trade union officials, to Peter Saunders ($9043) for researching the effect of social security on private savings, and for Martin Painter ($9712) for a comparative analysis of policy coordination of Australian governments. The Reserve Bank of Australia that year announced a grant of $17,150 for Murray Wells to investigate accounting standards for government authorities and a further $8000 to Flora Gill in support of her study of the Australian arbitration system. In 1983, Trevor Matthews obtained substantial ARC support for a study of the political activities of business and employers organisations; in 1984 Ken Turner gained a further grant for preparing a history of the Labor Party in New South Wales, while the Department of Industrial Relations secured funding from the Bureau of Labour Market Research for a study of professional scientists.

Faculty over this period arranged eight R.C. Mills Memorial Lectures (reprinted in Groenewegen, ed. 2004, chapters 6–13). The first, given in 1974, was by faculty graduate, student and colleague of R.C. Mills, Sir John Crawford, on the subject, 'The Malthusian Spectre Today'. In 1975, Joan Robinson addressed contemporary contradictions of capitalism and in 1976 two future Nobel Prize winners in Economics presented lectures: Sir John Hicks addressed the question, 'Must Demand Stimulate Inflation?' (April) and Friedrich von Hayek lectured on 'The Atavism of Social Justice' (October). In 1977, Russell Mathews lectured on 'Issues in Australian Federalism', a major topic in Mills' research interests; in 1980 Paolo Sylos Labini discussed an 'Economist's View on Technological Change Under Contemporary Conditions'; in 1982 John Pitchford examined problems of Australian macro-economic policy in the 1970s, while in 1983 Donald Winch appraised higher maxims in political economy by looking at Malthus' and Ricardo's views on wealth and happiness. The continuing viability of this series of tributes to a former dean of the faculty that commenced in the 1958 (see Chapter 3) forms a fitting conclusion to this tale of increasing success in research by members of the faculty.

Towards a Faculty of Economics and Business

The turmoil in the faculty, a recurring theme of this chapter, generated various moves towards creating a 'professional' faculty from the business subjects, Accounting and Commercial Law, which attracted the majority of students in the faculty. In 1974, Warren Hogan and Colin Simkin had proposed separation of the professional from the social sciences subjects in the faculty; in 1977, Simpson-Lee, as dean floated the idea of a separate degree in accounting, while John Ward as vice-chancellor in 1984 had expressed a wish for generalist faculties to separate from the professional ones in order to achieve their different objectives more efficiently. Ward's proposal was taken up in 1984 by a large and somewhat unwieldy faculty committee, but its preliminary meetings achieved nothing positive. However, steps towards this end continued to be fiercely debated during the 1980s and 1990 and are discussed in the next chapter. These culminated in 1999 with the transformation of the Faculty of Economics into a Faculty of Economics and Business.

CHAPTER 6

Towards a Faculty of Economics and Business: new degrees and increased opportunities for specialisation, 1985–99

The last fifteen years of the Faculty of Economics, that is, before its replacement by a Faculty of Economics and Business from the start of 2000, saw the creation of several new degrees. These were designed to improve opportunities for specialisation in the social sciences, or to sharpen the focus of the degree and make it more attractive to students taking the Accounting–Commercial Law stream with the intention of pursuing a business or management career. New departments were therefore also established in the faculty. During the 1990s, departments of Finance and of Marketing were added to the six long-established departments of Accounting, Econometrics, Economic History, Economics, Government and Public Administration, and Industrial Relations. By 1999 the faculty was offering four undergraduate degrees — Bachelor of Economics, Bachelor of Economics (Social Sciences), Bachelor of Commerce and Bachelor of Commerce (Liberal Studies) — in addition to its postgraduate offerings at master and doctoral level and the very popular combined Economics/Law degree. The higher doctorate was occasionally awarded and new combined postgraduate degrees were introduced. They included the Master of Industrial Relations, Master of Public Policy, Master of International Relations, Master of Public Affairs, Master of Commerce and Master of Economics (Social Sciences) as well as a joint masters degree in Economics and Econometrics, and diploma courses in Economics, Industrial Relations and International Studies. In addition to the MBA and doctoral studies, the Graduate School of Management began to offer diplomas in Business Administration and in Transport Management, a certificate course in Business Management as well as a Master of Transport Management degree. The reintroduction of diploma courses by faculty seems ironical, given their abolition in the immediate post-World War II period as unbecoming to a modern university. However, it is yet another illustration of how history can often repeat itself, a phenomenon of which other examples are found in this chapter.

The fifteen years ending in December 1999 witnessed other significant changes. Enrolments and staff numbers in the faculty increased considerably. In 1985, there had been 83 full-time academic members of staff, including eight professors; by 1999 there were 117 full-time academic members of staff of whom fourteen were professors. Some of these additional chairs were sponsored. Examples are the Arthur Young chair of Accounting and the National Australia Bank chair of Finance. Undergraduate enrolments in 1985 amounted to 1386 students studying for either the BEc or the BEc (SocSci) or the BEc/LLB degrees. By 1999, these enrolments had more than doubled to 3150 students.

Extra-mural activities were also briefly on the agenda. In 1987 faculty was requested to take on responsibilities for commercial and economics teaching at Chifley University College.

Its rapid transformation into the University of Western Sydney meant that this faculty teaching in the end did not eventuate. However, faculty member Helen Nelson did assist with the new university's initial administrative development by serving as a member of its council. Moreover, for several years from 1994, faculty was involved in teaching first-year courses at Penang University College in Malaysia.

Growth in staff and student numbers placed increasing pressures on the physical resources available to the faculty within the Merewether Building, particularly staff office space, teaching rooms and library resources. The last problem was eliminated for the faculty when Wolstenholme Library closed its doors in 1998 after a half century of service to students and staff. The space the library had occupied was refurbished to become the Wolstenholme Study Centre, a place where students could study quietly between lectures and other classes. In 1999 it became a computer centre, giving students internet access, an increasingly important part of their tools for study and research. Growing use of computers by staff and student meant that special computing laboratories were also required from the early 1990s and, to assist in servicing them and their users, technical computer staff was hired at both faculty and departmental level.

The faculty enters the computer age: a computing room in Merewether.

Other significant changes took place in these years. By 1999, the academic year was subdivided into two semesters, with mid-semester breaks and a vacation between semesters, as well as the usual summer holidays from mid-December to end February. Twice-yearly examinations became par for the course under semesterisation, and semester courses completely replaced full-year courses by the mid-1990s. The three-term academic year in force since the 1850s was formally abandoned in 1989 to accommodate changes in the school year to a four-term system. Many older staff members regretted the change. It reduced flexibility in dividing teaching, increased examination loads and made greater demands on student, and staff, concentration. Government intervention via a newly created Department of Employment, Education and Training became more intrusive from the end of the 1980s, affecting student entry standards, pass rates, research funding and many other matters, not least of which was the imposition of the Higher Education Contribution Scheme (HECS) for students, payable in instalments on graduation.

During 1990 Senate decided in favour of appointed deans instead of deans elected by the membership of a faculty. This change was considered essential in the new world of financially devolved faculties, when far greater responsibilities were placed on deans as executive officers assisting the vice-chancellor. Appointments of deans would be made from applicants obtained either through internal or external advertisements for the position, a practice which had existed in the Medical Faculty for some time. The new appointed deans would hold office for a period of five years as compared with the two-year terms for the elected deans. Pro-deans and sub-deans (from the early 1990s called associate deans) continued to be elected by faculty for two-year terms.

This chapter examines these changes in the following manner. Enrolments, curriculum changes and staff changes (1985–99) are examined first. A more detailed look at faculty deliberations and administration for the period follows. This includes changes in housing the faculty; the introduction of the two new departments, Finance and Marketing; a review of faculty graduates and students (1985–99); the progress of the Sydney University Economics Society; attempts at revitalising of the alumni association by resuscitating the University of Sydney Economics Graduates Association; and research and scholarship in the faculty. The chapter concludes with a brief discussion of deliberations on the change to a Faculty of Economics and Business. It may be noted that the high incidence of turmoil which had plagued the faculty during the 1970s and early 1980s had virtually disappeared by 1985. There were no staff or student strikes, student representation and consultation had become part of the established administrative procedures in the university while the political economy dispute was more or less resolved during 1985. A *de facto* separation of the P-teachers from the Department of Economics gradually evolved, starting with Frank Stilwell's appointment in 1983 as director of P-studies, a virtual head of department position, and by creating an Economics (P) major through formally adding Economics III(P) and IV(P) to the syllabus. From 1997, political economy was recognised as a separate program within the Department of Economics and, at the time of completing the final manuscript (2009), had been a separate discipline group for some years. As indicated in the Epilogue, both Government and the Political Economy departments transferred to the Faculty of Arts in January 2008.

Enrolments, curriculum and staffing, 1985-99

Enrolments over these fifteen years continued to grow steadily. Part of this growth came from the faculty's wider range of its course and degree offerings, and from the expansion of the effective pool from which potential students could be attracted. Overseas fee-paying students, mainly from South-East Asia, were one profitable source of expanding student intake, particularly after the introduction of the Bachelor of Commerce degree in 1993. Other curriculum developments, especially those arising from the establishment of the departments of Finance and Marketing, also generated growing student numbers, when Sydney's universities, increased to five during the 1990s, needed to compete actively for students. One sign of this competitive framework was the employment from 1998 of a faculty marketing and planning manager, Virginia Bleasel, with two marketing assistants, Melinda McMullen and Karin Osterhoff.

The increase in postgraduate degree offerings mentioned at the start of this chapter helped shift the composition of faculty enrolments more in the direction of postgraduate studies. The ratio of postgraduate to undergraduate students changed from 1:6.3 in 1985 to 1:3.7. in 1999. The age structure of postgraduate students also changed. Many of the new, more business-oriented postgraduate courses and diplomas were successfully targeted at mature age, part-time students who were primarily interested in raising the level of their qualifications.

Faculty enrolment of women students increased at both graduate and undergraduate level. In 1985, 39 per cent of undergraduates and 22 per cent of postgraduate students in the faculty were women; by 1999, women accounted for a majority of undergraduates (51.7 per cent) and 46.7 per cent of postgraduates. The days when the Faculty of Economics was a male bastion became a dim memory for only the oldest academic faculty staff of the 1990s. As shown later in this section, the same shift in gender balance applied to academic staff, though it should be immediately added with as yet relatively little effect on senior academic staff positions. In 1999, for example, there was only one woman among the fourteen faculty professors, Patricia Springborg, and only four women among its 22 associate professors, of whom two were in the Department of Economics (Flora Gill and Judy Yates) and two in the Government Department (Helen Nelson and Linda Weiss).

The increase in faculty staff, explored more fully later in this section, owed as much to the growth in curriculum as to the expansion in student numbers. At the undergraduate level, course offerings in all departments expanded considerably, in particular the number of optional courses at senior level. The highly structured Economics degree with little room for internal choice with which the faculty started had by the end of the 1990s virtually disappeared. Opportunities for greater specialisation started earlier and earlier, involving the creation of new departments and sub-departments, and multiplication of the optional courses open to students in second and third year. The details of this by department can be briefly indicated.

In 1985, the Accounting major at pass level consisted of three compulsory pass courses, with three special advanced courses for honours students from second year. In 1999, completing the Accounting major involved a first year of two compulsory semester courses (Accounting IA and IB), a second year when students could specialise in either Financial Accounting or Management Accounting, while third year had to be completed by taking sequential semester courses in Financial Statement Analysis and Auditing. Honours students took a final honours year for the whole of this period, but in 1999 could attempt joint honours in Accounting and Finance. In addition, two terminating first-year semester courses were offered by then for those only interested in a brief introduction to the subject. By 1985, Commercial Law had three *de facto* sequential courses for its students; it formally became a major sequence from 1991.

The Econometrics major in 1985 still required a compulsory Economic Statistics course in first year and three term modules to be completed in both second and third year chosen from a possible four in Econometrics II and five in Econometrics III. The department offered an alternative sequence in Operations Research at third- and fourth-year level. By 1999, semesterisation meant that first year was completed by two sequential semester courses, Econometrics IA and IB. The same applied to Econometrics II. For third year, a compulsory Econometrics IIIA was taken in first semester while a second semester course was chosen from eight possible third-year options. Alternatively, students could take the sequence Operations Research A and B. Honours students had to complete additional work but, as in 1985, were able to chose between Econometrics IV and Operations Research II.

Economic History in 1985 consisted of a compulsory course in first year; second- and third-year students chose two options from a total of 15 and needed to complete the two courses in Early, and Modern, Australian Economic History. Honours students took an additional fourth year. By 1999, first year contained two compulsory semester courses on economic history of Europe and the Asia-Pacific area. Second and third year was completed by taking two optional courses in each of these years, to be chosen from a total 24 options listed for that year. Honours students took additional courses from second year as well as Economic History IV. By 1999, Australian Economic History had become an optional subject, and departmental emphasis was on Asia, Africa, Europe, and the Pacific.

In 1985, Economics required a compulsory first-year course, a compulsory second-year course for two lectures per week in the year plus a one lecture a week option, to be chosen from five. Third year consisted completely of optional courses, of which two had to be chosen from a pool of fourteen options. There were separate required courses for honours students from second to fourth year, with Economics IV permitting considerable choice in the manner by which it could be completed (thesis and coursework, long essay and coursework, coursework only). All fourth-year honours students had to take an Australian Economic Policy seminar. In addition, the department in 1985 continued to offer two self-standing courses, The Australian Economy in first year, and in third year History of Economic Thought. It also gave Economics II(P). None of these self-standing courses in 1985 offered internal choice. In 1999, Economics I and Economics I(P), Economics II and II(P) were offered in first and second year with no internal choice. For third year, Economics III and III(P) students had to chose two options from a total of eighteen (of which six were (P) options and two optional semester courses covered the former History of Economic

Thought syllabus). Honours students needed to take additional work from second year and complete either Economics IV or IV(P).

A Government major in 1985 required Government I as a compulsory first-year course. Government II and III could be completed by taking two short courses in each year, chosen from an offering of 27 short courses. These were subdivided into five groups (Political Theory, Comparative Politics, Public Policy, International Politics and Political Sociology) with the proviso that the four short courses selected came from at least two of these groups. The honours program in Government started in third year (two additional advanced courses) and was virtually completed by thesis in Government IV. By 1999, first-year students had to take two semester courses from a list of eleven junior semester courses; while second- and third-year students had to complete one course per semester (that is, two each year) chosen from a list of 51 optional senior semester courses. Honours students did additional work in third year and completed a thesis in Government IV.

In 1985, an Industrial Relations major was completed by taking its first- and second-year courses which offered no internal choice; Industrial Relations III consisted of two options to be chosen from a total of four. Honours students took Industrial Relations IV as well. By 1999, the Industrial Relations major still required a first year with no internal choice, though now consisting of two semester courses. In second and third year, students had to complete two optional semester courses per year to be chosen from a list of fifteen. These enabled students to specialise in Human Resources Management and other management studies, or in Labour History, Labour Economics or further Industrial Relations studies. Honours courses were offered for three years from second year onwards, ending with Industrial Relations IV (completed by coursework and thesis with the primary focus on the thesis).

Majors in Finance and in Marketing were introduced in 1994. In 1999, the Finance major consisted of first- and second-year courses, Corporate Finance I and II, with no internal choice. Finance III enabled students to choose one semester course out of three for first semester, and one out of two for second semester. Honours courses were offered from second year, and required completion of Finance IV by writing a research report and taking several courses. Joint honours opportunities were offered with candidates eligible for final-year honours in Accounting, Econometrics or Marketing. In 1999, the Marketing major commenced in second year with four compulsory semester courses to be completed in that year and the third year, together with one optional marketing course to be chosen from two such courses. A Marketing honours program was also offered consisting of two semester seminar courses plus the completion of a research report (or thesis) during the second semester of Marketing IV.

By 1999 all faculty course majors had introduced far greater choice than existed in 1985. This was achieved either by reducing the number of compulsory course offerings with no internal choice in any one year, or by expanding the range of options from which students could choose. Where many options were listed, departments invariably warned that not all options were necessarily available in any one year. Accounting and Commercial Law offered the least amount of choice to the pass student, followed by Marketing, Finance and Econometrics. After all, these were the more professional training courses in the faculty, with a substantial core to be mastered. Subjects from the humanities and social sciences, such as Economic History and Government, offered most choice, while the semi-professional courses of Economics and Industrial Relations confined choice to the senior year(s). This was also the practice in the more social science orientated (P) courses whose first and second year offered no internal choice. Honours was also offered by every department, generally starting with additional studies in second year (Government alone excepted), and requiring the completion of a thesis or other form of major research work (Economics alone excepted).

As noted earlier, financial devolution, faculty's growth in size and responsibilities (including marketing its courses) meant an increase in faculty administrative staff and in other staff assisting the dean. By 1985 faculty had already been electing two sub-deans responsible for undergraduate and postgraduate studies. Faculty support staff then consisted of two secretaries, of whom one was graduate assistant to the dean. In addition, faculty employed a Wolstenholme Librarian and two attendants who had general caretaking duties for the faculty building including provision of staff services such as setting up equipment used in lectures. By 1999, when financial devolution had become an established fact of life, being dean was a full-time responsibility, entailing abandonment of most, if not all, teaching. A pro-dean had been elected from 1987, while sub-deans (whose title was changed to associate deans in 1991) were by then well-established positions.

Non-academic faculty staff by 1999 had increased beyond administrative and secretarial assistance. It had doubled to four, including the dean's graduate assistant. Faculty attendants stayed at two, but the faculty librarian position vanished when the Wolstenholme Library ceased to operate from 1998. More complexity in the degree and course choices offered by the faculty, together with increased inter-university competition in attracting the best possible students, meant that the faculty now employed four student advisers (two for undergraduate, two for postgraduate studies), as well as a marketing and planning manager with two assistants. Greater emphasis on securing high standards of university teaching created a faculty need for an undergraduate teaching quality officer. It may be noted here that Michael Jackson (Government), Frank Stilwell (Political Economy) and Linda English (Accounting) won university awards for excellence in teaching in 1989, 1991 and 1998 respectively. Increased administrative responsibilities for the dean from financial devolution — faculty had effectively become a medium sized 'business unit' with around 150 staff on its payroll — entailed that faculty employ a non-academic executive officer and a faculty manager to help the dean's oversight of faculty resources. Rapid growth of computer use in the faculty by staff and students, with concomitant growing needs for maintenance and supervision of substantial computer laboratories, made employment of a team of four faculty computer systems managers mandatory. Between 1985 and 1999 faculty administrative and support staff grew from four to twenty, a neat five-fold increase.

Between 1985 and 1999 faculty academic staff grew much more slowly, from 91 to 117. This was despite the addition of two new departments employing nineteen new staff altogether (twelve in Finance and seven in Marketing for 1999). Average academic staff numbers per department actually fell from 15.2 in 1985 to 14.6 in 1999, and student–staff ratios rose as a consequence. They more than doubled for Accounting from 16.8 to 38.0, almost trebled for Econometrics from 14.0 to 41.2, nearly doubled for Industrial Relations from 16.4 to 27.7, for Economic History from 16.3 to 26.5 and for Government from 15.5 to 28.3, while for Economics they rose from 20.0 to 28.3. In 1999, Finance and Marketing had student–staff ratios of 38.3 and 27.0, while (P) staff, no longer included with Economics in the official university statistics, had the most favourable ratio in the faculty of 20.9. Over this fifteen-year period, Accounting academic staff rose from 21 to 22, that of Econometrics from 7 to 9, Economics from 27 to 30, and Industrial Relations from 5 to 13. Two departments declined in terms of academic staff members: Government from 22 to 20; Economic History staff halved from eight to four.

At the individual departmental level, there was considerable turnover of staff from both retirements and resignations. Details of staff changes for the eight faculty departments in existence in 1999 are provided in what follows.

Accounting had the greatest turnover of staff between 1985 and 1999. By 1999, its three professors — Allen Craswell, Stephen Taylor and Terry Walter — had replaced the two 1985 professors, Murray Wells and Greg Whittred. Craswell had been appointed to his professorship in 1989, he was a senior lecturer in 1985 and had been promoted to associate professor in 1987. Terry Walter was appointed to a chair in 1990 while Stephen Taylor was promoted to professor in 1996 after his appointment as associate professor in 1992. Murray Wells resigned his Accounting chair in 1997 to go to the Graduate School of Management, Greg Whittred resigned his chair in 1989. Of the two associate professors in 1985, Ron Bowra retired in 1989 while Frank Clarke resigned in 1986 to take up a chair at the University of Newcastle. Graeme Dean, the only associate professor in Accounting in 1999, was promoted to that position in 1990.

Of the senior lecturers on the Accounting staff in 1985, Alan Craswell by 1999 was a professor and Graeme Dean associate professor. Of the other five, Sri Ramanathan retired in 1989, John Oxley-Oxland was promoted to associate professor in 1990 before resigning in 1993, Michael Gaffikin resigned in 1988, Geoffrey Hart stayed on as senior lecturer and Peter Wolnizer resigned in 1988 to return as appointed Dean of the Faculty of Economics at the end of 1998. Of the Accounting lecturers in 1985, Roger Burritt resigned in 1987, Cynthia Coleman was promoted to senior lecturer in 1990 , David Johnstone resigned in 1987, Stephanie Rees resigned in 1989 and Stephen Taylor had become a professor. Of the eight 1999 Accounting lecturers reported in the *Faculty Handbook*, Paul Blayney was appointed in 1989, Isabel Gordon in 1996, Patty Kamvounias in 1993, Philip Lee in 1990, Barbara Mesher in 1995, Joanne Pickering in 1992, Qingliang Tang in 1996 and Mary Wyburn in 1996.

Much Accounting staff was appointed and resigned between 1985 and 1999. These included Michael Aitkin, associate professor in 1993, who left Accounting in 1994 to join the newly formed Finance Department; Baijit Kaur, appointed in 1987, left in 1993 to join the Graduate School of Management; Craig Deegan, appointed lecturer in 1987, resigned in 1989; Martin Dubler, appointed in 1990, resigned in 1992; Linda English, appointed in 1990, resigned in 1994; Helen Fielder, appointed in 1990, resigned in 1993; Mary Louise Brien, appointed as lecturer in 1994, resigned in 1995; Scott Richardson, appointed lecturer in 1996, resigned in 1997; and John Trowell, appointed lecturer in 1991, resigned in 1996. The department hosted several visiting professors, among whom Professor E. Emanuel (University of Auckland) in 1987, Professor Chee W. Chow in 1992 and Professor Jere Francis (University of Iowa) in 1997.

In Econometrics, Alan Woodland was sole professor for the whole of the period covered by this chapter. Moshe Haviv, the department's only reader, was promoted to that position in 1994 from the senior lectureship to which he had been appointed in 1992. Bob Bartels and Denzil Fiebig, the department's two associate professors in 1999, were both promoted to that position from senior lectureships in 1990; Ernie Houghton remained as senior lecturer from 1985 to 1999; Murray Smith, appointed lecturer in 1987 was promoted to senior lecturer in 1994. John Goodhew remained a lecturer for the period. Other staff resigned. Dilip Madan, a senior lecturer in 1985, did so in 1990; Andy Tremayne, promoted to associate professor in 1989, resigned in 1998. The department hosted several visiting professors: A. Parley and D.M. Waterson, both in 1990; Peter Schonfield, a German exchange scholar, in 1997.

As already indicated, Economic History lost half of its staff between 1985 and 1999. Its only professor, Steve Salsbury, the dean for most of this period, died from cancer in March 1998. Three other senior staff members in Economic History in 1985 retired: Ken Buckley in 1987, Peter Hall in 1989 and John Drabble in 1994 (after having been promoted to associate professor in 1987). Another senior lecturer of 1985, Gary Wotherspoon, resigned in 1998. The department's two associate professors in 1999, Robert Aldrich and Ben Tipton, in 1985 were both senior lecturers and were promoted in 1989. Diane Hutchison, the department's only senior lecturer in 1999, was appointed as lecturer in 1990 and promoted in 1992. Lily Rahim, the department's only lecturer in 1999, was appointed in 1996. Mathew Allen, appointed lecturer in 1990, resigned in 1994.

Economics also experienced many staff changes. Of the three Economics professors in 1985, only Peter Groenewegen remained in that position in 1999, although by then on a half-time contract. Warren Hogan and Gordon Mills both retired in 1998. Bill Schworm, the other Economics professor in 1999, was appointed in 1995. Of the four associate professors in 1985, two (Ted Wheelwright and Jim Wilson) retired in 1986, Viv Hall resigned in 1989 to take up a chair in New Zealand, while Frank Stilwell remained as associate professor and director of (P) Studies in 1999. In 1999 other associate professors were Tony Aspromourgos (lecturer in 1986, senior lecturer in 1989 and associate professor in 1998), Debesh Bhattacharya (promoted in 1992 from senior lecturer), Flora Gill (promoted from senior lecturer in 1994), Tony Phipps (promoted from senior lecturer in 1995), Russell Ross (promoted from senior lecturer in 1998), Jeffrey Sheen (appointed senior lecturer in 1989, promoted to associate professor in 1992) and Judy Yates (promoted from senior lecturer in 1992). There were twelve senior lecturers in the department in 1999. Three of these, Gavan Butler, Louis Haddad and Evan Jones, were senior lecturers in 1985; Dilip Dutta was promoted to senior lecturer in 1994 after his appointment to a lectureship in 1988; Steffan Ziss was promoted to senior lecturer in 1996 after his appointment as lecturer in 1989; Joseph Halevi, Dick Bryan and Bruce Ross were promoted to senior lectureships in 1985, 1987 and 1989; Don Wright was promoted to senior lecturer in 1995 (from the lectureship to which he was appointed in 1988); Surinder Joson was promoted to senior lecturer in 1986, Stuart Rosewarne in 1993 (lectureship in 1987), Elizabeth Savage was appointed to a senior lectureship in 1990 and Yanis Varoufakis was promoted to senior lecturer in 1992 (from the lectureship to which he had been appointed in 1988). Of the eight lecturers in 1999, John Carson had been appointed in 1994, Pamela Cawthorne in 1994, Denise Doiron in 1995, Nils-Peter Lagerhof in 1998, Pushkar Maitra in 1997, Gabrielle Meagher in 1996, Abhijit Sengupta in 1996 and Graham White in 1990.

In the intervening period, a considerable number from the Economics staff resigned, sometimes within a short period from their initial appointment. Of those on the staff in 1985 but no longer there in 1999, who have not already been mentioned, Michael Blad died in 1989, Sol Kiew Kim retired in 1989, John Piggott in 1986, Peter Saunders resigned in 1989 to take up positions at the University of New South Wales, Margaret Power retired in 1994, John Stuckey resigned in 1986, Eric Kiernan resigned in 1988, Noreen Cooray, a former senior tutor, was made a lecturer in 1988 before her retirement that year, and Pak Wai Lui resigned in 1987. Other Economics Department staff members in the period covered by this chapter include Kit Chin Vam, a lecturer from 1986 to 1987; Geoff Kingston, a senior lecturer from 1987 to 1989; Luigi Ermini, a lecturer from 1988 to 1989; Costas Karfakis, a lecturer from 1990 to 1994; William (Billy) Jack, a lecturer from 1991 to 1992; and Shaun Hargreaves-Heap, a visiting senior lecturer for one year in 1989.

The Department of Economics hosted many academic visitors. These included Professor Simon Domberger in 1985 (he was appointed Bowater Professor of Management in the faculty in 1987); Professor Andrea Maneschi, Professor Michael Waterson and Professor Gerard Debreu (Nobel Laureate in 1983) visited for various periods during 1987; Professor F. Shup (University of Illinois) and Professor Bob Rowthorn (Cambridge University) visited during 1989; in 1990 Mr Simon Mohun was a visiting senior lecturer and Professor V.M. Kollontai visited the department for a month. Mr S. Khazed was visiting senior lecturer during 1992, Professor Luigi Pasinetti (Università Cattolicà, Milan) was a visiting professor in 1993, Professor John Harsanyi (a former student in the faculty and Nobel Laureate in 1994) was visiting professor in 1995, as were Professor Robert Casson, Professor W. Bussert (University of Waterloo) and Dr Patricia Tiberi (University of Udine); Professor J. Melvin (University of Waterloo) visited during 1996, Professor Mario Floro (American University) visited in 1997, and Dr Gautam Bose (University of Cairo), Professor Carmen Carrera (University of Madrid), Professor Monojit Chatterji (University of Dundee), Professor Russell Cooper (University of Dundee), Professor Anthony Creane (Michigan State University), Dr Christian Ausperger (Catholic University, Louvain) and associate professor Geoffrey Kingston (University of New South Wales) visited in 1999.

The Department of Government also experienced significant staff changes. Its one professor in 1985, Christopher Hood, resigned in 1989 to return to England. Alistair Davidson, appointed professor in 1989, resigned in 1993 to go back to Melbourne. Of the two readers in 1985, Carole Pateman resigned in 1989 to take up a professorship at the University of California (Berkeley) while Fred Teiwes stayed in the department, becoming professor in 1992, one of four Government professors in 1999. The other three professors in 1999 were Graeme Gill (appointed in 1990), Michael Jackson (appointed 1993) and Patricia Springborg (appointed 1997). Three of the four 1985 associate professors in Government left during the period, while Terry Irving remained as associate professor in 1999. Ken Turner retired at the end of 1986, Michael Leigh (who was professor and academic director of the International College, Penang, in 1994–95), retired as associate professor in Government in 1997, as Trevor Matthews had done in 1996. Associate professors in Government in 1999 other than Terry Irving were Helen Nelson (promoted in 1991), Martin Painter (promoted in 1992), Rodney Tiffen (promoted in 1993) and Linda Weiss (promoted in 1996, following her appointment as lecturer in 1991 and promotion to senior lecturer in 1994). John Ravenhill, promoted to associate professor in 1989, resigned in 1990, and Michael Hogan (promoted to associate professor in 1993) retired during 1997.

Of the thirteen senior lecturers in Government in 1985, eight (Graeme Gill, Michael Hogan, Michael Jackson, Helen Nelson, Martin Painter, John Ravenhill, Patricia Springborg and Rodney Tiffen) had become professor or associate professor by 1999; the remaining five had either retired or resigned. Ernie Chaples and Ian Grosart retired in 1990, Ross Curnow and Peter King both retired in 1996 and Barbara Page (lecturer in 1989, senior lecturer in 1995) retired in 1998. Of the five senior lecturers in Government in 1999, Randall Stewart had been appointed in 1992, Deborah Brennan in 1993, Lex Watson in 1994, Diarmuid Maguire in 1995 and M. Ramesh in 1998. Lex Watson was the only lecturer in Government in 1985. In 1999 there were five: Louise Chappell, appointed in 1994; Devin Hagerty, John Hobson and Darryl Jarvis, all appointed in 1997; and Peter Dauvergne, appointed in 1998.

Other members of the Government Department between 1985 and 1999 included Peter Nelson, a lecturer in 1985, resigned in 1986; Martin Laffin, appointed lecturer in 1987, resigned in 1990; Felix Patrikeeff, appointed lecturer in 1990, resigned in 1998; Ian Bell, appointed lecturer in 1991, resigned 1996; Qingguo Jia, appointed lecturer in 1993, resigned in 1998; Lisa Hill, appointed lecturer in 1994, resigned in 1996; Ivan Molloy, appointed in 1994, resigned in 1997; Roderic Pitty, appointed in 1994, resigned in 1996; and Jayasuriya Ankres, appointed in 1995, resigned in 1996. The Government department also hosted various visiting professors, including Hu Hua (1986), Sydney Tarrow (1993), Robert Wood (1993–94), Rawdon Dalrymple (1995) and Professor Henri Albinski (University of Pennsylvania) in 1999.

In 1985, the Department of Industrial Relations had a vacant professorship, one senior lecturer (Richard Morris) and four lecturers (Alice Coolican, Ron Callus, Greg Patmore and Keith Whitfield). In 1999, the Professor of Industrial Relations was Russell Lansbury (appointed in 1987), Ron Callus and Greg Patmore were its two associate professors (promoted to senior lecturer in 1987 and 1990, and to associate professor in 1990 and 1997). There were three senior lecturers in Industrial Relations in 1999: Bradon Ellem (appointed in 1997), Suzanne Jamieson (appointed lecturer in 1990, promoted to senior lecturer in

1993) and Jim Kitay (appointed lecturer in 1990, promoted to senior lecturer in 1993). In addition, there were five lecturers in 1999: Marian Baird (appointed in 1997), Susan McGrath-Champ (appointed in 1995), Grant Michelson (appointed in 1996), Nick Wailes (appointed in 1998) and Mark Westcott (appointed in 1995). Of the 1985 lecturers, Alice Coolican resigned in 1990 and Keith Whitfield in 1989 after promotion to senior lecturer in 1986. Richard Morris, who as senior lecturer was the senior member of the department in 1985, retired in 1994. Some Industrial Relations staff who were appointed and resigned during this period should also be mentioned. They include Mark Bray (appointed lecturer in 1987, promoted to senior lecturer in 1992 and to associate professor in 1996, retired in 1998), Robyn Kramar (a lecturer from 1988 to 1990), Joe Zappala (a lecturer from 1989 to 1992) and John Campling (a lecturer from 1994 to 1998).

The Industrial Relations Department has a strong tradition of having honorary appointments on its staff drawn from the practising industrial relations community. Over this period, they include Pauline Griffin, Peter Harley, the Hon. J.T. Ludeke, the Hon. James Macken, Sir John Moore and Vic Techritz. In 1986 its visiting professors included George Strauss; in 1997 Dr Andrew Pendleton (Bradford University) and Dr Robin Archer (Oxford); in 1998, Bert Evans and the Hon. Bob Hawke (former prime minister and industrial relations specialist as trade union leader and advocate). Hawke was also a visiting professor in the department in 1992, when he delivered the first Kingsley Laffer Memorial Lecture in honour of the founder of the Industrial Relations Department, who had also been its first teacher during the 1950s.

The Finance Department, which commenced operations in 1994, by then had appointed Peter Swan as its foundation professor, and Juliane Wright as an associate lecturer. By 1995, the department had added Michael Aitkin (formerly in Accounting) and Gerard Garvey as associate professors (Garvey resigned in 1997); Alex Frino (first appointed in Accounting in 1993, promoted to senior lecturer in Finance in 1998, associate professor in 1999) and Michael McCorry as lecturers. In 1996, Finance added two professorial fellows to its staff: Peter Marshman and Bryce Wauchope. By 1998, two additional lecturers had been appointed, Elvis Jarcenic and Roland Winn, as well as a research fellow, Xianming Zhou. By 1999, the department added Jayarim Muthuswamy to Alex Frino as new associate professors, while the lecturing staff was increased by the appointment of Xianming Zhou and Tro Kourtian, a former honours graduate. This made total staff in the Finance department for 1999 two professors, two associate professors and five lecturers, a quite rapid growth rate for five years, but nevertheless not really matching its substantial enrolments.

The Marketing Department also began operations in 1995 with only its foundation professor, Jordan Louviere, appointed in 1994. Three other staff had been appointed by 1995: Pamela Morrison as senior lecturer, and lecturers Jeffrey Blazel and Thomas Crook. In 1996, Benedict Dellaert joined the staff as an additional senior lecturer. Terence Beed and Bernard Pailthorpe (only for 1998) had been appointed associate professors in 1998, having been visiting professors during 1997. By 1999 the Marketing Department retained its foundation professor, employed one associate professor and five senior lecturers (Charles Areni, Sandra Burke, Pamela Morrison, Harmen Oppewal and Rohit Verma) of whom three were promoted lecturers. Visiting staff in 1998 had included Professor David Bunch from the University of California, Davis.

Although the postgraduate programs, Master of Business Administration and Master of Public Policy, were transferred to the Graduate School of Management and Public Policy before 1985, some of its staff continued to serve as faculty members. A prominent example is David Hensher, appointed in 1990 as professor and head of a new Transport Policy Research Unit in the Graduate School of Management and Public Policy. Postgraduate programs mounted by the eight departments with primary location in the faculty from 1994 were staffed by these departments with the teachers enumerated in this section.

Faculty deliberations and administration, 1985–99

Semesterisation in 1989 brought with it fewer faculty meetings. The six meetings which took place in 1985 were reduced to three meetings over the next three years (with four taking place in 1988 because a special meeting was also called). From 1989, if special meetings are ignored (not easy to do since such meetings were called during 1989, 1991, 1993 and 1994), two faculty meetings a year, that is, one in each semester, were called on dates announced at the end of the previous year.

Attendance at faculty meetings continued to fluctuate widely. For 1985–99, maximum attendance of 75, close to three-quarters of faculty membership, was recorded for the special faculty meeting of 27 September 1991 largely devoted to the introduction of the Bachelor of Commerce degree proposed for 1993. A minimum attendance of 22 was reported for a special meeting (24 September 1993) devoted to the non-controversial topic of implementing a unit system for the faculty, a change recommended by the Academic Board to facilitate the administration of student results following the standardisation of semester courses. Most of the faculty meetings for the period covered by this chapter debated new course and degree initiatives, the consequences of semesterisation and, especially towards the end of the period, the move towards a Faculty of Economics and Business which began in earnest during the final years of the 1990s. The resolution of the political economy dispute during 1985 explains why that year was the last year in faculty's 80 year history when two faculty meetings per term had to be called.

The first (special) faculty meeting of March 1985 was called to debate an important, but far from unanimous Academic Board report on Faculty of Economics restructuring as a possible solution to the long-standing political economy dispute. Three alternatives were discussed in this report. The first proposed splitting the faculty into two. The second proposed replacing the faculty by three boards of studies (that is, a board of studies in economics comprising Accounting, Econometrics and Economics; a board of studies in social sciences comprising Government, the (P) teachers in a new department as yet unnamed and a department of sociology when it was established; and a board of studies in social work comprising the Arts department of that name). The third option suggested the relocation of some Faculty of Economics staff (the Government Department and the designated (P) teachers) to the Faculty of Arts. It may be noted this scheme left Economic

History in limbo, since members of that department were strongly divided on which of the three boards of studies was the most appropriate for them. The same faculty meeting discussed an outline for a revised Economics II(P) as a more suitable sequel to the common Economics first-year course implemented in 1984 at the request of the Academic Board. It also proposed a new Economics IV(P) course, Neo-Marxist Political Economy, an important part of the proposed resolution of the dispute. None of these suggestions was accepted by the meeting. However, a proposal by Michael Hogan from Government to solve the problem by the introduction of a new degree was accepted by the faculty after much debate. A committee was set up to report on a new degree structure for consideration by faculty at its July meeting.

The proposed new degree became the Bachelor of Economics (Social Science) by the end of the year. However, the committee set up by faculty to make recommendations on the matter initially suggested a revised BEc degree together with a new BEconomic Studies degree. This second degree made Economics II(P) and III(P) alternative ways of completing the compulsory Economics requirement of the degree and introduced a different Economics I course from that offered in the BEc. The July faculty meeting which debated this proposal failed to reach agreement. No vote was taken after lengthy but inconclusive debate during which many different preferences were expressed by those present. Lack of support for the two degree structure proposed is partly explained by the fact that one of the degrees, the revised BEc, was seen by many faculty members as a narrow degree in Business Studies. Faculty therefore resolved to send the report back to the committee for further deliberation and revision.

The next faculty meeting (11 October 1985) considered a new report from the committee, which in the meantime had set up two working parties to deliberate on the details for the two degrees. Apart from submitting reports of its two working parties, the committee proposed three resolutions for adoption by faculty: one seeking in principle support for a two degree structure in the faculty, the second seeking support for a new BEc (SocSci) and the third proposing the establishment of a joint board of studies with the Faculty of Arts to inquire into the possibility of creating a bachelor of social sciences degree. After prolonged debate, faculty decided by 28 votes to 22 that the 'Faculty of Economics approve the proposal for a new BEc (Social Sciences) degree as set out in scheme 1 of the working party on the second degree'. This scheme suggested an eleven-course degree with three compulsory courses in Economics. These compulsory requirements could be met either by taking Economics I, II and III or by taking a new Economics I (Social Sciences), Economics II(P) and III(P). Students in this degree were unable to take Accounting and Commercial Law courses, or to complete Econometrics II and III. Second major sequences proposed for the second degree were Economic History, Government, Industrial Relations, as well as Geography, Philosophy, Psychology, Religious Studies and Social Anthropology. New by-laws and resolutions for the two degrees were approved by faculty at a special meeting (11 December 1985). By officially recognising a separate (P) stream as a means of satisfying the compulsory Economics requirement for the new BEc (Social Sciences) degree, the two-degree structure adopted by faculty also took much of what heat remained from the political economy dispute.

Among other items of business, the three faculty meetings in 1986 planned, if at all possible, to extend the Merewether Building, partly to accommodate the growing space requirements of the Graduate School of Management. The space occupied by the Wolstenholme Library was noted as a potential site.

During 1987 faculty adopted a Quinquennial Plan. This highlighted faculty's inadequate resources in terms of staff, space and library facilities, as well as the urgent need for a safer method of crossing City Road for students between lectures. A proposal by Accounting in 1988 to change its name to Accounting and Finance was narrowly lost with 25 votes in favour, 27 against. Faculty also debated ways to solve growing national problems in accounting education. A faculty management committee was established as part of the administrative response to financial devolution. At its last meeting in 1988, faculty approved fees for all master and diploma students, a sign of things to come over subsequent years. Four faculty meetings were held during 1989. They introduced semesterisation and a concomitant unit system for measuring student progress in the degree, discussed a cooperative scheme for accounting education, reiterated the problem of space shortage indicated by grossly overcrowded lecturing theatres and listened to Alan Craswell's proposal for a Faculty of Commerce and a change of name for the Accounting Department to Commerce Department. This was rejected. Faculty did approve entry for 50 full-fee paying overseas students and a quota on Accounting enrolments to commence in 1991.

Faculty meetings in 1990 debated a new degree, the Bachelor of Commerce. The intention of the new degree was to make Accounting and Commercial Law the key specialisations, thereby enabling the BEc to cater more effectively for students wishing to specialise in the other faculty courses, Industrial Relations and Economic History. The new degree required 22 units (or eleven full-year courses). In addition, it made two units each compulsory from Economics, Accounting and Econometrics, allowed no more than ten units to be taken as first-year courses and required two major sequences of six units each for satisfactory completion. A further distinguishing feature of the new degree was that the second major sequence could come from a non-faculty course such as Asian Studies, a modern language, or other prescribed courses offered at the university which would satisfy an individual student's needs in taking the degree. A summary of the courses of study required for the new degree was presented as follows:

Semester	1	2	3	4	5	6	Units
	Acc.	Acc.	Acc.	Acc.	Acc.	Acc.	6
	Econ.	Econ.					2
	E'trics	E'trics					2
			Law	Law	Law	Law	4
			Invest.	Audit.			2
	Option	Option	Option	Option	Option	Option	6
				Total units over six semesters/three years:			**22**

The six optional units in this table constituted the second major to be taken in the degree. The Commerce degree enabled four units of Commercial Law to be taken, as well as the compulsory two units each of Economics, Econometrics and Accounting, and contained only ten units of first-year subjects: the eight units taken in the first and second semesters and the two units of Commercial Law taken in the third and fourth semesters.

A special faculty meeting (27 September 1991) recommended introduction of the BCom degree from the start of the 1993 academic year, though with a number of changes from those initially proposed. One major change was to make Economics I (Social Sciences) an alternative for the compulsory Economics subject, another was rephrasing the opportunity to select the second major sequence from a non-faculty course by requiring that sixteen units in the degree had to come from faculty courses. Faculty voted in favour of the new degree by 39 votes to 33 (with two abstentions). Moreover, the dean announced that he would let faculty decide on the opportunities for currently enrolled students to take the new degree after its resolutions had been confirmed by Senate. The new degree began in 1993. It proved to be a very attractive faculty offering for students interested in pursuing a business career, including many full-fee-paying overseas students.

During 1990 and 1991 faculty legislated for full semesterisation of all its courses; approved reorganisation of both the joint Economics/Econometrics Master degree and that in Industrial Relations; and drew up procedures for the appointment of deans after internal and, if necessary, external advertisement. The last faculty meeting in 1991 introduced the Penang venture as a potentially profitable faculty project in exporting its teaching.

In 1992, faculty altered its unit system by differentiating between first year (twelve-unit) and senior year (sixteen-unit) courses as a more sophisticated quantification of the faculty's various degree requirements. In addition, it debated a proposal for a combined Bachelor of Engineering/Commerce degree to be completed over five years, and welcomed the introduction of a full sequence of Sociology courses (I–IV) for students enrolled in the BEc (SocSci) degree.

At a special meeting (23 April 1993), faculty was given more details about the Penang venture. Various problems facing the scheme were raised, including those for junior staff giving lectures in a strange cultural environment and the extra costs of that teaching, as well as the flow-on from the scheme in terms of senior faculty enrolments from students who had successfully completed the first-year Penang program. Some of these problems, it was argued, could be resolved through using the services offered by the university's Centre for Teaching and Learning. In September 1993, the faculty's unit system was revised to allow for four unit courses and to check the relative weights of the faculty degree relative to others in the university (the 22 units required by the faculty as against the twenty units more generally required for a university degree). At the October 1993 meeting, the dean reported on the inaugural meeting of his advisory committee, initiated as yet a further administrative response to financial devolution. Faculty now also needed to prepare an annual budget. In 1994, a special faculty meeting approved the introduction of a Master of Commerce and Diploma of Commerce as special fee-paying degrees largely geared to the overseas student market. By 1996, they proved an extraordinary success, financially and academically, with enrolments trebling. The ordinary June 1994 faculty meeting was informed that student evaluation of teaching on a regular basis was now official faculty policy, and that grades in examinations and final results were to be standardised across the university. In November 1994 Senate approved the resolutions for the Master of Commerce degree, the Graduate Diploma in Commerce and the Master of International Relations degree.

During 1995 the faculty received a proposal from the Faculty of Arts for a combined Bachelor of Arts/Bachelor of Commerce degree. It followed a proposal for a Bachelor of Commerce (Liberal Arts) degree suggested by the dean in 1994 and debated during 1995. This was a scheme in which Commerce subjects (Accounting, Econometrics and Economics) could be combined with subjects from Arts or from Science. A novel feature in the proposal was the introduction of a one-semester first-year course on expository writing. Resolutions for the new degree were approved by Senate during 1996. During 1995, largely from an initiative of the dean, faculty organised academic staff exchanges with Saint-Petersburg State University, and established a technical aid program for St Petersburg which airlifted three tonnes of computing equipment in its first year of operation (reported in the *Australian*, Higher Education Supplement, 26 July 1995).

Apart from approving a substantial number of course changes, faculty meetings in 1996 debated yet another proposal for a name change when Terry Walter and Peter Swan recommended Faculty of Commerce and Economics as a name better reflecting faculty's current activities. This proposed name change was defeated by 28 votes to 20. However, it anticipated events in the second half of the 1990s when the gradually growing emphasis on business studies in the faculty was recognised by both a faculty name change and plans for its structural reorganisation.

The years 1997 to 1999 achieved just that. In 1997, faculty formed a subcommittee to examine its future role and functions, as well as the proposed merger of its Graduate School of Business and the Australian Graduate School of Management at the University of New South Wales (FM: 19 September 1997). That meeting also reported strong departmental support for a faculty summer school, to run over seven weeks in January and February, enabling students to speed up completion of their degree. A fee of $1375 was envisaged for a first-year level unit of study, and $1575 for a senior unit. A new building proposal was also announced. An additional faculty building was to be constructed on vacant land known as the 'stone yard', almost adjacent to the Merewether Building in Codrington Street. The Merewether Building would be kept as a faculty location but no decisions had been made as yet as to which departments would move from Merewether into the new building. This proposal marked the end of faculty's search for additional space in the Institute Building. Finally, a Curriculum Committee report noted the state of play over the introduction of the BCom (Liberal Studies) degree and its draft resolution.

A special faculty meeting on 24 April 1998 debated new academic structures and governance for the faculty in terms of establishing schools. At this meeting, the Economics Department proposed either a three-school model (Economics, Commerce and Social Sciences) or simply a School of Social Sciences. Economic History preferred a Faculty of Social Sciences with support from the Faculties of Arts and Science to a new schools structure. Industrial Relations supported creation of a new school of Industrial Relations and Management. The Department of Marketing and the Institute of Transport Studies expressed a strong desire for a School of Commerce. No views were expressed at this stage by Econometrics, Government and Accounting. The subsequent May 1998 meeting paid tribute to Steve Salsbury's services to the university as dean and Professor of Economic History, in response to his death from cancer in March. In the interim, Terry Walter was appointed as acting dean, to hold office until a new dean was appointed at the end of 1998. The meeting also discussed details of the proposed joint BE/BCom degree enabling students to combine commerce with engineering studies.

On 21 July 1999, a special meeting debated faculty's proposed new structure and name. Faculty's restructuring committee recommended in the first place that from 1 January 2000 the faculty be called the Faculty of Economics, Politics and Business. Secondly, it proposed that faculty divide into two schools: Economics and Political Science (consisting of the departments of Economics, Political Economy, Economic History, Government, Econometrics and Business Statistics) and a School of Business (consisting of the departments of Accounting and Business Law, Finance, Marketing, Transport and Logistics and Industrial Relations under its new name, Work and Organisation Studies). The 7 December 1999 faculty meeting was informed that Senate, at its meeting of 6 September, had approved Faculty of Economics and Business as the new name for the Faculty of Economics and Business from 1 January 2000, and that the names of its two schools were to be as recommended. Perhaps in response, the Department of Government and Public Administration also adopted a name change: Government and International Relations, a more adequate reflection of its current interests and expertise. Faculty therefore initiated debate at this meeting on a new constitution designed to incorporate these changes with respect to membership and associated matters. This new constitution was finalised at the first meeting of the Faculty of Economics and Business held on 14 April 2000.

In the year of its 80th birthday, the Faculty of Economics therefore ceased to exist under its original name and structure. It started the new millennium as the Faculty of Economics and Business. Its two schools, Economics and Political Science and Business, were to be housed in the Merewether Building and in the new Business Building erected, as proposed, in Codrington Street. Although there was a great deal of continuity between the two faculties, it can also be said that the Faculty of Economics and Business marked an important new beginning designed to cope more effectively with the demands of economics and associated business studies in the 21st century.

A new economics precinct of Merewether Building and Institute

By the mid-1980s space was at a premium within the Merewether Building, given the growth in staff and student enrolments. Room shortages came to a head in 1989. The Economics Faculty was initially promised relief from a proposed new general-purpose building to be called the Madsen Building. Tutorial rooms used in the basement of the Merewether Building, known colloquially as the 'dungeon tute rooms', were declared to be a potential safety hazard, with no satisfactory exits in case of fire. Staff, in such an eventuality, were said to carry legal liability. Good news on this front came at the March 1989 faculty meeting. First of all, air-conditioning was to be provided for the faculty's two large lecture theatres, MLT1 and MLT2, an essential improvement given their very substantial overcrowding, especially for first- and second-year Economics lectures. In May 1989, the dean reported that the university was not able to provide a new building for the Faculty of Economics in the near future. Its offer of temporary relief was to make space available in the adjoining Institute Building. Industrial Relations became the first department to be moved to this building, which would also provide new lecture and tutorial rooms. To alleviate overcrowding in the large Merewether Lecture Theatres, the vice-chancellor offered use of the Wallace Theatre. This offer had to be rejected, given the distance students would then have to travel between classes from one end of the university to the other, including crossing busy City Road. The rapid growth in Arts students taking faculty courses was seen as a major part of the overcrowding problem, for which the Faculty Management Committee could only see an immediate answer through enrolment quotas. In 1991, the first of these quotas was applied to Accounting.

By 1992, the Institute Building increasingly provided space for faculty purposes. A new Stock Exchange Materials Library was opened on 11 November 1992; the upper Institute's advanced computer laboratory started on 8 December 1992. More space for faculty purposes was provided when the Geography Department vacated the Institute in early 1993. In the meantime, faculty obtained additional space for postgraduate students and some staff in the Darlington Road terrace houses at the rear of the Merewether Building. This additional accommodation proved to be rather unsatisfactory because good lines of communication between it and the Merewether Building were virtually non-existent.

In June 1993, the dean announced that new postgraduate facilities were to be provided in Room 333 of the Institute Building. These gave 24-hour access for students to the 40 study carrels available there for their use. Much of the unsatisfactory postgraduate accommodation in the Darlington terrace houses was thereby replaced. In December 1995 the new Finance Department was housed in the Institute Building following completion of refurbishing its lower ground floor. More general refurbishment of parts of the Merewether Building likewise took place during 1995. These included redecoration of Room 397 as a general committee meeting room, of the staff common room (tea room) and of some additional office space for faculty's expanding administrative staff.

A memorandum (dated 30 September 1994) highlights the inadequacy of teaching space for tutorials within what was now called the Economics Precinct. During 1994 the Faculty of Economics was using space for tutorials not only in the Merewether and Institute Buildings but to a significant extent in the Madsen and Carslaw Buildings, in Biochemistry, in Architecture and even in Fisher stacks. In addition, some of these buildings provided lecture rooms for the large number of courses the faculty was now offering to its students. The Institute Building became increasingly important over the next few years as a provider of space to the faculty for both teaching and staff accommodation. It initially provided accommodation for the new departments of Finance and of Marketing as well as for Industrial Relations, while its associated manager's residence for a while housed staff from the Political Economy Group, which by the end of the decade became the Department of Political Economy.

However, space problems for the faculty were not adequately solved until 2002, when the newly completed Economics and Business building was able to house the new Business School including the three departments formerly housed in the Institute Building. This left the Merewether Building to the School of Economics and Politics, while faculty administrative staff was located in both venues. The dean's office went into the Business School building, befitting the incumbent dean's discipline of Accounting.

Two new Business Studies departments: Finance and Marketing

Two new departments joined the six long-established ones in the faculty during the mid-1990s. The introduction of Finance and Marketing courses reflected the growing emphasis on business studies in the faculty. Their creation, as previously mentioned, inspired a move within very few years to alter faculty's name to recognise this change explicitly, together with a division of faculty into schools of Business and of Economics and Political Science. Since details of the new departments' staffing and broad course structures have already been outlined, this section only discusses the creation of the new departments and associated matters.

Creating a Finance Department for the faculty was on the agenda from the beginning of the 1990s. A selection committee for a chair in Finance was set up in July 1991, and Peter Swan was appointed its first incumbent in December 1993. He came with very substantial academic credentials from the University of New South Wales. Other teaching staff and an administrative assistant were appointed during 1995. The new department itself officially commenced in June 1994, and was highly successful in attracting able students. It was initially housed in the west wing of the Institute Building. From the outset, it offered its courses for both the BEc and the BCom degree. Moreover, from the beginning it provided for postgraduate studies leading up to the research degrees of MEc and PhD.

Second-year courses in Corporate Finance started the new major sequence. These required as prerequisites satisfactory completion of Accounting IA or Financial Accounting Concepts, Economics I and Econometrics I. The Corporate Finance courses dealt with investment decision making, the Australian capital market, equity finance versus debt, and issues in capital allocation, derivatives and futures markets, and foreign exchange and debt markets. Honours studies in Finance also started in second year, requiring advanced work on these topics, and a high aggregate first-year mark. Second-year first-semester courses in Finance (taken in third year) included more detailed study of derivative securities (options, futures and swaps), as well as Corporate Control, with honours students in addition required to take a weekly seminar concentrating on topics in Corporate Governance and Control. In second semester, student had to take courses in trading and dealing in security markets, as well as in Advanced Corporate Finance Theory including the capital asset pricing model, arbitrage pricing theory, dividend policy and other corporate finance topics. Second-year honours in Finance required taking a weekly seminar program largely devoted to the topic, Security Market Pricing Structure. Final-year honours for Finance student entailed satisfactory completion of a substantial piece of research and could be taken jointly with Accounting or Marketing honours.

From the early 1990s, faculty also actively contemplated the formation of a marketing department. The university established a chair in Marketing in September 1991 but initial advertisements failed to attract qualified applicants. The chair was therefore re-advertised in April 1993 and Jordan Louviere was appointed to the foundation chair at the end of that year. Other teaching staff was appointed in 1994 and thereafter as needed. The new department was officially inaugurated on 4 May 1995, and an advisory board to guide and assist its operations was set up the following August consisting of academics drawn from other universities and from practitioners. In December 1995, the department proposed establishment of an institute of retail and services studies for the Faculty of Economics. Like the Finance Department, Marketing was housed in the Institute Building though it was situated on the third level of the Merewether Building for a brief period in 1995. It attracted a large number of academic visitors, drawn mainly from North American universities. The department developed a strategic plan in 1997 to signal its major emphasis on teaching, and attracted satisfactory student numbers in its early years.

The Marketing Department only offered courses from second year, with units available in Marketing Principles, Consumer Behaviour and Marketing Research. Prerequisites for the courses were satisfactory completion of Economics I and Econometrics I. In third year, the department offered a continuation of its Marketing Research course, together with courses in Marketing Communications, Retail and Services Marketing, and New Products Marketing. Marketing courses were only available to Bachelor of Commerce students, and the department therefore also contributed to courses for the Master and Diploma of Commerce. By 1996, honours courses in Marketing were available to its students, requiring additional advanced work as part of its first- and second-year courses and the completion of a major marketing research project in the final honours year.

The establishment of Finance and Marketing departments greatly increased the opportunities for business studies in the faculty, facilitating the drive towards renaming the faculty as one of Economics and Business. However, it is appropriate to recall at this stage that this enhancement of business studies within the faculty also marked a return to its early beginnings. After all, these had simply consisted of re-organising the commercial teaching responsibilities within the original Department of Economics from 1906 to 1920 under the direction of Robert Irvine as its foundation professor.

Graduates and students, 1985–99

The veritable explosion in both undergraduate and postgraduate degrees during the final fifteen years of the Faculty of Economics by that name was mentioned at the start of the chapter. Needless to say, this had a major effect on both the quantity and type of graduates the faculty was producing. The 1985 *Annual Report of the University* indicated that in its first 65 years the faculty had conferred just over 8000 degrees on aggregate; in the following fifteen years it almost matched this figure with the conferring of 7702 degrees. The faculty was now the fourth largest in the university on this criterion; that is, after Arts, Science and Medicine.

Given the growing variety of the type of degree offered by the faculty, these graduation data need to be disaggregated. In 1985, the university conferred over 400 faculty degrees of which almost 95 per cent were BEc degrees. Three PhDs were conferred, eleven MBAs and nine masters degrees. Just over one-third of the postgraduate degrees and a fraction under one-third of the BEcs went to women in those years. Twenty-seven degrees were awarded with honours, of which two went to masters students. There was only one university medallist in 1985, Robert Dubler, an Industrial Relations student. There were four other first-class honours graduates, fourteen with upper seconds, five with lower seconds, and one with third-class honours. The last grade of honours, it can be noted here, was eliminated *de facto* by faculty from 1996. No further third-class honours degrees were awarded after that year.

In 1991, the first full cohort of BEc (SocSci) degrees were conferred, 55 in all, of which ten were awarded at honours level. Twenty-three pass BEc (SocSci) degrees had been conferred the year before. Most of the recipients of the new degree were women, the case for most years up to 1999. However, the two first-class honours degrees, including a medallist (Scott Eden in Economics P), went to men; the five women honours graduates were awarded second-class honours results. The BEc in 1991 was conferred on 34 students at honours level, including two medallists (Jason Murray and Kyle Oliver), nine other first-class honours graduates, sixteen with upper seconds and seven with lower seconds. The number of postgraduate degrees conferred in 1991 was 35, among whom sixteen were MBAs, and seven Master of Public Policy graduates. For the year as a whole, a total 471 degrees were conferred; of which 185 (or over 39 per cent) on women graduates.

The first BCom degrees (at pass level) were conferred in 1996, 197 in all, close to half of the total 418 pass bachelors degrees awarded by faculty in that year. By 1997, the Commerce degrees had become even more popular, and 254 BComs were conferred, including 21 at honours level (one medallist, Robin Balcomb, seven other first-class honours graduates, thirteen second-class honours graduates), so that the first medallist in the new Commerce degree was a woman. This compared with 122 BEcs conferred (of whom 35 at honours level including five medallists) and 97 BEc (SocSci) degrees, of which nine were awarded with honours. The Master of Commerce degree was conferred on 21 students (five had received this new degree in 1996), part of a vastly growing number of postgraduate degrees conferred in 1997 (333, or over 40 per cent of all faculty degrees for that year). Over 90 of these postgraduate degrees were MBAs, sixteen were PhDs, while other master degrees, postgraduate diplomas and certificates made up the remainder. The small percentage (22.2) of women recipients among the postgraduate degrees conferred helped lower the overall percentage of faculty degrees conferred on women to 32 per cent, a reversal of previous trends.

In 1999, its final year of existence as a Faculty of Economics, faculty conferred 1286 degrees, 41.7 per cent of which were postgraduate. At the undergraduate level, 163 students graduated BEc, 125 BEc (SocSci) and 461 BCom, the newest degree accounting for more than 60 per cent of faculty undergraduate degrees conferred. Women received 35.7 per cent of these degrees, and 27.2 per cent of the 537 postgraduate degrees. Three medals were awarded, 22 other first-class honours degrees, 23 upper seconds and eight lower seconds or a total of 56 honours (7.5 per cent of the 749 bachelor degrees conferred). Honours degrees were awarded at virtually equal numbers for the three types of undergraduate degrees: nineteen each in the BEc and the BEc (SocSci), eighteen in the BCom. Postgraduate degrees included seventeen PhDs, 58 MBAs, four Masters of Public Policy, eleven MEcs, three MEcs (SocSci), and 213 MComs, together with 50 Masters of International Studies, 22 Masters of Transport Management, seven Masters of Public Affairs, sixteen Masters of Industrial Relations and 89 graduate diplomas (three in Economics, two in Industrial Relations, five in Transport Management, four in International Studies, seven in Commerce and 68 in Business Management) as well as 39 Graduate Certificates (two in International Studies, 29 in Management, one each in Industrial Relations and in Transport Management, four in Marketing and 21 in Commerce).

Before looking at major individual performances on an annual basis, some general remarks on honours awards may be made. Honours numbers fluctuated widely in both absolute and relative terms over the fifteen year period ending in 1999. For the BEc, annual awards ranged from 19 to 61, an average of 36 per annum; for the BEc (SocSci) annual honours awards ranged from 9 to 23, averaging 16.2; while for the three years of the BCom, honours awarded ranged from 18 to 31 with an average of 23.3.

In terms of total graduates, this averaged out at 11.4 per cent for the BEc, 22 per cent for the BEc (SocSci) and 6.5 per cent for the BCom. The incidence of honours therefore varied considerably between the three undergraduate degrees conferred by the faculty.

Two PhDs were conferred in 1985: Alan Craswell, a staff member and later professor in Accounting, gained his doctorate for research on 'the impact of changes in Auditors' legal and professional Obligations on the frequency of Audit Reports' while Mohamed Haque gained his in Econometrics for 'An Analysis of Australian Family Budgets'. Nine Master of Economics degrees were conferred, including one to Jayne Godfrey, later Professor of Financial Accounting at Monash University, and two at honours level to Irene Adraskelas (Economics) and Sally Thorpe (Econometrics). Twelve MBAs were conferred and 391 BEcs, of which 25 were at honours level. The medal was awarded to Robert Dubler (Industrial Relations), four other first-class honours were equally shared between Economics (Evan Jones and Mathew Ryan) and Geography (Paula Douglas and Michael Hughes). Fourteen upper seconds were awarded, nine in Economics, two in Industrial Relations and three in Government. Six students received lower honours grades. Of the 366 pass graduates, several distinguished themselves in later careers. Anthony Albanese was elected MHR for Grayndler in 1996, after a period as policy adviser to the New South Wales premier and as New South Wales party officer, and since 2002 served as shadow minister for various portfolios. In 2007 he was appointed Minister for Infrastructure, Transport, Regional Development and Local Government in the Rudd Labor government elected that November. Robert Ryan built a financial management career in the credit union sector and George Argyrous an academic career. The 1985 graduation list also included a 64-year-old BEc, Leo Tutt, a mature-age student who attended university simply for the pleasure of studying.

Four PhDs were conferred during 1986: on Tony Aspromourgos (Economics) for a thesis on 'Sir William Petty and the Origins of Classical Political Economy'; on Richard Kuhn (Government) for research on economic thought of the labour movement 'Between the Depression and Long Boom'; on Barry Moore (Government) for work on administrative style and its effect on functioning of an organisation; and on Greg Patmore (Industrial Relations) for his thesis on industrial relations in the New South Wales Railways (1875–1929). In addition four MEcs were conferred, three at honours level (Graham White in Economics, Kevin Baker in Economic History and Maurice Peat in Econometrics) as well as nine MBAs. Of the 384 BEcs conferred, 32 were awarded with honours. The one university medallist was Stephen Donald (Econometrics). There were fifteen other first-class honours graduates (John Kirkness in Accounting, Rex di Bona and Luke O'Connor in Computer Science, Lisa Bacigalupo and Peter Skib in Econometrics, Charles Taylor, Susan Thorp and Malcolm Wood in Economics, Tony Darwell and Glenn Dennett in Geography, Ann Harding and Philip Strickland in Government, Louise Thornthwaite and Chris Wright in Industrial Relations, and Veronica Tseng in Operations Research). In addition, there were ten upper seconds, five lower seconds and one graduate with third-class honours. Three of the 1986 postgraduate degree recipients became noted faculty teachers: by 2006, Tony Aspromourgos was professor in Economics, Greg Patmore was associate professor (Industrial Relations) and Graham White a senior lecturer (Economics). Chris Wright, after first-class honours in Industrial Relations, lectured in that subject for some time. Ann Harding, with first-class honours in Government in 1986, became Professor of Applied Economic and Social Policy at the University of Canberra in 1993; Donald Harwin (with an upper second in Government) became a prominent Liberal politician in the New South Wales Legislative Council; Michael Sherris, a 1986 MBA, became Professor of Actuarial Studies at the University of New South Wales after a career in the financial sector; Susan Spence, another 1986 MBA, after teaching Psychology at Sydney University for some years, became Professor of Psychology at the University of Queensland in 1995; and Carmel Tebbutt, a pass graduate, commenced a political career in state Labor politics as Member of the Legislative Council (1998–2005), MLA for Marrickville from 2005, and Deputy Premier from 2008. For 1986 the faculty graduate list was therefore particularly productive of future academics and state politicians.

In 1987 there were only two PhDs produced for the faculty: Frank Carrigan and Frank Gelber, the second with a thesis on 'The Influences of Income Competition on Inflation'. Three MEcs were conferred, two at honours level to Nigel Ray and Lyndell Davies, both in Economics, and 24 MBAs. Of the 329 BEcs conferred, 32 were awarded at honours level. Again, there was only one university medallist, Michael Sofair (Economics), and eight other first-class honours graduates (Tracy Conlan in Economic History, John Greenfield in Geography, Stephen Borthwick and Simon Lovell in Econometrics, Stephen Fisher and Philip Moffitt in Economics, Michael Blazey and Brett Evans in Government), fifteen gained upper seconds and eight lower seconds. Jusuf Hariman, who added a BEc in 1987 to his other degrees, later distinguished himself sufficiently in his chosen fields of hypnotherapy and psychotherapy to enter *Who's Who* in 2004, the only tangible benefit from his economics studies an attempt at linking management problems with psychology. Other 1987 faculty graduates mentioned by name in this paragraph had careers in the Commonwealth Public Service (Nigel Ray), banking (Lyndell Davies) and economic consulting (Frank Gelber).

No PhDs were conferred in 1988, and only six MEcs of which two were with honours (to Phillip Minns and Paul Gavell). In addition, seventeen MBAs were conferred as well as the first three Master of Public Policy degrees. Three hundred and thirty-seven BEcs were conferred, 32 at honours level. They included two medallists, Mark Blair in Accounting and Anthony Corke in Econometrics. Eight other first-class honours degrees were conferred (Paul Durham in Accounting, Stuart Pook in Computer Science, Deborah Yan in Econometrics, Kieran Sharpe and Collette Young in Economics, Ian Dallen and Robyn Dowling in Geography, and Joe Zappala in Industrial Relations). Fourteen honours degrees awarded were upper seconds, seven lower seconds, with one third-class honours. Of the 305 BEc pass graduates, only one has distinguished himself sufficiently to enter *Who's Who* at the time of writing. This was Ross Cameron, Liberal MHR for Parramatta from 1996 to 2005 and parliamentary secretary to the treasurer from 2003 to 2005. Joe Zappala, it may be recalled, lectured for some time in Industrial Relations.

Three PhDs were conferred in 1989: Lola Antrobus for a thesis on 'The Rural and Industrial Development Authority in Malaya (1950–1965)', Bruce Duncan for one on 'The Social and Political Thought of Catholic Opinion Makers in Sydney During the 1930s', and Asheq Rahman with one on the Accounting Standards Review Board. In addition, Noel Foley, a faculty benefactor and prominent businessman was given a Doctor of the University *honoris causa*. Nine MEcs were conferred, six with honours (to Sylvana Caloni, Peter Docherty, Tony Jensen, Kristi Needham, Walter Setkiewicz and Mathew Smith), as well as seventeen MBAs and seven Masters of Public Policy. During 1989, the first five BEc (SocSci) degrees were also conferred, as well as 395 BEcs, of which 31 were awarded with honours. No university medals were awarded in 1989, and six first-class honours results (to James Goth, Gerard Ryan and Catherine White in Economics, Kathleen Mee is Geography, and to Andrew Fitzmaurice and David Matheson in Government). In addition, there were seventeen upper seconds and eight lower second among the honours students. No student from this cohort has become sufficiently distinguished as yet to gain an entry in *Who's Who*, not surprising when the average lead-time for this distinction is around two decades following graduation.

During 1990, the faculty conferred the DSc (Econ) on Barry Gordon (a graduate of the 1950s and Professor of Economics at the University of Newcastle) for his books on classical and pre-classical economic thought. Three PhDs were conferred: on Graham Bornholt with a thesis on the relative plausibility of competing hypotheses, on Robin Kumar for one on policies and practices determining the employment of managers, and one on John Shields for his thesis, 'Craft Work, Craft Unions and the Survival of Apprenticeships in New South Wales (1860–1914)'. Six MEcs were conferred, three with honours (to Greg Jarjoura, Keith Latty and Patricia Todd), as well as fourteen MBAs and four Master of Public Policy degrees. Twenty-three BEc (SocSci) degrees were conferred, and 348 BEcs, of which 28 were at honours level. Angus Taylor and Chris Wilkins, both in Economics, received university medals, while the seven other first-class honours went to Leon Wong in Accounting, Nadima el Hassan in Computer Science and Operations Research, Martijn Wilber in Economic History, Andrew Tiffin and Joe Tripodi in Economics, Michael Kulper in Geography and Michael Wilcox in Government). There were also eighteen upper seconds and one lower second-class honours awarded. Richard Mackay, one of the 1990 MBAs, a heritage consultant, gained an AM in 2003 for services to the community in relation to heritage; Joe Tripodi, Labor MLA for Fairfield from 1995, became Minister for Roads in the 2005 and in 2009 was Minister for Finance, Infrastructure, Regulatory Reform, and Ports and Waterways.

In 1991, three PhDs were awarded: to Verna Rutnam for a thesis on decision making on medical research policy in Australia; to Virginia Teodosio for work on tripartism and the imperatives of development in the Philippines, and to Chris Wright for work on the rise of modern labour management. Twelve MEcs were conferred, eight with honours (to Michael Fassler, David Gentle, Peter Gunning, Jae-Hoon Kim, Suk-Joong Kim, Kristi Needham, Paul O'Brien and Yun Zhang). In addition, 40 MBAs were conferred, twelve Masters of Public Policy, seven Masters of International Studies, as well as one Graduate Diploma in Public Management, seven Diplomas in Economics and five Diplomas in Industrial Relations. Three hundred and fifty-six BEcs were also conferred, including 34 with honours, as well as 55 BEc (SocSci) degrees, ten with honours. For BEc honours graduates, there were two university medallists (Jason Murray and Kyle Oliver), nine other first-class honours graduates (Andrew Campbell, Han Meng Chan, David Corby, Marc Innes-Brown, Jennifer Kelly, Mark Latina, Jillian Lockman, Colin Rose and John Tate) as well as seventeen upper seconds and seven lower seconds. For the BEc (SocSci), one university medal was awarded (to Scott Eden) and one other first-class honours (to Neil Ackland). No graduate from the 1991 cohort had as yet gained an entry in *Who's Who* by 2006 as a sign of post-university distinction.

At the 27 March 1992 graduation ceremony, faculty and the university acknowledged the services of a prominent faculty staff member, Betty Johnson, an administrative officer (secretary) in the university from 1964 to 1991, mainly in the Government Department. After retirement, she became a National Secretary in the Older Women's Network (1998) and during her long university career was also an active staff unionist. It was therefore most appropriate that the vice-chancellor presented her with the degree of Master of Industrial Relations, *honoris causa*. In addition, the faculty in 1992 conferred three PhDs: on Mark Blair for a thesis on choice of ownership in the Australian life insurance industry; on Siosaia Kami for one on determinants and special features of consumer demand in Tonga; and on Chris O'Donnell for work on the effects of partial lamb prices stabilisation on lamb and wool prices, production, and producer welfare. Faculty conferred eight MEcs, four at honours level (to Michael Dobbie, Jim Farrell, Keiran Sharpe and Sunbyn Shynn), 75 MBAs, seven Masters of Public Policy, two Masters of Industrial Relations, as well as nine Diplomas in Economics, three Diplomas in Industrial Relations, three Diplomas in International Studies, one Diploma in Public Management and three Diplomas in Transport Management. In addition, 423 BEcs were conferred, 61 at honours level, as well as 65 BEcs

(SocSci) of which twelve were at honours level. For the BEc, four university medals were awarded (to Kin Wai Lee in Accounting, to David Murphy in Econometrics and Economics, and to John Romalis and Geoff Shuetrim in Econometrics) as well as sixteen other first-class honours (to Jeff Coulton and Richard Saywell in Accounting; Anders Linstrom in Computer Science; Alexandra Heath in Econometrics; Tim Beresford, Maric Fleming, Kristen Heazlewood, Natalie Medlicott, Tim Rocks, Annabel Spring and Catherine Wright in Economics; Timothy Dixon, John Rieler and Monique Rotic in Government; and to Rohan Garnett and Helen Paul in Industrial Relations). There were in addition 29 upper seconds, nine lower seconds and three thirds. For the BEc (SocSci) Gabrielle Meagher was awarded the university medal, with one other first-class honours awarded to Jennifer Fleming. There were also seven upper, and two lower seconds awarded. As previously mentioned, Gabrielle Meagher joined the Political Economy staff as a teacher later during the decade.

At the 26 February 1993 graduation ceremony, the vice-chancellor presented Bert Evans and Robert Reid with the degree of DSc (Econ) *honoris causa* for services to business and the university. Two PhDs were also awarded in 1993: to Paul Augumeri for a thesis on the economic ideas of Antonio Genovesi (1713–69) and to Baljit Kaur for one on the role of political costs in the tax effect accounting policy choice; Kaur, it may be recalled, was a staff member at the time in Accounting. Thirteen MEcs were awarded, five at honours level (to Therese Chan, Hyeon Seung Huh, Catherine Lee, Paul Oslington and Berenice Spencer) one MEc (SocSci) at honours level (to Bill Lucarelli), as well as 71 MBAs, eleven Masters of Public Policy, sixteen Masters of Industrial Relations, 24 Masters of Transport Management, seven Masters of International Studies and two Diplomas in Economics, two Diplomas in Industrial Relations, three Diplomas in International Studies and four Diplomas in Transport management. Three hundred and seventy-one BEcs were conferred, 58 at honours level. University medals went to Akrum Geha (Accounting) and Mark Jason (Economics), and twelve other first-class honours degrees were conferred (on Stuart Sayers and Eugene Wong in Accounting, Yu Ming Yung in Economics and Econometrics, Stephen Cheung, Peter Cooper, Philip Dean, Adrian Hart, Steven Kennedy in Economics, to Michael di Francesco and Edwin Nelson in Government and to Emma Malden and Warwick Yonge in Industrial Relations). In addition, 25 upper and nineteen lower seconds were conferred. There were also two university medallists among the 50 new BEc (SocSci) degrees: Christopher Briggs and Sean Scalmer. Other first-class honours degrees went to Deborah Biancotti, Verity Carney, Nadja Diessell, Elizabeth Hill, Kurt Iveson, Belinda Smith and Virginia Williams, while ten upper seconds, three lower seconds and one third-class honours were also conferred. Two of the 1993 recipients of degrees have appeared in *Who's Who* so far: David Bell, one of the new MBAs, for distinguished business management in banking, transport and communications, as well as Bert Evans, whose services to business and the university were mentioned at the start of the paragraph.

Once again, a DSc(Econ) *honoris causa* was awarded in 1994, this time to Laurence Short, for services to trade unionism and industrial relations. Five PhDs were conferred: to Sang Hee Han for a thesis on an econometric general equilibrium model for a small open economy with an application to Australia; to Chris Keane for work on the housing reform movement (1900–15); to Evandor McMicken for research on rescheduling credit worthiness and market prices; to Colin Rose for a thesis on hills, humps and other non-linear oddities; and to Hume Winzar for a Monte Carlo evaluation of conjoint preference simulators. Twelve MEcs were conferred, two at honours level (to Jeakyu Lim and Simon Wedde) as well as one MEc (SocSci), thirteen Masters of Industrial Relations including two with honours (Kerry Burke and Lillian Durent), as well as 88 MBAs, three International MBAs, twelve Masters of Public Policy, 22 Masters of Transport Management, eleven Masters of International Studies, together with seven Diplomas in Economics, three in Industrial Relations, five in International Studies, one in Transport Management, thirteen in Corporate Management and four in Public Policy. Four hundred and nine BEcs were conferred, including 45 at honours level. These included two medallists (Sally Auld and Michael Plumb, both in Economics), and seven other first-class honours degrees (to Carolyn Kenny, Rod McKensey, Diane Saw, Roland Winn [Accounting], Claire Johnson [Computer Science], Stephen Groenewegen [Government] and Hayden Fox [Industrial Relations]). In addition, 24 upper seconds, eleven lower seconds and one third-class honours were conferred. Of 72 BEc (SocSci) degree, seventeen were conferred with honours. These included two university medallists (Jodie Ball in Economics, Social Sciences, and Tianbiao Zhu in Government) as well as four other first-class honours degrees (Vanessa Jackson and Danielle Spruyt in Economics Social Sciences, Olivia Jenkins in Geography and Jane Southwell in Psychology). There were nine upper, and two lower second-class honours degrees conferred as well.

In 1995, PhDs were conferred on Neil Hardie, for a thesis entitled, 'A Framework to integrate Models and Definitions of Quality', on Paul Hooper for research on the strategic role of transport packages and their impact on consumer demand, and on Farzana Naqvi for a computable general equilibrium model of energy economy interaction in Pakistan. Eight MEcs were awarded, two at honours level (to Muhammed Khan and Shailendra Singh), one MEc (SocSci) at honours level (to Anthony Stokes), twelve Masters of Industrial Relations including two at honours level (to Jeffrey Braithwaite and John Elder), as well as 86 MBAs, five international MBAs, five Masters of Public Policy, 24 Masters of Transport Management, eight Diplomas in Economics, four in Industrial Relations, seven in International Studies, eleven in Transport Management, 44 in Management and two Certificates in Business Management. Three hundred and forty-five BEcs were conferred, 45 at honours level. These included one university medallist (Justin Wolfers in Economics), and fourteen other first-class honours graduates including Matthew Duffy and Bronwyn Sneddon, Accounting; Bernard Conlon and Keven Fitzgerald, Econometrics; Colleen Cassidy, Economics and Econometrics; Francis Kwok and Kellie Spence, Economics; Alexander Maroya, Government; and Nikola Balnave and Sarah Barnes, Industrial Relations). Twenty-one upper seconds, seven lower seconds and two third-class honours degrees were conferred. Of the 83 BEc (SocSci) degrees conferred, 21 were at honours level. One of these was a university medallist, Maya Andreassen (in Economics Social Sciences), and there were five other first-class honours degrees conferred (to Nicholas Jordan, Katherine O'Rourke and

Sacha Vidler in Economics Social Sciences, and to Julia Cummins and Murray Woodman in Industrial Relations). In addition, three upper seconds and three lower seconds were conferred.

Five PhDs were conferred by the faculty during 1996, three from its Graduate School of Business. Alex Frino (a staff member) received his in Finance for a thesis on the determinants of intraday bid ask spreads on the Australian Stock Exchange, Daehoon Nahm in Econometrics for research on quasi-separability and monetary aggregation, Alan Fish for one on expatriate career management practices, Wendy Spinks for one on office-based telecommuting and Michael Nyathi for a thesis on strategic alliance partner choice in international aviation. Thirteen MEcs were awarded including four at honours level (to Andrea Graziani, Milovan Lucich, Michael Plumb and Valerie Severin), four MEcs (SocSci) including two honours (Adam Rorris and Adrienne Tan) as well as five MComs, 100 MBAs, two Masters of Public policy, 36 Masters of Industrial Relations, six Masters of Transport Management, two Masters of Management and six Diplomas in Economics, seven Diplomas in Industrial Relations, three Diplomas in Transport management, 47 Diplomas in Business Administration and one Certificate in Business Administration. In addition 176 BEcs were conferred, 34 at honours level including two university medallists (Adrianne Croft in joint Economics/Econometrics and Philip Chung, Operations Research and Computer Science) while other first-class honours degrees went to Harishand Madhoo and Scott Richardson in Accounting, Meredith Beechey in joint Econometrics/Economic History, David McAndrew in joint Econometrics/Operations Research, Sonia Lopes, Deborah Smith and Daniel Yeung in Economics, Michael Chaaya and Rebecca Hindwood in Government; twenty upper seconds and three lower seconds. There were 98 BEc (SocSci) including nineteen at honours level with one university medallist (Christina Ho in Economics Social Science) and four other first-class honours results (to Paula Mottek in Economic History, Vanessa Boyle and Michael Sutton in Economics Social Science and Alexandra Gartrell in Geography); eleven upper seconds and three lower seconds; and 197 BComs.

In 1997, Faculty conferred the DSc (Econ) *honoris causa* on James Wolfensohn for outstanding services to international finance, the arts and charitable organisations. In addition, PhDs were conferred on Jonathan Batten for a thesis on financial risk management of Australian financial institutions, to Poming Chan for one on the structure and market efficiency of Hong Kong foreign exchange markets; to Peter Cooper for work on systematic inequality and market failure, to Ian de Mellow on cost efficiency of New South Wales rail passenger services, on Ann Hodgkinson for research on corporate organisational change in the global market, to Armal Karunaratne for work on a control-relational model of the exporter foreign channel intermediary relationship, to Roderick Katz for a thesis on demand for bicycle use, to Jae Hoon Kim for work on bootstrapping in vector auto-regressive models, to Suk-Yoong Kim for research on the role of economic news and expectations in Australian financial markets, to Sean Scalmer for a thesis on 'the cancer of class', to Rhonda Sharp for research on Labor's occupational superannuation policy, to Andrew Tan for a thesis on the ASEAN states since 1975 and to Philip Toner for work on main currents in the theory of circular and cumulative causation. Seven MEcs were conferred including two at honours level (to Pierre Uldry and Alison Vicary), four MEc (SocSci) including two at honours level (to Chris Dunstan and Kiri Evans), 91 MBAs, five Masters of Public Policy, 32 Masters of International Studies including two at honours level (to Karen Chan and David Connery), 25 MComs, seven Masters of Industrial Relations, 28 Masters of Transport Management, three Masters of Management, one Master of Public Affairs as well as seven Diplomas in Economics, three Diplomas in International Studies, ten Diplomas in Transport Management, 61 Diplomas in Business Administration, one Graduate Diploma in Public Policy, one Graduate Diploma in Commerce, 26 Graduate Certificates in Business Administration and one Graduate Certificate in Commerce. One hundred and twenty-two BEcs were conferred, 35 with honours. These include five university medallists (Maria Abbonizio, Michele Laidlaw and Mark Melatos in Economics; Richard Holden, the 1996 joint winner of Business student of the year in Economic History; and Jane Toman in Econometrics), as well as six other first-class honours (Angus Boyd in Finance, Andrew Hetzberg, Fathima Salih, Tim Peterson, Martin Toner and Luke Willard in Economics) plus twenty upper seconds and three lower seconds. There were also 97 BEcs (SocSci) including nine at honours level of which one with first-class honours (Carolyn Deere); and 254 BComs of which 21 were at honours level including one university medallist (Robin Balcomb), seven others with first-class honours (Carole Forde, Peter Lambousis, Mia Prodigalidad, Jason Shailer, Jason Watson, Andrew West and Valerie Youngman) as well as eight upper seconds and five lower seconds. By 2004, Mark Melatos had become a lecturer in Economics in the faculty.

In 1998 three DScs (Econ) were conferred, two *honoris causa*. The two honorary doctorates were awarded to Professor Muhammed Yunus for innovative banking and one-use micro-credit for the world's poor and for advocacy of social justice, and to William Fisher. The third went to David Johnson. PhDs were conferred: on Neal Arthur for a thesis on Economic determinants of corporate boards' compositions, Nadira Barkatullah for work on pricing demand analysis with an application to a water utility, Jeroen Bijleveld for a thesis on dilemmas of human rights in foreign policy, on Peter Docherty for research on money and employment, on Grant Michelson, on Anja Morton for a thesis on audit service quality, on Paul Oslington for work on unemployment in an open economy, on Shane Ostenfeld on lesbian liberation and Labor in Australia, on Habibolah Shirazi, on Frank Vigneron and on Mark Westcott for research on workplace industrial relations at the Clyde refinery 1974–94. Eighteen MEcs were conferred including twelve at honours level (to Michael Boeiovsky, John Bridges, Khurelbataar Chomed, Mathew Crowe, Narantuya Chuluunbat, Jifong Du, Anthony Housego, Kishore Karunakaran, Charles Littrell, Saime Pollack, Kishti Sen and Ai Zhou). Five MEcs (SocSci) were conferred including two at honours level (to Thirunavukarasu Sundaram and Chris Dunstan), 161 MComs, 99 MBAs, two international MBAs, three Masters of Management, twelve Masters of Industrial Relations including two at honours level (Tilda Khoshaba and William Ward), 36 Masters of International Studies including one at honours level (Andrew Heys), two Masters of Public Policy, four Masters of Public Affairs including one at honours level (to James McGillicuddy), thirteen Masters of

Transport Management as well as five Diplomas in Economics, four Diplomas in Industrial Relations, one Diploma in International Studies, one Diploma in Taxation, four Diplomas in Commerce, six Diplomas in Transport Management, 29 Diplomas in Business Management, one Graduate Diploma in Management, one Graduate Certificate in International Studies and 24 Graduate Certificates in Business Management. One hundred and eighty-two BEcs were conferred, 30 at honours level. These included three university medallists (Amelia Hill in Finance, Asley Lester and Kui Ng in Economics) as well as ten other first-class honours (to Derek Mak in Accounting, Claudia Certoma, Hiroshi Narushima, Nigel Semitecolos and Tet Far Soon in Economics, Peter Forrest in Finance and Keats Brydon, Chi Chem, Wee Koan Tok and Alexander Rock in Marketing), thirteen upper seconds and four lower seconds. One hundred and twelve BEcs (SocSci) were conferred, among them sixteen at honours level including three first-class honours (to Chris Martin in Economic History, Nocola Franklin in Geography and Dhananjayan Sriskandarajah in Political Economy), twelve upper seconds and one lower seconds. Three hundred and sixty-five BComs were conferred. These included 31 at honours level among whom one university medallist (Natalie Krestovsky) and ten other first-class honours graduates (Sascha Levitt in Accounting and Finance, Nell Carney in Economics and Econometrics, Paul Edney in Economics, Michael Chang, Laura Hayes and Rodney Saddington in Finance, Bentley de Beyer in Industrial Relations, Rodrigo Balart, Lisa Coggan and Angela Yeoh in Marketing).

The last Faculty of Economics graduation ceremonies under this name took place in 1999. They likewise included a DSc (Econ) *honoris causa*, this time conferred on His Excellency Phan Van Khai, Vietnamese prime minister. In addition, seventeen PhDs were conferred, three by the Graduate School of Management (on Ghulam Mian for a thesis on the short-run dynamics of the Australian Stock Exchange, on Lesley White for research on perceived relative influence to joint decision making in a professional services context, and on Jianlin Xu for a thesis on bus routing strategies). Faculty of Economics PhDs were conferred on Muhammad Akhter, on Brett Carroll, on Robert Christie for a thesis on organisational and institutional influences on rotating saving and credit associations, on Carolyn Currie for a thesis on the regulation of the Australian financial system, on Mark Donoghue for research on the history of the classical wage fund doctrine, on Chris Guest for a thesis on the market and the role of government in the political economy of Smith, Mill, Marshall, Keynes and Hayek, on Gabrielle Meagher for a thesis called 'The Ultimate Lousy Job: Evaluating the Construction of Paid Housework', on Mahamad Nassar, on Nicholas Pappas for research on the French occupation of Castellorizo (1915–21), on Teresa Poon for research on inter-firm networks and the dynamic process of industrial upgrading, on Michael Rafferty, on Stuart Sharp for a thesis titled, 'Destined to Fail: Management of the New South Wales Railways (1877–1995)', on John Tate for a thesis on the formative context of Kant's moral philosophy and on Yun Zhang for a thesis on data envelopment analysis operating environment sample size and application to electricity distribution.

Eleven MEcs were conferred, six at honours level (to Philip Haywood, Paul Kitney, Katsuyuki Meguro, Kamala Holla, Chen Leu and Shi Cheng Kao); three MEcs (SocSci), one at honours level (to Wooi Syn Tan); 213 MCom degrees (including two at first-class honours level to Mei Ling Chen and Yvonne He); 46 Master of International Studies degrees including eight at honours level (to Rebecca Davies, Kikue Hamayotsu, Sylvia Marfori, Bridie Nolan, Ramiro Ruedi, Katrina Sauvides, Leila Shashahani and Peter Strauss); sixteen Masters of Industrial Relations including one at honours level (to Sylvia Falzon), 58 MBAs, four Masters of Public Policy, seven Masters of Public Affairs, four Masters of Management, 22 Masters of Transport Management, as well as three Diplomas in Economics, two Diplomas in Industrial Relations, four Diplomas in International Studies, seven Diplomas of Commerce, five Graduate Diplomas of Transport Management, 68 Diplomas of Business Management, one Graduate Certificate in Industrial Relations, two Graduate Certificates in Commerce, four Graduate Certificates in Marketing, one Graduate Certificate in Transport Management and one Graduate Certificate in International Studies. One hundred and sixty-three BEcs were conferred, including nineteen at honours level among whom university medals went to Yane Svetiev (in Economics) and Melanie Wyld (in Government) with other first-class honours to Damien Boey, Ben Dudley, Andrew Harpham, Andrew Krestovsky and Rebecca Stoeckel, all in Economics, and Paul Burke, in Marketing. Nine upper seconds and two lower seconds were also awarded. Of the 125 BEc (SocSci) degrees conferred, nineteen were at honours level including six first-class honours (to Paul Hunyor and Adrienne Whitby in Economic History, to Natasha Cortis and James Fletcher in Economics Social Sciences, and to Dale Kreibig and Craig Reucassel in Government), nine upper seconds and three lower seconds. Of 213 BCom degrees conferred, eighteen were at honours level of which ten were first-class honours (to Changsen Wu in Accounting, to Yuen Leong, Stephen Smith and Nicholas Steiner in Accounting and Finance, to Sheila Mong in Economics, to Anthony Charara and Roger Feletto in Finance, to Joanne Katsiaris in Government, and to Victor Leung and Kathy Sigouras in Marketing) as well as five upper second and three lower seconds.

Given the increased number of higher degrees in the period covered by this chapter, it is not surprising that some of the personal recollections from past students came from postgraduate students. One detailed reminiscence was from a student taking the Master of Public Policy as a part-time evening student during the first year it was taught. Dawn Linklater, a policy analyst in the NSW Public Service, was awarded the Master of Public Policy in 1988. At 50, she was among the oldest members of the class. She noted that students in particular found the substantial economic component of the degree quite heavy going but also very useful 'to make sense of the various trends and public announcements from financial commentators. Indeed, the whole degree was the most useful in practical terms of all my studies ... And I have a real feeling of gratitude for the staff who struggled to instil so much into our heads already so full of our work and pre-conceived ideas.' She recalled with pleasure Michael Jackson's lectures on ethics, those by Martin Painter and Helen Nelson on organisational theory, Gordon Mills on cost/benefit analysis and cost-effectiveness studies, classes by Russell Lansbury on industrial relations and more generally, human resources management, and my own lectures on public finance, especially those on Australian inter-governmental relations (letters to the author, 6 November, 6 December 2004).

Paul Oslington, now a senior lecturer in the School of Business at the Australian Defence Force Academy (Canberra) completed first a joint masters degree in Economics/Econometrics, followed by PhD in international economics supervised by Alan Woodland and Jeff Sheen. Of the masters course, he recalled with pleasure Robert Rowthorn (a visitor in the Economics Department at the time) and his 'excellent' teaching in advanced economic theory, Denzil Fiebig's 'well taught' Econometrics classes, the 'awful' lectures on Economic Development, and my lectures in the history of economic thought which stimulated him to write his masters thesis on aspects of Max Weber's thought. His PhD thesis on general equilibrium trade modelling with unemployment was a theoretical exercise designed to improve his knowledge and skills in mainstream theory and its application to real problems. Its successful completion in 1997 meant he was able to obtain one of the few academic posts in Economics advertised in Australia in that year.

Six graduates from the 1990s sent brief reminiscences of their Faculty of Economics studies. One student of 1992–94, Janine Mills, recalled the 'proliferation of paper planes, particularly during Economics I and II, sometimes the floors would be covered by them'. In third year, however, an unnamed lecturer collected a plane thrown at him during a lecture. He then threw it back, with the astonished class watching its rapid descent 'into the cleavage of one of the few students not paying attention to what was going on. She casually removed it and threw it towards the back of the lecture room.' Janine Mills also recalled Yanis Varoufakis as by far 'her favourite lecturer', and Bruce Ross for his ability to entertain a large, two-hour third-year option on Business Enterprise on Fridays from 3 to 5 pm (letter to the author, 1 August 2003). A friend of hers, Elen Seymor, an Economics students from 1991 to 1993 and now a legal officer, likewise recalled Yanis Varoufakis as her most inspiring teacher. She also remembered an attempt by an unnamed teacher to disprove mathematically 'Marx's labour theory of value'. This made her so depressed about the subject — 'universities after all were supposed to be radical places' — that she decided to become a lawyer instead of an economist. Or at least that is how she now explains her choice of occupation to her friends (letter to the author, 4 August 2003).

'A very mature age student in 1997', that is, one is his early seventies, Henry Linney largely recalled his course in the History of Economic Thought as an interesting reflection on the difference in longevity of thought depending on its application to different scientific fields. His example was Malthusian population theory, no longer very highly regarded in economics and the social sciences, but revered as very inspirational by biology students of Darwinian evolution theory (letter to the author, 12 October 2002).

A final honours-year student in Economics in 1997, Jeremy Bray, now an economic analyst in the Office of National Assessments, recorded several aspects of his economics teaching. One was the constant challenge to Tony Aspromourgos during his honours seminar on macro-economic theory not to light up his cigarette kept at the ready behind his ear, and make do with sipping black coffee instead. Another was the declaration by Joseph Halevi in lectures on economic growth in Economics III that only his students in France could understand the Kaldor-Pasinetti growth model, not they, 'because they were all totally *bourgeois*!' He also recalled Halevi's confessions of faith, 'Pasinetti is my religion' and 'I am a Keynesian-Leninist'. Jeremy remembered my seminar on Marshall's *Principles of Economics* in the Economics IV course, Economic Classics, as one instilling several minutes of profound silence after the presentation of the paper, though also that this disappeared when the class 'became more comfortable in your presence and gained confidence … making the discussion much more fruitful' (letter to the author, 29 October 2004).

Jeremy Martin, likewise a student in 1994–97, took Economics honours and tutored first-year classes for a couple of years. After working at the Commonwealth Bank, he completed an MBA at the Australian Graduate School of Management and is now working for Westfield. From his first year, he recollected Yanis Varoufakis, 'long haired with a leather jacket and tight denim jeans … an instant hit with the female students … and quickly nicknamed the Greek God'. More seriously, Martin was astounded at the fast pace of university teaching, in the first two weeks of lectures the entire HSC micro-economics syllabus was fully covered. Social aspects of university life were not forgotten. The Economics revue, *Skase Ventura*, was a major event for him in first year, in which he participated on the production side. Later, his economics honours class celebrated the end of semesters by eating at the Buon Gusto restaurant in Darlington, often with some of their teachers. Smokos in first year, with a barbecue and drinks on the Merewether lawn were also fondly remembered as creating a 'wonderful atmosphere with lots of free beer in plastic cups.' Louis Haddad's fourth-year course in Economic Planning ('which seems like a strange subject to study today in the world of capitalism') was memorable for its 'invaluable teaching style' which helped to develop students' confidence in their own ability. Overall, Jeremy Martin recalled the Economics honours course as 'a wonderful experience' with its 'small classes', preparation of case studies and papers 'and then discussing your ideas and thoughts with the rest of the class'.

Finally, Ian Gutierrez, a joint Economics/Econometrics masters student in 1997 from the Philippines, remembered both the delightful course and his 'enriching stay at International House'. Needless to say, he took the two required courses (Mathematical Methods for Economic Analysis and Econometric Applications) and in addition the following options: Econometric Theory, Economic Systems, Corporate Structure and Strategy, Public Economics and Economic Classics. This rich array of subjects was not something he would have easily found in the United States. He particularly enjoyed Louis Haddad's teaching in Economic Systems because of his interesting approach to the subject. In fact, Gutierrez used this approach in his preparation of the written research assignment which he completed on the Philippine economy during the Marcos era. From Economic Classics he recalled the hefty weekly reading (sometimes 200–300 pages each week) and the benefit of studying the whole of both Marshall's *Principles of Economics* and Keynes' *General Theory*. However, most unforgettable about this course was that its final examination in Merewether coincided with a bomb threat, thereby slowly diminishing the 90 minute gap between that and the afternoon's examination on Corporate Structure and Strategy held a good walking distance away at the Sports Centre close to Sancta Sophia College. Gutierrez has now happily settled in Sydney in the professional services industry, after work with Accenture and in telecommunications in the Philippines. The wide range of disciplines he studied for his masters helped him greatly to 'cope with the demands of corporate life where business problems and people are as varied as they can be'. It also taught him to 'analyse problems from different perspectives, that is, the quantitative, the historical, the socio-political, the systemic and even the philosophical'. For some students, faculty's postgraduate offerings clearly were very rewarding.

The demise of the Wolstenholme Library

On 12 March 1998, the Wolstenholme Library ceased to operate as a faculty library, a function it had by then fulfilled for over half a century with varying degrees of success. During the second half of the 1980s, its useful role in assisting study was still mentioned in faculty publications on courses. Thus the 1985 *Faculty Handbook* described it as 'supplementing the Fisher Library undergraduate collection for courses in the Faculty of Economics' and as holding the research collections of accounting and industrial relations. Hours of opening were still five days a week, starting at 9 am and finishing at 5 pm on Mondays and Fridays and at 7 pm midweek. The strong support from outside organisations was mentioned, as was the regular assistance from graduate donations of both books and money. However, 1985 Wolstenholme Library Committee meetings discussed requests from Fisher Library to cancel serial subscriptions, an ongoing saga during the 1980s given the financial restraint placed on university library funding. In spite of this, the Wolstenholme Library in 1985 committed to new serial subscriptions in every faculty discipline. More ominously, in March 1986, the faculty library committee was asked to consider plans for the Wolstenholme Library's future, given the space and study room requirements of the Graduate School of Management, and for housing research collections held within departments such as the Spann Collection in Government and that of the Accounting Research Centre.

In May 1987, plans for extending the Merewether Building noted the plight of the Wolstenholme Library. They also acknowledged its need for further resources given its recognised shortcomings in providing satisfactory reader services for undergraduate and postgraduate students. These problems remained on the agendas for faculty library committee meetings up to the first half of the 1990s. Their magnitude grew in line with the expansion of courses and the additional demands on library resources from the new Commerce degree. In June 1992, faculty appointed a new committee (chaired by Alan Craswell) to investigate the future of the Wolstenholme Library. Both the implications of making the library a major faculty priority and the manner in which the library could best serve the changing needs of the faculty were major items on the committee's agenda. Little seems to have come from its deliberations, however, and library committee reports rarely made it to the agenda of faculty meetings at this time. Nevertheless, new courses continued to proliferate and library resources continued to be heavily stretched. A subsequent report on the library situation (dated 10 May 1995) recognised what had become obvious and recommended as follows:

> The Wolstenholme Library was no longer capable of being the primary library for many of the faculty's undergraduate students and a more appropriate use

for the area would be as a study space with carrels, closed reserve books and multiple copies of journal material relevant to current undergraduate teaching. The consensus was that general library facilities were more appropriately and economically provided ... by Fisher Library ... The Faculty would need to make a proposal to Fisher Library concerning the housing of journals currently held in Wolstenholme Library. The Committee agreed to **recommend** to the Faculty that Wolstenholme Library become a study centre for students. [The committee needed to consult on this with the University Librarian, Dr Neil Radford, particularly on management responsibility for the change and the timetable for reorganisation].

[Secondly,] the Committee agreed that the new library should be primarily for postgraduate students, and for staff and postgraduate research needs. The Committee agreed to **recommend** ... that planning for the proposed new building allocate sufficient space to provide a satisfactory postgraduate and staff research facility capable of meeting the needs of projected student and staff numbers.

Only the first recommendation was acted upon. A report to the dean from the chair of the library committee, tabled in faculty on 21 May 1999, confirmed the closure of the Wolstenholme Library as a library and its refurbishment as a student study centre. This preserved the name commemorating 1930s graduate and staff member, S.H. Wolstenholme. Few faculty members appear to have regretted the Wolstenholme Library's final passing.

The Sydney University Economics Society, 1985–99

As the 1998 *Faculty Handbook* put it, Sydney University Economics Society (ECOSOC) continued to be 'responsible for making students' lives outside of lectures and tutorials more fun and exciting through a host of different events'. It continued its operations for virtually the whole period covered by this chapter (only the 1999 *Faculty Handbook* did not give it official recognition) using the facilities provided by faculty for this purpose. These included the students' common room with its coffee shop, as well the society's office in Room 250 of the Merewether Building. It will be recalled from Chapter 5 that student representation on faculty introduced during the 1970s partly relied on the use of office bearers of the Student Economics Society ex officio and this practice continued. Organisation of faculty's sport teams for rugby, soccer, tennis, golf, basketball and cricket remained as important parts of Economic Society activities. These teams participated in inter-faculty competitions and even in inter-university ones, such as the rugby match organised for many years with the Faculty of Commerce Society at the University of New South Wales.

On the social side, ECOSOC continued to organise many of its traditional activities. These included the annual ball, or formal, held at venues like the Sheraton Wentworth Hotel (as in 1985) or the Opera House (in 1988), the President's Dinner, harbour cruises, as well as the mid-term parties and smokos with their free beer recalled by Jeremy Martin. During the late 1980s and for most of the 1990s an annual revue was organised at the Union's Footbridge Theatre. The 1998 *Faculty Handbook* described this event as 'a musical, theatrical and humorous extravaganza' when commemorating the last time this once regular event took place. The society also published a regular newsletter, called *Dollars and Sense*, during part of the 1980s and *Merewether 90210* during part of the 1990s. No runs of copies of these newsletters appear to have been preserved. For much of the 1990s ECOSOC also regularly organised career evenings and afternoons at which representatives of major employers of faculty graduates were generally invited to speak. This likewise was an activity which the Student Economics Society had sponsored in the past.

Material on only a few aspects of ECOSOC's activities of the 1980s remains in the university Archives and absolutely nothing seems to have survived for the 1990s. Preserved information is confined to the names of its five presidents, in office from 1984–85 to 1988–89, that is, Steven Hocking (1984–85), Rod O'Connor (1985–86), L. Edwards (1986–87), Robert Sadleir (1987–88) and Sharron Peirce (1988–89).

The University of Sydney Economics Graduates Association

Attempts during the early 1980s by Steve Salsbury as dean to revive the graduates association (USEGA) in the hope of fostering a North American style alumni society were mentioned in Chapter 5. Presumably for that reason, *Faculty Handbooks* from 1984–85 (but not in 1999) mentioned the association as both a bridge between faculty and its graduates and as a meeting place where faculty graduates could keep in touch with each other. Both objectives were to be achieved by the organisation of regular meetings at which notable speakers addressed issues in economics and allied subjects. In addition, the association's newsletter, *The Sydney Economist*, was reactivated for some years (1987–90). To facilitate membership by recent graduates, the *Faculty Handbook* provided the treasurer's postal address, replacing it from 1989 with the postal address of the convenor of its Membership Committee. However, my attempt in 2004 to use this address to inquire about the association's recent activities proved unsuccessful; the letter was returned by the post office. As is noted in the Epilogue, an attempt to breathe new life into a Faculty Alumni Association with a well-attended function in 2007 proved more successful, at least in the short run.

Some information on the association's activities, especially for the 1980s, is preserved in the university Archives. The annual general meeting (28 October 1986) was appropriately addressed by a member of the registrar's staff (and former graduate) Phil Westlake, on the topic, 'the Future of USEGA'. On the record, that future must have seemed bleak. A subsequent meeting of faculty and association representatives (20 November 1986) produced the dismal conclusion that the association's failure was largely attributable to lack of contact between these two parties. At the start of the 1987 academic year, the association's existence was publicised by Jeremy Steele at a 'welcome to freshers' function organised by the student's economics society. A dinner was held by the association (26 May 1987) subsidised to the tune of $700 by John Ward as vice-chancellor. In June 1987 Phil Westlake wrote to John Ward drawing his attention to the association's new constitution, which Senate approved the following month (7 July 1987). This had been preceded by a meeting in April at the Commonwealth Bank of a new Graduates Association Committee comprising Tom Togher, Noel Baker, K. Lloyd, Frank Perry, Phil Westlake, Ms T. Hong, Ms Nyole Vaiciurgus and Mrs V. Roberts, following which Baker and Roberts attended the May faculty graduation ceremonies on behalf of the association.

Under Murray Wells as dean in 1987–88, a graduate newsletter was initiated, edited by Graeme Dean, Peter Hall (staff members) and by Mrs Fabian Babich. A new council was elected during 1987 comprising Fabian Babich (a 1977 graduate), Martin Hoare (1956), David Hobbs (1956), B.T. Johnson (1972), David Martin (1973), John Pearson (1966), Frank Perry (1972), Anne Rolfe (1959), Tom Togher (1961) and Nyole Vaiciurgus (1963). However, the Association's 1987 financial statement reported a deficit of $7933. The association also conducted a survey of graduates during 1987. Interestingly, this had a response rate of 36.1 per cent for graduates of more than 20 years standing, and of only 25.2 per cent for more recent graduates. It also provided data on graduate employment. This indicated that 8.2 per cent of faculty graduates had found employment in accounting, 8.2 per cent in banking, 4.8 per cent in other financial institutions, 10.9 per cent in law, 12.2 per cent in the public service and 10.2 per cent in education. These data, it should be noted, left almost half of graduates' occupations (45.5 per cent) unaccounted for.

Despite this hectic activity and official encouragement of the association during 1987, new attempts at reviving it had to be made in 1989, and again in 1990, 1993 and 1997. The first of these included an evening in October 1989 with John Howard, then shadow minister for Industrial Technology and Commerce, as the guest speaker. The association's 1990 Annual Report surprisingly revealed a rather negative attitude to the mutual interests of faculty and its graduates, not a recipe for a successful and thriving graduates association. The 1997 attempt at establishing a vibrant Faculty Alumni Association proved as unsuccessful as those of its predecessors in 1989, 1990 and 1993.

Faculty scholarship and research, 1985–99

In absolute numbers, research and publications produced by members of the faculty increased dramatically over the period covered by this chapter. This was partly the result of increased numbers of staff, partly the consequence of the introduction of additional departments in Finance and Marketing during the mid-1990s. Government remained the most productive research unit of the faculty for most of this period, particularly with respect to the number of books published. Official university publication of departmental research performance ceased with its 1991 Research Report. However, every department continued to file their annual research record by type of publication with the university's Research Office, which is the source of the information used in this section for the period commencing 1994. For this reason, faculty's research performance in this chapter is discussed in two discrete periods: the seven years from 1985 to 1991 and the six years from 1994 to 1999. It was impossible to gain access to comparable data for the two intervening years. Moreover, the official statements on the nature of their research prepared annually by departments for the official University Research Report are unavailable for the second period.

Over the seven years from 1985 to 1991, faculty members published 1029 items, of which 129 (12.5 per cent) were books, 287 (27.9 per cent) were chapters in books, and 613 (59.6 per cent) were refereed journal articles. The Government Department produced 38.5 per cent of this research, Economics 25.9 per cent, Accounting 12.1 per cent, Industrial Relations (including the Australian Centre for Industrial Relations Research and Training, or ACIRRT) 11.0 per cent, Economic History 6.8 per cent and Econometrics 6.3 per cent. These data of course indicate nothing about research productivity of individual staff members, an index in terms of which some members of the smaller departments easily outstripped many of those from the two largest faculty departments. Nor does it say anything about the quality of the research, or that of its place of publication, nor for that matter do these data distinguish between books, book chapters, articles and conference papers.

The Accounting Department included the following major research interests over these years: inflation accounting, explanations of accounting choices in terms of their economic consequences, the interface of finance theory with the accounting policy decision making process, and the principle and practice of auditing. In addition, the Commercial Law staff of the department listed taxation law as their major research field. In later years, these interests expanded to include management accounting, public and private accountability, and the underpricing phenomenon when issuing new securities on the stock exchange, an issue of particular relevance to privatisation of government assets at the state and federal levels. Chambers (as an honorary associate in the department) continued to be an active researcher for the whole of this period. Other key researchers in Accounting were Alan Craswell (with seventeen items), Graeme Dean (with eight) and Cynthia Coleman with seven, of which six were books. The Accounting Department's publication record on average was eighteen items per annum.

The Econometrics Department's research concentrated on labour supply issues, tariff reform, the multilateral transfer problem, option pricing, dynamic modelling and the testing of time series models. Most of the Econometrics research was published in the form of journal articles, its three most productive researchers — Bob Bartels, Denzil Fiebig and Alan Woodland — publishing 31 articles and five chapters in books between them. Total items published by the department averaged 9.4 per annum, and its total research of 66 items accounted for 6.7 per cent of total faculty output over these years. However, for 1985, this averaged out at 1.66 items per staff member, the second highest departmental publication rate in the faculty.

The economic historians in the faculty researched business, industrial and social history, with special reference to Australia, France, Germany, Mexico, China, Japan and South-East Asia. Over the period as a whole, members of the department published an 69 items (9.9 per annum). Robert Aldrich, with a total of 29 publications including five books, produced over 40 per cent of this total. Ben Tipton, with one book and nine chapters in books, was the next most prolific. Salsbury, who for most of these years was also dean of the faculty, still managed to publish his *History of the Sydney Stock Exchange* as well as four chapters in books. An aspect of social history on which some members of the department concentrated at this time was gay history, with special reference to 'gay Sydney' as an urban sub-culture, a topic on which Gary Wotherspoon published several books, while Robert Aldrich also published on this subject.

Economics, still by far the largest department in terms of staff members, published 266 items in aggregate over the seven years ending 1991, or an average of 38 per annum which amounted to approximately 1.4 per staff member, the case in 1985. Little of this research focused on key issues in which the department was claiming to specialise, although labour economics, the broader political economy area and the history of economic thought were research topics on which individual departmental members frequently published. In its 1987 research report, the department drew attention to the fact that four members of the department (Tony Aspromourgos, Peter Groenewegen, Joseph Halevi and Warren Hogan) had contributed 32 entries to *The New Palgrave. A Dictionary of Economics* out of a total 2000 prepared by 900 contributors world wide, 'a sign of the degree of international recognition the Sydney Economics Department enjoys'. Peter Groenewegen, who remained the most prolific researcher in the department, published 34 items (five books, eleven book chapters and eighteen refereed articles) in his research fields of Australian public finance (taxation policy and intergovernmental financial relations) and the history of economic thought. Frank Stilwell (28 items) concentrated on various political economy issues and on urban and regional research; Warren Hogan (22 items) focused on money, finance and banking as well as policy issues such a deregulation; while Judy Yates (with eleven items) continued her research work on housing economics. Together, these four members of the Economics staff produced more than a third (35.7 per cent) of the department's research.

The Government Department remained by far the faculty's most productive research department. It produced over a third of the faculty's research, or 395 items, and seven members of the department reported more than ten items over this period. Michael Jackson was the most prolific faculty researcher for these seven years, listing 51 items, of which two were books, seven book chapters, and the other 42 journal articles. Graeme Gill published 34 items; Martin Painter seventeen, Carole Pateman and Patricia Springborg sixteen each, and Terry Irving thirteen. Rodney Tiffen published ten items in his field of media policy. Areas on which members of the department continued to specialise in their research were summarised as Australian political institutions and sociology, Australian public administration and public policy, comparative politics (with special reference to the USSR and China), international relations, and political theory. Average publications per staff member per year exceeded three items, almost twice that of the next department (Econometrics) on this manner of ranking research performance.

Despite then being still the newest department in the faculty, just ten years old in 1985, Industrial Relations showed a very acceptable research record by that year. Over the seven years, its members published 97 items, or 13.8 per annum, the fourth highest average for the faculty. In terms of the average number of publications per staff member, it ranked third in the faculty, behind Government and Econometrics. Two members of the department published more than ten items over this period: Russell Lansbury published 24 (four books, ten book chapters and ten articles); Ron Callus published thirteen (two books, two chapters in books and nine articles). Special research interests as reported by the department included aspects of labour history such as the history of specific trade unions, issues in labour economics and wage determination, as well as more specialised topics: equal employment opportunity, industrial democracy, and employment resources in small business, to name but a few.

For most of the six years ending in 1999, there were eight departments in the faculty which filed details of their research. Finance, it will be recalled, had become a department in the faculty from 1994, Marketing from 1995. Faculty reported 887 items of research over these six years, or 147.8 per annum. These comprised 90 books (or 10.1 per cent of the total), 206 chapters in books (or 23.2 per cent of the total) and 601 articles (or 67.8 per cent). Departmental ranking on the basis of research productivity altered over this period. Economics was now first, with 30.1 per cent of the total; Government was second with 24.5 per cent; Industrial Relations, again including the research reported by ACIRRT, was now third with 13.5 per cent. Accounting slipped to fourth with 8 per cent, Finance was fifth with 6.9 per cent Econometrics sixth with 6.8 per cent, Marketing seventh with 3.9 per cent, and Economic History last with 3.7 per cent. The Centre for Micro-Economic Policy Analysis, set up in the 1980s under the direction of Professor Gordon Mills, reported four items of published research (0.5 per cent of the total) while the Institute of Transport Studies (directed by David Hensher) reported seventeen items (or 1.9 per cent of the total). Other centres established in the faculty by this time tended to report their publications with the department in which they were located.

For the final six years of the 1990s, the major publishers in the Accounting Department were Graeme Dean with eleven items and Stephen Taylor with ten. Members of the Accounting staff for less than the full six years such as Alan Craswell and Linda English, both with six items, can also be mentioned, as can Michael Aitkin (with five articles in Accounting to his credit and many more in Finance, the department he joined in 1996). Departmental research concentrated on topics in auditing, ethical standards in accounting practice, accounting education and associated matters, company collapses, as well as issues of company and taxation law.

Research output from the Econometrics Department continued to be largely confined to articles. Denzil Fiebig and Bob Bartels, two key departmental researchers for the earlier period, reported twelve and ten items respectively for the six years commencing 1994. They were joined as key researchers in Econometrics by newcomer to the department Moshe Haviv (appointed senior lecturer in 1992 and promoted to reader in 1994) who reported thirteen articles for the period in question. Ernie Houghton, who reported virtually no publications from the early 1970s, listed nine items of research from 1994. Professor Alan Woodland reported five. No special research interests of the department are easily identifiable from the material recorded by the Research Office apart from energy demand modelling and associated topics.

Economic History, whose staff numbers were declining over this period, reported 30 research items in total, of which six were books, fourteen were chapters in books and ten were journal articles. Robert Aldrich remained the department's most productive researcher with three books, four chapters in books and four articles; he was followed by Ben Tipton with one book, six book chapters and two articles. Gary Wotherspoon before his resignation from the department reported one book (on minorities and cultural diversity in Sydney) and two book chapters; Salsbury reported one further article before his death in 1998. Newcomers to the Department, Lily Rahim and Dianne Hutchison, reported a book (on aspects of development in Singapore) as well as two book chapters, and an article on Australian economic history. The department therefore retained some interest in Australian economic history, but more generally specialised on France and its colonies (Robert Aldrich) and Asian economic history (Tipton and Rahim) as well as work on 'social and cultural history' in the form of gay studies.

The 271 research items reported by the Department of Economics were substantially produced by the small minority of six who reported more than ten published items over this period. Together, these six persons accounted for 46 per cent of departmental publications with two of them, Peter Groenewegen with 45 items and Frank Stilwell with 26, being responsible for just over a quarter of that output. Judy Yates stayed in third place with fourteen items, jointly in that position with Joseph Halevi, likewise with fourteen. They were followed by Yanis Varoufakis with thirteen items and Dick Bryan with ten. Given that 33 departmental members over that period reported some research, the annual average per staff member can be estimated at 1.4 items, a statistic which ranks the Economics Department somewhat lower in faculty research performance. History of economic thought, political economy issues, housing economics, game theory and labour economics were key research topics. The Political Economy Group, still formally part of the Economics Department by the end of 1999, produced a quarter of departmental research in this period.

The 65 items of research reported by the Finance Department were largely in the form of articles (a total of 59 were listed), although its also produced two books and four chapters in books. Of the books, one was a collection of essays reviewing the performance of Australian financial markets; the other provided an introduction to Corporate Valuation by Alex Frino, who recorded eighteen articles but no book chapters. Peter Swan, before he left the department in 1999, reported eight articles; Michael Aitkin reported fifteen, and Gerard Garvey, fourteen. The remaining articles were published by a further six staff members who, with one exception, reported only one or two publications for the period. Much of the new department's research performance was therefore attributable to a few key researchers.

With 217 published items, the Department of Government remained a formidable producer of research. Its members published nearly half of the faculty's books (that is, 38), a good third of its chapters in books (69) but less than one-fifth of its articles (110). The most productive member of the department in terms of published research was Terry Irving with 21 items (comprising two books, nine book chapters and ten articles), followed by Martin Painter with nineteen items (five books, eight book chapters and six articles), Linda Weiss with thirteen (two books, three chapters and seven articles) and Michael Jackson with twelve items (three book chapters and nine articles). Three other department members reported ten publication, that is, Patricia Springborg, Tim Rowse and Fred Teiwes. Some of the other earlier high performers such as Graeme Gill, Michael Hogan and Rod Tiffen dropped back to nine published items for the first, and to six items for the two others. Those publishing ten items or above, collectively produced just under two-fifths (39.2 per cent) of the department's output, but average performance for staff members per annum fell to less than one (or 0.9 to be more precise), well below the 1.4 recorded for the Economics Department. Research interests remained similar: Australian politics, sociology, public administration and public policy, comparative political systems, political theory and the media.

Industrial Relations published 117 items over the period, or 13.2 per cent of faculty's published research. Most of these publications appeared as book chapters (42 items) or journal articles (69), and only six were published as books. Russell Lansbury published just under one third of this research with 37 items (four books, eighteen book chapters and fifteen articles). Only one other member of the department, Jim Kitay, published more than ten items (eight chapters and seven articles) with the next four, in terms of research output, Grant Michelson (nine articles and a joint book chapter), John Campling (one book, a joint book chapter and five articles), Greg Patmore (one book chapter and five articles) and Suzanne Jamieson (four book chapters and two articles). Members of the department also contributed to the preparation of several reference books in their discipline. Key research areas for the department were comparative industrial relations or its global context, workplace relations, personnel management and, more generally, aspects of trade unions policy and labour economics.

The last department added to the Faculty of Economics, that of Marketing, reported its first research output in 1996. Over its five years existence until the end of 1999, it generated 35 published items of research consisting of one book, five book chapters and 29 articles. The book was an edited work with only one of the editors a member of the department at the time of its publication in 1997. Of the five chapters in books reported, three were by Jordan Louviere, one by Benedict Dellaert and one by John Clark. More than half the 29 articles came from Jordan Louviere and Benedict Dellaert (eight each), with another six reported by Harmen Oppewal. The other seven articles were published by the other five members of the department reporting research. The resulting departmental publication average per annum was seven, or less than one publication per staff member per year. For the years 1996 and 1997 Marketing in addition reported seven and ten conference contributions, a research category instituted for only four of the six years in question, and hence not mentioned so far in this chapter.

As indicated previously, some research was published by centres, of which ACIRRT, the Micro-Economic Policy Unit and the Transport Economics Research Unit were three instances previously mentioned. In 1989, a Centre for the Study of the History of Economic Thought was set up within the Economics Department, which published a series of reprints of economic classics as well as half a dozen volumes of the proceedings of workshops edited by its director, Peter Groenewegen, and included with his research output. Other centres were created within other departments or, occasionally, on an interdepartmental basis. These included the Accounting Research Centre and the Economic and Regional Restructuring Unit (with Geography), a Research Institute for Asia and the Pacific, the Centre for European Studies, the Centre for Peace and Conflict Studies (within the Government Department) and the Public Affairs Research Centre.

Several departments of the faculty continued to be responsible for editing journals. The Accounting Department remained in charge of editing *Abacus* and of the *Australian Accounting Review* but added a third publication, the *Accounting, Auditing and Accountability Journal*, which it manages jointly with University of Adelaide accounting academics. From the late 1980s, members from the Government Department and from Industrial Relations edited *Labour History*, the Political Economy Group within the Economics Department edited the *Journal of Australian Political Economy*, members of the Industrial Relations Department edited the *Economics and Labour Relations Review* (the successor to the long established, *Journal of Industrial Relations*).

Moreover, two departments published series of working papers or continued previously established series for at least part of this period. The Economics Department published its series of working papers, by the late 1980s amounting to about twenty per annum. The research they contained was subsequently published in refereed journals for close to half the papers issued in the series. The series stopped in 1999 due to lack of resources, particularly the hefty labour input from research assistants required in their preparation. From 1987, the Department of Industrial Relations also initiated a working papers series. This contained three papers in its first year, four in 1988, two in 1989 and seven in 1991.

University Research Reports up to 1991 also show reasonable success rates by departments in attracting research funds both from the Australian Research Council and from other sources. Only a sample of some of the financial research assistance faculty members obtained in this period needs to be given to give an indication of its diversity. For example, in 1986, Russell Ross (Economics) obtained $26,750 from the Department of Aboriginal Affairs to research labour market policy for Aboriginals; Peter King (Government) obtained $12,350 from the Department of Foreign Affairs for his International Year of Peace project; Bob Bartels (Econometrics) added a grant of $5000 from the Department of Resources and Energy to the 1985 grant of $15,000 he had received to research Australian energy demand; while Ross Curnow obtained $300,000 from the Premier's Department for a Bicentennial History of the New South Wales government. In 1989, Lex Watson (Government) obtained over $170,000 from five different sources to research aspects of AIDS prevention.

Some further examples of faculty successes with respect to Australian Research Council funding can be given. In 1989, Alan Woodland (Econometrics) received a $33,000 grant to investigate residential demand for electricity and gas; Elizabeth Savage obtained $120,000 for research on reform to the Australian taxation and social security systems; Graeme Gill (Government) obtained $20,000 to study the Communist Party in the Soviet Union as an instrument for change in the USSR, and Russell Lansbury (with Joe Isaac from Monash) obtained $28,000 for research on workplace industrial relations. Two years later, in 1991, Accounting reported two ARC grants (combined value of $118,000) for Michael Aitkin,

Terry Walter, Greg Whittred and Steve Taylor; ACIRRT reported ARC support of more than $200,000 to establish it as a key centre of industrial relations research; Economic History reported three ARC Grants (to Robert Aldrich, John Drabble and Diane Hutchison) of $29,000 each; Economics and Government reported that Peter Groenewegen (Economics) and Fred Teiwes (Government) were among the first ten recipients of ARC senior research fellowships for five years, together with five ARC grants (to Peter Groenewegen, Graeme Gill, Terry Irving, Martin Painter and Fred Teiwes) while Russell Lansbury (Industrial Relations) received a $52,000 ARC grant for research on case studies in workplace industrial relations in Australia. In 1996, a record ARC grant of $700,000 was awarded to Denzil Fiebig, Peter Swan, Jordan Louviere and Michael Aitken for developing a national micro-economic modelling laboratory (MEMlab), the largest grant ever received by members of the faculty, and expected by the researchers to be more than matched by private enterprise. In 1997, large ARC grants went to Bob Bartels, Benedict Dellaert and Denzil Fiebig ($250,000), to Graeme Gill ($170,000) and to Terry Walter and Da Silva Rosa ($150,000).

Given this research record, it is surprising that at the Senate meeting in December 1995 the faculty was criticised by the Dean of Science, Professor Robert Hewitt, as being the worst performing faculty in the university in terms of research. No real evidence apparently supported this charge, which in any case was easily challenged by recent work published on the research record of Australian economics and econometrics departments over the six years 1988–93 (Towe and Wright 1995) and on that of Australian accounting and finance departments for 1990 to 1994 (Towe 1996). These studies demonstrated the very high ranking (first) of the Accounting, Econometrics and Finance departments in Australian university research, as well as the far lower ranking (fourth) of the Economics Department (which did however improve its relative research standing in the faculty during the second half of the 1990s).

Research quality in the faculty over this period can also be demonstrated by the election of six of its members to the Academy of Social Sciences in Australia to join the two members of faculty elected in 1982 (Peter Groenewegen) and 1984 (Murray Wells), not to mention previous faculty members such as Ray Chambers, Henry Mayer, Colin Simkin and Dick Spann. Alan Woodland (Econometrics) was elected in 1985, Graeme Gill (Government) in 1994, David Hensher (Transport Management) in 1995, Peter Swan (Finance) in 1997, Russell Lansbury (Industrial Relations) and Patricia Springborg (Government) in 1999. Although this made Sydney University's membership of the academy still relatively small as compared to the Australian National University and the University of Melbourne, it was a considerable improvement over the situation of the 1970s when Sydney's Faculty of Economics had only few persons elected to this body (as shown in Chapter 5).

Moreover, individual researchers in the faculty received many other honours. In March 1989, Alan Woodland was made a fellow of the Econometric Society. In 1992, Peter Groenewegen was appointed as corresponding member of the Royal Dutch Academy of Sciences. In 1994, Murray Wells was named Accountant of the Year. Two faculty members received Choice's Academic Book of the Year Award: John Ravenhill in 1989 for *Politics and Society in Contemporary Africa* and Peter Groenewegen in 1995 for his biography of Alfred

Marshall. In 1996, Tony Aspromourgos was honoured by the Academy of Social Sciences with its first Young Scholar of the Year award. In November 1996 the *University News* reported that Murray Smith and Colin Rose 'had found original and creative mathematics solutions to age-old statistical problems in economics' published in a chapter they had contributed to Hal Varian's *Computational Economics and Finance*.

Towards a Faculty of Economics and Business

The gradual move towards a Faculty of Economics and Business was outlined earlier in this chapter as part of the section devoted to faculty deliberations. During 1999 a series of special faculty meetings brought the process to a conclusion, partly by adopting the proposals of the Faculty Restructure Working Party chaired by the new dean, Peter Wolnizer. This working party, it may be recalled, had proposed a name change for the Faculty to Faculty of Economics, Politics and Business. It also proposed departments were to be organised within a two-schools system, comprising a School of Economics and Politics Science, and a School of Business. Departments would be transformed into discipline groups. The new School of Economics and Political Science would house the discipline groups of Economics, Political Economy, Economic History, Government and Econometrics and Business Statistics. The School of Business would house the discipline groups of Accounting and Business Law, Finance, Marketing, Transport and Logistics, and Work and Organisational Studies (formerly Industrial Relations). The School of Business would also house ACIRRT and the Institute of Transport Studies. It was also proposed that the existing eight departments would become five, that is, Accounting, Economics, Finance, Management Studies and Political Science, but this failed to eventuate.

The September 1999 meeting of Senate endorsed the two-school model proposed by faculty and the simplified name ultimately adopted, Faculty of Economics and Business. A faculty meeting on 7 December 1999 then debated two options for a new faculty constitution, with the final vote not taken until 2000, when the Faculty of Economics and Business held its first meeting on 14 April. By then, the new faculty was up and running and had enrolled its first students. Continuity was preserved by the fact that the last Dean of the Faculty of Economics, Peter Wolnizer, also became the first Dean of the Faculty of Economics and Business. Moreover, most of the changes were nominal and organisational, though the new School of Business building in Codrington Street meant that the institutional and academic division into schools was given a concrete reality. Their geographical proximity preserved the ease of communication essential to maintain the two schools as important and complementary parts of a single faculty.

EPILOGUE

The Faculty of Economics and Business in its first decade

In January 2000, the Faculty of Economics and Business commenced operations under its new name and with a new organisational structure. During its first two years it remained housed within the Merewether Building and the adjoining Institute Building. During 2002 the School of Business together with the office of the dean moved into a new building in Codrington Street, separated from its former home by the Darlington Road terraces. Over these initial, formative years, faculty continued to be guided by Peter Wolnizer as its dean but by 2009, when this volume was being completed, leadership of its initial component schools had already changed several times, and governance structures had significantly changed.

Over the early years of the new faculty, governance structure rested on a broad division of subject between two schools: the School of Business and the School of Economics and Politics. Foundation head of the School of Business was Bob Bartels (Econometrics) and for the School of Economics and Politics, Graeme Gill (Government and International Relations). They were replaced in 2003 by Sid Gray, Professor of International Business, and Stephen Nicholas, a former Professor of Economic History at the University of New South Wales, with Graeme Dean serving as acting head of the School of Business from December 2002 to July 2003. As an organisational structure, schools were abandoned by the faculty in 2007, and with them, heads of schools, leaving governance responsibilities in the faculty to heads of disciplines and the dean's office, broadly construed to include the four sub-deans in the faculty.

On approaching its first decade, the new Faculty of Economics and Business has also seen important changes in its composition, in addition to reaping considerable awards for its programs. The most startling change is undoubtedly the major alteration in its academic structure following the creation of a new School of Social and Political Sciences in the Faculty of Arts. This school incorporates the former Faculty of Economics departments of Government and International Relations, and of Political Economy. From 2008 they join the departments of Anthropology, Sociology and Social Policy, and the Centre for Peace and Conflict Studies for this purpose, a change adopted by the university's Senate at its September 2007 meeting. This change, among other things, therefore entails the removal from faculty of its second oldest department, that is, Government, established in the 1920s with an emphasis on teaching public administration. In some respects, Government's departure from the Faculty of Economics is less drastic than appears at first sight. For a long time, members of the Government Department had enjoyed dual membership of both the Faculties of Economics and of Arts, and many of its members felt closer affiliation with the Arts Faculty than with Economics, especially on its transformation to a Faculty of Economics and Business. The departure of Political Economy to the School of Social Sciences in the Faculty of Arts will neither be mourned by the majority membership of the Faculty of Economics and Business nor by its own members. This is evident from a remark made by Frank Stilwell when these changes were approved by Senate: 'I find [them] challenging and welcome' (*University News*, 21 September 2007). It may also be noted briefly that this change has returned the essential scope of faculty's teaching responsibilities to its original foundations in economics and commerce, established in the first decade of the previous century.

Additional matters relating to the new Faculty of Economics and Business in its first decade need to be recorded. Their more detailed analysis, however, awaits its future historian. The following pages can therefore only be described as an attempt to highlight some major developments and achievements of the first decade of the faculty in the new millennium.

In 2004, the Faculty of Economics and Business scored a first for any Australian faculty of economics, commerce or business by gaining accreditation for both its business and accounting programs from the premier international accrediting body, the Association of Advanced Collegiate Schools of Business. The faculty thereby joined 950 educational institutions in the world, of which 466 hold business accreditation and only 163 have gained accreditation for their accounting programs. This prestigious accolade embraces undergraduate, masters and doctoral courses of study and their associated degrees, and is a remarkable tribute to the faculty's excellence in teaching, research and community related programs.

The new Faculty of Economics and Business from its beginnings was assisted by a Faculty Board of Advice, comprising leading figures in Australian business, government, economics and education. For 2009, chairman of the Advisory Board is Mr John Egan (the chairman of Egan Associates). Its members (in alphabetical order) are Mr David Anstice, President, Human Health; Mr George Frazis, Group Executive GM, Development and New Busines; Mr Bill Forrest, company director; Mr Charles Littrell, executive general manager, Policy Research and Consulting, Australian Prudential Regulation Authority; Adjunct Professor Wayne Lonergan, managing director Lonergan Edwards & Associates; Gillian Moore, principal, Pymble Ladies College; Mr Bernard Newsom, past principal, North Sydney Boys High School; Mr Des Pearson, Auditor General, Victoria; Adjunct Professor Stephen Roberts, chief executive office, Citigroup Global Markets & Banking, Australia and New Zealand; Adjunct Professor Robert Savage, company director David Jones; Dr Alastair Stone, managing director, Pacific Infrastructure Corporation; Bryce Wauchope, company director; and Terry Williamson, company director. This innovation in faculty administration contributes to ensuring that the dean and his staff receive the best possible advice when formulating appropriate strategies, policies and practices for the faculty. This in turn enabled it to draw the best students for its programs from both Australia and Asia. Such administrative changes also help to enhance relationships with key institutions in education and business, including especially the various universities with which the faculty has a major association.

Irrespective of this advisory assistance for faculty and dean, governance of the faculty continues to incorporate regularly scheduled meetings of faculty and meetings of its many committees in the manner in which that system of governance gradually evolved from its beginnings in 1920. Faculty governance, including that of its two schools until 2007, has reverted to faculty administration and departmental governance and administration within identified 'discipline groups'.

The listing of these discipline groups in the 2009 *Faculty Handbook* for its two broad segments indicates some significant changes from those prevailing in 1999. This is only one sign that the new Faculty of Economics and Business constitutes more than just a name change. For example, the new faculty has considerably extended the array of opportunities on offer for education in economics and business.

The Business segment of the faculty now contains eight disciplines, as well as the Centre for International Securities Studies, the Institute of Transport and Logistics Studies and the Work Place Research Centre. These discipline groups, or departments, are Accounting, Business Information Systems, Business Law (formerly the Commercial Law section of the Accounting Department), Finance, Graduate School of Government, International Business, Marketing, and Work and Organisational Studies (the former Department of Industrial Relations).

At the start of 2009, the non-Business segment of Faculty comprised the two disciplines of Economics and Operations Management and Econometrics. The Government and Political Economy departments had transferred to the Arts Faculty by the start of 2008 and it may be noted again that Economic History, for so long a major area of study in the faculty, disappeared as a separate discipline group in 2006. One of its former teaching staff members, Diane Hutchison, joined the Economics discipline and Ben Tipton that of International Business, while others preferred joining the History Department within the Faculty of Arts. Lack of students made continuation of Economic History as a separate discipline group no longer feasible.

Despite the elimination of Economic History as a separate discipline in the faculty, and the transfer of both Government and Political Economy to the Faculty of Arts, the number of broad specialisations in the Faculty of Economics and Business expanded from eight at the end of the 1990s to ten in 2009. The great majority of these are now housed in Business, a sign of how the educational winds are blowing in the new millennium. The first decade of the 'new' faculty's existence have also seen tremendous growth in staff numbers, courses on offer and opportunities for students to expand their educational horizons by participating in exchange programs with other universities, enabling them thereby to take part of their studies elsewhere.

Staff growth in these early years of the faculty can be briefly indicated for comparison with that described in Chapter 6. Take first faculty's administrative staff. The dean's staff still includes an executive [graduate] assistant (Hazel Latoza), and four associate deans drawn from the academic staff (that is, for 2009, Carole Comerton-Forde, Mark Freeman, Sid. Gray, and David Hensher). In addition, the faculty employed an executive officer, a business manager, a finance officer, several administrative assistants, as well as more than a dozen staff members devoted to marketing, special projects, research coordination, and various other administrative duties. Faculty, moreover, appoints a teaching quality fellow and a director of doctoral studies from the academic staff. In addition, faculty administration in 2009 included a student information office staff of sixteen persons, an Information Technology Department comprising twenty persons, an Office of Teaching and Learning in Economics, and a Business Planning and Development staff consisting of twenty persons including some of the faculty officers previously mentioned. There were also eight attendants, including Frank Kambosus (attendant in charge) serving both the new Business Building and the Merewether Building.

Academic staff in the two faculty groups of subjects has also expanded. At the start of 2009, Business had twenty-five professors (including two women), that is, six in Accounting (including the dean), two in Business Information Systems, two in Business Law, two in Finance, three in International Business, two in Marketing, two in Work and Organisational Studies, five in the Institute of Transport Studies, and one in the Graduate School of Government. In the Economics group of two disciplines, there were four professors (all male), that is, one in Operations Management and Econometrics, and three in Economics. It has to be noted with regret that women continue to be very poorly represented at the most senior academic level in the Faculty of Economics and Business.

There were sixteen associate professors (including four women) in the group of Business disciplines. Four were in Accounting, one in Business Information Systems, two in Finance, two in Marketing, and seven in Work and Organisational Studies. The Economics group of disciplines had six associate professors, all in Economics. The number of women associate professors in the faculty total of twenty-two in this position implied a slightly better relative position than at the professorial level, particularly within the School of Business. However, for the Faculty of Economics and Business in 2009 it remained very true to say that women were under-represented at the senior academic staff level, just as had been the case for the Faculty of Economics in 1999.

At the more junior staff level, the Business disciplines in 2009 employed 39 senior lecturers: eleven in Accounting, four in Business Information Systems, four in Business Law, five in Finance, six in Marketing, seven in Work and Organisational Studies and two in the Institute of Transport and Logistics Studies. Fifty lecturers taught in the group of Business subjects (twelve in Accounting, four in Business Information Systems, six in Business Law, nine in Finance, seven in International Business, six in Marketing, four in Work and Organisational Studies and two in the Institute of Transport and Logistics Studies). In its two disciplines, the group of Economics subjects employed twenty-one lecturers (six in Operations Management and Econometrics and fifteen in Economics). It also employed nine senior lecturers (six in Economics and three in Operations Management and Econometrics). Overall, faculty employed 170 persons as full-time, tenured academic staff in the form of 29 professors, 22 associate professors, 48 senior lecturers and 71 lecturers. Of this staff, the School of Business accounted for 130, or 76.5 per cent. With its 30 staff members, Economics was no longer the largest discipline group in the faculty, it was surpassed by Accounting (with a permanent full-time academic staff of 33). Work and Organisational Studies had twenty, Finance had eighteen. Of the remaining discipline groups, Marketing employed sixteen academic staff, Business Law twelve, Operations Management and Econometrics ten, Business Information Systems eleven and International Business twelve.

Not surprisingly, this substantial growth in staff produced a considerably increased volume of research, supporting the quality improvement of which the Faculty of Economics and Business justifiably boasted in its annually published research reports and its occasional publications on special expertise within its discipline groups. The most recent Faculty Research Review at the time of writing (January 2009) covered research for 2007. It reported twenty-eight ARC Discovery Project grants, thirteen ARC Linkage Project grants, as well as many research grants from bodies other than the ARC. In addition, the group of Business subjects reported nine research centres, groups and foundations, and six academic journals edited from within the school as well as two on-line publications. The group of Economics subjects reported one research centre and editorial responsibility from within the school for one journal.

As compared with the one successfully completed PhD candidate for the faculty by 1964, the Faculty of Economics and Business reported in 2007 that it enrolled more than 160 doctoral students. Of these, the group of Business subjects had 131 PhD candidates on its books (27 in Accounting, seven in Business Information Systems, two in Business Law, 24 in Finance, three in the Graduate School of Government, eight in International Business, seventeen in Marketing, 28 in Work and Organisational Studies, twelve in the Institute of Transport and Logistics Studies and three in the Centre for International Security Studies). In addition, the Economics subjects enrolled 31 doctoral students (ten in Operations Management and Econometrics and 21 in Economics). The wide variety of masters degree coursework programs on the faculty's books, together with the number of students they attracted, made its postgraduate endeavours very substantial indeed even when compared with the late 1990s.

The publication record of the faculty for 2007 as reported in Faculty's Research Review was also extensive. On aggregate, faculty members recorded the publication of five books and edited books, 27 chapters in books, and 212 journal articles. Extensive conference participation and published conference proceedings were reported as well. With respect to the three key publication categories, members of the Business group of disciplines were responsible for all five books, 14 chapters in books and 162 journal articles; those from the Economics group reported three chapters in books and 50 journal articles. The three major publishing discipline groups were Accounting (one book, one chapter and 39 journal articles); the Institute of Transport and Logistics (eight chapters in books and 31 journal articles) and Work and Organisational Studies (two books, four chapters in books and 18 journal articles). Other Business subjects showed the following publications by type: Business Information Systems (four articles), Business Law (three chapters and sixteen articles), Finance (one chapter and 22 articles), International Business (one book, one chapter and four articles), Marketing (three chapters in books, seventeen articles), Work and Organisational Studies (two books, four chapters and seventeen articles), Work Place

Research (one chapter and eight articles). Finally, the Economics group of disciplines reported three book chapters and 35 articles (Economics) and fifteen articles (Operations Management and Econometrics). Compared to 1999, this was a considerable increase, matching the growth in staff.

In this context, reference can also be made briefly to the manner in which, at one stage, the new faculty advertised its available expertise to the community at large. A brochure, *Faculty of Economics and Business Experts* (published September 2001), first listed the experts on its staff in alphabetical order and then the areas of expertise of which these collectively could boast. This listing of experts and their fields of expertise was accompanied with a photograph, and ways they could be contacted individually (that is, email address, telephone number and fax number). Not surprisingly, such a guide was quickly out-of-date through staff resignations and retirements as well as by the appointment of new staff, the reason presumably why this exercise was not repeated. Alphabetically, faculty's range of expertise in 2001 commenced with 'Aboriginal people, labour market status of', and ended with an example of Chinese politics expertise with the entry, 'Zhou Enlai'. In between, among many other things, the faculty named five experts on 'corporate governance', half a dozen on environmental issues, two on housing economics as well as five on 'takeovers, mergers and acquisitions'.

The contents of this brief epilogue suggest that at its centenary (or perhaps its golden jubilee), a future historian of the Faculty of Economics and Business at the University of Sydney will have a great deal to talk about. More importantly, this Epilogue implies that the Faculty of Economics did not really disappear in 1999. It simply continued with a new name, some significant, new, business-oriented disciplines, and a new form of organisational structure. All of these are liable to change over time. The enormous growth potential through innovative teaching and research demonstrated by the new structure befits the new millennium, during which it appropriately opened for business.

BIBLIOGRAPHY

Arndt, H.W. (1985), *A Course through Life. Memoirs of an Australian Economist*, Canberra: Australian National University.

Benham, F.C. (1928), *The Prosperity of Australia*, London: P.S. King and Sons.

Black, H.D. (1970), 'Undergraduating in the 1920s', *Economic Review '70, Jubilee Supplement*, pp. 14–15.

Black, H.D. (1988), 'Fragments of an education in the dismal science', *The Sydney Economist*, Part 1, 2(1), pp. 3–4; Part 2, 2(2), pp. 2–4.

Braddon, H.Y. (1909), *Business Principles and Practice*, Sydney: William Brooks.

Braddon, H.Y. (1912), *Australian Company Law and Sidelights on Modern Commerce*, Joseph Fisher Lecture on Commerce, 25 April 1912, Adelaide: University of Adelaide.

Braddon, H.Y. (1914), *The Modern World of Credit*, Sydney: Angus and Robertson.

Braddon, H.Y. (1925), *The Guilds*, Joseph Fisher Lecture on Commerce, 6 May 1925, Adelaide: University of Adelaide.

Braddon, H.Y. (1930), *Essays and Addresses*, Sydney: Angus and Robertson.

Brown, Nicholas (2001), *Richard Downing. Economics, Advocacy and Social Reform in Australia*, Melbourne: Melbourne University Press.

Buckley, K.D. (1957), 'The Australian University Scene', *The University Review* 29(2), February, pp. 48–55.

Buckley, K.D. and Wheelwright, E.L. (1998), *False Paradise: Australian Capitalism Revisited 1915–55*, Melbourne, Oxford University Press (Australia).

Butlin, Judith, '*Vale* Joyce Fisher (1914–1997)', unpublished obituary, March.

Butlin, N.G. (1978), 'A Fraternal Farewell: Tribute to S.J. Butlin', *Australian Economic History Review*, 18(2), September, pp. 99–118.

Butlin, S.J. (1953), 'Richard Charles Mills', *Economic Record* 29957) November, pp. 177–88.

Butlin, S.J. (1955), *War Economy 1939–1942, Australia in the War 1939–1945*, Series 4, vol. 3, Canberra: Australian War Memorial.

Butlin, S.J. (1962), Frederic Benham 1900–1962', *Economic Record* 38(83), September pp. 386–8.

Butlin, S.J. (1970), 'The Faculty's Fifty Years', *Economic Review '70. Jubilee Supplement*, pp. 8–13.

Butlin, S.J. (1983), 'Australian Central Banking 1945–1959', *Australian Economic History Review* 23(2), September, pp. 95–192.

Butlin S.J. and Schedvin, C.B. (1977), *War Economy 1942–45. Australia in the War of 1939–*

1945, series 4 (civil), volume 4, Canberra: Australian War Memorial.

Clark, Colin and Crawford, J.G. (1938), *The National Income of Australia*, Sydney: Angus and Robertson.

Connell, W.F., G.F. Sherrington, B.H. Fletcher, C. Turner and U. Bygott (1995), *Australia's First. A History of the University of Sydney 1940-1990*, Sydney: Hale and Iremonger, volume 2.

Cornish, Selwyn (1993), 'Sir Leslie Melville: An Interview', *Economic Record*, 69(207) December, pp. 437–57.

Crawford, R.M. (1975), 'A Bit of a Rebel'. The Life and Work of George Arnold Wood, Sydney: Sydney University Press.

Curnow, Ross (1993), 'Bland, Francis Armand (1882-1967)', *Australian Dictionary of Biography*, Melbourne: Melbourne University Press, Vol. 13, pp. 202–04.

Eddy, W.H.C. (1961), *Orr*, Brisbane: Jacaranda Press.

Goodwin, C.W.D. (1966), *Economic Inquiry in Australia*, Durham N.C.: Duke University Press.

Groenewegen, P.D. (1986), 'Richard Charles Mills (1886-1952), *Australian Dictionary of Biography*, Vol. 10, Melbourne: Melbourne University Press, pp. 517–19.

Groenewegen, P.D. (1990), 'Neoclassical Value and Distribution Theory: the English speaking Pioneers', in *Neoclassical Economic Theory 1870 to 1930*, edited by K. Hennings and Warren J. Samuels, Boston: Kluwer Academic Publishers, chapter 2, pp. 13–51.

Groenewegen, P.D. (2002), 'R.C. Mills and Australian Fiscal Federalism, with special reference to the work of the Grants Commission', *History of Economics Review* No. 36, Summer, pp. 66–76.

Groenewegen, P.D. (2003), 'Teaching the History of Economic Thought at the University of Sydney: Some Reflections', *History of Economics Review* No. 36, Summer, pp. 109–25

Groenewegen, P.D., ed. (2004), Australian Economic Policy, Economic Theory and Economic History. Nineteen R.C. Mills Memorial Lectures 1958–2003, Sydney: Faculty of Economics.

Groenewegen, Peter and Bruce McFarlane (1990), *A History of Australian Economic Thought*, London: Routledge.

Irvine, R.F. (1914), The Place of the Social Sciences in a Modern University, Sydney: Angus and Robertson.

Irvine, R.F. (1916), *The Veil of Money*, Sydney: The Review Company.

Irvine, R.F. (1933), *The Midas Delusion*, Adelaide: privately printed for the author by the Hassell Press.

Jevons, H.S., *Essays in Economics*, Sydney: Angus and Robertson.

Jones, Evan and Stilwell, Frank (1986), 'Political Economy at the University of Sydney', in Brian Martin *et al.*, *Intellectual Suppression. Australian Case Histories, Analyses and Responses*, Sydney: Angus and Robertson.

Keynes, J.M. (1936), The General Theory of Employment, Interest and Money, London: Macmillan.

Laffer, Kingsley (1981), 'The Development of the Industrial Relations School in the University of Sydney 1953–1971', Sydney: University of Sydney, Department of Industrial Relations, *Occasional Paper No. 1*, March.

La Nauze, J.A. (1949), *Political Economy in Australia. Historical Studies*, Melbourne: Melbourne University Press.

Lodewijks, John (2007), 'A Conversation with Warren Hogan', *Economic Record* 83(263), December, pp. 445–59.

McCredie, H. (1979), 'Braddon, Sir Henry Yule (1863–1955), *Australian Dictionary of Biography*, Vol. 7, Melbourne: Melbourne University Press, pp. 380–81.

McCullough, Colleen (1998), *Roden Cutler V.C. The Biography*, Milsons Point: Random House Australia Limited.

McFarlane, B.J. (1966), *Professor Irvine's Economics in Australian Labour History 1931–1933*, Canberra: Australian Society for the Study of Labour History.

McFarlane, B.J. (1983), 'R.F. Irvine (1861–1941), *Australian Dictionary of Biography*, Vol. 9, Melbourne: Melbourne University Press, pp. 438–39.

McLeod, A.L. (1955), *Evening Studies at the University of Sydney: 1884–1954*, Sydney: Sydney University Evening Students Association.

Mill, J.S. (1873), *Autobiography*, London: Longmans, Green, Reader and Dyer.

Mills, R.C. (1915), *The Colonisation of Australia*, London: Sidgwick and Jackson.

Mills, R.C. (1940), *The University and Business. A Lecture*, Sydney: Australasian Medical Publishing Company Limited.

Mills, R.C. and Benham, F.C. (1925), The Principles of Money, Banking and Foreign Exchange, and their Application to Australia, Sydney: Angus and Robertson.

Mills, R.C. and Butlin, S.J. (1948), 'Bland and the University', *Australian Journal of Public Administration* 7(3) New Series, September, pp. 129–43.

Mills Report (1973), Committee Appointed to Consider and Report on all Matters relating to the Studies, Lectures and Examinations in the Course Economics I, II, III and IV, (Chair: C.P. Mills), Sydney: Faculty of Economics.

Passmore, John (1997), *Memoirs of a semi-detached Australian*, Melbourne: Melbourne University Press.

Schedvin, C.B. (1970), *Australia and the Great Depression*, Sydney: Sydney University Press.

Schedvin, C.B. (1993), 'Butlin, Sydney James Christopher Lyon (1910–1977), *Australian Dictionary of Biography*, vol. 13, Melbourne: Melbourne University Press, pp. 320–22.

Stilwell, F.J.B. (2001), 'Obituary of G.A.J. Simpson-Lee', *Sydney Morning Herald*, 15 May 2001.

Towe, Jack (1996), 'The Ranking of University Accounting and Finance Departments in Australia 1990–1994).

Towe, Jack and Wright, Don (1995), 'Research published by Australian Economics and Econometrics Departments 1988-93', *Economic Record* 71(212) March, pp. 8-17.

Turner, Clifford, Ursula Bygott and Peter Chippendale (1991), *Australia's First. A History of the University of Sydney, Vol. I, 1850-1939*, Sydney: The University of Sydney in conjunction with Duncan & Iremonger.

Ward Report (1976), *Report of the Committee appointed by the Academic Board to enquire into Political Economy*, Chair: John M. Ward, Sydney: University of Sydney Academic Board, 10 May, 15 June, 16 July, 10 August.

Wilkes Report (1982), Report of the Committee to Report on the Preset State of Political Economy within the University, Sydney, University of Sydney Academic Board, 28 May.

Williams, Sir Bruce (2005), *Making and Breaking Universities*, Sydney: Macleay Press.

INDEX

Abbonizio, Maria 204
Abbott, Tony 164
Able, Chu Chown 183
Academy of Social Sciences in Australia membership of Faculty staff 125, 170, 219
Ackland, Neil 200
Ackland, Richard 121
Adam, Stewart 151
Adams, Robert 74, 82
Agafonoff, A.F. 74
Aitken, Maxwell 112
Aitken, Michael 182, 186, 215, 216, 218, 219
Akther, Muhammed 205
Albanese, Anthony 197
Albert, Frank 10, 14, 28, 47
Albinski, Henry 139, 185
Aldcorn, Dr. xiv
Aldcroft, Derek 98, 108, 140, 171
Aldrich, Robert 140, 171, 183, 213, 214, 216, 219
Allard, G.M. xx, 3
Allen, Bruce 27, 124
Allen, Mathew 183
Allen, Percy 111, 121
Altman, Dennis 97, 115, 139, 172
Anderson, Allan 140, 172
Anderson, Chris 113
Anderson, Neil 82
Anderson, Professor John 17, 42, 63
Andraskelas, Irene 197
Andreassen, Maya 202
Andrews, Gregory 113
Andrews, P.W.S. 86
Andsure, Denis 167
Angus, Ian 82
Ankres, Jayasuriya 185

Anschau, John 163
Anstice, David 222
Antrobus, Lola 199
Archbold, D.A. 74
A.R.C. Funding of Faculty staff 172-73, 218-19
Archer, Robin 186
Areni, Charles 186
ARGC funding of Faculty staff 127
Argy, Fred 74, 82
Argy, Victor 74, 81, 86, 97, 114, 120, 126
Argyrous, George 197
Arndt, H.W. 60, 61-62, 67, 68, 69
Arthur, Neal 204
Asimus, David 68
Aspromourgos, A. xi, 183, 198, 207, 214, 220
Atkin, Stacy 4, 10, 17, 18-20
Atkins, Ruth 35, 42
Augumeri, Paul 201
Auld, Sally 202
Ausberger, Christian 184
Austin, John 112

Ba, Neyin 47
Babich, George 161, 172
B.Ec requirements xxi-xxii, 77-78
B.Ec Soc. Sci. 188
Bacigalupo, Lisa 198
Baikovsky, Eugene 84
Baird, Marian 186
Baker, Kevin 198
Baker, Noel 168, 212
Balart, Rodrigo 205
Balcomb, Robin 196
Ball, Desmond 97
Ball, Jodie 202
Balnave, Nikola 202

Bannon, Anthony 163
Barclay, Alan 82
Barff, H.E. 6, 7, 8
Barkatullah, Nadira 204
Barnard, Alan 61, 67
Barnes, Sarah 202
Barraclough, Sir Samuel xxi
Barry, Margaret 47–48
Bartels, Robert 140, 161, 172, 183, 213, 215, 218, 219, 221
Bartlett, Kerry 110
Barton, Allen 61, 68
Barton-Taylor, Nicholas 161
Batten, Jonathan 203
Baxt, Robert 98, 121, 125
Baxter, Colin 112
Beeby, G.S. xxi
Beechey, Meredith 203
Beed, Terence 186
Beelaerts, C.W.F. 121
Berg, Tony 112, 120
Bell, Carol 74, 98, 125
Bell, David 201
Bell, Ian 185
Benham, F.C. 9, 10, 15, 16, 17, 19, 20, 21, 22, 23, 28, 51
Benjafield, O.G. 74
Bennett, Fred 82
Bennett, Roy 121
Bentley, Phillip 98
Bernasek, Mike 75
Berry, Michael 112, 121
Bevan, Norm 82
Bhattacharya, Debesh 97, 117, 121, 126, 130, 137, 168, 171, 183
Biancardi, Paul 112
Biancotti, Deborah 201
Bijleveld, Jeroen 204
Binns, David 165
Birch, Alan 59, 61, 64, 74, 84, 86, 88, 98, 125
Birkett, William 81, 98, 112, 120, 125, 170
Black, Sir Hermann 4–5, 6, 13, 14, 16, 17, 18, 28–29, 36, 38, 40, 47, 49, 50, 52, 59, 60, 62, 63, 64, 65, 69, 70, 72, 74, 75, 84, 85, 86, 92, 97, 114, 115, 117, 118, 120, 121, 122, 124, 168
Blad, Michael 137, 184
Blair, Mark 199, 200
Bland, F.A. xvii, xviii, 3, 9, 10, 17, 20, 21, 22, 23, 24, 29, 30, 31, 32, 33, 37, 41, 43, 47, 49–50, 51, 52, 59, 60, 63, 69, 70, 71, 78
Blayney, Paul 182
Blazel, Jeffrey 186
Blazey, Michael 198
Bleasel, Virginia 178
Blunt, Charles 110
Boardman, Ian 162
Boeiovsky, Michael 204
Boey, Damien 206
Bondar, Gregory 162
Booker, John 157
Booth, Anna 163
Booth, Peter 162
Borkovic Kathryn xii
Bornhold, Graham 199
Borrie, Mick 131
Borthwick, Stephen 198
Bose, Gautam 184
Bouckley, Merrill xii
Bowra, Ron 98, 102, 125, 139, 170, 182,
Boyle, Vanessa 203
Boyd, Angus 204
Bracken, Keith 124
Braddock, George 120
Braddon, Henry xv, xvii, xviii, xxi, 3, 8, 9, 19, 20, 21, 22
Bradford, John 110
Bradley J. 20, 29
Bragg, John P. 82
Braithwaite, Jeffrey 202
Bray, Jeremy 207–08

Bray, Mark 186
Breen, Michael E. 48
Brennan, Christopher 7
Brennan, Deborah 185
Brezniak, Michael 145
Bridge, Alan 59, 61
Bridges, John 204
Brien, Mary Louise 183
Brigden, James 17
Briggs, Christopher 201
Broadhead, Ken 120
Bromley, J.E. 87
Bronwich, Michael 140
Brooker, Bill 120, 121
Brooker, Robert 98
Brown, Robert (MHR) 82
Brown, Robert C. xii, 115–18, 161, 162, 165–66
Brown, Ron 59, 61, 74, 98, 139
Brown, Russell 163
Brown, S.R. 63
Bryan, Richard 137, 184, 216
Bryant, Ann 151
Bryant, Peter 109
Brydon, Keats 205
Buckley, Ken D. xii, 59, 61, 62, 70, 74, 77, 86, 98, 108, 125, 140, 143, 145, 171, 183
Bucklow, Maxine 74, 75, 98, 117, 125–6, 140, 153
Bullivant, Graeme 161
Bunch, David 187
Burgess, John 161
Burke, Kerry 202
Burke, Paul 206
Burke, Sandra 186
Burritt, Roger 139, 182
Burrowes, Mark 163
Burrows, Peter 112
Bury, Leslie 120
Bush, Michael C. 74
Business Administration Diploma mooted 44 *See also:* M.B.A.

Butcher, D.M. 168
Butler, Gavin 97, 117, 118, 126, 137, 146, 167, 171, 183
Butler, Ira 29, 35, 38
Butler, R.W. 85
Butler, Richard 111
Butler, Thomas xiv
Butlin, Judith xi, 67
Butlin, Noel G. 35, 42, 60, 61, 62, 66–67, 69, 70, 71
Butlin, S.J. 14, 27, 28, 30, 31, 35, 38, 39, 40, 43, 46, 47, 48, 50, 51, 52, 57, 59, 60, 61, 63, 64, 66–67, 69, 71, 72, 74, 76, 77, 78, 84, 85, 86, 89, 92, 93, 99, 102, 103, 105, 108, 114, 118, 119, 124, 125, 126, 129, 140, 148
Buttrose, William 112

Cahill, Anthony 157
Callus, Ron 140, 163, 172, 173, 185, 214–15
Caloni, Sylvana 199
Campbell, Andrew 200
Campbell, Ian 87, 98
Campbell, Jeremy 164
Campbell, John 113
Campbell, Keith O. 75
Cameron, Ross 199
Campling, John 186, 217
Cannan, Edwin 9, 10, 21, 39
Carney, Nell 205
Carney, Verity 201
Carlsberg, Bryan 140
Carreras, Carmen 184
Carrick, Sir John 35
Carrigan, Frank 198
Carroll, Brett 205
Carroll, Lyn 120
Carsaro, Francesco 163
Carson, John 164, 184
Carter, P.I. 98
Carver, S.R. 52
Cassidy, Brian 162

Cassidy, Colleen 202
Casson, Robert 184
Cavalier, Rodney 158
Cawthorne, Pamela 184
Certoma, Claudia 205
Chaaya, Michael 203
Chaffer, Barry 85
Chaffey, Sheila 124
Chambers, R.J. 35, 59, 60, 64, 68, 70, 71, 74, 75, 76, 77, 79, 83, 85, 86, 89, 91, 98, 101–02, 114, 121, 122, 125, 126, 132, 139, 140, 141–2, 145, 148, 149, 150, 160, 170, 172, 213, 219
Chambers Memorial Lecture 142
Chan, Han Meng 200
Chan, Karen 204
Chan, Pomeng 203
Chan, Therese 201
Chandler, Phillip 113, 120
Chang, Michael 205
Chann, Kenneth 91
Chaples, Ernie 138, 185
Chappell, Louise 185
Charara, Anthony 206
Chatterji, Monjit 184
Chaudari, Rica 98
Chem Chi 205
Chen, Mei Ling 206
Cheung, Stephen 201
Chia, Swee-Eng 139
Chislett, Gerard D'A 85
Chodkowiecz, David 110
Chomed, Khurelbatar 204
Christie, Robert 205
Chua, Wai Fong 139
Chuluunbat, Narantuya 204
Chung, Phillip 203
Clark, Colin 14
Clark, David L. 110
Clark, John 217
Clarke, David 112
Clarke, D.S. 81

Clarke, Frank xi, 98, 110, 121, 125, 139, 168, 170, 182
Clarke, Peter 137
Cleary, W.J. xx, 10, 13, 17, 19, 30
Clim, P.J. 84
Clunies-Ross, A. 38, 46, 47, 48, 60
Coady, A.W.B. 42
Cocks, Grahame 109
Coggan, Lisa 205
Cohen, André 110
Cole, Tony 111
Coleman, Cynthia 139, 182, 213
Coleman, William 164
Collins, Jock 97, 146, 161
Collis-George, Professor N. 158
Commerce teaching curriculum xix
Commerce teaching staff xx-xxi
Comerton-Forde, Carole 223
Computerisation, growth of in Faculty 176
Conen, Jean 14, 35, 48
Conlan, Tracey 198
Conlon, Bernard 202
Conn, Neil xii, 74, 97, 81, 116, 126, 127, 138
Connell, Bob 98, 115, 125, 170
Connery, David 204
Connors, B.T. 85
Coolican, Alice 172, 185, 186
Coombs, H.C. 29, 88
Cooper, Peter 201, 203
Cooper, Russell 184
Cooray, Noreen 184
Corby, David 200
Cordes, Claude 121
Cordoni, René 118, 138
Corina, John 140, 153, 172, 173
Corke, Anthony 199
Cortis, Natasha 206
Costello, C. 168
Cotman, Nigel 111
Cotton, G.W. xxii

Coulton, Jeff 201
Cox, Allaster 165
Craswell, Alan 98, 139, 170, 172, 182, 189, 197, 209, 213, 215
Crawford, Sir John 14, 29, 32, 35, 42, 47, 50, 52, 91, 173
Crawford, R.M. 47
Creane, Anthony 184
Croft, Adrienne 203
Crook, Thomas 186
Cross, R.F. 59, 61
Crough, Greg 162
Crowe, Mathew 204
Cujes, George 161
Cummins, Julia 203
Curnow, Ross 97, 125, 138, 170, 185, 218
Currie, Carolyn 205
Curthoys, Jean 154
Cutler, Sir Roden 35, 37, 48, 120

Dallen, Ian 199
Dalrymple, Rawdon 185
D'Alton, Stephen 112
Dalziel, Robert 113
Dan, Malcolm 82
Danes, Michael T. 161, 162
Darby, Douglas 83
Darwell, Tony 198
Da Silva, Rosa 219
Dauvergne, Peter 185
Davidson, Alistair 184–5
Davidson, Sydney 140
Davies, Lyndall 198, 199
Davies, J.G. 98
Davies, Rebecca 206
Davis, Edward 147
Davis, Jeremy 109
Dean, Graeme xi, 62, 139, 142, 161, 163, 168, 170, 182, 212, 213, 215, 221
Dean, Philip 201
Deans, appointed rather than elected 177

Debenham, Mary 14, 35, 47
De Beyer, Bentley 205
Debreu, Gérard 184
Deegan, Craig 183
Deek, Fred 131
Deer, A.F. 14, 35, 85, 129
Deere, Carolyn 204
Defina, George 140
De Haas, Eric 101, 120
De Jong, Piet 109, 140, 172
Dellaert, Benedict 186, 217, 219
De Mellow, Ian 203
Dennett, Colin 114
Dennett, Glenn 198
Departmental system, introduction of 57, 78–79
Department of Finance 177, 180, 193, 194–95
Deutsch, Robert 163
De Viana, Robert 83
Di Bona, Rex 198
Diessell, Nadja 201
Di Francesco, Michael 201
Diploma of Economics and Commerce xvi, xvii, xviii, xix, 8, 9, 32, 34, 43
Diploma of Public Administration 33–34, 43–44, 76–77
Dixon, Peter 82
Dixon, Timothy 201
Dobbie, Michael 200
Docherty, Peter 164, 199, 204
Doiron, Denise 184
Domberger, Simon 184
Donald, Stephen 198
Donald, Susanne 139
Donnelly, M.F.S. 168
Donnelly, Sandra 138
Donoghue, Mark 205
Donovan, Brian 161
Donovan, Jack 61, 68
Donovan, John 83
Dougherty, Sir Ian 14
Dougherty, Ivan 85

Douglas, Paul   197
Douglas, Robert   121
Dowcras, George   81
Dowling, Robyn   199
Dowsett, W.T.   42
Drabble, John   140, 171, 183, 219
Drane, N.T.   59, 60, 61, 64, 67, 70, 71, 74, 85, 86, 88, 97
Du, Jifong   204
Dubler, Robert   196, 197
Dubler, Martin   183
Dudley, Ben   206
Dudley, Glen   113
Duffy, Matthew   202
Duncan, Bruce   199
Duncan, George   13
Duncan, W.G.K.   47, 50
Dunne, Edward   82
Dunstan, Chris   204
Dunstan Vane, H.   xx
Durent, Lillian   202
Durham, Paul   199
Dutta, Dilip   183–4
Dwyer, Terry   162, 165

Eades, Warren   164
Eames, A.   109
Economic Review   84–85, 120–123
Economics courses in 1913   xv–xvi
Economics (P) as alternative stream to Economics   134, 135–6, 146, 147, 156–7
Eden, Scott   200
Edney, Paul   205
Edwards, H.R.   59, 60–61, 64, 67, 70, 71, 74, 86, 88, 97, 99, 114, 126, 127, 168
Edwards, L.   211
Eedy, Arthur   8
Egan, John   222
Elder, John   202
Eldershaw, Flora   15
El Hassan, Nadima   200

Eleem, Braden   185
Ellis, Kevin   35
Else-Mitchell, Rae   62
Emanuel, E.   183
Emerson, Craig   163
English, Linda   181, 183, 215
Ermini, Luigi   184
Evans, Brett   198
Evans, Kiri   204
Evans, William   161
Evening Lectures   4–5,
    changes in   75–76
    disadvantages of,   71–72
Evening students   36–37, 45, 63, 68, 145
Evening Students Association   17–18, 32
Eyers, E.J.   124

Faculty administration   65–6
Faculty by-laws   1–2, 5–6, 11–13, 76, 77
Faculty Committee system   91–2, 102–03
Faculty course structure   changes 28–29, 32–34, 44–46, 58–59, 94–96, 128, 187–8
Faculty degrees   175
Faculty enrolments   38, 40–42, 58–59, 93–94, 160, 175, 178–9
Faculty Golden Jubilee (1970)   118–19
Faculty governance problems   154–55
Faculty graduates   13–15, 35–37, 67–68, 79–83, 108–14, 149, 195–6
Faculty meetings   31–34, 98–102,
    student representation at   100–101
Faculty publications committee   64
Faculty Research and Publications   20–22, 49–51, 70–71, 86–88, 124–7, 169–72, 212–18
Faculty Research funding   172–3
Faculty staffing   3–4, 10–11, 28–29, 38, 51, 59–61, 74–75, 96–98, 136–7, 181–7
Faculty of Economics and Business
    associate deans of   223

board of advice of 222
governance of 221, 223–4
research and publications 225–6
staff numbers 224–5
student enrolments of 225
Faculty of Economics and Social Sciences 132, 143
Fair, Patrick 164
Falzon, Sylvia 206
Faminsky, A.A. 47
Farrell, Jim 200
Fassler, Michael 200
Feleto, Roger 206
Ferguson, Laurie 158
Ferguson, Martin 163
Ferguson, Robert 112
Fernandez, Roy 61, 68
Ferris, Bill 110, 113, 120, 121
Fiebig, Denzil 140, 172, 183, 207, 213, 215, 219
Fielder, Helen 183
Fields, Richard 167
Finch, Stephen 163
Firth, Robert 47
Fish, Alan 203
Fisher, A.G.B. 47
Fisher, Joyce 65–6, 83, 102, 105, 151
Fisher Lectures on Commerce xviii
Fisher, Stephen 198
Fisher, William 204
Fitzgerald, Sir Alexander 88
Fitzgerald, J.B. xx
Fitzgerald, Kevin 202
Fitzgerald, Tom 35
Fitzmaurice, Andrew 199
Flanagan, Kerry 162
Fleming, Brian 27
Fleming, Bruce 35
Fletcher, James 206
Flood, Phillip 82
Floro, Mario 184
Foley, Noel 199

Forbes, Eric 121
Ford, Arthur 68
Forde, Carole 204
Foreman, Ken 61, 68
Forrest, Bill 222
Forrest, Peter 205
Forsyth, Peter 110, 120, 121
Foster, George 109, 125
Fox, Hayden 202
Francis, Jeremy 183
Franklin, Nicola 205
Frazis, George 222
Freeman, Mark 223
Frenkel, Stephen 172
Frino, Alex 186, 203
Frisch, Jack 110, 121

Gadson, John 124
Gaffikin, Michael 139, 170, 182
Gardiner, Gregory 113
Gardiner, Margaret 161, 162
Garnett, Roman 201
Gartrell, Alexandria 203
Garvey, Gerard 186, 216
Gates, Barbara 73
Gates, R.C. 59, 61, 70, 71, 74, 83, 84, 86, 88, 97, 114
Gavell, Paul 199
George, Henry 20
Geha, Akrum 201
Gelber, Frank 162, 198, 199
Gentle, David 200
Gentle, Tony 162
Giezelt, Ray 158
Giles, Thomas 163
Gill, Flora 137, 171, 172, 173, 178, 183
Gill, Graeme 138, 170, 185, 214, 217, 218, 219, 221
Ginswick, Jules xii, 59, 61, 64, 74, 75, 92, 98, 108, 126, 140, 145, 152
Gleeson-White, M.A. 68
Gluskie, Laurie J. 82

Godfrey, Jayne 197
Gold, Hyam 109, 110
Goodhew, John 74, 81, 98, 102, 114, 140, 165, 183
Goodwin, B.W. xxi
Goodyer, T.W. 74
Gordijew, Igor 72, 81
Gordon, Barry 68, 75, 199
Gordon, Isabel 182
Gorton, Senator John 105
Goth, James 199
Goth, R. 74
Graduates Association, *see* USEGA
Granger, C.W.J. 140
Gray, A.C. 85
Gray, Sidney 112, 120, 140, 221, 223
Graziani, Andrea 203
Greiner, Nick 110, 120, 121
Grenville, Stephen 110
Greenfield, John 198
Greenhalgh, Alan 35, 42
Grey, Peter 111
Griffin, Pauline 186
Graham, J. 168
Groenewegen, Peter 81, 85, 97, 102, 120, 126, 127, 137, 166, 167, 170, 171, 183, 206, 207, 208, 214, 216, 217, 219, 220
Groenewegen, Stephen 202
Grogan, Peter 83
Groom, Eric 163
Grosart, Ian 97, 125, 138, 170, 185
Grose, Simon 167
Guest, Chris 205
Gunn, J.A.L. 29, 38, 51
Gunning, Peter 200
Guthrie, F.B. xx, xxii, 3, 20, 21, 22
Gutierrez, Ian 208–09

Haddad, Louis xii, 81, 85, 97, 130, 137, 166, 171, 183, 208
Haddad, Maurice 81, 85, 97, 102, 130, 137, 146

Hagerty, Devin 185
Hale, Ken 139
Haley, W.J. 140
Halevi, Joseph 137, 171, 184, 207, 214, 216
Hall, Alan 61, 67
Hall, Chris 121
Hall, Leigh 112
Hall, Peter 98, 108, 122, 140, 171, 183, 212
Hall, V.B. 118, 126, 137, 166, 171, 183
Hamayotsu, Kikue 206
Hambly, Gail 162
Hamilton, Clive 164
Han, Sang Hee 201
Hancock, Keith 156
Hannes, Simon 164
Haque, Mohamed 197
Harcourt, G.C. 156
Hardie, Neil 202
Harding, Ann 198
Hargreaves, Alan 167
Hargreaves-Heap, Shaun 184
Hariman, Jusuf 198
Harley, Peter 186
Harpham, Andrew 206
Harris, Stuart 68, 80
Harrison, Steven 98, 112, 117, 166
Harrison-Ford, Carl xii
Harsanyi, John C. 138, 184
Hart, Adrian 201
Hart, Geoffrey 139, 182
Hartwell, Max 61, 71
Harwin, Donald 198
Hatzistegos, John 164
Haviv, Moshe 183, 215
Hawke, Robert 186
Hayek, F.A. von 88, 173
Hayes, Laraine 161
Hayes, Laura 205
Haywood, Philip 205
He, Yvonne 206
Healey, Mark 167

Heaton, C.L. 74
Heazlewood, Kristen 201
Hedley, Maureen 37
Heeley, G.F. 82
Hely, Tony 111
Henningham, John 162
Hensher, David xii, 187, 215, 219, 223
Herbertson, John 74
Herries, O. 74
Hertzberg, Andre 204
Hewitt, Robert 219
Hewson, John R. 110
Heynes, Warren 82
Heys, Andrew 204
Hiatt, Les 147
Hicks, Sir John 88, 166, 173
Hickson, William 97
High, Nina 167
Hill, Amelia 205
Hill, David 93, 111, 114, 121, 128, 129
Hill, Elizabeth 201
Hill, Geoffrey 113
Hill, Lisa 185
Hinchy, Michael 109
Hindwood, Rebecca 203
Hoare, Martin 212
Hobbs, David 212
Hobson, J.A. 185
Hocking, Steven 211
Hodgkinson, Ann 203
Holla, Kamela 205
Hogan, Bruce 162
Hogan, Kerry 163
Hogan, Michael xii, 138, 151, 185, 188, 217
Hogan, W.P. 96, 102, 108, 118, 119, 121, 126, 127, 128, 129, 130, 137, 143, 144, 145, 155, 156, 166, 167, 170, 171, 174, 183, 214
Holden, Richard 204
Holman, William 8
Holmes, J.D. 48, 69, 168

Hong, T. 212
Hood, Christopher 184
Hooper, Paul 202
Horn, Audrey 65
Horn, R, 74
Horner, Derek 74, 97, 114
Horner, F.B. 32, 35, 83
Horrigan, Bill 97, 129
Houghten, Ernie 91, 98, 117, 140, 183, 215
Housego, Anthony 204
Howard, Bob 138
Howard, John 212
Howell, Gordon J. 82
Hua, Hu 185
Hudson, H.R. 67
Hudson, M.A. 81
Hughes, Michael, 197
Huh, Hyeon Seung 201
Hunter, Thelma 74, 87
Hunter, William George 82
Hunyor, Paul 206
Hurd, Debbie 138
Hutcheson, Ross 120
Hutchins, Ian 111, 120
Hutchinson, Belinda 163
Hutchinson, Diane 183, 216, 219, 223
Hytten, Torlein 38, 47

Iemma, Morris 165
Illife, John 82
Indyk, Martin 121
Industrial Relations, studies in 65, 76, 152–4
Innes-Brown, Marc 200
Invasion of Vice Chancellor's office 147
Irons, Stephen 145
Irvine, Robert F. xvii, xxiii, xix, xx, xxi, xxii, 2, 3, 4, 5, 6, 7, 8, 9, 15, 20, 21, 118, 195
Irving, Terry 115, 116, 125, 138, 170, 172, 185, 214, 216, 219

Isaac, Joe 218
Ives, Walter 42
Iveson, Kurt 201

Jack, Sybil 98, 108, 125
Jack, William 184
Jacka, Liz 154
Jackson, Michael xvi, 138, 170, 181, 185, 206, 214, 216
Jackson, Robert 91
Jackson, Vanessa 202
Jacobs, D.H. 121
Jameson, Suzanne 185, 217
Jans, Sophie 137
Jarcenic, Elvis 186
Jarjoura, Greg 199
Jarvis, Darryl 185
Jason, Mark 201
Jenkins, C.N. 168
Jenkins, Olivia 202
Jensen, Tony 199
Jepson, George 111
Jevons, H.S. xiv, xv
Jevons, W.S. xiv
Jia, Quinggo 185
Jilek, T.S. 85
Johnson, Brian 112–13
Johnson, B.T. 212
Johnson, Clarke 202
Johnson, David 204
Johnston, Betty 200, 138
Johnston, Ian 111
Johnstone, Diane 121, 161
Jones, Evan 97, 159, 171, 183, 117, 118, 137
Jones, Evan [not the staff member] 197
Jones, Valerie 137
Jordan, Nicholas 202
Joson, Surinder 137, 161, 171, 184

Kain, John 167
Kaldor, A.G. 110

Kambosus, Frank 224
Katsiarris, Joanne 206
Kami, Siosaia 200
Kamvounias, Patty 182
Kannangara, D.M. 97, 116
Kao, Shi Sheng 205
Karfakis, Costas 184
Karunakaran, Kishore 204
Karunaratne, Armaz 203
Katz, Roderick 203
Kaur, Baijit 182–3, 201
Keane, Chris 202
Keene, R.A.C. 109
Keene, Steven 145
Kells, Geoff 113
Kelly, Jennifer 200
Kennedy, Stephen 201
Kenny, Carolyn 202
Kent, Albert 48
Kent, Warwick 82
Kerr, Donald 27
Kerr, Ivo 10, 13, 37, 46, 51, 60, 68, 69, 85
Kerridge, Graham 145, 163
Kewley, Tom 35, 38, 48, 51, 52, 59, 60, 63, 74, 84, 87, 125, 138
Keynes, J.M. 19, 27–28, 208
Khai, Phan Van 205
Khan, Muhammed 202
Koshaba, Tilda 204
Kidd, Arthur 42
Kiernan, Eric 137, 171, 184
Kiklhorn, Vladimir 84
Kim, Jae-Hon 200, 203
Kim, Sol Kiew 91, 97, 126, 184
Kim, Suk-Joong 200, 203
Kincade, Allen 163
King, David 112
King, Peter 97, 115, 116, 125, 138, 185, 218
Kingston, Geoffrey 137, 184
Kirby, Michael 93, 111, 120
Kirkness, John 198

Kitay, Jim 186, 217
Kitney, Paul 205
Kmenta, Jan 68, 69, 74, 84, 85, 86, 87, 98
Knowles, Lillian 9
Kohli, Ulrich 138, 171
Kollontai, V.M. 184
Kolsen, Helmut 68, 74, 84, 85, 86, 97, 120, 126
Kommer, Walter 82
Konijn, Henk 86, 87
Kourtian, Tro 186
Kramar, Robyn 186
Kreibig, Dale 206
Krestovsky, Andrew 206
Krezniarik, P. 168
Kriesler, Peter 161, 163
Kuhn, Richard 198
Kulper, Michael 200
Kumar, Robin 199
Kwok, Francis 202
Kyan, Nyun 47

Laffer, Kingsley 38, 50, 51, 59, 60, 61, 62, 64, 65, 69, 71 74, 75, 85, 86, 88, 98, 117, 125, 126, 140, 152, 153, 154
Laffin, Martin 185
Lagerhof, Nils-Peter 184
Laidlaw, Michele 204
Laker, John 109
Lambert, Michael 111
Lamberton, Don 61, 67
Lambousis, Peter 204
La Nauze, John 38, 41, 42, 46, 47, 50, 51, 52, 60, 61, 63, 69, 70
Lancaster, Harry 35
Lance, Donna 114, 120
Lane, David 82
Lansbury, Russell xii, 185, 206, 214, 217, 218, 219
Larcombe, Fred 42
Latham, Mark 165
Latina, Mark 200

Latoza, Hazel 223
Latty, Keith 199
Laurence, Peter 164
Laurence, Roy 113
Layard, M.W.T. 81, 98
Layton, Roger 74, 80
Leaver, John 113
Lee, Catherine 201
Lee, Kin Wai 201
Lee, Phillip 182
Leech, Stewart 139
Lees, Dennis 138
Leigh, Michael 97, 125, 138, 185
Lenzner, Graham 112
Leong, Yuen 206
Leplastrier, J.E. 85
Lester, Ashley 205
Leu, Chen 205
Leung, Victor 206
Lever, Frank 111
Levien, Harold 48
Levitt, Sasha 205
Levy, Harry 68–69
Lewis, Geoffrey 117, 126
Lim, Jeakyu 202
Limbrick, John 111
Linklater, Dawn 206
Linney, Henry 207
Linstrom, Anders 201
Linton, J.E. 37, 40
Little, Barbara 98, 108, 110, 125
Littlejohn, George xv
Littrell, Charles 204
Lloyd, Clem 113–14
Lloyd, K. 212
Lloyd-Ross, M. 75
Loader, Robert 121
Lockman, Jillian 200
Lodewijks, John 163, 166
Loginov, A.V. 120
Lonergan, Wayne 220, 222
Longley, James 164

Lopes, Sonia   203
Lord, Gillian   69–70
Louvière, Jordan   186, 195, 217, 219
Loveday, Peter   74, 87, 98
Lovell, H.T.   32
Lovell, Simon   198
Lucarelli, Bill   201
Lucich, Milovan   203
Luckett, Peter   139
Ludeke, J.T.   186
Lyle, Tom   109
Lyons, R.   168

McCafferey, Genia   163
McCallum, D.M.   71, 74, 84, 87
McCallum, Sir Munro   xvi
McCarthy, John   74, 86, 98, 125
McCrane, David   120
McCorry, Michael   186
McCredie, Hugh C.   59, 61, 74, 147
McCullough, Colleen   37
McDonald, A.H.   48
McDonald, Fergus   113
McDonald, Warwick   111
McDonald Holmes, John   32, 42
McFarlane, A.I.R.   85
McFarlane, Bruce   72, 80, 85
McGillicuddy, James   204
McGrath, John   167
McGrath, Kim   167
McGrath, Michael   82
McGrath-Champ, Susan   186
McGregor, Graeme, W.   82
McGregor, H.A.L.   74
McGregor, L.   105
McGuinness, P.P.   82, 168
McIntyre, A.P.   98
McInery, Jim   167
McKay, Brigadie-General Iven, G.   6
MacKay, Richard   200
McKensey, Rod   202
Mackerras, Malcolm   83

McLaurin, Sir Normand   xv, xxiii
McLennan, Brian   121
McMahon, Sir William   61, 68, 85
McMicken, Evandor   202
Macmillan, David   86, 88
McMullen, Belinda   178
McMullin, N.C.   67
McNair, Ian   82
McNamara, Ian [Macca]   162
McPhee, S.D.   48
Macken, James   186
Madan, Dilip   140, 172, 183
Maddocks, S.A.   47
Madgwick, R.B.   5, 6, 10, 13, 16, 17, 18, 28, 29, 32, 36, 37, 38, 40, 47, 49, 50–51, 52, 60
Mahdoo, Harishand   203
Maitra, Pushkar   184
Mak, Derek   205
Malden, Emma   201
Malliate, Paul   164
Maneschi, Andrea   184
Manna, Barbara   65
Manning, Richard   82
Marfori, Sylvia   206
Marketing, Department of   23, 177, 180, 191, 193, 195
Markos, Toula   140
Markham, Sheilah   139
Marnet, Helen   137
Maroya, Alexander   202
Marsden, Robin   73
Marshall, Alfred   208
Marshman, Peter   186
Martin, A.H.   32, 60
Martin, Barrie   82
Martin, Chris   205
Martin, Clarey   14, 15, 59, 62
Martin, David   162, 212
Martin, Gregory   164
Martin, Jeremy   208, 210
Martin, John   167

Martin, R.M. 87
Marx, K.H. 20
Mason, Arthur 151
Matheson, David 199
Mathews, R.H. 40
Mathews, Trevor 81, 97, 116, 138, 161, 173, 185
Matthews, Ken 162
Matthews, Russell 173
Maunder, G.D.B. 35
Maxwell, Phillip 112
May, Allen 85
May, R.J. 74, 81, 82, 85, 87
Mayer, Henry 59, 61, 69, 71, 74, 87, 88, 97, 115, 116, 125, 126, 132, 138, 154, 155, 170, 219
MBA 131, 134, 136, 147–48, 150, 161
Meagher, Gabrielle 184, 201, 205
MEc regulations 45–6, 64–5,
Medlicott, Natalie 201
Mee, Kathleen 199
Meguro, Katsuyuki 205
Melatos, Mark 204
Melham, Daryl 163
'Melville, Sir Leslie 7, 14, 16, 131
Melvin, J. 184
Mendelsohn, Ron 35
Menzies, R.G. 61, 68
Menzies, P.G. 168
Merewether Building 103–07, 151–2, 189
Merewether, Francis 105
Merrilees, Bill 97, 118, 137, 171, 172
Mesher, Barbara 182
Mian, Ghulam 205
Michelson, Grant 204, 217
Miles-Connolly, D. 84
Milgate, Murray 137, 138, 161, 171
Militon, Michael 167
Mill, J.S. xiv, 41–42
Miller. Phoebe 15
Miller, R.B.D. 35, 41–42, 48
Mills, C.P. 35, 74, 86, 98, 116, 125, 139, 145, 170
Mills, Gordon 137, 171, 183, 206, 215
Mills, Janine 207
Mills, R.C. 1, 3, 4, 5, 9, 10, 12, 14, 15, 16, 17, 18, 19, 20, 21, 22, 23, 27, 28, 28, 29, 30, 31, 32, 366, 237, 38, 39, 40, 43, 44, 46, 47, 48, 49, 50, 51, 52, 61, 63, 71, 88, 118, 119
Mills [R.C.] Building 71–73, 89
Mills [R.C.] Memorial Lectures 88, 173
Milston, Michael 121
Minns, Phillip 199
Mo, Myit 47
Moenting, H. 85
Moffit, Philip 198
Molloy, Ivan 185
Mong, Sheila 206
Moore, Andrew 140
Moore, Barry 198
Moore, Gillian 222
Moore, H.J. 15
Moore, Sir John 186
Moors, E.M. xvi, 3
Morris, Megan 167
Morris, Richard 140, 172, 185, 186
Morrison, Pamela 186
Mortimer, David 110, 121
Mortimer, Dennis 101, 161
Mortimer, Portia 36
Mortimer, Rex 97, 125, 133, 138, 145, 148
Morton, Anja 204
Mottek, Paula 203
Muir, Gloria 152
Muir, Ian 82
Munro, Kevin 168
Murphy, Chris 164
Murphy, David 201
Murphy, Helen 161
Murphy, M.E. 63
Murray, Jason 196, 200
Muscio, B. 16
Muthuswamy, Jayarim 186

Nahm, Deahoon 203
Naqvi, Farzana 202
Narushima, Hiroshi 205
Nassar, Mahamed 205
Needham, Kristie 199, 200
Neilson, David 112
Nell, Edward C. 157
Nelson, Edwin 201
Nelson, Helen 138, 176, 178, 185, 206
Nelson, Peter 97, 138
Neville, John W. 156
New, Victor 139
Newsum, Bernard 222
Ng, Kui 205
Ng, Yew Kwang 91, 112
Nicholas, Stephen 221
Nichols, W.F. 59
Nicholson, Douglas 47
Nielson, Robert 124
Nigam, B.M. Lall 139
Nobel, Jim 168
Nolan, Bridie 206
Norton, W.R. 138
Nugan, Ken 82
Nyathi, Michael 203

O'Brien, Paul 200
O'Connor, Luke 198
O'Connor, Rod 211
O'Donnell, Chris 200
O'Donnell, R.M. 163
O'Keeffe, Barry 74, 98, 114
Oliver, Kyle 196, 200
Oppewal, Harmen 186, 217
O'Rourke, Katherine 202
Osborn, Diane 108, 109
Oslington, Paul 201, 204, 207
Osmond, Warren 98, 116, 167
Ostenfeld, Shane 204
Osterhof, Karen 178
Oulton, Nick 138
Oxley-Oxland, John 182

Page, Barbara 161, 185
Pakthorbe, Bernard 186
Painter, Martin 138, 170, 173, 185, 206, 214, 216, 219
Pak, Wai Lui 184
Palmer, George 80
Pan, Swee Kuen 137
Pappas, Nicholas 205
Parley, A. 183
Parker, Ian Alexander 81–82
Parker, Ron 29, 35, 42, 52
Parkes, Sir Henry xiii, xiv
Partridge, Percy 60, 63, 64, 69, 71
Pasinetti, L.L. 207
Passmore, John 35, 40
Pateman, Carole 97, 138, 149, 170, 185, 214
Paterson, James xiv
Paterson, Robert 82
Patman, Raymond 151
Patmore, Greg xii, 140, 164, 172, 185, 198, 217
Patrikeeff, Felix 185
Patterson, Gordon 74, 81, 97
Paul, Helen 201
Pawley, W.H. 35, 38
Payne, Ian 112
Pearce, I.F. 138, 171
Pearson, Des 222
Pearson, John 109, 212
Peat, Maurice 137, 198
Peirce, Sharron 211
Pell, Maurice Birkbeck xiii
Penang University College 176, 190–91
Pendleton, Andrew 186
Perry, Frank 212
Perry, Tom 121
Perry, Warren 36
Pessley, Lindy 167
Peterson, E. Allen 48
Peterson, Tim 204
PhD program 63, 64–65, 91, 148, 160–61

Phelps-Brown, E.H.   126
Phillips, B.J.   98
Phillips, Sir John   14, 35, 126
Philpott, Les   119
Phipps, Tony   97, 116, 117, 137, 166, 171, 183
Pickering, Joanne   182
Piggott, John   137, 184
Pitchford, John   173
Pitman, David   163
Pitman, Michael   147, 157
Pitty, Roderic   185
Plimsoll, Sir James   35, 47, 131
Plumb, Michael   202, 203
Poggi, Giovanni   138, 139
Political Economy 'Day of Protest'   155–6
Pollack, Saime   204
Pollard, A.H.   59
Pook, Stuart   199
Poon, Teresa   205
Poon, Yu Can   140
Portus, G.V.   3, 5, 9, 10, 15, 16, 17, 20, 21, 22, 23, 32, 37, 50
Potter, Sir Ian   14
Powell, M.K.H.   84, 120
Power, John   97, 115
Power, Margaret   81, 97, 130, 137, 146, 171, 184
Pritchard, Hugh   74, 97, 126, 138, 161, 171
Prodogalidad, Mia   204
Public Administration studies   xix, 10, 24, 25, 29–30
Pullen, John   xii

Quinlan, Michael   161, 163
Quotas on enrolments   133, 143, 148

Radcliffe-Brown, Alfred   16
Radford, Neil   111–12, 210
Rafferty, Michael   205
Rahman, Asheq   199

Rahim, Lily   183, 216
Ramanathan, T. Sri   139, 182
Ramasubban, S.   172
Ramasubban, T.A.   98, 121, 127
Randall, Sir Richard   35
Randerson, R.   47
Rankin, Robert   163
Rappaport, Harry   139
Raskall, Philip   161
Ravenhill, John   185, 219
Ray, Nigel   164, 198, 199
Rees, Stephanie   139, 182
Renouf, Alan   168
Renwick, Cyril   36, 42, 59, 60, 63, 64, 69, 70
Reucassel, Craig   206
Rewell, Keith   163
Richards, Jeff   139
Richardson, Scott   203
Richardson, Jim   97, 139
Riches, Anne   139, 150, 151
Richmond, David   111
Rieler, John   201
Rimmer, Malcolm   98, 117, 126, 140, 153, 172
Rivett, D.M.   15
Rix, Stephen   162
Robinson, G.   84
Robinson, Joan   166, 173
Roberts, Paul   97, 146
Roberts, Stephen   222
Roberts, V.   212
Rochester, Stephen   111
Rock, Alexander   205
Rocks, Tim   201
Rolfe, Anne   212
Rolfe, Hylda   111
Romalis. John   201
Rorris, Adam   203
Rose, Colin   200, 202, 220
Rosewarne, Stewart   137
Ross, Bruce   97, 137, 184
Ross, Iain   164

Ross, K.M.J.   74
Ross, Russell   137, 171, 173, 183, 218
Rotic, Monique   201
Rowan, D.C.   84
Rowse, Tim   217
Rowthorn, Robert   184, 207
Ruddock, M.S.   36
Ruedi, Ramiro   206
Runcie, Neal   67
Rush, John G.   161
Russell, F.A.   xx, xxi, 3, 21, 22
Rutherford, R.G.S.   59, 61, 63, 64, 71, 74, 75, 77, 79, 86, 89, 98, 99, 117, 120, 121, 132, 140, 144, 148, 169
Rutnam, Verna   200
Ryan, Colleen   161
Ryan, Gerard   199
Ryan, Mathew   197
Ryan, Robert   197
Rybak, Janet   140
Rybak, Sheilah   172
Rydon, Joan   87

Saddington, Rooney   205
Sadleir, Robert   211
Sahuza, Jenny   120
St. Mortske, Kimberley   121
Salih, Fathima   204
Salsbury, Stephen   133, 140, 148, 149, 158, 168, 171, 183, 192, 211, 213, 216
Sanders, Don   61, 68
Sappey, Richard   122
Sappideen, T.R.   98
Saunders, Peter   137, 161, 171, 173, 184
Sauvious, Katrina   206
Savage, Elizabeth   184, 218
Savage, Robert   222
Saw, Diane   202
Sawkins, D.T.   10, 11, 36, 37, 46, 60, 63
Sayers, R.S.   126
Sayers, Stuart   201
Saywell, Richard   201

Scalmer, Sean   201, 203
Scanlan, Phillip   113
Scarf, David   120
Schedvin, C.B.   28, 66, 67, 72, 81, 85, 91, 98, 102, 108, 125, 127, 140
Scherer, Peter   140, 153
Schoffel, Claude   85
Schonfield, Peter   183
Schrapnell, Phillip   168
Schworm, William   183
Scott, Brian   82
Scott, Eric   14
Scott, Jennifer   137
Scott, R.   36, 98
Scott, Walter   xiv
Scotton, Robert   68, 74, 75
Sedgwick, Stephen   111
Semesterisation   177, 189–90
Semitecolos, Nigel   205
Sen, Kishti   204
Sengupta, Abhjit   184
Setkiewicz, Walter   199
Setton, Ellis   124
Severin, Valerie   203
Seymore, Elen   207
Shaller, Jason   204
Shann, E.O.G.   37, 47
Shaw, Alec   74, 98, 139
Sharp, Rhona   203
Sharp, Stuart   205
Sharpe, I.G.   97, 137–8, 166, 171
Sharpe, Kieran   199, 200
Sharpe, M.J.   82
Shashahani, Leila   206
Sheen, Jeffrey   183
Shepherd, Ian   161
Shepherd, Richard   110
Sherlock, Anthony   113
Sherris, Michael   198
Shirazi, Habibolah   204
Shields, John   199
Shields, R.J.   110

Short, Laurence   201
Shuetrim, Geoff   201
Shup, F.   184
Shynn, Sunbyn   200
Sieper, Ted   109
Sigouras, Kathy   206
Simkin, C.G.F.   96, 116, 117, 118, 119, 125, 126, 127, 128, 129, 130, 132, 137, 143, 155, 165, 166, 171, 174, 219
Simpson-Lee, Geelum   42, 48, 59, 60, 64, 69, 70, 71, 74, 77, 86, 96, 99, 116, 117, 118, 128, 133, 137, 145, 146, 147, 148, 168, 174
Singer, Kurt   59, 61, 69, 70
Singh, Shailendra   202
Skezely, Leslier   139
Skib, Peter   198
Skrzynskie, Joseph   113, 121
Sloan, B.P.   67
Small, Cecily   120
Smith, A.C.   74
Smith, Belinda   201,
Smith, Chris   167
Smith, Deborah   203
Smith, Graeme   162
Smith, Kerry   162
Smith, Mathew   199
Smith, Murray   220
Smith, Philippa   111
Smith, Stephen   206
Snedden, Billie   161
Snedden, Bronwyn   202
Sofair, Michael   198
Sommerlad, Ernest Lloyd   41
Soon, Tet Far   205
Sorrell, Geoff   98, 117, 126, 140, 153, 172
Southwell, Jane   202
Spann, Richard N.   59, 61, 64, 65, 71, 72, 74, 75, 76, 77, 84, 87, 88, 89, 97, 102, 125, 126, 132, 138, 149, 154, 170, 173, 219
Spasjovic, Janko   162
Spence, Cecilia   139

Spence, Kellie   202
Spence, Susan   198
Spencer, Berenice   201
Spiert, John   113
Spigelman, Jim   120
Spinks, Wendy   203
Spooner, E.S.   47
Spring, Annabel   201
Springborg, Patricia   138, 170, 178, 185, 214, 217, 219
Spruyt, Danielle   202
Sriskandarajah, Dhanan Jayan   205
Stamp, E.   140
Standish, Peter   74, 86, 98, 114
Stanley, Owen   109
Stanner, W.E.H.   47
Stanwell, Ian   82
Staunton, John   98, 125, 139
Stebbins, H.I.   74
Steeley, Jeremy   211
Steiner, Nicholas   206
Stephenson, Liz   151
Sterling, Robert   140
Stevens, Sir Bertram   30, 47, 48
Stevens, Glenn   164
Stevens, N.F.   59, 61, 68
Stewart, Randall   185
Still, Leonie   111
Stilwell, Frank J.B.   xii, 97, 116, 118, 122, 126, 137, 146, 155, 158, 159, 166, 167, 171, 181, 183, 214, 216, 222
Stoeckel, Rebecca   206
Stokes, Anthony   202
Stokes, Nigel   97, 110, 116, 120, 130
Stone, Alastair   222
Stout, A.K.   33
Strauss, George   186
Strauss, Peter   206
Strickland, Phillip   198
Stuckey, John   137, 184
Student dissatisfaction with faculty governance   131, 154–5
Sub-deans, introduction of   133, 150

Sullivan, Mark 162
Sutton, Michael 203
Svetiev, Yane 206
Swain, Edith xvi
Swan, Peter 186, 191, 194, 216, 219
Swan, Trevor 28, 36, 38, 42, 52, 60
Sydney University Economics Society 15–16, 46–49, 83–84, 119–120, 166–67, 210–11
Sylos Labini, Paolo 138, 173

Talunin, A. 140
Tan, Adrienne 203
Tan, Andrew 203
Tan, Wooi Syn 205
Tang, Qingliang 182
Tarrow, Sydney 185
Tate, John 200, 205
Taylor, Angus 199
Taylor, Michael 147
Taylor, Rae 82
Taylor, Robert 139
Taylor, Stephen 182, 215, 219
Tebbutt, Carmel 198
Techritz, Victor 186
Tedder, James 69
Teiwess, Fred 138, 170, 185, 217, 219
Teodoso, Virginia 200
Thomas, Charles 121
Thompson, Elaine 98, 161
Thompson, Graeme 161
Thornwaite, Louise 198
Thorpe, Sally 197
Thorpe, Susan 198
Throsby, David 156
Tiberi, Patricia 184
Tierney, John 110
Tiffin, Andrew 200
Tiffin, Rodney 138, 170, 173, 185, 214, 217
Tipton, Ben 140, 171, 183, 213, 216, 223
Todd, Patricia 199

Togher, Tom 212
Tok, Wee Koan 205
Toman, Jane 204
Toner, Martin 204
Toner, Phillip 203–4
Treloar, Ernie 98
Tremayne, Andy 183
Tripodi, Joe 200
Trowell, John 139, 183
Tseng, Veronica 198
Tucker, Barbara 98, 140
Tucker, G.L.S. 46
Turner, C.N. 168
Turner, Harry 140, 153, 172
Turner, Ken 68, 97, 115, 116, 125, 138, 143, 150, 170, 172, 173, 185
Tutt, Leo 197
Tweedie, Sandra 140

Uldry, Pierre 204
University of Sydney Economics Graduates Association 85–6, 124, 167–9, 211–12

Vaiciurgus, Nyole 212
Valentine, Tom 109
Vam, Kit Chin 184
Van Duren, Nancy 138
Varian, Hall 220
Varoufakis, Yanis 184, 207, 208, 216
Verma, Rohit 186
Vidler, Sacha 203
Vigneron, Frank 204
Vilary, Alison 204
Vohralik, F. 84

Wailes, Nick 186
Walder, E.J. 42
Walker, Alice 83
Walker, Judith 98
Walker, K.F. 29, 32, 38

Walker, Robert   98, 112, 125, 139, 160, 170
Walker, Sir Ronald   10, 13, 16, 17, 23, 28, 36, 37, 39, 47, 50, 52, 60, 131
Wallace, Sir Robert   33, 37
Wallas, Graham   9
Walsh, Max   113
Walsh, Michael   139
Walter, Terry   182, 191, 192, 219
Walton, John   82, 85
Walton, Michael John   164
Warburton, George   172
Warnken, Russell   121
Ward, John   147, 151, 156, 173–4, 211
Ward, William   204
Waters, Bill   93, 126, 128, 129, 130, 167
Waterson, D.M.   183, 184
Watson, Jason   204
Watson, John   48
Watson, Lex   98, 138, 218
Watts, P.R.   xxi, xxii, 3, 10, 33, 51
Wauchope, Bryce   186, 222
Weaver, James   122
Webb, Roy C.   156
Weddie, Simon   202
Weiss, Linda   178, 185, 216
Wells, Murray C.   132, 139, 141, 151, 160, 170, 182, 212, 219
West, Andrew   204
Westcott, Mark   186, 204
Westerway, Peter   74, 80, 84, 87, 98, 114
Westlake, Phil   211, 212
Wheelwright, E.L.   59, 61, 64, 69, 71, 74, 76, 84, 86, 96, 114, 115, 116, 117, 121, 126, 127, 137, 146, 147, 148, 155, 162, 166, 168, 170, 171, 172, 183
Whitby, Adrienne   206
White, Catherine   199
White, Graham   184, 198
White, Lesley   205
Whiteman, John   161
Whitfield, Keith   140, 172, 186

Whiteford, Donald   82
Whitred, Greg   182, 219
Whyte, Robert   113
Wiggins, L.R.   110
Wight, Bob   113
Wilber, Martijn   200
Wilcox, J.M.   15, 16
Wilcox, John   82
Wilcox, Michael   200
Willard, Luke   204
Wilkes, G.A.   149, 157, 158
Wilkins, Chris   199
Williams, Sir Bruce   128–9, 153, 159
Williams, C.B.   110
Williams, David   83
Williams, Neil   164
Williams, Tom   36
Williams, Virginia   201
Williamson, Terry   202
Willis, J.G.   74, 81
Wilmott, Garry   111
Wilson, J.R.   59, 60, 64, 67, 69, 74, 75, 86, 96, 117, 118, 126, 127, 137, 183
Wilson, J.S.G.   38, 50, 51, 60
Wilson, R.C.   47
Wilson, Max   120
Winch, Donald   173
Winn, Roland   186, 202
Winning, Bill   122
Winzar, Hume   202
Wise, Trevor   139
Wolfe, Digby   85
Wolfensohn, James   203
Wolfers, Justin   202
Wolnizer, Peter   xii, 139, 141, 161, 162–3, 170, 182, 220, 221
Wolstenholme Library   52, 57–8, 72–3, 102, 132, 148, 152, 181, 189, 209–10
Wolstenholme, S.H.   32, 50, 210
Wong, Eugene   201
Wong, Leon   200
Wood, Arnold   xiv

Wood, David 31, 42, 161
Wood, Greg 120
Wood, Malcolm 198
Wood, Robert 185
Woodhouse, Patricia 97
Wooding, Paul 97
Woodland, Alan 140, 148–9, 151, 169, 172, 183, 207, 213, 215, 218, 219
Woodman, Murray 203
Woolley, John xiii, xiv
Wormal, Peter 157
Wotherspoon, Gary 108, 140, 171, 183, 214, 216
Wright, Brian J. 82
Wright, Catherine 201
Wright, Chris 198, 200
Wright, Don 184
Wright, Jack 61, 68
Wright, Juliane 186
Wright, Michael 140
Wright, Peter 120, 129
Wu, Changssen 206
Wyburn, Mary 182
Wyld, Melanie 206
Wyllie, A.C. xiv

Xu, Jianlin 205

Yan, Deborah 199
Yates, Judy 97, 126, 137, 171, 178, 183, 214, 216
Yeoh, Angela 205
Yeung, Daniel 203
Yonge, Warwick 201
Young, Collette 199
Young, John 147
Youngman, Valerie 204
Yung, Yu Ming 201
Yunus, Muhamed 204

Zappala, Joe 186, 199
Zerby, John 97, 116, 130

Zhang, Yun 200, 205
Zhou, Ai 204
Zhu, Xianming 186
Zhu, Tianbiao 202
Ziss, Steffan 184